NBER Macroeconomics Annual 1986

Editor
Stanley Fischer

THE MIT PRESS
Cambridge, Massachusetts
London, England

Send orders and business correspondence to:
The MIT Press
28 Carleton Street
Cambridge, MA 02142

In the United Kingdom, continental Europe, and the Middle East and Africa, send orders and business correspondence to:
The MIT Press Ltd.
126 Buckingham Palace Road
London SW1W 9SD England

ISSN: 0889-3365
ISBN: hardcover 0-262-06105-8
paperback 0-262-56037-2

Since this volume is a record of conference proceedings, it has been exempted from the rules governing critical review of manuscripts by the Board of Directors of the National Bureau (resolution adopted 8 June 1948, as revised 21 November 1949 and 20 April 1968).

Contents

Preface

The National Bureau of Economic Research (NBER) was founded in 1920 to do empirical economic research that would provide the basis for improved public and private decisions. Through the years, the Bureau has pursued that goal through a variety of research projects and conferences. The establishment of this new annual NBER macroeconomics conference promises to be an important milestone in that tradition.

The past several decades have seen substantial advances in macroeconomic theory, econometric methods and computing technology. Often, however, research in empirical macroeconomics has failed to live up to the potential suggested by these advances. Major economic issues of national importance have been debated publicly without the help of objective economic research, while much of the academic economic research has focused on relatively narrow and technical questions. Although there is obviously an important role for such basic research, it is important also for the economics profession to contribute serious research to the broader public policy debate. The purpose of this new NBER annual conference is to stimulate such empirical research on significant national issues.

I am grateful to Stanley Fischer for organizing this annual conference and for editing this volume. I have the highest expectations for the contribution of this series over the years ahead.

Martin S. Feldstein
President
The National Bureau of Economic Research

Editorial

This new journal aims to encourage and disseminate research on real macroeconomic problems. It will appear once a year, and will include two kinds of articles, the first directed to answering specific questions, the second showing the empirical relevance of potentially important new ideas in macroeconomics.

Three articles in this volume fall into the first category: Blanchard and Summers analyze the causes of high European unemployment; Hayashi examines the causes of high Japanese saving rates; and Feldstein seeks to establish, empirically, links between the budget deficit and the exchange rate. The articles by Martin Eichenbaum and Kenneth Singleton on real business cycles, Lawrence Katz on efficiency wage theory, and Martin Weitzman on profit sharing, are of the second kind.

The articles were invited for this volume, and were initially presented at a conference held in Cambridge, Massachusetts, in early March 1986. They have been revised in light of the incisive comments made by the formal discussants and the discussion at the conference. The discussants' comments and a brief summary of the discussion at the conference follow each article. To maintain the currency of the papers and the comments, the journal appears very rapidly after the conference.

Although each article sets its own scene well, I will briefly describe the motivation and the approach taken by the authors, starting with the paper by Olivier Blanchard and Lawrence Summers. European unemployment has been rising more or less steadily since 1970. European unemployment had been well below U.S. levels in the 1950s and 1960s, reached U.S. levels in the 1970s, and by now is well above U.S. rates in most countries—and almost double the U.S. rate in the United Kingdom.

Blanchard and Summers describe the problem and find that in the past there have been similar periods in which unemployment in both Europe and the United States has risen and stayed high. Indeed, they argue that the unemployment rate is so persistent that the standard textbook view that the economy, left alone, tends to revert to a stable "natural" rate of unemployment has to be questioned. They explain this persistence by the contrast between insiders (those with a job) and outsiders (the unemployed). Wage bargaining between the firm and its insider-workers results in a contract that takes into account the interests of the insiders but not the outsiders. Workers cease to influence wage bargains once they have lost their jobs, and therefore cannot take actions that will increase their chances of being employed. Thus the unemployment rate tends to stay at its current level, except for shocks such as unexpected changes in aggregate supply (increases or decreases in oil prices, for example) or demand. They explain rising European unemployment as the result of a sequence of adverse supply shocks in the 70's, and demand shocks in the 80's, particularly increasingly tight European fiscal policy.

The Blanchard-Summers article departs, by implication, from the previously standard view that European unemployment is in large measure the result of excessively high real wages. They do not focus on the behavior of real wages, emphasizing that both real wages and unemployment are endogenous and that it makes very little sense to blame unemployment on real wages. In their model, a union that is willing to incur a greater risk of unemployment in exchange for higher real wages will produce the unemployment but not higher real wages. Real wages in their model are determined by production conditions. They leave for future research an explanation of the joint movement of real wages and unemployment.

Martin Eichenbaum and Kenneth Singleton describe real business cycle theory. The theory is that business cycle phenomena can be understood as reflecting the effects of a variety of *real* disturbances on an economy in which markets are continuously *in equilibrium*. The theory is identified by both its italicized characteristics. The view is that monetary disturbances, changes in the money stock—or monetary policy more generally—do not affect real economic variables, such as the level of output, the real interest rate, or the real exchange rate. Second, the theory sees no need to assume that markets are in disequilibrium, since many of the phenomena that are usually viewed as reflecting disequilibrium, such as cyclical fluctuations, are potentially consistent with equilibrium. Eichenbaum and Singleton take a pragmatic approach to the nonmonetary aspect of the approach, arguing not that monetary disturbances inherently cannot affect real variables, but that they have not in practice done so in the postwar U.S. economy.

After constructing an equilibrium business cycle model that includes a potential role for monetary disturbances to affect output, Eichenbaum and Singleton concentrate on empirical work that examines the role of money in postwar U.S. cycles. Using vector autoregressions, they fail to find signs of monetary influences. These surprising results receive considerable attention both from the formal discussants and in the informal discussion. The discussants also noted that a failure to find monetary effects on real output bore on the first characteristic of real business cycle theory—that the cycle is not caused by monetary factors—but left open the second issue, whether the cycle is an equilibrium phenomenon driven mainly by shocks to productivity.

Extraordinarily high Japanese saving rates contrast remarkably with U.S. savings behavior. Observers who worry about lagging U.S. productivity growth and the need for modernizing investment hope that saving incentives will increase the supply of investment funds in this country. Fumio Hayashi's careful and informative paper seeking to explain the high Japanese saving rate first puts U.S. and Japanese savings data on a common statistical basis, thereby reducing some of the discrepancy. Even so, there is a large difference to explain.

Hayashi then turns to detailed cross-sectional Japanese data. The standard life-cycle model in which individual saving is driven by the need to finance retirement spending is shown not to account for the high Japanese saving rate, even when account is taken of the difficulty of borrowing to buy houses in Japan. Two striking features of the Japanese life-cycle pattern are that elderly parents tend to move in with their children and that housing (particularly the value of land) accounts for a large share of wealth. Hayashi attributes some of the high Japanese saving rate to these characteristics, arguing that parents appear to accumulate wealth in large part to make bequests, largely in the form of housing, to children.

The national saving rate in Japan declined substantially in the 1970s as the government started running large deficits, and the Japanese saving rate began to fall towards (but is still far from) the U.S. rate. Hayashi believes that this trend will continue, with part of Japanese saving behavior during the 1960s and 1970s reflecting an effort by individuals to raise their standard of living rapidly. His discussants raise the question of whether the high Japanese growth rate might not be responsible for the high saving rate, rather than vice versa, though the channels for that line of causation remain unclear.

Many theories attribute business cycle fluctuations largely to wage and price stickiness. If there is excess unemployment, firms would, according to these views, be willing to hire more workers if only wages could be cut. Although this argument is not watertight, it does focus attention on the behavior of wages. Efficiency wage theory is the view that firms do not cut wages because the efficiency with which labor works depends on the real or relative wage it receives.

Lawrence Katz describes several versions of efficiency wage theory. He starts from the strongest form of the theory relevant in poor countries where the physical health and efficiency of the worker depends on his or her earning enough to pay for food. He also discusses versions in which workers whose effort on the job is only imperfectly observable are paid above market wages so that there is a real penalty in the loss of a job if they are caught shirking. In addition to describing the theories, Katz draws out their empirical implications, many of which relate to differences in wages across different job categories. The alternative, standard theory ascribes wage differentials to differences in workers' abilities, rather than to, for example, the difficulty of monitoring effort on different jobs.

The macroeconomic implications of efficiency wage theory receive attention in both Katz's paper and the following discussion. The real wage rigidity implied by the theory may allow supply shocks to affect employment. It is more difficult to show that real wage rigidity can account for effects of nominal shocks, such as changes in monetary policy, on output. A recent development outlined by Katz is the "small menu cost" approach that shows that under certain circumstances, small costs of changing prices will lead to price rigidity that may have large impacts on the level of output. The merits of this approach too receive considerable attention in the discussion.

Martin Weitzman's work on the macroeconomic implications of alternative labor compensation arrangements has led him to the view that profit sharing would produce more stable employment with less inflation than the current wage system. His article develops the analytical basis for this conclusion. The analysis suggests that although the equilibrium level of unemployment might be similar under wage and profit sharing systems, responses of output and employment to shocks would be very different. In particular, with profit sharing, the incentive of firms to lay off workers in response to reductions in product demand is much reduced. In a useful question-and-answer section of the paper, Weitzman answers many of the questions typically raised about profit sharing. He then examines the Japanese bonus system, concluding that it can be viewed as a profit sharing system. He cautiously suggests it may have some responsibility for the superior employment performance of the Japanese economy.

Weitzman's work has received considerable public attention, and even recognition in the 1986 British budget. Discussants of course raised their doubts about the approach, many along the lines of "How come if this is a good idea it hasn't already been implemented?" In reply Weitzman emphasizes the possible divergence between private and social benefit: employment might be more stable in the economy as a whole with the implementation of profit sharing, even though no single firm might find it worthwhile to introduce if all other firms are on the wage system.

The extraordinary appreciation of the dollar between 1980 and the beginning of 1985 is the focus of Martin Feldstein's "The Budget Deficit and the Dollar." Conventional macroeconomic models predict that expansionary fiscal policy will produce higher real interest rates, an appreciation, and a current account deficit. Feldstein explores the exchange rate–budget deficit link in a series of regressions of the real exchange rate of the dollar against current and expected budget deficits, and a variety of other variables that might be expected to affect the exchange rate. These include the investment-incentive tax changes of 1981 that have been held partly responsible for the increase in demand for funds in the United States, and the growth rate of the monetary base, representing monetary policy.

Feldstein's results appear remarkably robust, with the budget variable almost inevitably significant in affecting the exchange rate. According to his regressions most of the appreciation of the dollar is accounted for by the change in U.S. fiscal policy. Some of the discussants accepted Feldstein's basic approach but probed the sensitivity of his conclusions. Others believed that to a first approximation, changes in taxes have no effects on interest rates or the exchange rate, but that changes in government spending do. This is the so-called Ricardian equivalence theory that holds that deficits merely represent future taxes, which have precisely the same effect on current actions as current taxes. Several discussants pointed out that changes in the mix of national spending—for instance, toward foreign goods—associated with fiscal changes could affect the real exchange rate even if Ricardian equivalence held. Whatever the doubts, Feldstein's regressions point to significant fiscal policy effects on exchange rates.

Stanley Fischer

Acknowledgments

The organization of the conference at which the articles in this volume were first presented and the rapid publication of this first *NBER Macroeconomics Annual* took the cooperation of several of the ever-efficient and ever-pleasant members of the National Bureau of Economic Research's Cambridge staff and the MIT Press. Kirsten Foss and Annie Spillane at the Bureau and Christine Lamb at the MIT Press deserve special thanks.

In future issues, it will go without saying that the authors and discussants have labored hard and well to produce articles and comments on time, and even more remarkably, to send them in on time. This time it deserves to be said, for the first volume sets a high standard for the future. Readers will certainly appreciate the high quality and the interest of the articles, as well as the serious thought that has gone into many of the formal discussants' comments.

Takeo Hoshi, of the MIT Economics Department, was invaluable in the editing process, both in checking the manuscripts and in writing up the reports of the discussion. I am grateful to him, and to the informal advisory committee for this first volume, Olivier Blanchard, Rudiger Dornbusch, and Lawrence Summers. Martin Feldstein's support was essential.

Stanley Fischer

Abstracts

Hysteresis and the European Unemployment Problem

OLIVIER J. BLANCHARD AND LAWRENCE H. SUMMERS

European unemployment has been steadily increasing for the last fifteen years and is expected to remain very high for many years to come. In this paper, we argue that this fact implies that shocks have much more persistent effects on unemployment than standard theories can possibly explain. We develop a theory that can explain such persistence, and that is based on the distinction between insiders and outsiders in wage bargaining. We argue that if wages are largely set by bargaining between insiders and firms, shocks which affect actual unemployment tend also to affect equilibrium unemployment. We then confront the theory with both the detailed facts of the European situation as well as those of earlier periods of high persistent unemployment, such as the Great Depression in the United States.

Do Equilibrium Real Business Cycle Theories Explain Postwar U.S. Business Cycles?

MARTIN EICHENBAUM AND KENNETH J. SINGLETON

This article presents and interprets some new evidence on the validity of the real business cycle (RBC) approach to business cycle analysis. The analysis is conducted in the context of a monetary business cycle model that makes explicit one potential link between monetary policy and real allocations. This model is used to interpret Granger causal relations between nominal and real aggregates. Perhaps the most striking empirical finding is that money growth does not Granger cause output growth in the context of several multivariate VARs and for various sample periods during the postwar period in the United States. Several possible reconciliations of this finding with both real and monetary business cycles models are discussed. We find that it is difficult to reconcile our empirical results with the view that exogenous monetary shocks were an important independent source of variation in output growth.

Why Is Japan's Saving Rate So Apparently High?

FUMIO HAYASHI

This article begins with a look at time-series data on aggregate saving for the United States and Japan. After showing that a resolution of conceptual differences substantially narrows the gap in the saving rates between the two countries, the article examines various explanations for Japan's high saving rate by confronting them with a wealth of tabulations from household surveys in Japan. The life-cycle explanation is found to be inadequate. The prevalence of the extended family and bequests are singled out as probably the most important factor contributing to higher saving. An attempt is made to estimate the flow of intergenerational transfers. It is argued at the end that Japan's recent large trade surplus is due more to her slumping investment than any increase in saving.

Efficiency Wage Theories: A Partial Evaluation

LAWRENCE F. KATZ

This paper surveys recent developments in the literature on efficiency wage theories of unemployment. Efficiency wage models have in common the property that in equilibrium firms may find it profitable to pay wages in excess of market clearing. High wages can help reduce turnover, elicit worker effort, prevent worker collective action, and attract higher-quality employees. Simple versions of efficiency wage models can explain normal involuntary unemployment, segmented labor markets, and wage differentials across firms and industries for workers with similar productive characteristics. However, deferred payment schemes can solve some efficiency wage problems without requiring job rationing. A wide variety of evidence on interindustry wage differences is analyzed. Efficiency wage models appear useful in explaining the observed pattern of wage differentials. The models also provide several mechanisms for cyclical fluctuations in response to aggregate demand shocks.

Macroeconomic Implications of Profit Sharing

MARTIN L. WEITZMAN

This article argues that substantial progress in the struggle for full employment without inflation will have to come largely from basic changes in pay-setting arrangements rather than from better manipulation of financial aggregates. My analysis suggests that widespread profit sharing, along the general lines practiced in Japan, represents a structural reform of the labor market that is likely to improve the unemployment-inflation trade-off. I attempt to place the problem of labor payment mechanisms in historical perspective; I then provide an analytic framework for comparing wage and profit-sharing systems. Major criticisms of profit sharing are discussed in a question and answer format. Profit sharing is then compared with three alternative and, I argue, less promising prototypes for structural reform of the labor market: incomes policy, two-tiered pay, and employee control. The Japanese experience is then examined with an eye to evaluating the possible macroeconomic impact of the bonus system and implications for profit or revenue sharing.

The Budget Deficit and the Dollar

MARTIN S. FELDSTEIN

This study examines the reasons for changes in the real exchange rate between the dollar and the German mark from the beginning of the floating rate regime in 1973 through 1984. The econometric analysis focuses on the effects of anticipated structural budget deficits and monetary policy in the United States and Germany and the changes in U.S. profitability induced by changes in tax rules. The possible impact of a number of other variables is also examined.

The evidence indicates that the rise in expected future deficits in the budget of the U.S. government has had a powerful effect on the exchange rate between the dollar and the German mark. Each one percentage point increase in the ratio of future budget deficits to GNP increased the exchange rate by about 30 percentage points. Changes in the growth of the money supply also affect the exchange rate. Changes in tax rules and in the inflation-tax interaction that altered the corporate demand for funds did not have any discernible effect on the exchange rate.

A separate analysis confirms that there is an equilibrium structural relation between the dollar-DM exchange rate and interest rates in the United States and Germany. An increase of one percentage point in the real interest rate differential has been associated with a rise in the DM-dollar rate of about 5 percent.

Olivier J. Blanchard and *Lawrence H. Summers*
MASSACHUSETTS INSTITUTE OF TECHNOLOGY AND NBER,
HARVARD UNIVERSITY AND NBER

Hysteresis and the European Unemployment Problem

After twenty years of negligible unemployment, most of Western Europe has since the early 1970s suffered a protracted period of high and rising unemployment. In the United Kingdom unemployment peaked at 3.3 percent over the period 1945–1970, but has risen almost continuously since 1970, and now stands at over 12 percent. For the Common Market nations as a whole, the unemployment rate more than doubled between 1970 and 1980 and has doubled again since then. Few forecasts call for a significant decline in unemployment over the next several years, and none call for its return to levels close to those that prevailed in the 1950s and 1960s.

These events are not easily accounted for by conventional classical or Keynesian macroeconomic theories. Rigidities associated with fixed-length contracts, or the costs of adjusting prices or quantities, are unlikely to be large enough to account for rising unemployment over periods of a decade or more. And intertemporal substitution in labor supply is surely not an important aspect of such a protracted downturn. The sustained upturn in European unemployment challenges the premise of most macroeconomic theories that there exists some "natural" or "non-accelerating inflation" rate of unemployment toward which the economy tends to gravitate and at which the level of inflation remains constant. The European experience compels consideration of alternative theories of "hysteresis" which contemplate the possibility that increases in unemployment have a direct impact on the "natural" rate of unemployment.

This article explores theoretically and empirically the idea of macroeconomic hysteresis—the substantial persistence of unemployment and the protracted effects of shocks on unemployment. We are particularly interested in the current European situation; we seek explanations for the pattern of high and rising unemployment that has prevailed in Europe for the past decade and for the very different performance of the labor markets in the United States and Europe, and we reach some tentative conclusions about the extent to which European unemployment problems can be solved by expansionary demand policies. The central hypothesis we put forward is that hysteresis resulting from membership considerations plays an important role in explaining the current European depression in particular and persistent high unemployment in general. The essential point is that there is a fundamental asymmetry in the wage-setting process between insiders who are employed and outsiders who want jobs. Outsiders are disenfranchised and wages are set with a view to ensuring the jobs of insiders. Shocks that lead to reduced employment change the number of insiders and thereby change the subsequent equilibrium wage rate, giving rise to hysteresis. Membership considerations can therefore explain the general tendency of the equilibrium unemployment rate to follow the actual unemployment rate. We adduce a number of types of empirical evidence consistent with our hypothesis. The paper is organized as follows:

Section 1 documents the dimensions of the current European depression. By looking at movements in unemployment in the United States and the United Kingdom over the past century, we show that high unemployment is in fact often quite persistent. We review and find lacking, standard explanations of the current European situation. We then consider a number of mechanisms through which a high persistence of unemployment could be generated.

Section 2 explores what we find the most promising of the possible mechanisms for generating hysteresis. It presents a formal model illustrating how temporary shocks can have a permanent effect on the level of employment in contexts where wages are set by employers who bargain with insiders. Persistence results in this setting because shocks change employment and membership in the group of insiders, thus influencing its subsequent bargaining strategy. We then discuss the role of unions and whether such effects can arise in nonunion settings.

Section 3 examines the behavior of postwar Europe in light of our theory of hysteresis. It presents direct evidence on the role of unions, on the behavior of wages and employment, and on the composition of unemployment. We find the European experience quite consistent with our model. Europe appears to have high hysteresis, much more so than the United States. High unemployment in Europe and low unemployment in the United States are well explained both by different sequences of shocks, especially in the 1980s, and by different propagation mechanisms, with Europe exhibiting more persistence than the United States.

Section 4 returns to an issue of fundamental importance for policy. Granting that Europe has more hysteresis than the United States, is it really due to unions or is hysteresis itself endogenous, being triggered by bad times? In an attempt to answer this question, we compare Europe now to Europe earlier when unemployment was low, and compare the current European depression to the U.S. Great Depression. The latter comparison is especially important, given the ability of the United States to decrease unemployment drastically in 1939 and 1940, mostly through aggregate demand. The conclusion summarizes our beliefs and doubts, and draws the implications of our analysis for policy.

1. The Record of Persistent Unemployment

We begin by documenting the dimensions of the current European depression, then demonstrate that Europe's current and persistently high unemployment is not historically unusual. Data for the past century suggest a surprisingly high degree of persistence in unemployment in both the United States and the United Kingdom. We argue that such persistence is not easily explained by standard natural rate theories and conclude that theories that allow for hysteresis—a very high dependence of current unemployment on past unemployment—[1] are required to explain such persistence.

1.1. THE EUROPEAN DEPRESSION

Table 1 presents some information on the evolution of unemployment in three major European countries as well as in the United States over the past twenty-five years. While European unemployment rates in the 1960s were substantially lower than in the United States, unemployment rates in Europe today are substantially greater than current U.S. rates. The unemployment rate in the United States has fluctuated considerably, rising from 4.8 to 8.3 percent in the 1973–1975 recession, then declining to 5.8 percent in 1979, rising to 9.7 percent in 1982 before declining to around 7.0 percent today. In contrast, unemployment in Europe has

1. Formally, a dynamic system is said to exhibit hysteresis if it has at least one eigenvalue equal to zero (unity, if specified in discrete time). In such a case, the steady state of the system will depend on the history of the shocks affecting the system. Thus, we should say that unemployment exhibits hysteresis when current unemployment depends on past values with coefficients summing to 1. We shall instead use "hysteresis" more loosely to refer to the case where the degree of dependence on the past is very high, where the sum of coefficients is close but not necessarily equal to 1.

risen seemingly inexorably since 1973. In France, the unemployment rate has increased in every single year since 1973, while it has declined only twice in Germany and the United Kingdom. The differences between the European countries and the United States are most pronounced after 1980. While the U.S. unemployment rate is at roughly its 1980 level, it has approximately doubled in the three European countries. The rapid decline in U.S. unemployment after 1982 contrasts sharply with the continuing increase in unemployment in Europe. The last line of table 1 gives European Commission forecasts of unemployment for 1986: they show little expected change. Longer-run forecasts are very similar: baseline projections by the European Commission put unemployment for the EEC as a whole at 10.4 percent in 1990, compared to 10.8 percent in 1985.

Differences in unemployment rates actually understate the differences in the performance of American and European labor markets over the past decade. Europe has suffered the concomitants of high unemployment—reduced labor force participation and involuntary reductions in hours—to a much greater extent than has the United States. Between 1975 and 1983, the labor force participation rate of men in the United States remained constant, while the corresponding rate in OECD Europe declined by 6 percent. Average annual hours worked declined by 2.7 percent in the United States between 1975 and 1982, compared with declines of 7.5 percent in France and 8.1 percent in the United Kingdom. Perhaps the most striking contrast of the labor market performances of Europe and the United States is the observation that between 1975 and 1985 em-

Table 1 EUROPEAN AND U.S. UNEMPLOYMENT, 1961–1986

	United States	*United Kingdom*	*France*	*West Germany*
1961–1970	4.7	1.9	.9	.8
1971–1975	6.1	2.8	2.6	1.8
1976–1980	6.7	5.2	5.3	3.7
1980	7.1	6.0	6.4	3.4
1981	7.6	9.2	7.7	4.8
1982	9.7	10.6	8.7	6.9
1983	9.6	11.6	8.8	8.4
1984	7.5	11.8	9.9	8.4
1985	7.3	12.0	10.7	8.4
1986*	7.2	11.7	10.9	8.0

Source. Annual Economic Review, Commission of the European Communities, 1986.
*Forecast.

ployment increased by 25 percent, or about 25 million jobs, in the United States while declining in absolute terms in Europe.[2]

1.2. UNEMPLOYMENT RATES IN THE UNITED KINGDOM AND THE UNITED STATES OVER THE LAST CENTURY

European unemployment has increased steadily and, pending an unexpected change in policy, is expected to remain at this new higher level for the foreseeable future. How unusual is such high and persistent unemployment? To answer this question, we will now examine the behavior of

2. This difference reflects different demographic trends in the two countries as well as differences in labor market performance.

Figure 1   U.K. UNEMPLOYMENT RATE

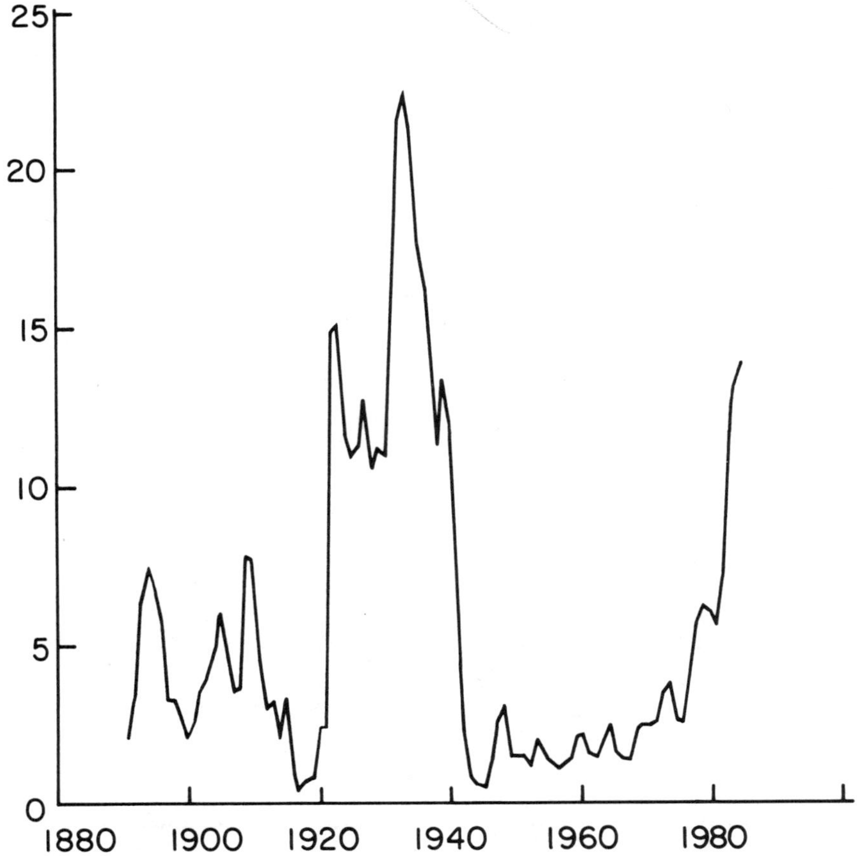

unemployment over the last century in both the United Kingdom and the United States.

Figures 1 and 2 plot unemployment for each of the two countries, for the period 1890–1985 for the United Kingdom, and 1892–1985 for the United States.[3]

Estimation of an AR(1) process for the whole sample for each country gives:

$$\text{UK: } u = \underset{(.04)}{.93}\, u(-1) + e;\ \sigma_e = 2.1\%$$

3. For the United States we made use of the revised unemployment rates calculated by Romer (1986) for the 1890–1929 period.

Figure 2 U.S. UNEMPLOYMENT RATE

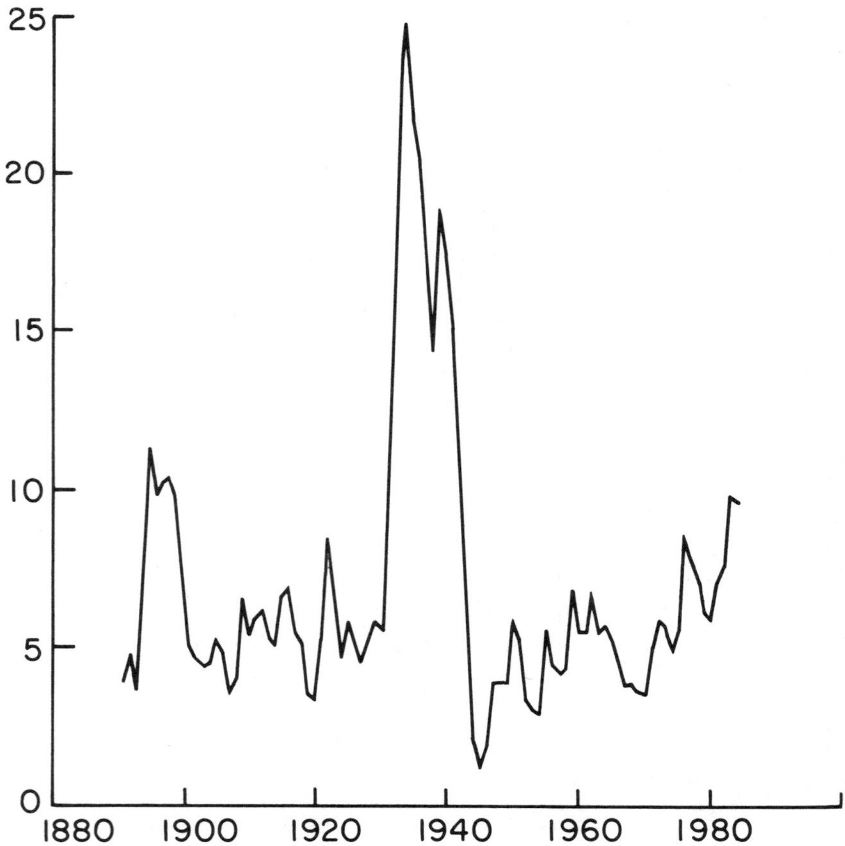

$$\text{US:} \quad u = \underset{(.04)}{.90}\, u(-1) + e; \sigma_e = 2.0\%$$

In both cases, the degree of first-order serial correlation is high. Unemployment is indeed surprisingly persistent. It exhibits at best a weak tendency to return to its mean.

Examination of the two figures—as well as statistical work—suggests that the evolution of the unemployment rate over the past century is not well captured by any simple linear autoregressive representation. The degree of persistence as captured by the degree of first-order serial correlation reported above arises largely from relatively infrequent changes in the level around which unemployment fluctuates. In the U.K., when unemployment goes up from 1920 to 1940, it shows little tendency during that period to return to its pre-1920 level; it then returns to a low level during World War II, to stay there until the 1960s. The current episode, both past and forecast, is a second instance in which unemployment, after having sharply increased, stabilizes at a new, high level. The United States experienced a sustained increase in unemployment from 1929 to 1939, only to see it drop sharply during and after the war to a new, much lower, level. When the degree of persistence in unemployment is estimated separately for periods of high and low average unemployment, there is some weak evidence of greater persistence within periods of high average unemployment.

Time series studied in isolation give little indication as to the cause of the changes in the mean level, which account for much of the persistence in unemployment. They could be exogenous or be triggered by unemployment itself, with a few years of high unemployment triggering an increase in the mean level of unemployment, a few years of low unemployment in turn triggering a decrease. Lacking a tight specification of how this triggering occurs we do not believe that the data can easily distinguish between these two possibilities, so we shall not attempt to do so.

Our finding that unemployment exhibits a very high degree of persistence over the past century parallels the findings of Nelson and Plosser (1982), Campbell and Mankiw (1986) and others that a variety of economic variables follow random walks or other nonstationary processes. In many cases such findings can be easily rationalized by recognizing that the level of technology is likely to be nonstationary and that other variables such as the level of output depend on productivity. But the failure of unemployment to display more of a mean-reverting tendency is troubling. It is unlikely that nonstationarity in productivity can account for the persistence of unemployment since the secular increase in productivity has not been associated with any trend or upward drift in unemployment.

1.3. DIAGNOSING UNEMPLOYMENT PROBLEMS

What sort of theories can account for persistent high unemployment in general and the current European experience in particular? We highlight the general difficulties one encounters in explaining persistent unemployment by focusing on the problem of explaining the current European situation. The central puzzle it poses is its persistence. While it is easy to point to substantial adverse supply and demand shocks over the last fifteen years, we argue that our standard theories do not easily explain how they have had such enduring effects on the level of unemployment.[4]

Aggregate Demand There is little question that Europe has been affected by large adverse demand shocks, especially since 1980 (see, for example, Dornbusch et al. (1983)). In the 1980s, Europe has to a large extent matched tight U.S. monetary policy while at the same time engaging in a major and prolonged fiscal contraction (see Blanchard and Summers 1984 for the U.K., Germany and France; see Buiter 1985 for a more detailed study of U.K. fiscal policy).

But to the extent that aggregate demand shocks do not affect the equilibrium or natural rate of unemployment, one would expect sustained high unemployment to be associated with rapid declines in the rate of inflation. More generally, standard models of the effects of aggregate demand shocks would not predict that previous estimates of the relationship between inflation and unemployment would break down. There is, however, substantial evidence that this relation has broken down and that the decline in inflation has been much smaller than would have been predicted by past relationships. The relation between wage inflation and unemployment will be examined in detail later, but the basic point that previous relations have broken down is evidenced in table 2, which gives the rates of inflation and unemployment in 1984 and 1985 for the United Kingdom, France, and Germany. Despite the high rates of unemployment, there is no sign of disinflation, with the United Kingdom and Germany seeing a small increase in inflation and France a small decrease. Econometric estimates of the rate of unemployment consistent with stable inflation show rapid increases over the past decade. Layard et al.

4. This section relies heavily on the empirical work presented for individual European countries at the Chelwood Gate Conference on Unemployment, to be published in *Economica*, 1986. The reader is referred to individual country papers for further evidence.

(1984), using crude time trends in a Phillips curve relation, find the unemployment rate consistent with steady inflation to have risen from 2.4 in 1967–70 to 9.2 in 1981–1983 in Britain, from 1.3 to 6.2 in Germany, and from 2.2 to 6.9 in France. Coe and Gagliardi (1985), also within the framework of the Phillips curve but using instead of a time trend a battery of potential determinants of equilibrium unemployment as right-hand side variables, obtain roughly similar results. Aggregate demand shocks have clearly played a role in explaining the increase in European unemployment, but they cannot be the whole story, given the increase in the rate of unemployment consistent with steady inflation.

Aggregate Supply Aggregate supply explanations appear more promising if the goal is to explain an increase in equilibrium unemployment. This is indeed the approach followed by much of the recent research. Sachs (1979; 1983) and Bruno and Sachs (1985) have argued that unemployment in Europe is largely the result of a combination of adverse supply shocks and real wage rigidity. The argument is that real wages do not adjust to clear the labor market so that adverse supply shocks that reduce the demand for labor at a given real wage create unemployment. This argument has two parts, real wage rigidity and the occurrence of adverse supply shocks. We start by reviewing the evidence on the second.

Table 3 presents some information on the behavior of various supply factors with a potential bearing on unemployment in the United Kingdom since 1960.[5]

A first candidate is *unemployment benefits*. Unemployment insurance may raise unemployment if it causes workers to search longer or less intensively for jobs, reducing the pressure that unemployment puts on

5. We focus on the United Kingdom because detailed data are easily available. Available data for France and Germany tell a very similar story.

Table 2 INFLATION AND UNEMPLOYMENT IN THE UNITED KINGDOM, FRANCE, AND GERMANY, 1984–1985

	United Kingdom		*France*		*Germany*	
	π	U	π	U	π	U
1984	4.4	11.8	7.0	9.9	1.9	8.4
1985	5.5	12.0	5.7	10.7	2.1	8.4

π = Rate of change of GDP deflator.
U = Unemployment.

Source: Annual Economic Review, Commission of the European Communities, 1986.

wages. The second column of table 3 gives the average replacement ratio, the average ratio of after-tax unemployment benefits to earnings for different categories of workers; it shows no clear movement over time. This is not necessarily conclusive evidence against a role for unemployment benefits: one can easily envision mechanisms through which increases in unemployment benefits lead to higher real wages and higher unemployment but little or no change in the replacement ratio. Indeed, another way of reading the column is that it shows an increase in real unemployment benefits of roughly 30 percent since 1970. Furthermore, it has been argued that the principal changes in unemployment insurance have occurred through changes in eligibility rules rather than benefit levels. Attempts to estimate the effect of unemployment benefits on unemployment have not been very successful (see Minford (1982) and Nickell (1984)) and one is led to conclude that the increase in unemployment benefits probably does not account for a large portion of the increase in unemployment.

A second candidate explanation is *structural change*. The argument is

Table 3 SUPPLY FACTORS AND U.K. UNEMPLOYMENT

Year	*Unemployment Rate (%)*[a]	*Replacement Rate (%)*[b]	*Mismatch Index (%)*[c]	*Productivity Growth (%)*[d]	*Change in Tax Wedge (%)*[e]
1960	2.3	42	—	1.9	.0
1965	2.3	48	41	2.8	1.0
1970	3.1	51	38	3.2	1.0
1975	4.7	49	43	2.7	.8
1976	6.0	50	38	1.5	2.8
1977	6.4	51	35	1.7	1.9
1978	6.1	50	35	1.4	−.9
1979	5.6	46	35	2.1	1.3
1980	6.9	45	37	1.5	1.3
1981	10.6	50	41	1.4	2.6
1982	12.8	54	37	1.1	1.0
1983	13.1	54	—	.5	−1.8

a. Standardized unemployment rate; source OECD.
b. Weighted average of replacement rates relevant to families of different sizes. Source: Layard and Nickell (1986).
c. Index constructed as $\Sigma \mid u_i - v_i \mid$ where u_i and v_i are the proportions of unemployment and vacancies in occupation *i* respectively. Source: Layard, Nickell, and Jackman (1984).
d. Rate of change of total factor productivity growth, derived by assuming labor augmenting technical change. The first four numbers refer to the rate of change (at annual rate) over the previous five years. Source: Layard and Nickell (1986).
e. The tax wedge is the sum of the employment tax rate levied on employers and of direct and indirect tax rates levied on employees. The first four numbers refer to the rate of change (at annual rates) over the previous five years. Source: Layard and Nickell (1986).

that the need for large-scale reallocation of labor associated with structural change tends to increase unemployment. Often it is suggested that the energy shocks of the 1970s increased the rate of structural change and so led to higher unemployment. The adjustment to structural changes may be complicated by real wage rigidity. The third column of table 3 presents the index of "mismatch" developed by Layard, Nickell, and Jackman (1984). This index tries to represent the degree of structural change in the economy by examining the extent to which unemployment and vacancies occur in the same sectors. The results in the table look at occupational mismatch, but results are largely similar when industrial and regional measures are used.[6] There is little evidence of an increase in the rate of structural change since the 1960s, when the unemployment rate was consistently low.

Perhaps the most common supply-based explanations for persistent high unemployment involve factors that reduce labor productivity or drive a wedge between the cost of labor to firms and the wage workers receive. The fourth and fifth columns of the table give time series for *total factor productivity growth* and the change in the *tax wedge*.[7] It is clear from the table that there has been a substantial reduction in the rate of total factor productivity growth in the wake of the oil shocks. Over the years the total tax wedge has also risen substantially, by 30 percent since 1960, by 10 percent since 1970. While it is still true that the real after-tax wage consistent with full employment has risen fairly steadily, it has increased more slowly than it had in the first half of the postwar period.

The Problem with Aggregate Supply Explanations We have now documented the presence of adverse supply developments relative to what might have been expected in the early 1970s. But for these shocks to have a long-lasting effect on unemployment, there must be long-lasting real wage rigidity. If and when labor supply becomes inelastic, supply shocks are then reflected in real wages, not in unemployment. Surely, individual labor supply is inelastic in the long run. As with aggregate demand explanations, we face the problem of explaining the mechanism that causes shocks to have long-lived effects.

Recent models of union behavior (notably McDonald and Solow (1981)) have addressed this problem by showing that if wages are the result of bargaining between unions and firms, the result may be real wage

6. The mismatch index by industry goes up, however, in 1981 and 1982—the last two years for which it has been computed.

7. Let a be the rate of growth of productivity and θ be the change in the tax wedge. Then the rate of growth of the after-tax real wage consistent with a given capital/labor ratio is approximately given by $a - \theta$.

rigidity, with shocks affecting employment only. There is, however, a fundamental difficulty with this line of argument. To take the model developed by McDonald and Solow, if real wages were truly rigid at a rate determined by the interaction of union preferences and firms' production technology, employment would steadily increase and unemployment steadily decrease through time. Annual productivity improvements due to technical change are equivalent to favorable supply shocks. As long as productivity increments and capital accumulation lead to the demand curve for labor shifting outward faster than the population grows, unemployment would decline. This appears counterfactual.[8] Even over the last decade, the cumulative impact of productivity growth has almost certainly more than counterbalanced the adverse supply shocks that occurred.

To rescue this line of thought, it must be argued that real wages are rigid along some "norm," which may increase over time. But this has two implications. The first is that the dynamic effects of supply shocks on employment then depend on the way the norm adjusts to actual productivity—this is left unexplained. The second and more important here is that adverse supply shocks have an effect only as long as the norm has not adjusted to actual productivity. Thus, unless the norm never catches up with actual productivity, adverse supply shocks cannot affect unemployment permanently. It seems implausible that the current persistence of high unemployment can all be attributed to lags in learning about productivity. Both the United Kingdom and the United States have experienced enormous productivity gains without evident reduction in unemployment over the last century. High unemployment therefore cannot be blamed simply on poor productivity performance. It can only be attributed to *surprises* in productivity performance. But then it is hard to see how to explain protracted unemployment from lower productivity growth.

Where does this leave us? We have argued that there is plenty of evidence of adverse shocks, whether it be lower-than-expected productivity growth, increases in the price of oil or in the tax wedge in the 1970s or contractionary aggregate demand policies in the 1980s. But we have also argued that standard theories do not provide us with convincing explanations of how these shocks can have such a sustained effect on unemployment. Put differently, it is difficult to account for the apparent increase in the equilibrium rate of unemployment—or equivalently, in the unemployment rate consistent with stable inflation—by pointing to

8. When a time trend is added to the AR(1) specification of unemployment estimated above, its coefficient is both small and insignificant, for both countries.

these shocks. Borrowing from business cycle terminology, it is not difficult to find evidence of negative impulses—the difficulty is in explaining the propagation mechanism. This leads us to look for mechanisms that can explain the propagation of adverse supply or demand shocks over long periods of time. These include the possibility that current unemployment depends directly and strongly on past unemployment.[9] We now consider various channels through which this may happen.

1.4. THEORIES OF HYSTERESIS

Three types of explanation which, loosely speaking, might be referred to as the "physical capital," "human capital," and "insider-outsider" stories can be adduced to explain why shocks that cause unemployment in a single period might have long-term effects.

The physical capital story simply holds that reductions in the capital stock associated with the reduced employment that accompanies adverse shocks reduce the subsequent demand for labor and so cause protracted unemployment. This argument is frequently made in the current European context where it is emphasized that, despite the very substantial increase in the unemployment rate that has occurred, capacity utilization is at fairly normal levels. For the EEC as a whole, capacity utilization has shown no trend over the last decade. It currently stands at 81 percent, compared with 76 percent in 1975, 83 percent in 1979, and 76 percent in 1983. It is then argued that the existing capital stock is simply inadequate to employ the current labor force.

We are somewhat skeptical of the argument that capital accumulation effects can account for high unemployment, for two reasons. First, as long as there are some possibilities for substitution of labor for capital ex post, reductions in the capital stock affect the demand for labor just as adverse supply shocks do. As we have noted, it is unlikely that an anticipated supply shock would have an important effect on the unemployment rate. Second (see section 4), substantial disinvestment during the 1930s did not preclude the rapid recovery of employment associated with rearmament in a number of other countries. Nor did the very substantial reduction in the size of the civilian capital stock that occurred during the war prevent the attainment of full employment after the war in many countries.[10] The argument that reduced capital accumulation has an important effect on the level of unemployment is difficult to support with historical examples.

9. This is also the direction of research recently followed by Sachs (1985) to explain European unemployment.
10. Unemployment remained high—around 10 percent—in Italy until about 1960 but other factors are thought to have been at work in that case.

A second and perhaps more important mechanism works through "human capital," broadly defined. Persuasive statements of the potentially important effects of unemployment on human capital accumulation and subsequent labor supply may be found in Phelps (1972) and Hargraves-Heap (1980).[11] Some suggestive empirical evidence may be found in Clark and Summers (1982). Essentially, the human capital argument holds that workers who are unemployed lose the opportunity to maintain and update their skills by working. Particularly for the long-term unemployed, the atrophy of skills may combine with disaffection from the labor force associated with the inability to find a job to reduce the effective supply of labor. Early retirement may for example be a semi-irreversible decision. More generally, if for incentive or human capital reasons employers prefer workers with long horizons, it may be very difficult for middle-aged workers to find new jobs. A final point is that in a high-unemployment environment, it will be difficult for reliable and able workers to signal their quality by holding jobs and being promoted. The resulting inefficiencies in sorting workers may reduce the overall demand for labor.

Beyond the adverse effects on labor supply generated by high unemployment, the benefits of a high-pressure economy are foregone. Clark and Summers (1982) demonstrate that in the United States at least, World War II had a long-lasting effect in raising female labor force participation. Despite the baby boom, in 1950 the labor force participation of all female cohorts that were old enough to have worked during the war was significantly greater than would have been predicted on the basis of prewar trends. The causal role of participation during the war is evidenced by the fact that the participation of very young women who could not have worked during the war was actually lower than would have been predicted on the basis of earlier trends. Similarly, research by Ellwood (1981) suggests that teenage unemployment may leave some "permanent scars" on subsequent labor market performance. One channel through which this may occur is family composition. The superior labor market performance of married men with children has been noted many times. The effect of the Great Depression on fertility rates, both in the United States and in Europe has often been noted.

Gauging the quantitative importance of human capital mechanisms generating hysteresis is very difficult. Some of the arguments, early retirement for example, suggest that labor force participation should decline rather than that unemployment should increase in the aftermath of

11. Drazen (1979) constructs a related model, based on learning by doing, that also generates hysteresis. Hall (1976) explores the possibility that unemployment has long-lasting effects on productivity, and its implications for economic policy.

adverse shocks. Perhaps a more fundamental problem is that to the extent that there is some irreversibility associated with unemployment shocks, it becomes more difficult to explain why temporary shocks have such large short-run effects. If early retirement is forever, why should it be taken in response to a temporary downturn? Overall, while it seems likely that human capital mechanisms can explain some of the protracted response to shocks, it is doubtful that they are sufficient to account completely for the observed degree of persistence.

A third mechanism that can generate persistence and that we regard as the most promising relies on the distinction between "insider" and "outsider" workers, developed in a series of contributions by Lindbeck (see, for example, Lindbeck and Snower (1985)) and used in an important paper by Gregory (1985) to explain the behavior of the Australian economy. To take an extreme case, suppose that all wages are set by bargaining between employed workers—the "insiders"—and firms, with outsiders playing no role in the bargaining process. Insiders are concerned with maintaining their jobs, not insuring the employment of outsiders. This has two implications. First, in the absence of shocks, any level of employment of insiders is self-sustaining; insiders just set the wage so as to remain employed. Second, and more important, in the presence of shocks, employment follows a process akin to a random walk; after an adverse shock, for example, which reduces employment, some workers lose their insider status and the new smaller group of insiders sets the wage so as to maintain this new lower level of employment. Employment and unemployment show no tendency to return to their preshock value, but are instead determined by the history of shocks. This example is extreme but nevertheless suggestive. It suggests that, if wage bargaining is a prevalent feature of the labor market, the dynamic interactions between employment and the size of the group of insiders may generate substantial employment and unemployment persistence. This is the argument we explore in detail in the next section.

2. *A Theory of Unemployment Persistence*

Here we develop a theory of unemployment persistence based on the distinction between insiders and outsiders. As the example sketched at the end of section 1 makes clear, the key assumption of such a theory is that of the relation between employment status and insider status. We can think of this key assumption as an assumption about *membership rules,* the rules that govern the relation between employment status and membership in the group of insiders. The possibility of persistent fluctuations in employment arises because changes in employment may change the group's membership and thereby alter its objective function.[12]

First, we develop a partial equilibrium model of bargaining between a group of insiders and a representative firm and characterize employment dynamics under alternative membership rules. (We use the term "group" rather than the more natural "union" to avoid prejudging the issue of whether the membership considerations we stress are important only in settings where formal unions are present.) Second, we extend the analysis to a general equilibrium setting and show how both nominal and real shocks can have permanent effects on unemployment. Third, we consider two issues: endogeneity of membership rules, and whether our analysis is indeed relevant only or mostly in explicit union settings.

2.1. A MODEL OF MEMBERSHIP RULES AND EMPLOYMENT DYNAMICS

To focus on the dynamic effects of membership rules on the decision of the group of insiders (the "group" for short), we formalize the firm as entirely passive, as presenting a labor demand on which the group chooses its preferred outcome.[13] We start by characterizing employment and wages in a one-period model. In a one-period model, initial membership is given and membership rules are obviously irrelevant. But it is a useful intermediate step, which will allow us to contrast our later results with traditional ones that treat membership as exogenous. Throughout, we make no attempt at generality and use convenient functional forms and some approximations to retain analytical simplicity.

The One-Period Model The group has initial membership n_0 (in logarithms, as are all variables in what follows, unless otherwise mentioned). It faces a labor demand function given by:

$$n = -cw + e \quad (2.1)$$

where n is employment, w is the real wage and e is a random technological shock, with mean Ee, uniformly distributed between $[Ee - a, Ee + a]$. The coefficient a captures the degree of uncertainty associated

12. The issue of membership and membership rules is clearly closely related to the issue of union size and union membership in the union literature. See Farber (1984, section 6) for a survey. This literature has not, however, focused on the dynamic implications of membership rules.

13. Formalizing the firm as passive allows us to concentrate on the effects of alternative membership rules on the decisions of the group of insiders. Allowing for wage bargaining between the firm and insiders as well as for some control of employment ex post by insiders introduces additional issues which we shall discuss later.

with labor demand. The group must decide on a wage w before it knows the realization of e. Given w and the realization of e, the firm then chooses labor according to the labor demand function. If n exceeds n_0, $n - n_0$ outsiders are hired. If n is less than n_0, $n_0 - n$ insiders are laid off. The probability of being laid off is the same for all insiders.

Before specifying the objective function of the group, we can derive, for given w and n_0, *the probability of being employed.* The probability of being employed for an insider is equal to 1 if $n > n_0$. For $n < n_0$, we approximate the probability (which is not in logarithms) of being employed for an insider by $1 - n_0 + n$. This approximation will be good as long as n is not too much smaller than n_0. Under these assumptions, the probability p of being employed is given by

$$\begin{aligned} p &= 1 - (1/(4a))\,(n_0 + cw - Ee + a)^2 \qquad &&\text{for } n_0 + cw \geqslant Ee - a \\ &= 1 &&\text{for } n_0 + cw \leqslant Ee - a \end{aligned} \tag{2.2}$$

(All derivations are in the Appendix.)

If even under the worst outcome —which is $e = Ee - a$ and thus $n = -cw + Ee - a$— n is larger than n_0, then the probability of employment is clearly equal to 1. Otherwise, the probability is an increasing function of expected productivity Ee, a decreasing function of initial membership n_0, and of the wage w. It is also a decreasing function of the degree of uncertainty a; the larger a is, the lower the probability of being employed in bad times, while the probability remains equal to 1 in good times.

The second step is to derive the choice of w. This requires specifying the utility function of the group. The group maximizes the utility function of the representative group member, which we specify as

$$U = p + bw$$

Utility is linear in the probability of employment and the wage. This specification is not the most natural but it is attractive, for two reasons. The first reason is that, as we will see, it implies, together with the specification of probabilities given above, that the group exhibits the stochastic equivalent of inelastic labor supply, that is, an increase in Ee is entirely reflected in an increase in real wages and leaves the probability of employment unchanged. We have argued previously that this is a desirable feature of any model of wage determination given the absence of major trends in unemployment rates over long periods of time.[14] Note, however, that our assumption of stochastically inelastic labor supply is the opposite of that used by McDonald and Solow (1981). Where they postulate a rigid real wage so that the labor supply curve is perfectly elastic, we postulate perfectly inelastic labor supply. The second reason is that it is analytically convenient.

Replacing p by its value from equation (2.2) and solving for the optimal wage w gives:

$$w^* = (1/c)(-n_0 + Ee + a(2(b/c) - 1))$$

Replacing in labor demand gives

$$n = n_0 - a(2(b/c) - 1) + (e - Ee)$$

Replacing w^* in equation (2.2) and rearranging gives the optimal probability:

$$p^* = 1 - a(b/c)^2$$

Thus the wage depends negatively on initial membership. As, by definition, $E(e - Ee) = 0$, whether expected employment exceeds membership depends on the sign of $a(2(b/c) - 1)$, thus on whether b/c is less than ½ or not. The lower b is, the more importance workers attach to employment protection as opposed to the wage; the higher c is, the smaller the wage reduction required to increase expected employment. If b/c is less than ½, workers set a wage low enough to imply expected net hirings of outsiders by the firm. Note, as we have mentioned, that the optimal probability of being employed depends neither on the initial membership nor on expected productivity.[15]

Until now, the analysis has been rather conventional—given the initial membership, insiders choose a wage. This wage and the realization of a disturbance determine employment. But when we go from this one-period model to a dynamic one, there may well be a relation between employment in this period and membership in the next. This relation will depend on the form of membership rules. We now examine how this affects employment dynamics.

We first define *membership rules*. We can think of various membership rules as being indexed by m. Those workers who have been working in the firm for the last m periods belong to the group; they are insiders. Workers who have been laid off for more than m periods lose member-

14. The assumption of stochastically inelastic labor supply maintained here is not realistic for a single firm. It is best to think of the firm under consideration as a representative firm, facing the same shocks as other firms.

15. Because we use a log linear approximation to define p, p^* as defined can be negative. But the approximation is only acceptable for p close to 1, that is, for values of $a(b/c)^2$ not too large.

ship[16] and become outsiders. There are two extreme cases: the first is the case where m is equal to infinity, so that the initial membership never changes. The second is the case where $m = 1$ so that membership always coincides with current employment. The extreme cases highlight the effects of alternative membership rules; we consider them before turning to the more difficult intermediate case.

THE CASE OF A CONSTANT MEMBERSHIP (m = INFINITY) Let us denote by $\bar{n}_i$ beginning of period i membership, and by n_i realized employment in period i. In the present case, membership is equal to $\bar{n}_0$ forever. So, in each period, if n_i exceeds $\bar{n}_0$, all members work; if n_i is less than $\bar{n}_0$, the probability of being employed is given for each member by (approximately) $1 - \bar{n}_0 + n_i$. We assume that the one-period utility function of a worker is given, as above, by $(p_i + bw_i)$ and that the workers' discount factor is equal to θ. Thus the utility of a member at time zero is given by

$$U_0 = E_0 \sum_{i=0}^{\infty} \theta^i \, [p_i + bw_i] \text{ where } \theta \text{ is less than one.}$$

Assume for the moment that the shocks affecting labor demand are uncorrelated over time, or more precisely that e_i is independent and identically distributed, uniform on $[-a, +a]$. (We shall return to the case of serially correlated shocks.) Then by the previous analysis, the probability of being employed in period i, conditional on w_i is given by (using the fact that $Ee_i = 0$),

$$\begin{aligned} p_i &= 1 && \text{for } \bar{n}_0 + cw_i \leqslant -a \\ &= 1 - (1/4a)(\bar{n}_0 + cw_i + a)^2 && \text{for } \bar{n}_0 + cw_i \geqslant -a. \end{aligned}$$

Given that employment outcomes do not affect future membership, and given the assumption that shocks are white noise, the problem faced by members is the same in every period, and thus its solution is the same as that derived above:

$$\begin{aligned} w_i^* &= (1/c)(-\bar{n}_0 + a(2(b/c) - 1)) \text{ and} \\ n_i &= \bar{n}_0 - a(2(b/c) - 1) + e_i \quad (2.3) \end{aligned}$$

In response to white noise shocks, employment will also be white noise. Whether employment is on average larger or smaller than mem-

16. We may also think of asymmetric rules where it takes m_1 periods to acquire membership, and m_2 periods to lose it. We shall briefly return to their likely implications later.

bership depends on whether (b/c) is smaller or larger than ½. If the insiders want strong employment protection, they will choose a wage so that, on average, employment exceeds membership and the firm has a cushion of outsiders who are laid off first in case of adverse shocks.

It is easy to see that the result that employment is white noise will continue to hold regardless of the stochastic process followed by e. As shown above, our assumptions ensure that labor supply is stochastically inelastic. Changes in the expected value of e affect real wages but do not affect the level of employment. Only the deviation of e from its expected value affects the level of employment. By the properties of rational expectations, the unexpected component of e must be serially uncorrelated.

THE CASE WHERE MEMBERSHIP EQUALS EMPLOYMENT ($m = 1$) We now go to the opposite extreme, in which membership comes and goes with employment. In this case membership at time i is simply given by employment at time $i - 1$: $\bar{n}_i = n_{i-1}$. If the group kept the same decision rule as in equation (2.3) but applied it to $\bar{n}_i$ rather than to $\bar{n}_0$, equation (2.3) would become

$$\omega_i^* = (1/c)(-n_{i-1} + a(2(b/c) - 1))$$
$$n_i = n_{i-1} - a(2(b/c) - 1) + e_i. \quad (2.3)'$$

Thus, employment would follow a random walk, with drift. Optimal wage behavior under the assumption that membership equals beginning-of-period employment is, however, not given by equation (2.3′). Unlike the behavior implied by equation (2.3′), current members should recognize their inability to commit future memberships to wage policies. The subsequent policies of the group will depend on its then-current membership. This fundamentally changes the character of the maximization problem. The group membership, when taking wage decisions today, knows that wage decisions will be taken in the next period by a membership which will in general be different from that of today. This implies in particular that if an insider is laid off, he becomes an outsider and thus considerably decreases his chances of keeping employment with the firm; this presumably leads him to choose a lower wage than in the previous case, where being laid off in the present did not affect his chances of being hired in the future.[17]

17. There is another effect that works in the opposite direction. Choosing a high real wage leads to lower expected employment, thus lower membership and higher expected real wages in the future. This effect however turns out to be dominated by that emphasized in the text.

The formal solution to this problem is treated in the appendix. Even with the simplifying assumptions we have made so far, the problem is intractable unless we further simplify by linearizing the group's intertemporal objective function. Let w' be the wage around which the objective function is linearized and let the shocks to labor demand be white noise. The solution to the maximization problem is then

$$w_i^* = (1/c)\,(-n_{i-1} + a(2(b/c)\,(1/(1 + b\theta w')) - 1))$$
$$n_i = n_{i-1} - a(2(b/c)\,(1/(1 + b\theta w')) - 1) + e_i. \quad (2.4)$$

The probability of employment for a member is a constant and is given by

$$p_i^* = 1 - a[(b/c)\,(1/(1 + b\theta w'))]^2.$$

Thus, under this membership rule, employment follows a random walk with drift. For a given labor force, there is unemployment hysteresis. Uncorrelated shocks to labor demand affect current employment, and through employment, membership and future expected employment. The drift is positive if (b/c) is less than $(1 + b\theta w')/2$, if workers care sufficiently about the probability of employment as compared to the wage. In such a case, although they do not care about the unemployed, they will set the wage each period so as to have the firm hire, on average, new employees. For a given membership, the wage is always set lower than in the m = infinity case and thus the probability of employment is set higher; this is because being laid off implies a loss of membership and imposes a much larger cost than before.

This analysis can again easily be extended to the case where labor demand shocks are serially correlated. The results remain the same; employment continues to follow a random walk. This is a consequence of our maintained assumption that expected changes in labor demand have no effect on the level of employment.

The Intermediate Case (m between 1 and infinity) The intermediate case, where workers remain insiders for some time after losing their jobs and where newly hired workers eventually but not immediately become insiders, raises an additional conceptual problem. There will no longer be unanimity among insiders. Those who have already experienced some unemployment, or those who have been working in the firm for a short period of time, will be more apt to favor more cautious wage-setting policies than those who have not. A theory of behavior in the face of conflict between members is beyond the scope of this article.[18] A plausible conjecture is that allowing for values of m between 1 and ∞ leads to wage-setting policies that are less cautious than in the $m = 1$ case but more cautious than in the $m = \infty$ case.

More important, rules corresponding to m between one and infinity are likely to generate unemployment behavior such as that shown in Figs 1 and 2, namely infrequent but sustained changes in the level of unemployment. Short sequences of unexpected shocks of the same sign have little effect on membership and thus on mean employment. In the case of adverse shocks, insiders are not laid off long enough to lose insider status; in the case of favorable shocks, outsiders do not stay long enough to acquire membership. But long—and infrequent—sequences of shocks of the same sign have large effects on membership and may lead to large effects on the mean level of employment. The length of the shock necessary to cause a permanent change in employment depends on the membership rules. In general, there is no reason for these rules to be symmetric. The length of time after which an unemployed worker becomes an outsider need not equal the length of time after which a new worker becomes an insider. Hence favorable and unfavorable shocks may persist to differing extents.

We have derived the results of this section under very specific assumptions: fixed membership rules; the firm is passive; outsiders play no role, direct or indirect, in the negotiation process. We must return to these assumptions. Before we do so, however, we must first show how the model of this section can be used to generate permanent effects on aggregate employment of both nominal and real shocks.

2.2. PERSISTENT EFFECTS OF NOMINAL AND REAL DISTURBANCES ON UNEMPLOYMENT

We now assume that there are many firms in the economy, each dealing with its own group of insider workers. We further assume that wages are set in nominal terms, so that nominal disturbances can affect employment. We then characterize the effects of nominal and real disturbances on employment and real wages.

THE DERIVED DEMAND FOR LABOR FACING EACH GROUP The economy is composed of many firms indexed by j, each selling a product which is an imperfect substitute for all others, but being otherwise identical. The demand facing firm j is given by

18. Farber (1984) reviews the research on union behavior when members have different seniority status, and thus conflicting interests.

$$y_j = -k(p_j - p) + (m - p), \quad k > 1.$$

All variables are in logarithms and all constants are ignored for notational simplicity. The variables y_j and p_j denote the output and the nominal price charged by firm j respectively; m and p denote nominal money and the price level. Demand for the firm's output depends on the relative price as well as on aggregate real money balances. The restriction on k is needed to obtain an interior maximum for profit maximization.

Each firm operates under constant returns to scale; the relation between output and employment is given by $y_j = n_j$. If w_j is the wage that firm j pays its workers, constant returns and constant elasticity of the demand for goods imply that prices are given by $p_j = w_j - e$, where e is a random technological shock, which is assumed common to all firms.[19]

Each firm j faces a group of insiders with the same objective function as above, which chooses a nominal wage and lets the firm determine employment. Given the relation between p_j and w_j, we can think of each group j as choosing w_j subject to the demand function

$$n_j = -k\,(w_j - e - p) + (m - p). \quad (2.5)$$

THE CHOICE OF THE WAGE AND EMPLOYMENT We now characterize the decisions of each group j at time zero (and for the moment we do not introduce the time index explicitly). We assume each group to operate under the membership rule $m = 1$, so that at time zero, membership in group j is given by $n_j(-1)$. The group now chooses a nominal rather than a real wage, based on its expectations of the price level, Ep, nominal money, Em, and the expected value of the technological shock, Ee, which all enter the derived demand for labor. As we have shown earlier, given such a demand function and its objective function, it chooses a wage so that the expected level of employment is equal to its membership plus a constant term. Again ignoring the constant, this implies

$$-k(w_j - Ee - Ep) + (Em - Ep) = n_j(-1) \quad (2.6)$$

which implicitly defines w_j as a function of $n_j(-1)$, Em, Ep and Ee.

19. Thus, we assume implicitly that the technological shock affects costs, but not the relation between output and employment. This is the case, for example, if output is produced with two inputs, labor and a nonlabor input, according to a Leontief technology, and the technological shock reflects changes in the relative price in the nonlabor input. A change in productivity growth would instead affect both the relation between output and employment, and between prices and wages. Allowing the technological shock to affect the relation between output and employment in the model is straightforward but introduces ambiguities in the effects of supply shocks on employment which are not central to our argument.

To solve for w_j, we must solve for the value of Ep. We do so under the assumption of rational expectations. As all firms and groups are the same, and are all affected by the same aggregate nominal shock, all groups have the same membership, $n_j(-1) = n(-1)$. Furthermore, all nominal prices are the same and equal to the price level, so that the first term in equation (2.6) is equal to zero. Thus, from equation (2.6)

$$Ep = Em - n(-1) \quad \text{and}$$
$$w_j = Ee + Em - n(-1)$$

The expected price level depends on expected nominal money and negatively on membership. The nominal wage in turn depends positively on expected nominal money and the expected technological shock, and negatively on membership. Replacing w_j and Ep by their values in equation (2.5) and aggregating over j gives the equation characterizing the dynamic behavior of aggregate employment

$$n = n(-1) + (m - Em) + (e - Ee)$$

or, if we reintroduce the time index i,

$$n_i = n_{i-1} + (m_i - Em_i) + (e_i - Ee_i). \quad (2.7)$$

SHOCKS, EMPLOYMENT AND WAGES From equation (2.7) only unexpected shocks affect employment. In the case of real shocks, this comes as before from the assumption of inelastic labor supply, which implies that each group sets wages so as to leave employment unaffected by anticipated real shocks. In the case of nominal shocks, the result is the same as in other nominal contract models (Fischer 1977) and the intuition is straightforward. Workers set a nominal wage which, in view of expected aggregate demand, will maintain last period's level of employment. Firms simply mark up over this nominal wage. Unexpectedly low aggregate demand leads to unexpected decreases in output and employment, with no changes in nominal wages (by assumption) and in prices (because of constant returns).[20]

These unexpected nominal and real shocks, unlike other contract models, have, however, permanent effects on employment. This is the result of our assumptions about membership rules. Once employment has decreased, it remains, in the absence of other shocks, permanently at

20. As in other contracting models, staggering of wage decisions across unions would lead to effects of even anticipated nominal shocks. See Taylor (1979).

the lower level. A sequence of unexpected contractions in aggregate demand increases equilibrium unemployment permanently. If we assumed that m, the length of membership parameter, was greater than 1, we would again obtain the result that while short sequences of adverse shocks have no effect on equilibrium unemployment, a long sequence of such shocks would increase equilibrium unemployment permanently.

While the implications for employment are straightforward, the model implies that there is no simple relation between employment and real wages. Consider in particular the effects of nominal shocks. By our assumption of constant returns to scale and constant elasticity of demand, they leave the markup of prices over wages unaffected. Equivalently, they leave the real wage unaffected. Thus, a sequence of adverse nominal disturbances will decrease employment, with no effect on the real wage. This lack of a simple relation between real wages and employment comes from our assumptions of monopolistic competition and constant returns, not from our assumptions about insiders and outsiders. As our focus is on the dynamic effects of membership rules, we will not further explore the relation between real wages and employment. But it is an important caveat to the line of research which has focused on the role of real wages in "explaining" high European unemployment. In the model constructed here, it is quite possible to have sustained high unemployment without high real wages. It is also possible for expansionary policies to raise employment without altering real wages.

2.3. THE ENDOGENEITY OF MEMBERSHIP RULES

We now return to the original model and examine various extensions. We first focus on the determination of the membership rules.

We have shown that the time-series evolution of employment depends critically on the nature of these rules. To the extent that insider status is closely linked with employment, substantial persistence is likely to result. If membership does not change or changes relatively little when employment changes, employment is likely to be much less persistent.

It is clear that at any given time the currently employed would find it optimal to commit the group to maximizing their interests indefinitely, while ignoring the welfare of those currently laid off. That is, they would like to apply the rule $m = 1$ this period and $m = \infty$ hereafter. But this means that if the currently employed are those who decide about membership, the only time-consistent rule is $m = 1$, which is always the best current-period rule for the currently employed. The issue is therefore whether the group can precommit itself, or, more accurately, whether the currently employed can commit the group to take care of their interest in the future whether or not they are still employed by the firm.

Achieving the $m = \infty$ solution is probably not feasible. But it seems plausible that the group will be able to commit itself at least to some extent. The factor limiting the commitment will be the degree of divergence between the original membership and the group of employed workers in some subsequent period. Where the divergence is too great, current employees will wrest control of the group from those controlling it in the interests of some group of past workers. The extent to which groups can commit themselves is probably greatest where demand shocks are small so that level and composition of employment change relatively little from period to period.

This suggests that m will depend on the distribution of the shocks. If shocks have large variance, m may have to be close to 1 to avoid large differences between membership and the employed. Or m may instead be a function of the realization of the shocks. A sequence of large positive or negative unexpected shocks may lead to the takeover of the group by the then-current employees. When a large fraction of an original labor force is on layoff, the incentive for the workers still employed to ignore them and thus not take the pay cut required to get them back may be strong. This is much less likely in the face of small shocks. Changes in the value of m associated with major shocks provide another possible explanation for the coincidence of persistent and high unemployment.

Our model thus suggests two alternative explanations for the empirical observation that unemployment remains at high levels for long periods of time. First, for a given fixed value of m greater than 1 but less than infinity, a sequence of adverse shocks will lead to a change in membership and therefore alter the level of employment permanently. Second, in bad times currently employed workers are more likely to take over and disenfranchise the unemployed, thus reducing the value of m and increasing persistence. The two differ in their implications for the process for unemployment at high levels. In the first, after the level change, the process for unemployment will have a higher mean but the same degree of persistence around the new mean as it had before. In the second case, unemployment will not only be higher but exhibit more persistence.

2.4. LIMITATIONS AND EXTENSIONS OF THE MODEL

In developing our analysis, we have made a number of simplifying assumptions regarding functional forms and the structure of bargaining between workers and firms. The question arises of how sensitive our results are to these assumptions. We have also carefully avoided using the term "union" to refer to the group of insiders. But it is clear that "union" would often have sounded more appropriate and the issue arises of whether our analysis is actually relevant in nonunion contexts. We now discuss these issues informally.

OTHER BARGAINING STRUCTURES It is well known that even in a one-period model, it is in general inefficient to let the firm choose employment unilaterally, given the wage (see, for example, Oswald (1985)). In our multiperiod model the assumption that the firm chooses employment according to its short-run profit maximizing labor demand is even more questionable. Even if bargaining takes the form of the union setting a wage and allowing the firm to control the level of employment, firms will not choose to operate on their short-run labor demand curves. Through its employment decision, the firm can affect future membership (unless $m = \infty$). By employing more workers in this period, it can increase membership in the next period and thus lower the expected cost of labor. This will lead the firm to choose a level of employment higher than that implied by short-run profit maximization. We suspect that taking account of this consideration would not substantially alter our analysis of employment dynamics. Rather, it would simply shift each period's labor demand curve outward.

Another important possibility would be for the firm to introduce two-tier systems, where newly hired workers get lower wages than those hired previously. Under such systems, insiders should have no reluctance to let firms hire more workers, and employment should increase until new workers are paid their reservation wage. The general reluctance of unions to accept such arrangements, especially in Europe, suggests that a central issue is that of what happens over time to those hired at lower wages. Unions do not encourage two-tier arrangements at least partly because of the fear that second-tier workers will come to control the wage-setting process. Indeed, the rarity of two-tier arrangements is strong evidence for the relevance of the membership considerations stressed here. Without some such consideration, it is difficult to see why unions do not always favor such systems as a way of maximizing the rents that they can capture.

Going back to the setting of the wage, if we allow the wage not to be set unilaterally by the insiders but to be determined by bargaining between insiders and the firm, wages will depend both on the utility of insiders and on the present discounted value of profits to the firm. Profit is a decreasing function of the wage. Thus, the larger the weight of the firm in bargaining, the lower the wage, and thus the higher the average level of employment. The implications for employment persistence depend on the weight of the firm in bargaining when the wage is far from the reservation level of workers. If the firm is relatively more powerful when the wage is much above the reservation wage, then the wage will tend to decrease when it is high, employment will tend to return to a higher level. Whether or not this happens depends on the structure of bargaining between insiders and the firm.

The specific utility function we have used for insiders is also important for our results. Its main implication, which we have argued is a desirable one, is that the probability of employment chosen by the group is invariant to the size of the group of insiders, or to the level of productivity. If instead an increase in membership, given productivity, led the group to choose both a lower wage and a lower probability of employment—which we can think of as the stochastic equivalent of elastic labor supply—employment would depend on both the anticipated and unanticipated components of productivity and may show less persistence. Even under the rule $m = 1$, an unanticipated increase in employment would, if the increase in productivity was temporary, lead to the choice of a lower wage and a lower probability of employment in the following period, implying an expected return to the initial level of employment over time. The same effects would also arise if, as unemployment became larger and being unemployed became more costly, the group chose a higher probability of employment, leading to an expected increase in employment over time.

Groups or Unions? Is our analysis still relevant when workers are not formally organized in unions, when, for example, wages are simply set unilaterally by the firm?

The work of Lindbeck and Snower (1985) suggests that even in the absence of formal unions current workers have some leverage vis á vis firms. And Slichter (1950) provides confirming empirical evidence suggesting that even before unions were economically important, wages tended to be high in industries with relatively inelastic labor demand.

In many nonunion settings, current incumbent workers and prospective workers cannot be regarded symmetrically. The requirement of cooperation among workers and the collective knowledge possessed by incumbent workers make their position very different from that of prospective new workers. This leads us to suspect that the membership considerations we have stressed are at least somewhat applicable even in nonunion contexts. The potential applicability of our analysis to nonunion settings may be argued informally as follows. Imagine a firm facing a collection of insider workers. The firm must choose a wage and an employment level. It cannot credibly threaten to lay off all its workers and replace them, except at very high cost, because of the specialized expertise of its labor force. On the other hand, the firm cannot credibly threaten to replace workers individually with lower-wage workers because the remainder of the labor force will not tolerate the hiring of "scabs." Under these conditions, wages and expected employment will be set in some way so as to divide the surplus resulting from a continued relationship between workers and firms. Workers will in general be able to extract some surplus even when they are unorganized. If firms make an "inadequate" wage offer, the workers can refuse to work. As long as workers have specific capital, it will be preferable for management to make another higher offer rather than lay the worker off.

If agreements are renegotiated only periodically and firms are permitted to vary employment in the interim, shocks will in general influence the level of employment. Even without a formal model of the bargaining process between workers and firms, it seems reasonable to expect that a reduction in the number of incumbent workers will lead to the setting of a higher wage and a lower level of expected employment. Thus persistence in employment, though not necessarily as much as with unions, may result even in that case. This also may help explain what goes on in the nonunion sector of economies with large unions.

This argument is clearly tentative. But we conclude from it that, while the effects we have described are more likely to be present when there are explicit unions, they may also arise in settings in which insider-outsider considerations are important.

The Presence of a Nonunion Sector Finally, we consider how our conclusions must be modified if part of the labor market is neither unionized nor subject to insider-outsider considerations.

The simplest analysis of a setting with a competitive sector would hold that there was no involuntary unemployment. Wages in the nonunion sector would fall to the point where all those workers ejected from the union sector could find employment.[21] There are at least three reasons why even granting the existence of a competitive sector, this analysis is suspect. First, competitive firms may be reluctant to lower wages because of the fear of being unionized after they have alienated their current labor force. Second, unemployment benefits may be high enough so that the market-clearing wage in the nonunion sector is below some workers' reservation wage. In one sense their unemployment is voluntary since jobs are available. In another sense the unemployment is involuntary since the unemployed may envy workers with the same skill in the union sector. The general consideration is that when there are wage

21. There is some evidence that this has actually occurred in Britain. Despite the legal changes which have decreased the legal power of unions in the last decade, the size of the union wage differential appears to have risen sharply in recent years.

differentials across jobs, the concept of involuntary unemployment becomes elusive (see Bulow and Summers (1985) for an elaboration of that theme). Third, unemployment may occur even with a competitive sector if remaining unemployed is in some sense useful—or thought to be useful by workers—in getting a union job. This may occur if substantial search effort or queuing is required, or alternatively, if accepting a low-quality job sends a bad signal to employers. This unemployment is related to that of Harris and Todaro (1970) where workers must migrate to urban areas to have a chance at high-wage urban jobs.

There is a more fundamental point regarding the inability of a nonunion sector to prevent unemployment. As Weitzman (1982) persuasively argues, there are strong reasons to believe that most economic activity involves fixed costs and monopolistic competition. Imagine a monopolistically competitive economy with fixed costs of production and constant marginal costs where there is initially no involuntary unemployment. Suppose that an adverse demand shock reduces the demand for goods in this economy but that nominal wages remain constant in all existing firms. Then employment and output will fall as will the profitability of existing firms. Will it pay new firms to enter the market and hire the unemployed at low wages? It may not, because unlike incumbent firms, new firms must cover fixed as well as variable costs. Particularly in settings where labor costs do not represent a large fraction of sales, entry may not be able to ensure the employment of the unemployed.[22] These considerations may enhance the power of unions because they reduce the incentive to start up new nonunion firms.

3. *Empirical Evidence on Hysteresis Theories*

Having developed a formal theory of hysteresis, we now examine whether the model is consistent with the observed patterns of persistently increasing unemployment in Europe and whether it can illuminate the very different behavior of unemployment in Europe and the United States in the recent past. We start by giving direct, institutional evidence on the strength of unions in Europe. We then estimate wage and employment equations implied by our model, for both Europe and the United States. We finally examine patterns of labor market turnover, in the United Kingdom and the United States.

22. Consider a simple example. Suppose restaurant wages were rigid, and a big decline in the demand for restaurant meals took place so there were unemployed chefs. Would it pay to open a new restaurant with a low-paid chef? Probably not if fixed costs were high. These considerations may have something to do with why in bad times employment growth may be concentrated in small establishments.

3.1. THE ROLE OF UNIONS IN EUROPE

The Size of the Union Sector Our model suggests that, even if hysteresis may arise in nonunion contexts, it is probably the more likely to arise the stronger and the larger the union sector. Thus, we start by reviewing the role of unions in Europe. As before, we limit our investigation to the United Kingdom, France and Germany.[23]

Membership figures indicate a union density of approximately 45 percent for the United Kingdom, 20 percent in France, and 38 percent for Germany. But these figures give very limited information as to the strength of unions. A better indicator is union coverage, that is, the proportion of workers covered by some form of collective bargaining. For the United Kingdom, coverage is approximately 70 percent for manual workers, and 55 percent for nonmanual workers. For France and Germany, the proportion of all workers exceeds 80 percent. But even coverage numbers are misleading. To understand why, one must have some institutional background.

On the surface, the three countries appear to be very different. In France there are three main national unions. In Germany, there are only industry unions. In the United Kingdom, there is a maze of craft and industry unions. But the structure of bargaining is in fact quite similar and can be described as follows: in all three countries, most of the formal bargaining is done at the industry level. But in all three countries, wages are determined mostly at the company or plant level.

In the United Kingdom, industry bargaining sets rates, which are usually floors that have little effect on actual wages. Until the Employment Act of 1980, there was scope for extension, that is, for provisions to extend the terms of the agreement to the whole sector. These provisions were eliminated in 1980. In the last twenty years, there has been an increase in the amount of bargaining, both formal and informal, at the plant level, between shop stewards and employers. Given that plant/company bargaining is the really important level of bargaining, it is relevant to look at how many workers are covered by industry and/or plant/company level bargaining. In 1978, the number of workers covered by at least a company agreement was 33 percent for all industries and 47.7 percent for manufacturing. Given the importance of informal bargaining, these figures understate the importance of unions in setting wages.

In France, the "Conventions collectives," which are usually but not always at the industry level, form most of the formal bargaining. These

23. Given that this article is written primarily for an American audience, we do not review the role of unions in the United States in any detail. As will be clear from our description of Europe, unions in the United States play a much more limited role than they do in Europe.

agreements are signed between a "representative" union and a "representative" employer and apply even if not all unions sign it (which is frequently the case). Subject to some minor conditions, they can be extended to all firms in the industry, by decision of the Minister of Labor. As in the United Kingdom, however, the importance of industry agreements with respect to wages should not be exaggerated. They usually set floors, that do not appear, either directly or indirectly, to have a large effect on actual wages. As in the United Kingdom, a growing portion of the bargaining takes place at the company level, although often in haphazard fashion. Until 1982, wages were largely determined unilaterally by firms, or in response to complaints of union representatives in the plant, with little bargaining or even consultation; local strikes were a standard instrument used by unions to achieve a better deal. Since 1982, there has been a change in the law (Lois Auroux) which requires annual bargaining at the company level on pay and other matters. The result has been a drastic increase in the number of company-level agreements.

In Germany, most of the formal bargaining takes place at the industry level. Agreements can be extended—either to firms in the same industry or to nonunion workers in firms which sign the agreements—by the state or federal Minister of Labor if (1) half of the employees of the sector are employed by firms which have signed the agreement and (2) extension is approved by both unions and employers who have signed.[24] But as in the other two countries, bargaining is increasingly taking place at the company level and there is general agreement that pay is very largely determined at the company level.

To conclude, it is difficult to give an exact estimate of the "union sector" in these countries. To the extent that much bargaining over wages in fact takes place at the company level, union coverage numbers, which are based on both company and industry-level bargaining, probably overstate the number of workers for whom the wage is determined as a result of bargaining between unions and employers. Even with this adjustment, the size of the union sector still remains high, much higher than in the United States. Also, if we believe that the more disaggregated the level of bargaining the less likely it is to take into account the interests of the unemployed as a whole, then these countries are good candidates for hysteresis in the union sector.[25]

24. Actual extensions are rare but the threat of extension is considered to be very effective in making all firms respect the content of these agreements.

25. In future research, it would be valuable to study Japanese labor-market institutions with a view to evaluating the theories of persistent unemployment put forward here. There are a number of similarities between Japanese and European institutions, including the importance of company-level bargaining. There may however be important differences as well, particularly in the attitude of Japanese unions toward outsiders.

An alternative approach is to ask the question, can a firm be nonunion? can a firm become nonunion? In the United Kingdom, the answer is yes: a firm can be or can become nonunion. Nothing in the law prevents it. There are some well-known examples of nonunion firms, most often subsidiaries of U.S. companies. There are very few examples of firms going nonunion.[26] In France and Germany, extension agreements put some constraints on firms in a given sector. There are nonunion firms in both countries; in France, these are nearly exclusively small firms. In France, furthermore, various requirements are imposed on firms with more than 50 employees. In particular they must allow for the presence of *délégués du personnel* who are union representatives within the firm. All national unions have a right to be represented. Since 1978, firms must also allow for the presence of a *section syndicale d'entreprise*, for the presence of the union inside the firm. Together, these facts suggest that it is difficult to be or become nonunion in these countries.

Finally, there is the question of how different the nonunion sector is from the union sector. A study by Kaufman (1984) of the competitive sector in the United Kingdom finds relatively little difference in wage behavior across the two sectors. Together with the arguments given previously, this suggests that the size of the formal union sector may not be a major determinant of the extent of hysteresis. We shall return to this question in the next section.

Membership Rules Membership rules determining who the union represents at any particular time play an important role in our analysis. The empirical evidence on actual membership rules is fairly clear. Workers have the right to join unions if they want to. Workers who are laid off can remain in the union, although they often lose the right to vote; this may happen either because of formal restrictions, or because voting takes place inside the plant. But this tells us little about the question of in whose interest the union actually acts. A study of the unemployed and the unions in the United Kingdom (Barker et al. 1984) gives some information. It finds that, while laid-off workers are officially encouraged to remain in the union and have their union fees waived, they do not, for the most part, see reasons to stay in the union.[27] This provides support for the idea that the union cares mostly about the currently employed.

26. Two recent cases have been those of British Petroleum which has gone nonunion for some of its shipping operations, and that of Robert Murdoch who has in effect gone to a more accommodating union.

27. The reason unions encourage the unemployed to remain in the union appears to be due in part to their desire to increase membership figures, and through these, their role in the national union movement.

3.2. WAGE AND EMPLOYMENT EQUATIONS

Theory We now derive, and then estimate later, the wage and employment equations associated with an expanded version of the model of the previous section. There are two extensions. First we allow for a dynamic specification of labor demand; the reason for introducing it will be clear below. Second, we specify explicitly an alternative hypothesis to that of hysteresis.

We thus specify labor demand as[28]

$$n = s\,n_{-1} - (1 - s)b(w - p) + e. \quad (3.1)$$

Following the analysis of the previous section, we assume that the union acts to set expected employment according to the relation

$$En = (1 - a)n^* + an_{-1}. \quad (3.2)$$

The case where $a = 1$ corresponds to the case where $m = 1$ in the preceding section and there is hysteresis; the case where $a = 0$ corresponds to the case where the union's policy is independent of history and so there is no hysteresis. Clearly, intermediate outcomes are also possible.[29]

Finally, let the wage which satisfies equations (3.1) and (3.2) be denoted by w^*. We assume the actual wage to be given by

$$w = w^* + u,$$

where the disturbance term u is assumed to be white, uncorrelated with w^* and reflecting factors outside the model. Combining this assumption with equations (3.1) and (3.2) yields a wage and an employment equation:

$$\begin{aligned} w &= Ep + (1/b(1 - s)) \\ &\quad \times [-(1 - a)n^* + (s - a)n_{-1} + Ee] + u, \quad (3.3) \\ n &= (1 - a)n^* + an_{-1} \\ &\quad + [e - Ee + (1 - s)b(p - Ep - u)]. \quad (3.4) \end{aligned}$$

28. Allowing labor demand to depend on current and expected real wages, as it should under costs of adjustment, would complicate our task here. John Kennan takes up this issue in his comments on our paper.

29. Note that a between 0 and 1 does not correspond exactly to m between 1 and infinity. As we have argued before, m between 1 and ∞ leads to a more complex, nonlinear specification.

The wage equation holds that the wage of the union is a decreasing function of n^*. When the union is larger, it is more cautious in setting wages. The impact of n_{-1} is ambiguous. A larger value of n_{-1} raises the size of the group in whose interest the union is maximizing wages but it also increases labor demand.

The employment equation, on the other hand, implies that employment follows a first-order process. The degree of persistence depends only on a, not at all on s. Unexpected movements in employment are due to price and productivity surprises, and deviations of wages from target. Equation (3.4) can be estimated by ordinary least-squares (OLS). This is, however, not the case for equation (3.3): expected productivity is likely to be correlated with past productivity and thus with past employment. Therefore we now derive the reduced-form wage equation. To do so requires an assumption about the process followed by e: we assume that e follows a random walk.[30] Lagging equation (3.1) and substituting it in equation (3.4) yields

$$w - w_{-1} = k + (Ep - p_{-1}) + (1/b(1 - s)) \times [(1 + s - a)n_{-1} - s\, n_{-2}] + u, \quad (3.5)$$

where $k \equiv -(1/b(1 - s))\,(1 - a)n^*$.

This equation can be estimated by OLS. It gives the rate of wage inflation as a function of expected price inflation, and employment lagged once and twice. It is worth examining further.

Consider first the case where there are no costs of adjustment in labor demand. In this case the equation gives a relation between expected real-wage growth and lagged employment only. If $a = 1$, then expected wage growth does not depend on employment but if $a < 1$, it does. After an unexpected decline in productivity, which leads to lower employment, the remaining workers accept a cut in real wages only to the extent that they care about the workers who have been laid off.

If there are costs of adjustment to employment, then expected real-wage growth depends on employment lagged both once and twice. If $a = 0$, then the ratio of employment lagged twice to employment lagged

30. This is a plausible and convenient assumption. Suppose we assumed instead that productivity was the sum of a linear function of observable variables and a stationary or borderline stationary process, say an AR(1) process with coefficient ρ. The wage equation would then differ from that in the text in several ways. One would be the presence of lagged real wages, with coefficient $\rho - 1$. Another would be the presence of the ρ first differences of the observable variables affecting productivity. We have explored these more general specifications empirically for the United Kingdom and found our simple wage equation not to be misleading.

Table 4a WAGE EQUATIONS, 1953–1984

Country	π_{t-1}	$logE_t$	$logE_{t-1}$	$logE_{t-2}$	Time × 100	θ	DW	R^2	Z
Germany									
(1)	.6*	—	.92	−.80		.07	1.99	.54	.87
			(4.0)	(−4.2)		(.3)			
(2)	.6*	—	.71	−.57	−.12	.04	2.03	.59	.80
			(2.4)	(−2.2)	(1.5)	(.2)			
(3)	.6*	1.12	−.89			−.10	2.00	.74	.79
		(9.6)	(−8.9)			(−.5)			
(4)	.6*	.96	−.74		−.07	−.13	2.01	.76	.77
		(6.2)	(−5.1)		(−1.5)	(−.7)			
United Kingdom									
(5)	.75*	—	.67	−.76	—	.25	2.01	.23	1.13
			(2.6)	(−2.5)		(1.5)			
(6)	.75*	—	.86	−.84	.19	.09	1.97	.31	.98
			(3.2)	(−2.8)	(1.9)	(.5)			
(7)	.75*	.13	−.08	—	—	.21	1.83	.07	.62
		(.4)	(−.2)			(1.0)			
(8)	.75*	.34	−.19	—	.20	.16	1.84	.15	.56
		(1.0)	(−.5)		(1.5)	(.7)			

France									
(9)	.8*	—	.58 (1.5)	−.39 (−.9)	—	—	2.03	.12	.67
(10)	.8*	—	.61 (1.2)	−.42 (−.7)	.00 (.0)	−.05 (−.2)	1.92	.13	.69
(11)	.8*	.97 (2.9)	−.74 (−2.1)	—	—	—	2.04	.29	.76
(12)	.8*	1.28 (3.1)	−1.16 (−2.1)	—	.12 (1.2)	—	2.09	.33	.91
United States									
(13)	.7*	—	−.07 (−.8)	.00 (.0)		.54 (2.2)	2.03	.26	.00
(14)	.7*	—	−.07 (−.8)	.00 (.0)	.00 (.0)	.54 (2.2)	2.02	.26	.00
(15)	.7*	.24 (4.6)	−.25 (−4.8)	—	—	.48 (2.5)	1.98	.49	1.04
(16)	.7*	.28 (5.9)	−.16 (−3.3)	—	−.13 (−3.9)	.34 (1.7)	1.99	.63	.57

$\dot{w}$: rate of change of average hourly earnings in manufacturing.
π: rate of change of the consumer price index.
E: manufacturing employment.
t-statistics in parentheses.
All equations for Europe are run with a first order autocorrelation correction (θ = AR1 coefficient).
All equations for the U.S. are run with a first order moving average correction (θ = MA1 coefficient).
Z is the absolute value of the ratio of the coefficient on Log E_{t-1} to the coefficient on log E_t (or of the coefficient on log E_{t-2} to the coefficient on log E_{t-1} as the case may be).

Source: OECD data bank, extended back to 1950 by D. Grubb. See Grubb (1984).

once cannot exceed ½ (in absolute value). But as *a* increases, the ratio tends to 1. If $a = 1$, the ratio equals unity, that is, expected real-wage growth depends on the change rather than on the level of employment.

Note that we cannot identify *a* and *s* separately from estimation of the wage equation. But *a* must be positive if we find the ratio described above to be larger than ½. Furthermore, *a* can be directly obtained from the employment equation.

While we have derived the wage equation (3.5) from a rather specific theory of union behavior, it can be motivated in other ways. Following the logic of the monopolistic competitive model (see the preceding section) just as we have followed the logic of the competitive model, gives rise to an equation for wage inflation paralleling equation (3.5). Much more generally, equation (3.5) is very close to a standard Phillips curve which allows for a rate-of-change effect, a la Lipsey. The only real difference is the presence of employment rather than unemployment on the right-hand side. We now turn to estimation of the wage and employment equations.

Results The results of estimation of the wage equations for the United Kingdom, France, Germany, and the United States, for the period 1953 to 1984 are reported in tables 4 and 5.

In table 4a, four alternative specifications of the wage equation are estimated for each country. Because the appropriate timing is unclear with annual data, we estimate the equations using alternatively contemporaneous and once-lagged employment, and once- and twice-lagged employment.[31] We also estimate each equation with and without a time

31. Because our wage data refer to manufacturing wages, we use manufacturing employment as the employment variable in the results reported here. Very similar results were obtained using total employment.

Table 4b WAGE EQUATION RESIDUALS, 1953–1984

Year	*Germany*	*United Kingdom*	*France*	*United States*
1980	−1.91	1.7	1.6	−1.2
1981	−.32	−4.1	1.4	−.8
1982	−.75	3.9	−.0	−.1
1983	.57	−2.7	.1	−.9
1984	−.44	1.1	−1.5	.3
	$\sigma = 1.87$	$\sigma = 3.2$	$\sigma = 3.9$	$\sigma = 1.5$

Residuals from equations 3, 5, 11 and 15 in table 4a.

trend. Many researchers have captured the shift of the Phillips curve by a time trend, that is, by an increase over time unrelated to the history of unemployment and it is interesting to see what happens to our specification when a time trend is allowed. This gives us the four alternative specifications. Finally, we use for expected inflation the forecast of inflation obtained from estimation of an AR(1) process for inflation over the sample period and constrain the coefficient on expected inflation (which is therefore equal to a constant plus a scalar times lagged inflation) to equal unity.

In table 5, we perform the same set of estimations, but using unemployment rather than employment as a right-hand-side variable. We do this because unemployment is the variable used in standard Phillips curve specifications. Some theories of hysteresis such as the idea that the long-term unemployed exert less pressure on wages than those recently laid off also suggest that unemployment is more appropriate than employment in the Phillips curve.

Tables 6 and 7 give the results of estimation of the employment and unemployment processes for each country for the period 1953 to 1984. Here again, while our theory has implications only for employment, we think it is useful to report results for unemployment as well.

The results are fairly clear-cut and indicate that there are substantial differences between the European countries and the United States. Starting with the wage equations, one can draw the following conclusions:

1. Virtually all specifications for Germany, France, and the United Kingdom in tables 4 and 5 suggest a substantial degree of hysteresis.

Let us denote by Z the absolute value of the ratio of the coefficient on lagged employment/unemployment to the coefficient on contemporaneous employment/unemployment (or of the coefficient on employment/unemployment lagged twice to the coefficient on employment/unemployment lagged once as the case may be). As we have seen, under strict hysteresis ($a = 1$) this ratio should be equal to unity. Z is indeed close to unity for nearly all specifications; it is not affected by the inclusion of a time trend, or by the use of employment versus unemployment. There is little difference across countries: Z is higher in the United Kingdom, sometimes exceeding unity. It is closer on average to 0.85 for Germany and France.[32]

32. All these findings are quite robust. The value of z is substantively the same if, following the argument of footnote 30, the lagged real wage, current and lagged values of the capital-labor ratio, the price of oil, and a proxy for productivity growth (when available) are added to the regressions. The results are also robust to changes in the coefficient on lagged inflation, say within 0.2 of the values used in the table.

Table 5 WAGE EQUATIONS, 1953–1984

Country	π_{t-1}	U_t	U_{t-1}	U_{t-2}	*Time* × *100*	ρ	*DW*	R^2	*Z*
Germany									
(1)	.6*	—	−2.86	2.62	—	.30	1.97	.57	.92
			(−4.3)	(3.8)		(1.6)			
(2)	.6*	—	−2.41	2.12	−.08	.27	1.94	.59	.88
			(−3.0)	(2.6)	(−1.1)	(1.4)			
(3)	.6*	−2.39	1.68	—	—	.06	1.99	.50	.70
		(−4.0)	(2.6)			(.3)			
(4)	.6*	−1.60	.95	—	−.10	.08	2.00	.54	.59
		(−2.1)	(1.2)		(−1.5)	(.4)			
United Kingdom									
(5)	.75*	—	−2.31	2.58	—	.04	2.02	.33	1.17
			(−3.6)	(3.4)		(.2)			
(6)	.75*	—	−2.57	2.46	.14	(−.03)	2.02	.37	.96
			(−4.0)	(3.3)	(1.4)	−.2			
(7)	.75*	−.96	.78	—	—	.22	1.83	.12	.81
		(−1.0)	(.7)			(1.0)			
(8)	.75*	−1.43	.62	—	.28	.13	1.85	.25	.43
		(−2.0)	(.8)		(2.4)	(.6)			

France									
(9)	.8*	—	−1.42	1.35	—	.07	1.93	.03	.95
			(−.7)	(.6)		(.4)			
(10)	.8*	—	−3.01	2.10	.25	−.10	1.86	.15	.70
			(−1.3)	(.9)	(2.1)	(−.5)			
(11)	.8*	−3.57	3.78	—	—	.13	1.99	.14	1.06
		(−1.97)	(1.8)			(.7)			
(12)	.8*	−4.97	4.12	—	.33	−.10	1.91	.33	.83
		(−2.9)	(2.2)		(3.0)	(.5)			
United States									
(13)	.7*	—	−.07	−.06	—	.40	1.99	.21	.86
			(−.2)	(−.1)		(1.3)			
(14)	.7*	—	.11	.07	−.07	.47	2.01	.24	.64
			(.3)	(.2)	(−1.7)	(1.6)			
(15)	.7*	−1.02	.47	—	—	.41	1.99	.62	.46
		(−6.0)	(2.9)			(2.2)			
(16)	.7*	−1.05	.43	—	—	.42	1.99	.63	.41
		(−5.8)	(2.4)		.02	(2.2)			
					(.6)				

See Table 4.
U: standardized unemployment rate.
Z is the absolute value of the ratio of the coefficient on U_{t-1} to the coefficient on U_t (or of the coefficient on U_{t-2} to the coefficient on U_{t-1} as the case may be).

Source: OECD (1984) and Grubb (1984).

In most cases, the time trend contributes little. If the increase in unemployment was an autonomous increase in the natural rate over time, the coefficient on the time trend should be positive. It is in most cases insignificant and often negative. There are, however, two exceptions, for France and the United Kingdom when unemployment—rather than employment—is used as the right-hand-side variable. In both cases, the time trend is positive and significant and explains a large portion of the increase in nominal wages at given inflation and unemployment rates; in both cases, however, even when the time trend is allowed for, lagged unemployment still enters positively and the hysteresis ratio remains high.

Another way in which an autonomous but stochastic shift could manifest itself would be by the presence of high serial correlation in the estimated Phillips curve. Estimated serial correlation is, however, low in all cases.

A final piece of evidence is given in table 4b which reports the residuals associated with the best-fitting equations from table 4a, not in-

Table 6 EMPLOYMENT PROCESSES, 1953–1984

Country	ρ	θ	$\alpha \times 100$	R^2
Germany				
	.76	1.00	—	.96
	(22.3)	(5.3)	—	
	.86	.78	-1.9×10^{-2}	.97
	(26.7)	(3.9)	(.0)	
United Kingdom				
	1.07	.54	—	.96
	(23.3)	(2.6)	—	
	.95	.41	−.20	.94
	(16.3)	(2.0)	(−3.8)	
France				
	.94	.81	—	.94
	(19.5)	(3.0)	—	
	1.08	.48	−.13	.94
	(19.5)	(2.5)	(−4.0)	
United States				
	.82	.07	—	.72
	(7.5)	(.3)	—	
	.34	.46	.40	.77
	(1.5)	(1.6)	(2.5)	

Results of estimation of :
$\log E = \rho \log E(-1) + \alpha(\text{TIME}) + \varepsilon + \theta\varepsilon(-1)$
E : manufacturing employment.

cluding a time trend, for each country, for 1980 to 1984. There is little evidence of significant prediction errors in recent years. This is in sharp contrast to the performance of wage equations which do not allow lagged employment to enter.

2. In contrast to the results for Europe, the results for the United States provide evidence of much less hysteresis. There is evidence of a significant effect of either lagged employment or lagged unemployment. But, with the exception of one specification using employment, the value of z for the United States is smaller than for Europe, being in most cases around 0.5. There is also no evidence in favor of a time trend in the wage equation.

3. A comparison of the results of estimation in tables 4 and 5 does not give a clear answer as to whether employment or unemployment belongs in the wage equation. Using R^2's gives a draw, with employment doing better for France, unemployment doing better for the United Kingdom. Regressions, including current and lagged values of both unemploy-

Table 7 UNEMPLOYMENT PROCESSES, 1953–1984

Country	ρ	θ	$\alpha \times 100$	R^2
Germany				
	.92	.65	—	.91
	(14.8)	(3.4)	—	
	.94	.39	.06	.93
	(17.5)	(1.9)	(5.0)	
United Kingdom				
	1.02	.77	—	.95
	(20.9)	(3.9)	—	
	.81	.82	.09	.96
	(9.9)	(3.9)	(3.5)	
France				
	1.12	−.06	—	.97
	(32.7)	(−.3)	—	
	1.04	−.22	.02	.97
	(18.2)	(−1.1)	(1.4)	
United States				
	.72	.06	—	.58
	(4.5)	(.2)	—	
	.36	.31	.07	.63
	(1.4)	(.9)	(1.9)	

Results of estimation of :
$U = \rho U(-1) + \alpha(\text{TIME}) + \varepsilon + \theta\varepsilon(-1)$
U : standardized unemployment

ment and employment (or equivalently, employment and the labor force) give the same ambiguous answer, with the labor force being significant in the United Kingdom, but not in France or Germany. We see the U.K. results, however, as presenting a problem for our model.

The employment and unemployment equations reported in tables 6 and 7 confirm to a large extent the conclusions from the wage equations. Both unemployment and employment are more persistent in Europe than in the United States. In particular, the process generating unemployment appears nonstationary in all three European countries, whether or not a time trend is included in the regressions. The U.S. process is stationary. The data, however, strongly suggest that an ARMA(1,1), rather than the AR(1) process implied by our theory, is needed to fit the employment and unemployment processes of all four countries. This may reflect a difference between the length of a period in the model and the annual frequency of observation used in the estimation.

3.3. PATTERNS OF LABOR MARKET TURNOVER

A central element in our theory of hysteresis is the lack of concern of employed workers for the unemployed. It is the fear of job loss for current workers and not the outstanding labor-market pool that restrains wage demands. Indeed the formal model explains why firms hire at all only by assuming that wages which are set low enough to insure the jobs of current workers will sometimes make it profitable for firms to hire new workers. While this is clearly an oversimplification, the point remains that insider-outsider or union models of the type we have considered are really theories of why the unemployed are not hired, not theories of why layoffs take place. This suggests the utility of looking at data on labor-market turnover. A finding of high turnover with many workers having short spells of unemployment and then being rehired would tend to cast doubt on the relevance of insider-outsider formulations, while a finding that the rate of flow into and out of employment was relatively low but that the unemployed remained out of work for a very long time would tend to support these theories.

Table 8 presents some evidence on the rate of flow into unemployment in the United States and the United Kingdom over the past decade. The flow is measured as the number of persons becoming unemployed over a three-month period. For the United States, this is estimated as the number of unemployed reporting durations of less than fourteen weeks. For Britain it is the number of unemployment registrants over a three-month period.

Two conclusions emerge clearly. First, despite the much higher rate of unemployment in the United Kingdom than in the United States, the rate of flow into unemployment is actually lower in the United Kingdom. The implication is that the unemployment problem is not one of an excessive rate of job loss but of an insufficient rate of hiring of the unemployed. The second striking feature is that the rate of flow into unemployment in Britain has increased surprisingly little as unemployment has soared. Between 1970 and 1984 when the rate of unemployment in Britain rose more than 300 percent, the rate of flow into unemployment has risen by only about 75 percent. This pattern of rising unemployment with only a modest increase in the rate of inflow appears more pronounced in British than in American labor markets. In the United States, the inflow rate has accounted for a significant part of the increase in unemployment during recession periods. For example, between 1979 and 1982, unemployment increased by 67 percent and the inflow rate rose by 44 percent.

The OECD (1985) summarizes the fragmentary information available on labor market turnover for other European nations. The data in general parallel our findings for the United Kingdom—suggesting relatively modest increases in the rate of flow into unemployment starting from a very low base. They do, however, suggest that the composition of the

Table 8 PATTERNS OF INFLOW TO UNEMPLOYMENT

	United States	*Great Britain*
Year	Number unemployed less than 14 weeks as percent of employment	Quarterly inflow as percent of employment*
1970	4.4	3.3
1971	4.8	3.6
1972	4.5	3.6
1973	4.2	2.9
1974	4.8	3.2
1975	6.3	4.2
1976	5.7	4.9
1977	5.5	4.7
1978	5.0	4.5
1979	5.0	4.2
1980	5.8	4.9
1981	6.0	5.2
1982	7.2	5.5
1983	6.5	5.6
1984	5.5	

* Average of quarterly values.

newly unemployed has changed over time as the unemployment rate has increased. Lay-off rates have increased while quit rates have declined.

Given the magnitude of the increases in European unemployment rates and the relatively small increases in flow rates, it is inevitable that unemployment durations have increased substantially. Table 9 presents some information on the increasing importance of long-term unemployment in Europe. Along with information on the average duration of unemployment, it presents estimates of the fraction of all unemployment due to persons whose total length of unemployment exceeds various threshold lengths.[33] The data demonstrate that at the same level of unemployment, long-term unemployment is much more important in Europe than in the United States. In 1980, when the American unemployment rate was 7.2 percent, only an estimated 15 percent of all unemployment was due to persons out of work for more than a year. The corresponding percentages were 74 percent, 59 percent and 75 percent in the United Kingdom, Germany, and France even though the unemployment rates were lower. The data also show that long-term unemployment has increased in importance as overall unemployment rates have risen in Europe. Indeed, the increase in duration of unemployment is almost proportional to the increase in unemployment.

Summary We have shown that unions play an important role in Europe and that the behavior of European unemployment is consistent with our hypothesis about hysteresis. It is obviously tempting to conclude that unions are at the root of the European problem; but the temptation must be strongly resisted. First, even if unions create hysteresis, they only create a channel for persistence, which implies that both favorable and adverse shocks will both have long-lasting effects. The sequence of unfavorable shocks, at least some of which are the consequence of policy, may equally well be said to be the cause of persistent high unemployment. Second, it is yet unclear whether the cause of hysteresis in Europe is unions or the sequence of adverse shocks which has caused high unemployment.

4. *Is Eurosclerosis Really the Problem?*

We have seen that our model of persistent unemployment may explain important aspects of the current European depression and the very dif-

33. The motivation for calculations of this type is laid out in Clark and Summers (1979). In performing the calculations, we have assumed that the exit rate from unemployment is not duration-dependent. If, more realistically, we allowed for it to decline, the estimated concentration of unemployment in long spells would show up even more clearly.

Table 9 THE IMPORTANCE OF LONG TERM UNEMPLOYMENT

	United States		*United Kingdom*		*Federal Republic of Germany*		*France*	
	1980	1984	1980	1984	1980	1984	1980	1984
Unemployment rate	7.2	7.5	6.5	12.7	3.4	8.1	6.6	10.0
Average duration of unemployment for adult men currently unemployed	3.6	5.8	12.2	19.4	8.6	12.6	12.6	14.4
Percent contribution to adult male unemployment of those unemployed at least:								
6 months	50	72	91	96	85	92	92	93
12 months	15	39	74	87	59	75	75	80
18 months	4	18	57	76	38	58	58	64
24 months	1	8	41	65	23	43	43	56

Source: Based on authors' calculation.

ferent behavior of European and American labor markets. The evidence presented so far leaves open a crucial question, however. Is the presence of hysteresis in European unemployment a consequence of the heavily regulated and unionized character of European labor markets? Alternatively, is hysteresis the result of a sequence of adverse shocks to employment? The case that major structural reforms are needed if full employment in Europe is to be restored depends on an affirmative answer to the first question, while the case for expansionary macroeconomic policies is more compelling if the second question can be given a positive answer.

Deciding whether the source of hysteresis lies ultimately in European institutions or in the sequence of adverse shocks that have buffeted European economies requires comparisons of the current situation with situations where only one of these elements is present. Comparison with the United States at present cannot resolve the issue because the American economy lacks institutions like those in Europe and has not suffered a sequence of contractionary aggregate demand shocks like those experienced by Europe in the 1980s. But we are able to make two comparisons that can shed some light on the sources of hysteresis. The first is a comparison of the behavior of European labor markets in the recent period with their behavior over the 1953–1968 period. Broadly speaking, labor market institutions were similar in the two periods but the pattern of shocks was very different.[34] The second comparison is between the current European depression and the U.S. Great Depression of the 1930s. At the time of the U.S. Depression, unions were weak and social programs and labor-market regulations were a small factor. The U.S. Depression may also shed light on the role of expansionary policies in alleviating persistent high unemployment. We consider these comparisons in turn.

4.1. EUROPEAN LABOR MARKETS BEFORE THE CURRENT DEPRESSION

We have examined the persistence of unemployment and the behavior of wages in Europe over the past thirty-five years. This long interval contains the current depression period and the period of unparalleled growth of the 1950s and 1960s. We now examine the extent to which hysteresis is a product of bad times by considering labor-market behavior separately over each of the two periods. Table 10 presents estimates of the stochastic process followed by unemployment separately for the

34. Some of the institutional rigidities of European labor markets date, however, from social policies introduced in the 1960s and 1970s.

1952–1968 and 1969–1984 periods.[35] The degree of persistence in unemployment in Europe is much higher in the latter period. Similar but somewhat less dramatic results are obtained using employment rather than unemployment figures. For the earlier period, unemployment appeared to have been more persistent in the United States than in the United Kingdom or France. These results tend to suggest that hysteresis is a feature of bad times rather than a consequence of the structure of European labor markets.

Table 11 presents estimates of wage-change equations paralleling those reported in table 5, but using annual data for the 1953–1967 period. Taken together, the results suggest somewhat less hysteresis in the 1953–1967 period than over the whole sample period, with the difference being pronounced in the United Kingdom where the ratio Z, which

35. It is clear that with such short samples, and such a drastic increase in unemployment in the second subsample, estimation cannot be very precise.

Table 10 THE PERSISTENCE OF UNEMPLOYMENT IN GOOD AND BAD TIMES

Country	ρ	θ	*SE regression*
France			
1952–1968	.41	.81	.3
	(1.1)	(1.8)	
1968–1984	1.11	−.48	.4
	(5.0)	(1.4)	
Germany			
1952–1968	.86	.22	.5
	(12.3)	(.9)	
1968–1984	1.07	.51	.8
	(5.1)	(1.4)	
United Kingdom			
1952–1968	.01	.97	.5
	(.0)	(2.5)	
1968–1984	1.0	.99	.9
	(27.6)	(3.8)	
United States			
1952–1968	.75	−.37	1.0
	(1.6)	(−.7)	
1968–1984	.59	.50	1.1
	(1.7)	(1.1)	

The results represent estimates of an ARMA (1,1) process for the unemployment rate.

Table 11 WAGE EQUATIONS, 1953–1967

Country	π_{t-1}	U_{t-1}	U_{t-2}	*Time* × *100*	ρ	*DW*	R^2	*Z*
Germany								
(1)	.6*	−6.48	5.86	—	−.14	1.91	.55	.90
		(−3.7)	(3.7)		(−.4)			
(2)	.6*	−6.25	4.53	−.60	−.14	2.07	.60	.72
		(−3.6)	(2.2)	(−1.1)	(−.4)			
United Kingdom								
(3)	.75*	−2.91	1.89	—	−.00	1.71	.50	.65
		(−3.2)	(2.0)		(.0)			
(4)	.75*	−3.49	1.74	.16	−.17	1.71	.57	.50
		(−3.8)	(1.9)	(1.4)	(−.5)			
France								
(5)	.9*	−6.11	4.53	—	−.47	2.18	.61	.74
		(−3.8)	(2.8)		(−1.8)			
(6)	.9*	−6.25	4.12	−.06	−.50	2.19	.62	.66
		(−3.8)	(2.3)	(−.5)	(−1.9)			
United States								
(7)	.7*	−1.23	.37	—	.73	2.05	.66	.30
		(−5.2)	(1.7)					
(8)	.7*	−1.25	.57	−.17	−.04	1.90	.86	.46
		(−7.0)	(3.2)	(−4.2)	(−.1)			

See Table 4a and Table 5.

was close to 1 for the full sample is now close to 0.5. However, the results for the 1953–1967 period, like those for the entire period, suggest a greater degree of hysteresis in Europe than in the United States. The fact that persistence is present in the earlier period in Europe to a greater degree than in the United States but becomes increasingly important as the unemployment rate increases makes it difficult to draw any firm conclusion about its causes.

On balance, evidence on the changing behavior of European labor markets suggests that bad times as well as unions account for findings of hysteresis. But this evidence is not sufficiently powerful to permit a judgment about their relative importance.

4.2. A TALE OF TWO DEPRESSIONS

Salient features of many discussions of the current European depression include pessimistic forecasts that unemployment will never return to earlier levels, concern that reduced investment and lower capital stocks have made it impossible to employ the entire labor force, and fears that expansionary policies will lead directly into inflation with little or no favorable impact on output or employment. These pessimistic views are premised on the conviction that structural problems are central to high unemployment in Europe, and that the causes of persistent high unemployment go beyond a sequence of adverse shocks. Yet the American depression of the 1930s was ended by the expansion in aggregate demand associated with rearmament. Unemployment recovered to pre-Depression levels. Recovery was not inhibited by an insufficient capital stock or by the overly rapid adjustment of wages and prices. Are this experience and the current European experience sufficiently comparable to permit the inference that hysteresis arises from a sequence of adverse shocks rather than from structural problems in the labor market? Or do major differences in the character of the American and European depressions render the American experience irrelevant for thinking about current European problems?

We begin by briefly reviewing the record of the American economy over the 1925–1945 period. A number of basic economic statistics are presented in table 12. The outstanding feature of the period is, of course, the dramatic upsurge in unemployment that began in 1929. Unemployment rose from levels comparable to those in Europe in the late 1960s and early 1970s to 25 percent in 1933 and remained above 14 percent until 1940. As in Europe today, employment actually declined over a ten-year period. Beginning in late 1939 with the declaration of war in Europe, unemployment began to decline rapidly as rearmament stimulated the economy. The benefits of increased defense spending spilled over into the rest of the economy. While there were only 822,000 men in the army in November 1940 and 2.1 million a year later, nonagricultural employment increased by 16 percent (6 million persons) between 1939 and 1941. Production of a variety of nondefense goods increased rapidly. Mitchell (1947) reports that between 1939 and 1941 sales of automobiles rose by 35 percent, refrigerators by 69 percent and washing machines by 63 percent. Overall industrial production rose by 20 percent.

These rapid improvements in economic performance were unexpected. Indeed, in the wake of the 1937 recession many observers had despaired of any eventual return to full employment. Paul Samuelson noted in 1944 that "in the years just prior to 1939 there were noticeable signs of dwindling interest in the problem of unemployment which took the form of ostrich-like attempts to think away the very fact of unemployment by recourse to bad arithmetic and doubtful statistical techniques. And even among economists there was increased emphasis on the recovery of production and income to 1929 levels." Such pessimism was pervasive even among those charged with alleviating the situation. Harry Hopkins, a

Table 12 THE AMERICAN ECONOMY, 1925–1945

Year	*U*	*$\dot{w}$ (all workers)*	*$\dot{p}$ (CPI)*	*Index of productivity*	*Nonresidential capital (1958$)*
1925	3.2	.9	4.0	92.6	211.0
1926	1.8	1.5	0.0	95.0	218.7
1927	3.3	3.2	−6.0	95.4	223.9
1928	4.2	.3	−1.0	96.1	229.3
1929	3.2	3.5	−1.0	100.0	236.6
1930	8.9	−0.6	−3.0	97.0	238.8
1931	16.3	−5.0	−8.3	98.5	233.5
1932	24.1	−8.9	−9.0	95.4	222.8
1933	25.2	−5.8	−5.0	93.2	212.2
1934	22.0	12.0	2.6	103.3	203.9
1935	20.3	2.3	2.6	106.7	198.3
1936	17.0	1.9	1.2	111.3	197.0
1937	14.3	5.9	3.7	110.4	198.4
1938	19.1	1.8	−2.4	113.5	194.5
1939	17.2	1.2	−1.2	117.6	192.2
1940	14.6	2.4	1.2	122.2	193.6
1941	9.9	9.7	4.9	124.2	198.3
1942	4.7	26.9	10.5	123.3	193.5
1943	1.9	10.6	6.3	124.6	186.5
1944	1.2	7.8	2.0	134.4	183.0
1945	1.9	9.0	1.9	142.0	185.5

Source: Bailey (1983) and *Historical Statistics of the United States.*

liberal confidante of Franklin Roosevelt, wrote in 1937 that "it is reasonable to expect a probable minimum of 4 to 5 million unemployed even in future prosperity periods" (Leuchtenberg (1963) p. 263). Similar sentiments were echoed by others, including New York Mayor Fiorello LaGuardia who concluded that the situation had passed from being an emergency to being the new norm.

Similar pessimism is often expressed in Europe today. The pessimism reflects the view that unlike the U.S. Great Depression's persistent unemployment, persistent unemployment in Europe is caused by structural problems which are not merely the residue of adverse shocks. H. Giersch has coined and popularized the word "eurosclerosis" to denote these structural problems. Is there some important difference between the two situations that suggests that rapid expansionary policies would fail in Europe today even where they succeeded so spectacularly in the United States in 1940? There are surprisingly many similarities between the two experiences. The failure of inflation and real wages to recede more rapidly is an often-noticed aspect of the current European experience. Indeed, it is this observation that leads to conclusions that problems are structural and that the equilibrium rate of unemployment has increased. In the latter half of the depression, a similar pattern appeared in the United States. Between 1936 and 1940 unemployment fluctuated around a very high mean but there was essentially no deceleration in inflation and real wages rose by about 10 percent, close to the normal rate of productivity growth. Before the 1930s, periods of steady inflation had had much lower average unemployment rates.

Just as unemployment in Europe is highly persistent today, it appeared highly persistent during the American depression. The autocorrelation of unemployment was 0.87 in the United States over the 1919–1941 period. In table 13, we examine further the issue of hysteresis during the depression and present some estimated wage equations for the 1920–1941 period. The war years are omitted because of the influence of controls. The results dramatically suggest hysteresis paralleling that found in Europe today. When only contemporaneous employment or unemployment is entered into the equation, it is insignificant, but the change in employment or unemployment is strongly associated with changes in the rate of wage inflation.[36] These results are robust to a variety of ways of treating expected inflation. While paralleling our results

36. A similar finding is emphasized by Gordon and Wilcox (1981) who also provide evidence that it holds for Europe during the depression period. Gordon (1983) emphasizes the importance of the rate of change effect in the Phillips curve during the depression period in both the United States and the United Kingdom but finds the level effect to be dominant outside of this interval.

Table 13 WAGE EQUATIONS, 1920–41 AND THE AMERICAN DEPRESSION

	U_t	U_{t-1}	$logE_t$	$logE_{t-1}$	π_{t-1}	R^2	DW	Z
(1)	−.06	—	—	—	.22	0.0	1.71	—
	(.2)				(.8)			
(2)	−1.13	1.26	—	—	.50	.29	2.13	1.12
	(2.9)	(3.2)			(2.1)			
(3)	—	—	.67	—	.24	.03	1.75	—
			(.50)		(.9)			
(4)	—	—	2.71	−2.72	.38	.36	1.99	1.00
			(.74)	(3.2)	(1.7)			

The dependent variable is the rate of wage inflation. Data drawn from *Historical Statistics of the United States*.

for present-day Europe, these results differ from our results using American data for the postwar period. This may be taken as evidence that hysteresis is a phenomenon associated with bad times rather than with particular labor market institutions.

In considering contemporary European labor markets, we laid considerable stress on the importance of long-term unemployment, emphasizing that turnover rates were, if anything, lower in Europe than in the United States. Table 14 (from Woytinsky (1942)) presents some of the limited evidence available on patterns of labor-market turnover during the American depression. Again, the results parallel Europe today. There is little evidence of an increase in the flow rate into unemployment, though quits decline and layoffs increase. As in Europe today the duration of unemployment appears to have increased substantially. Woytinsky reported evidence from a 1937 Philadelphia survey that found that 61.7 percent of unemployed adult men had been out of work for more than a year. More generally, he concluded that the depression era saw the emergence of a new group of hard-core unemployed. Patterns in labor-market turnover do not appear to provide a basis for distinguishing European labor markets and American labor markets during the depression.

Hysteresis appears to be an important feature of American depression. Earlier, we suggested three possible sources of hysteresis. Of these, physical capital accumulation appears an unlikely culprit. As table 12 demonstrates, the real value of the nonresidential capital stock actually declined between 1929 and 1939. This reduction did not represent an important bar to full employment during or after the war when demand for goods was strong. This makes us somewhat skeptical of claims that insufficient capital is preventing a European recovery. However, it should be noted that Mitchell (1947) claims that capacity utilization rates were very low before the 1939 expansion. This is not true in Europe today. There is some evidence of human capital hysteresis in labor force participation. The U.S. labor force participation rate of men over 65 dropped from 54 to 42 percent between the 1930 and 1940 censuses.[37] This is considerably more rapid than its trend rate of decline. Between 1920 and 1930, it fell by only 1 percent, and it remained essentially constant between 1940 and 1950. It seems unlikely however that this could have had much effect on unemployment. Indeed, to the extent that marginal workers were induced to drop out of the labor force, bad times might have reduced subsequent unemployment.

37. This drop-off may to some extent reflect the effects of the introduction of Social Security. The program was sufficiently small in 1940 that this is unlikely to be the whole story. Moreover, the timing of its introduction surely had something to do with the fact of the depression.

Table 14 LABOR MARKET TURNOVER AND THE AMERICAN DEPRESSION

EXTENT OF LABOR TURNOVER FROM 1919 TO 1929
(Median monthly rates per 100 workers)

		Separations			
Year	*Accessions*	Total	Quits	Discharges	Layoffs
1919	10.1	7.5	5.8	1.1	0.6
1920	10.1	10.3	8.4	1.1	0.8
1921	2.7	4.4	2.2	0.4	1.8
1922	8.0	5.3	4.2	0.7	0.4
1923	9.0	7.5	6.2	1.0	0.3
1924	3.3	3.8	2.7	0.5	0.6
1925	5.2	4.0	3.1	0.5	0.4
1926	4.6	3.9	2.9	0.5	0.5
1927	3.3	3.3	2.1	0.5	0.7
1928	3.7	3.1	2.2	0.4	0.5
1929	4.4	3.8	2.7	0.5	0.6

Source: Monthly Labor Review, July 1929, pp. 64, 65; February 1931, p. 105.

EXTENT OF LABOR TURNOVER FROM 1930 TO 1940, BY YEARS
(Average monthly rates per 100 workers)

		Separations			
Year	*Accessions*	Total	Quits[a]	Discharges	Layoffs
			Median rates		
1929	4.4	3.8	2.7	0.5	0.6
1930	1.6	2.4	1.1	0.2	1.2
			Weighted average rates		
1930	3.1	5.0	1.6	0.4	3.0
1931	3.1	4.1	1.0	0.2	2.9
1932	3.4	4.3	0.7	0.2	3.4
1933	5.4	3.8	0.9	0.2	2.7
1934	4.7	4.1	0.9	0.2	3.0
1935	4.2	3.6	0.9	0.2	2.5
1936	4.3	3.4	1.1	0.2	2.1
1937	3.5	4.4	1.2	0.2	3.0
1938	3.8	4.1	0.6	0.1	3.4
1939	4.1	3.1	0.8	0.1	2.2
1940	4.4	3.35	1.0	0.15	2.2

a. Including miscellaneous separations because of death, retirement on pension, etc., reported separately since January 1940.
Source: Monthly Labor Review, 1930 to 1941. For a summary of labor turnover from 1931 to 1939, see *ibid.,* September 1940, pp. 696–704.

Source: Woytinsky (1942).

Our insider-outsider story of wage setting still remains. Beyond documenting the importance of hysteresis, and confirming its implications for wage equations, it is difficult to test the story directly. But the judgment of Leuchtenberg (1963) is perhaps revealing. "By Roosevelt's second term, as it seemed the country might never wholly recover, the burden of the unemployed had become too exhausting a moral and economic weight to carry. Those who drew income from other sources could hardly help but feel that the Depression had been a judgement which divided the saved from the unsaved. Increasingly, the jobless seemed not merely worthless mendicants but a menacing Lumpenproletariat." While Leuchtenberg is referring primarily to public attitudes toward the unemployed, similar private attitudes are the driving force behind the hysteresis mechanism we have stressed.

The finding of so many parallels between the current European depression and the American depression suggests to us that hysteresis in Europe may be more the result of a long sequence of adverse shocks than the result of structural problems. Perhaps most telling is the observation that the apparent natural rate of unemployment drifted upward following the actual unemployment rate during the American depression just as it has in Europe. Given the absence of structural explanations for this drift, the inference that it resulted from high past unemployment seems compelling. So too, the high apparent European natural rate of unemployment may be the result of hysteresis arising in the aftermath of a sequence of adverse shocks. This implies that expansionary macroeconomic policies may well work in reducing unemployment in Europe.

5. *Conclusions*

Periods of persistently high unemployment are not uncommon events in broad historical context, yet standard macroeconomic theories have a difficult time accounting for them. We have argued that they can only be understood in terms of theories of hysteresis that make long-run equilibrium depend on history. We have also argued that membership effects may well be important sources of hysteresis. Such effects appear to be an important source of persistence in unemployment in Europe today.

High unemployment is not, however, always persistent. Identifying the circumstances under which persistence is likely to arise is crucial. The main issue is whether hysteresis is the result of specific labor-market structures, of the presence of unions in particular, or whether it is itself the result of adverse shocks, which by increasing unemployment, trigger the insider-outsider dynamics we have discussed here. Our tentative conclusion, from the historical record, is that membership effects become important in bad times and are not crucially dependent on the presence of unions. We have not, however, provided a fully satisfactory theory of membership effects in nonunion settings.

Our theory permits a broad-brush account of the increase in unemployment in Europe over the past fifteen years. In the 1970s, European economies were hit with surprises in the form of rising oil prices, a productivity slowdown, and rapid increases in tax rates. With wages rigid in the short run, each of these types of shocks created unemployment. Because of the membership considerations stressed here, the decrease in employment was validated by higher wage demands. As a result, by the end of the 1970s the equilibrium level of unemployment had increased substantially. In the 1980s, the European economies, unlike the U.S. economy, experienced a series of adverse aggregate demand shocks as European monetary policies followed U.S. policies, but fiscal policies turned contractionary. This led to further unemployment which was then validated by wage demands by those who remained employed. At this point, unemployment will remain high even if there are no more adverse shocks, because of the power of insider workers to set wages.

Our argument is that Europe has experienced a sequence of adverse shocks during the past fifteen years, each of which had a fairly permanent effect on the level of employment. Current high unemployment can be blamed equally on a propagation mechanism that leads the adverse shocks of the past to have a lasting impact, or on the shocks themselves. Unlike simple Keynesian explanations for the European depression which stress only aggregate demand, our theory explains increases in the apparent natural rate of unemployment. Unlike some classical explanations for European unemployment which deny any role for demand management policies, our theory explains how aggregate demand can have protracted effects even in the absence of any long-lasting nominal rigidities.

This view of the European unemployment problem has a number of fairly direct policy implications. A first policy implication of our analysis is the desirability of using measures to "enfranchise" as many workers as possible. If work-sharing programs cause more workers to be employed and therefore represented in wage-setting decisions, they may lead to reduced wage demands and increased employment. Profit-sharing plans such as those proposed by Weitzman (1984) may also raise employment by making it possible for employers to reduce the cost of labor by increasing hiring. On the other hand, they would increase unions' resistance to hiring new workers and might thereby increase membership problems. An obvious alternative policy is to enact measures to reduce the power of unions and thereby allow outsider workers to have a larger impact on wage bargains. Our findings regarding the U.S. Depression where unions were probably not of great importance lead us to be somewhat skeptical of the efficacy of such measures. Certainly it does not yet appear that efforts to reduce the power of unions in the United Kingdom have borne (macroeconomic) fruit.

Our model suggests that shocks, positive or negative, are in a sense self-validating. If employment changes, wage-setting practices adapt to the new level of employment. This means that positive shocks contrived through demand management policies can reduce unemployment regardless of the source of the shocks that caused it. Even if unemployment initially originated from adverse productivity shocks, expansionary policies, if they succeed in raising the level of employment, will yield permanent benefits. Symmetrically, even if most of the increase in unemployment in the 1980s is due to demand, the large decrease in the price of oil may well decrease it permanently. At the same time the model suggests that only policies or shocks that are in some sense surprises will be efficacious. This means that it may be difficult to increase employment a great deal with expansionary policies. The crucial question becomes the length of time over which expansionary policies can "surprise" wage setters. To whatever extent they can, very long-lasting benefits will be derived.

Do the many parallels between the American and European depressions imply that a major expansion in aggregate demand would create the same miracles in Europe as it did in the United States? Unfortunately comparison of the two depressions cannot lead to a very definite answer. While it does dispose of the idea that the apparent increase in the natural rate of unemployment means that demand expansion cannot possibly succeed, and the idea that real wage growth must be restrained if expansion is to take place, an important problem remains. The likelihood of achieving a surprise for a protracted period through inflationary policies may well have been much greater in the United States after a decade including a major deflation than it is in Europe today after a decade of stagflation. On the other hand, the very political infeasibility of expansion in Europe suggests its possible efficacy. Certainly the protracted high unemployment caused by the deflationary policies of the recent past stands as a testament to the potent effects of macroeconomic policies.

We have benefited from the hospitality of the Center for Labour Economics at the London School of Economics. Richard Layard has been especially generous in helping us in a variety of ways. We thank David Grubb, John Martin and Andrew Newell for providing us with data, and Michael Burda, Robert Waldman, Changyong Rhee and Fernando Ramos for research assistance. We also thank David Metcalf, Steven Nickell, James Poterba, Andrei Shleifer, and participants in the NBER macroeconomics conference at which this paper was presented for useful discussions and comments.

APPENDIX TO SECTION 2

1. Derivation of the probability of being employed.

For a given realization of e, thus for a given $n = -cw + e$, the probability of employment is given by

If $n \geqslant n_0$, or equivalently for $e \geqslant n_0 + cw$, then $p = 1$

If $n \leqslant n_0$, or equivalently for $e \leqslant n_0 + cw$, then $p = N/N_0 \div 1 - n_0 + n$.

This implies that, for an arbitrary distribution of e, with density function $f(e)$, and support $[e^-, e^+]$, the probability is given by

$$p = \int_{e^-}^{n_0 + cw} (1 - n_0 - cw + e)f(e)de + \int_{n_0 + cw}^{e^+} 1\, f(e)de.$$

If, as assumed in the text, e is uniform on $[Ee - a, Ee + a]$, p becomes

$$p = (1/2a)\, \{[(1 - n_0 - cw + e/2)e]_{Ee - a}^{n_0 + cw} + (Ee + a - n_0 - cw)\}$$

$$= 1 \qquad \text{for } n_0 + cw \leqslant Ee - a$$

$$= 1 - (1/4a)(n_0 + cw - Ee + a)^2 \qquad \text{for } n_0 + cw \geqslant Ee - a.$$

2. Derivation of the solution in the case when $m = 1$.

We first derive the objective function maximized by the union at any given time.

We assume that, if laid off, the probability of being rehired by the firm is equal to zero. As in the text, we assume that the utility of being unemployed is equal to zero. Let p_i be, as in the text, the probability of being employed at time i for a member of the union at time i. Then, given the membership rule that membership depends on employment in the previous period, the probability for a union member at time zero to still be a union member in period i is given by $E_0(p_0 p_1 \ldots p_{i-1})$. Thus, the utility of the union member as of period 0 is given by

$$U_0 = E_0((p_0 + bw_0) + \theta p_0(p_1 + bw_1) + \theta^2 p_0 p_1 (p_2 + bw_2) + \ldots),$$

or, in recursive form, by

$$U_0 = p_0 + bw_0 + p_0E_0(\theta U_1).$$

Even under the assumption that the shocks are independently distributed through time, the random variables within the expectation operator above are not in general independent, making the maximization problem intractable. Thus, we solve instead the problem associated with the objective function linearized around some p', w'. This linearized objective function is given by the following recursion:

$$V_0 = (A + dp_0 + bw_0) + \theta p'E_0V_1,$$

where $A \equiv -\theta p'(p' + bw') / (1 - \theta p')$ and
$d \equiv 1 + \theta(p' + bw')(1 + \theta p' + \theta^2 p'^2 + \ldots)$
$= (1 + b\theta w')/(1 - \theta p')$.

The weight put on the probability of being employed, p_0, is now higher than in the previous case. This is because p_0 affects not only today's outcome but the probability of union membership and employment in the future.

We now derive the solution to the maximization using the linearized objective function. Under the assumption that shocks to labor demand are independent and uniformly distributed on $[-a, +a]$, the solution to the linearized maximization problem is derived as follows:

We first guess that the maximized value V_0 is of the form

$$V_0 = \alpha - \beta n_{-1} \tag{a1}$$

with coefficients α and β to be determined. We then solve for optimal p_0 and w_0 given α and β, and finally solve for α and β.

If $V_0 = \alpha - \beta n_{-1}$, then $E_0V_1 = \alpha - \beta E_0 n_0 = \alpha + \beta c w_0$. Replacing in the recursive form which characterizes V_0 gives

$$V_0 = (A + \theta p'\alpha) + (b + \theta p'\beta c)w_0 + dp_0 \tag{a2}$$

The probability p_0 is given by

$$p_0 = 1 - (1/4a)(\bar{n}_0 + cw_0 + a)^2$$

Replacing p_0 in equation (a2) and solving for optimal w_0 gives

$$w_0 = (1/c)[-\bar{n}_0 - a + 2a(b + \theta p'\beta c)/dc]. \tag{a3}$$

This in turn gives

$$p_0 = 1 - a((b + \theta p'\beta c)/dc)^2. \tag{a4}$$

This gives us w_0 and p_0 as functions of structural parameters and of α and β. We now solve for the values of α and β. Replacing w_0 and p_0 in equation (a2) and comparing equations (a2) and (a1) gives the values of α and β. The value of α is of no interest here. The value of β is given by

$$\beta = (b/c)/(1 - \theta p').$$

REFERENCES

Bailey, M. N. 1983. The labor market in the 1930's. In *Macroeconomics, Prices, and Quantities*, ed. J. Tobin, 21–62. Washington, D.C.: The Brookings Institution.

Barker, A., P. Lewis and M. McCann. 1984. Trades unions and the organisation of the unemployed. *British Journal of Industrial Relations* 3:391–404.

Blanchard, O., and L. Summers. 1984. Perspectives on high world real interest rates. *Brookings Papers on Economic Activity* 2:273–334.

Bruno, M., and J. Sachs. 1985. *The Economics of Worldwide Stagflation*. Oxford: Basil Blackwell.

Buiter, W. 1985. A guide to public sector debt and deficits. *Economic Policy* 1 (November): 13–60.

Bulow, J., and L. Summers. 1986. A theory of dual labor markets with application to industrial policy, discrimination and Keynesian unemployment. *Journal of Labor Economics*. Forthcoming.

Campbell, J., and G. Mankiw. 1985. Are output fluctuations transitory? Harvard University. Mimeo.

Clark, K., and L. Summers. 1979. Labor market dynamics and unemployment, a reconsideration. *Brookings Papers on Economic Activity* 1:13–60.

———. 1982. Labour force participation: Timing and persistence. *Review of Economic Studies* 49 (159): 825–44.

Coe, D., and F. Gagliardi. 1985. Nominal wage determination in ten OECD countries. OECD Economics and Statistics Department Working Paper 19 (March).

Dornbusch, R., et al. 1983. Macroeconomic prospects and policies of the european community. Center for European Policy Studies, Discussion Paper 1. Brussels. Reprinted in *Restoring Europe's prosperity*, ed. O. Blanchard, R. Dornbusch, and R. Layard, 1–32. Cambridge: MIT Press, 1986.

Drazen, A. 1979. On permanent effects of transitory phenomena in a simple growth model. *Economics Letters* 3:25–30.

Ellwood, D. 1982. Teenage unemployment: Permanent scars or temporary blemishes? In *The youth labor market problem: Its nature, causes and consequences*, ed. R. Freeman and D. Wise. Chicago: University of Chicago Press and National Bureau of Economic Research.

Farber, H. 1984. The analysis of union behavior. MIT Working Paper 355 (November).

Fischer, S. 1977. Long term contracts, rational expectations, and the optimal money supply rule. *Journal of Political Economy* 85 (February): 191–205.

Gordon, R. 1983. A century of evidence on wage and price stickiness in the United States, the United Kingdom and Japan. In *Macroeconomics, Prices and Quantities*, ed. J. Tobin, 85–120. Washington, D.C.: The Brookings Institution.

Gordon, R., and J. Wilcox. 1981. Monetarist interpretations of the Great Depression, an evaluation and a critique. In *The Great Depression revisited.* K. Brunner, ed., 49–207. Martinus Nijhoff.

Gregory, R. 1985. Wages policy and unemployment in Australia. Paper presented at the Chelwood Gate Conference on Unemployment, Chelwood Gate.

Grubb, D. 1984. The OECD data set. LSE Centre for Labour Economics Working Paper 615.

Hall, R. 1976. The Phillips curve and macroeconomic policy. Carnegie-Rochester Conference on Economic Policy, vol. 1: 127–48.

Hargraves-Heap, S. P. 1980. Choosing the wrong natural rate, accelerating inflation or decelerating unemployment and growth. *Economic Journal* 90 (September): 611–20.

Harris, J., and M. Todaro. 1979. Migration, unemployment and development: A two sector analysis. *American Economic Review* 60 (March): 126–43.

Kaufman, R. 1984. On Britain's competitive sector. *British Journal of Industrial Relations* (March).

Layard, R., S. Nickell, and R. Jackman. 1984. On vacancies. LSE Centre for Labour Economics Discussion Paper 165 (August).

Layard, R., and S. Nickell. 1986. Unemployment in Britain. *Economica.* Special issue on unemployment (forthcoming).

Layard, R. et al. 1984. Europe: The case for unsustainable growth. Center for European Policy Studies 8/9 (May). Reprinted in *Restoring Europe's prosperity,* ed. O. Blanchard, R. Dornbusch and R. Layard, 33–94. Cambridge: MIT Press, 1986.

Leuchtenberg, W. 1963. *Franklin D. Roosevelt and the New Deal.* New York: Harper & Row.

Lindbeck, A., and D. Snower. 1985. Wage setting, unemployment and insider-outsider relations. Institute for International Economic Studies, Stockholm, Working Paper 344 (December).

McDonald, I., and R. Solow. 1981. Wage bargaining and unemployment. *American Economic Review* 71 (December): 896–908.

Minford, P. 1982. *Unemployment: Cause and cure.* Oxford: Martin Robertson.

Mitchell, B. 1947. *Depression decade: From New Era through New Deal.* New York: Holt, Rinehart

Nelson, R., and C. Plosser. 1982. Trends and random walks in economic time series: Some evidence and implications. *Journal of Monetary Economics* 10 (September): 139–62.

Nickell, S. 1984. A review of *Unemployment: Cause and cure* by Patrick Minford with David Davies, Michael Peel and Alison Prague. LSE Centre for Labour Economics Discussion Paper 185.

OECD. Employment Outlook, 1984.

Oswald, A. 1985. The economic theory of trade unions: An introductory survey. *Scandinavian Journal of Economics.* Forthcoming.

Phelps, E. 1972. *Inflation policy and unemployment theory.* New York: Norton.

Romer, C. 1986. Spurious volatility in historical unemployment data. *Journal of Political Economy* 94 (February): 1–37.

Sachs, J. 1979. Wages, profits and macroeconomic adjustment: A comparative study. *Brookings Papers on Economic Activity* 2:269–319.

———. 1983. Real wages and unemployment in the OECD countries. *Brookings Papers on Economic Activity* 1:255–89.

———. 1985. High unemployment in Europe. Harvard University. Mimeo.
Samuelson, P. 1966. *The collected scientific papers of Paul A. Samuelson*. Vol. 2. Cambridge: MIT Press.
Slichter, S. 1950. Notes on the structure of wages. *Review of Economics and Statistics* 31:283–88.
Taylor, J. 1979. Staggered wage setting in a macro model. *American Economic Review*, 69 (May): 108–13.
Weitzman, M. 1982. Increasing returns and the foundations of unemployment theory. *Economic Journal* 92 (December): 787–804.
———. 1984. *The share economy*. Cambridge: Harvard University Press.
Woytinsky, W. S. 1942. *Three aspects of labor dynamics*. Washington, D.C.: Social Science Research Council.

Comment

JOHN KENNAN
University of Iowa

This is a thought-provoking paper on an important topic. The main theoretical idea is that persistence in the level of unemployment may be traced to the influence of currently employed workers ("insiders") on wage rates. Wages are set so that the insiders have a high probability of continued employment in the face of random shifts in the labor demand function. When demand is realized employment may increase or decrease, and the new set of insiders then acts so as to perpetuate itself. In particular, a run of negative demand shocks will produce a shrunken group of insiders who will be able to maintain high wage rates without seriously jeopardizing their own employment prospects.

The basic model presented in section 2.1 of the paper uses a quadratic approximation for the probability of employment p, and a utility function which is linear in p and the log-wage w. This tends to obscure the results, which are actually fairly general. For example, if the utility function were literally linear in p then utility would be unbounded, since p could be set at zero and the wage could be set arbitrarily high. The main results can apparently be derived in a slightly different way, however.

Suppose that the union maximizes the expected value of a log-linear function of the number of members employed and the wage rate:

$$\max_w \mathrm{E}\, b\, w + n.$$

If there is no uncertainty and $b = 1$ this reduces to the standard (Dunlop) model in which the union maximizes the total income of its members. Union employment is limited by the membership n_0 (measured in logs) and by the stochastic log-linear demand curve, so that

$$n = \min(n_0, e - cw)$$

where e is a random variable with distribution function F. Thus the union acts so as to maximize the function $V(w)$, which is defined as

$$\begin{aligned} V(w) &= b\,w + E\min(n_0, e - cw) \\ &= b\,w - cw + E\min(n_0 + cw, e). \end{aligned}$$

The derivative of this function is

$$\begin{aligned} V'(w) &= b - c + c[1 - F(n_0 + cw)] \\ &= c\,[b/c - F(n_0 + cw)]. \end{aligned}$$

Evidently, if $c < b$ then $V'(w)$ is always positive (since $F \leqslant 1$). In this case the union would maximize utility by setting an extremely high wage, implying that virtually no one would be employed (that is, the union would act as a monopolist facing inelastic demand). Assume then that labor demand is relatively elastic, so that $c > b$. Then if there were no uncertainty about the position of the labor demand curve, the union would set a wage just low enough so that all of its members would be employed. More generally, the union chooses a wage w^* so that

$$F(n_0 + cw^*) = b/c.$$

To see whether employment will exceed the union membership, write the labor demand function as

$$n - n_0 = e - cw - n_0.$$

Then when the union sets the optimal wage w^* the result will be

$$n - n_0 = e - F^{-1}(b/c).$$

For example, the expected value of nonunion employment is

$$En - n_0 = Ee - F^{-1}(b/c).$$

If the median of e is equal to its mean (as in the case of the uniform distribution assumed in the article) then $Ee = F^{-1}(\tfrac{1}{2})$. Since F is an increasing function, this implies that expected employment will exceed union membership if b/c is less than ½.

Thus the static results presented in section 2.1 remain valid for a reasonable reinterpretation of the union's utility function. In addition, the results hold for more general specifications of the distribution of labor demand shocks. The most important substantive assumption seems to be that the elasticity of labor demand must be quite high (roughly speaking, if the union maximizes expected income, c must be above 2). Equation (2.4) indicates that this assumption can be weakened considerably in the dynamic case.

If the labor demand elasticity is sufficiently high, then the dynamic model sketched by Blanchard and Summers gives a plausible qualitative description of recent movements in European unemployment rates. The model suggests that wages are set so that the current group of insiders can expect to preserve their jobs, given an average realization of the labor demand shock, with perhaps a small expected cushion of nonunion employment. When there is a run of large unfavorable labor demand shocks (such as oil price increases) many insiders lose their jobs and thereby lose a good deal of their influence on how wages should be set. The new smaller group of insiders then sets wages so that employment can be expected to drift slowly back up toward the full-employment level.

Of course this model is still subject to the standard criticism that unemployment is inefficient. It is not clear why the union must set wages before the demand shock is realized, nor why the union cannot negotiate a Pareto optimal contract. In the absence of a convincing explanation of this inefficiency, policy recommendations based on this model are on shaky ground.

Additional Unemployment Data

In discussing "the European unemployment problem" it seems appropriate to summarize the unemployment data for as many European countries as possible. This is done in table 1a; for comparison, unemployment data for several non-European countries are also included. Evidently, the recent experience of Britain, France, and Germany, which Blanchard and Summers take to be representative, is not the whole story. Although there are undoubtedly serious questions about the comparability of data across countries, any convincing explanation of the persistently high unemployment recently experienced by Britain, France, and Germany must account for the low unemployment rates in Switzerland, Sweden, Norway, and Austria.

Blanchard and Summers emphasize the contrast between movements in European and U.S. unemployment rates, particularly after 1980. Table 1a indicates that a similar contrast exists between Canada and the United States. Ashenfelter and Card (1986) recently considered the list of obvious suspects here, and concluded that there was insufficient evidence to warrant any indictments. It is true, however, that unions are now much more important in Canada than in the United States. According to Ashenfelter and Card, union membership rose from about 33 percent of employed workers in 1970 to about 40 percent in 1984, while union membership in the United States fell from 27 percent to about 20 percent over the same period. These data might be used to support the Blanchard-Summers thesis that a higher degree of unionization is associated with more sluggish adjustment to labor demand shocks.

Employment and Real Wage Equations

In section 3.2, Blanchard and Summers present estimates of wage and employment equations which apparently provide some empirical sup-

Table 1a UNEMPLOYMENT RATES, 1960–1985

	1960–64	*1965–69*	*1970–74*	*1975–79*	*1980–83*	*1984*	*1985*
Ireland	6.0	6.3	7.5	11.3	16.5	23.1	—
Spain	1.8	1.2	1.9	6.4	16.2	20.6	21.9
Belgium	3.6	3.4	3.4	9.3	15.9	18.6	18.8
Holland	—	—	2.7	5.1	12.4	17.6	—
Britain	1.8	2.0	3.0	5.2	10.9	12.6	13.0
Canada	6.1	4.2	5.8	7.6	9.9	11.3	11.2
Denmark	—	—	1.6	6.7	9.4	10.5	11.0
Italy	4.7	5.6	5.8	6.9	9.1	10.4	10.5
France	—	—	2.6	4.9	7.9	9.7	10.1
Germany	0.9	1.2	1.3	4.4	7.1	9.1	9.6
Australia	1.4	2.2	2.2	5.9	7.6	9.0	8.7
U.S.	5.7	3.8	5.4	7.0	8.3	7.5	7.5
Finland	—	2.6	2.2	5.1	5.6	6.2	6.8
Austria	3.0	2.7	1.9	2.0	3.4	4.5	5.0
Norway	1.4	1.2	0.9	1.1	2.2	3.3	—
Sweden	1.6	1.8	2.2	1.9	2.8	3.1	2.8
Japan	1.4	1.2	1.3	2.0	2.4	2.7	2.7
Switzerland	—	—	—	0.4	0.6	1.1	1.1

The countries are sorted according to the 1984 unemployment rate. Unemployment is stated as a percentage of the (total or civilian) labor force, except for Ireland and Belgium, where it is a percentage of the insured labor force. The 1985 figures generally refer to the first six months of 1985.

Source: OECD Main Economic Indicators.

port for their "hysteresis" theory. Equations of this sort are generally open to several alternative interpretations. For example, similar equations can be derived from the equilibrium labor market model discussed by Sargent (1979, chapter 16). Allowing for the influence of expected future real wages (as suggested in footnote 28 of the article), the labor demand function may be written as

$$n(t) = s\,n(t-1) - (1-s)\,b \sum_{i=0}^{\infty} \beta^i E_t W(t+i) + e(t), \quad (3.1)$$

where W is the real wage, β is the discount factor, and constant terms are ignored. When utility is intertemporally nonseparable in leisure the labor supply function can be written symmetrically as

$$n(t) = a\,n(t-1) + (1-a)\,d \sum_{i=0}^{\infty} \beta^i E_t W(t+i) + f(t), \quad (3.2)$$

where d is a parameter representing the elasticity of labor supply, and $f(t)$ is a preference shock. When d is set to zero this equation can instead be interpreted as the union's rule for setting expected employment, as in the article.

Assume that both e and f follow AR(1) processes:

$$\begin{aligned} (1 - \sigma L)\, e(t) &= u(t) \\ (1 - \tau L)\, f(t) &= v(t). \end{aligned}$$

Then, as is shown by Kennan (1985) the reduced form is a VAR(2):

$$\begin{bmatrix} n(t) \\ W(t) \end{bmatrix} = \begin{bmatrix} A_{nn} & A_{nW} \\ A_{Wn} & A_{WW} \end{bmatrix} \begin{bmatrix} n(t-1) \\ W(t-1) \end{bmatrix} + \begin{bmatrix} B_{nn} \\ B_{Wn} \end{bmatrix} n(t-2) + \begin{bmatrix} E_n(t) \\ E_W(t) \end{bmatrix},$$

where the coefficients labeled A and B are complicated functions of the basic structural parameters. The vertical supply curve assumption ($d = 0$) used in the article implies $A_{nW} = 0$, $A_{nn} = a + \tau$, $A_{ww} = \sigma$, $B_{nn} = -a\tau$ and

$$A_{Wn} = \frac{[s - a + \sigma - \tau]\,[1 - a\beta s\tau] - a\beta s[a - \sigma]\,[s - a]}{b[1 - s]\,[1 - \beta s]}$$

$$B_{Wn} = -\frac{[\sigma s - \tau a - \beta a s \tau(\sigma - \tau + s - a)]}{b[1 - s]\,[1 - \beta s]}.$$

The case analyzed in the article corresponds to assuming $\beta = 0, \tau = 0$ and $\sigma = 1$. Then

$$A_{Wn} = \frac{[s - a + 1]}{b[1 - s]}$$

$$B_{Wn} = \frac{-s}{b[1 - s]}.$$

In particular, if there is "strict hysteresis" ($a = 1$) then the employment coefficients in the wage equation sum to zero. This is hardly a solid foundation for a test of hysteresis, however, since it depends crucially on assuming $\tau = 0$ and $\sigma = 1$. For example, if there is no hysteresis ($a = 0$) the employment coefficients will still sum to zero if $\tau = \sigma + s(1 - \sigma)$.

Even if the employment and real wage equations are open to alternative structural interpretations it is useful to compare the reduced-form estimates across countries, as is done in tables 4–7 in the article. Some variations on this theme are shown in table 2a, using monthly data sampled annually, for eight countries. It is by no means clear that the data-generating process is similar for the five European countries in this table. Any unified theory of unemployment movements in the various European countries seems likely to have trouble dealing with the diversity shown in table 2a, particularly if the theory is built around the relationship between employment and real wages, as in the Blanchard and Summers article.

A Policy Experiment

Finally, it seems appropriate to mention a conventional alternative to the Blanchard-Summers hysteresis theory, namely that there is a connection between high unemployment and the notoriously high rates of income taxation in Europe. A simple policy experiment could pay rich dividends here. Suppose it is announced now that next year's income tax liability for each worker will be capped at the (real) amount paid by this worker last year plus (say) 10 percent. This would mean a zero marginal tax rate for (all of) next year, provided that the worker expects to reach the cap. If high marginal tax rates are important in depressing the level of economic activity, this experiment should produce a surge in employment, as the net wage received by workers rises, while the gross wage paid by employers falls. If marginal tax rates are not important, the experiment will not have much effect on real activity, or on the government's tax revenue.

Table 2a EMPLOYMENT AND REAL WAGE EQUATIONS

	Employment (n)				*Real Wage (W)*				
	$n\ (t-1)$	$n\ (t-2)$	$W\ (t-1)$	Trend	$n\ (t-1)$	$n\ (t-2)$	$W\ (t-1)$	Trend	W/n
Canada	.83	−.62	.24	.02	.28	.26	.93	−.02	.18
1962–84	(4.5)	(2.5)	(2.9)	(2.7)	(1.1)	(0.8)	(8.1)	(1.9)	
Italy	.81	−.07	.01	.00	−.30	−.15	.75	.01	.45
1962–84	(4.0)	(0.3)	(0.1)	(0.3)	(0.5)	(0.2)	(4.3)	(1.3)	
France	.71	.14	.18	−.01	−.19	.58	.91	.00	.04
1962–84	(3.0)	(0.6)	(2.2)	(2.6)	(0.5)	(1.6)	(6.9)	(0.5)	
U.S.	.67	−.46	.08	.02	−.64	−.11	.82	.02	.03
1962–84	(2.8)	(1.6)	(0.7)	(3.3)	(1.9)	(0.3)	(5.1)	(2.4)	
Austria	1.38	−.72	.21	−.01	.26	.19	.64	.01	.05
1962–84	(7.7)	(3.5)	(1.6)	(1.6)	(1.1)	(0.7)	(3.7)	(1.8)	
Japan	.48	.23	−.05	.005	−.19	1.7	.90	−.01	.002
1962–84	(2.2)	(1.1)	(1.6)	(2.4)	(0.4)	(3.4)	(12.5)	(2.5)	
Britain	1.03	−.01	.14	−.005	.47	−.35	.43	.01	.19
1955–83	(5.1)	(0.0)	(1.1)	(1.8)	(1.6)	(1.1)	(2.3)	(3.0)	
Germany	1.08	−.76	.44	−.02	.38	−.28	1.03	−.00	.02
1963–83	(5.3)	(3.2)	(2.3)	(2.5)	(3.2)	(2.1)	(9.0)	(0.6)	

Explanation: These are VAR(2) estimates (t-statistics in parentheses). The variables $n(t)$ and $W(t)$ refer to employment and real wages in April of year t. The column "W/n" gives the significance level of the F-statistic for the hypothesis that employment does not cause the real wage. The employment variable covers the whole economy except for Austria (mining and manufacturing), Germany (manufacturing) and Britain (manufacturing). The real wage is hourly earnings in manufacturing deflated by the consumer price index, except for Japan, where the real wage is monthly earnings in manufacturing, deflated by the CPI. The wage for Germany is obtained from quarterly data.

In other words, this experiment will yield large returns in case marginal tax rates are important, and will not cost much in any case.

I thank Martin Sefton and Barry Sopher for valuable research assistance. This research was funded in part by the National Science Foundation under Grant SES-8309003.

REFERENCES

Ashenfelter, O. and D. Card. 1986. Why have unemployment rates in Canada and the U.S. diverged? Industrial Relations Section, Princeton University, Working Paper 204 (February).

Kennan, J. 1985. An econometric analysis of aggregate fluctuations in labor supply and demand. College of Business Administration, University of Iowa, Working Paper No. 83-16A (July).

Sargent, T. J. 1979. *Macroeconomic Theory.* New York: Academic Press.

Comment

ROBERT E. HALL
Stanford University and NBER

Macroeconomics is undergoing a painful adjustment to the growing realization that the evidence does not support conventional theories about macro fluctuations. By and large, when output suffers a shock, the effects of that shock are permanent. Theories of gradual wage-price adjustment, by contrast, teach us that the economy gradually adjusts to demand shocks, so the shocks have no lasting effect on output or employment. In those theories, output follows a cycle around a full-employment trend path.

The first evidence against the cycle-around-trend view was presented by Charles Nelson and Charles Plosser (1982). Recent results obtained by John Campbell and N. Gregory Mankiw (1986) strongly support Nelson and Plosser's findings. Real GNP does not follow a cycle around a stable growth trend. Instead, each random deviation lasts more or less forever. In fact, a simple random walk with drift is not a bad approximation to the stochastic character of real GNP in the United States. Preliminary work of my own suggests that the same conclusion holds even more strongly in all of the major OECD economies.

Blanchard and Summers look at the same issue with respect to unemployment. As they note, unemployment is the least likely macro variable to deviate from the cycle-around-trend type of stochastic behavior. If unemployment measures the gap between labor supply and demand, then events which make output and employment change permanently—such as random technological innovations—should change unemployment only temporarily. They show that unemployment has tended to revert to a "natural rate" in postwar U.S. experience, but they also show how atypical that experience has been. In earlier U.S. history, and in all recorded European history, unemployment has been highly persistent. Again, a random walk is not a bad stochastic model for unemployment.

Macro theorists have gone in two very different directions in creating models where output does not have cycles around a stable trend. Nelson and Plosser interpret their findings as strongly supporting the real business cycle models where markets always clear and output fluctuates because of random shifts in tastes and technology. Certainly that type of model is alive and well today, as the article by Martin Eichenbaum and Kenneth Singleton (in this volume) shows. But an interesting new literature is also developing which deals with models where markets never clear, thanks to sound microeconomic reasons having to do with noncompetitive markets. Papers by Oliver Hart (1982) and many others make the point that a full-employment equilibrium is a special feature of competition.

The theoretical work to date generally rests on standard models of market imperfections. For example, Hart relies on Cournot behavior in the product market on the part of a finite number of sellers, and similar behavior in the labor market on the part of a finite number of labor unions. The existing models explain why the economy does not drive to its full-employment point, but they do not explain why stochastic fluctuations in output should have a random-walk character. Blanchard and Summers have opened a new avenue of research which deals explicitly with the random-walk issue.

In the Blanchard-Summers model, the monopoly power of a labor union or other group of incumbent workers depends on the past history of demand shocks. A positive demand shock dilutes the strength of the union because it adds new workers to the union, and the new workers have voting power equal to that of the established workers. Hence employment remains high virtually forever after a positive shock. A negative demand shock pushes some workers out of employment and soon thereafter out of the union. With fewer workers, the union chooses to jack up the wage and keep employment lower, again virtually forever.

An essential adjunct of the theory is that displaced workers cannot find jobs in new firms or in other sectors. Blanchard and Summers argue, with some persuasive power, that fixed costs deter entry at times of low demand in some sectors. Even if a competitive sector exists, they say, when it is crowded with displaced workers, the competitive wage will fall to the point where many workers will be unemployed because they are queued up for jobs in the union sector.

To my mind, the only serious weakness in Blanchard and Summers's model is the willingness of the incumbent workers to allow a favorable demand surprise to dilute their effective shareholder interest in the firm. Why don't they impose a rule against hiring, so that every demand surprise can be translated into further wage increases? The all-powerful union in the model slips in only one respect, but it is a terribly important respect. The sensible union would pursue a policy described by Lloyd Ulman as the "Cheshire Cat" theory of unionism—union membership gradually declines through retirement and attrition, and wages rise along the demand curve for labor. Ultimately all that is left is the smile of the last member, who is paid an astronomical wage.

Obviously there are many blanks to fill in to make this new explanation of unemployment persistence credible. The article as it stands has only a tiny section on how European unions actually operate, yet this is crucial to empirical support for the theory. Moreover, as Blanchard and Summers note, a random-walk model well describes U.S. unemployment in eras when unionization was extremely low. The theory then requires that the incumbent workers have some of the power of a union, but we do not yet know how they achieve or exercise that power without a formal union.

To my mind, the strongest empirical backing for the basic idea of the article is the evidence of the extreme persistence of unemployment in most countries in most eras. In addition to presenting this evidence, Blanchard and Summers devote quite a bit of space to the study of a companion type of evidence, the relation between wage adjustment and unemployment (or employment). Under a Phillips curve, where wage inflation is increasingly negative whenever the unemployment rate exceeds the natural rate, unemployment cannot evolve as a random walk. Consequently, the wage adjustment equation that governs an economy with fully persistent unemployment has the rate of change of unemployment (or employment) on the right-hand side, rather than the level of change. Blanchard and Summers devote considerable effort to showing that this prediction is fulfilled. I do not disagree with what they do, but I think it is important to point out that their case does not depend on the wage-change equations. The finding of strong persistence in unemployment makes their case on its own, and is much less subject to econometric criticism than their wage-change regressions.

My general conclusion is that the absence of cycle-around-trend behavior in most economies most of the time is an established fact, and one that will have an important role in shaping the macro theories of the future. The labor-market membership model developed by Blanchard and Summers has some merit as an explanation, but I do not find it compelling as a unitary explanation. Until I find out why unions stand idly by when their incumbent interests are diluted, I will remain unconvinced that a positive demand shock can raise output. Instead, I will continue to examine carefully alternative explanations of the failure of market-clearing forces, grounded in the microeconomics of product markets.

REFERENCES

Campbell, J. and N. G. Mankiw. 1986. Are output fluctuations transitory? Princeton, Harvard, and the National Bureau of Economic Research (January).

Hart, O. 1982. A model of imperfect competition with Keynesian features. *Quarterly Journal of Economics* 97:109–38.

Nelson, C., and C. Plosser. 1982. Trends and random walks in macroeconomic time series: Some evidence and implications. *Journal of Monetary Economics* 10:139–62.

Discussion

Rudiger Dornbusch pointed out the difference between employment trends in manufacturing and in services in Europe. The negative trend of employment is strong in the manufacturing sector, but not in services. He suggested that European unions are reluctant to cut wages because they doubt employment will increase unless large-scale investment takes place. He argued that the Blanchard-Summers analysis favored more fundamental policy changes than they imply, for instance the wage tribunals suggested by James Meade or Martin Weitzman's profit-sharing scheme.

Arnold Kling commented that Europe is not the only place with high unemployment. The "fresh water belt" of the United States, such as Michigan, has the same problem. One reason unemployment persistence has been less of a problem in the United States may be the fortunate presence of a prosperous "salt water belt."

Martin Weitzman criticized Blanchard and Summers's reluctance to draw the conclusions their analysis implies. The paper implies that labor unions are the prime suspect in the crime of high unemployment in Europe, but Blanchard and Summers shrink from that conclusion. They do not, for instance, discuss the relative merits of a two-tier wage system versus profit sharing in the labor market. In addition, the paper is ambiguous about the merits of Keynesian demand expansion. The paper implies that since the old-style Phillips curve has broken down, demand expansion would lead to inflation. He saw no alternative to microeconomic measures to attack the unemployment problem in Europe.

In response, Lawrence Summers stressed the parallels he and Blanchard found between the United States in the 1930s, when unions were weak, and Europe currently. Those similarities made them hesitant to blame Europe's difficulties on the unions.

The authors' failure to close the model worried James Hamilton, who agreed with John Kennan's statement that the labor contracts considered by Blanchard and Summers are inefficient. He suspected that a complete model might produce a constant level of employment.

Paul Romer cited Ashenfelter and Card's comparison between United States and Canadian unemployment, suggesting that this may give a clue as to whether unionization as opposed to the insider-outsider distinction mattered. The different attitudes to unionization in the two countries were exemplified by the frequency and government tolerance of Canadian mail strikes compared with the firing of the air traffic controllers in the United States.

Stephen Zeldes thought the Blanchard-Summers model had more to say about the persistence of unemployment than its average level. In a full model, it was quite possible that equilibrium would show a higher average level of unemployment in competitive labor markets than in the type of market examined by Blanchard and Summers, but that persistence would be lower in a competitive labor market.

Differences in unemployment rates across industries might give a clue as to the importance of unions, James Poterba suggested. It was also possible that characteristics of the employer as well as the employees determined wage and employment characteristics. Japanese firms in Britain have not gotten rid of British workers, but of British managers.

Olivier Blanchard agreed with Kennan's doubts about the optimality of Blanchard and Summers's labor contract, but speculated that the result from a more complete model would not be very different. He commented that he and Summers estimated and discussed the Phillips curve because their Phillips curve has policy implications very different from the most-used alternative, a standard Phillips curve with a time trend. With a time trend, high unemployment reflects a high natural unemployment rate, and there is no room for aggregate demand policy to affect unemployment. Answering Martin Weitzman, he agreed that expansion now would lead to high inflation unless some incomes policy is introduced, but he stressed that high inflation may have to be accepted for some time as a trade-off for lower unemployment.

Martin Eichenbaum and Kenneth J. Singleton
CARNEGIE-MELLON UNIVERSITY AND NBER

Do Equilibrium Real Business Cycle Theories Explain Postwar U.S. Business Cycles?

1. *Introduction*

During the past decade there has been a resurgence of interest in equilibrium real business cycle theories. According to these theories, the recurrent fluctuation in outputs, consumptions, investments, and other real quantities—what we shall refer to as the business cycle phenomenon—is precisely what one should expect to emerge from industrial market economies in which consumers and firms solve intertemporal optimum problems under uncertainty. Moreover, fluctuations in real quantities are attributed to exogenous technological and taste shocks combined with various sources of endogenous dynamics including adjustment costs, time-to-build capital goods, and the non-time-separability of preferences (e.g., Kydland and Prescott (1982), Long and Plosser (1983), Kydland (1984), and Prescott (1986)). Common characteristics of these models are that there is a complete set of contingent claims to future goods and services, agents have common information sets, and the only "frictions" in the economy are due to technological factors. In particular, real business cycle (RBC) models abstract entirely from monetary considerations and the fact that exchange in modern economies occurs via the use of fiat money.

There are two interpretations of this modeling strategy. The first interpretation is that monetary institutions and monetary policy are assumed to be inherently neutral in the sense that real allocations are invariant to innovations in financial arrangements and monetary policy. Money is a veil regardless of how much the veil flutters. The second interpretation is that the market organizations and the nature of monetary policy in the sample period being examined are such as that an RBC model provides an accurate characterization of the real economy. Under this interpretation RBC models may be useful frameworks for examining the determination of real allocations for certain institutional environments and classes of monetary policies. Money may be a veil as long as the veil does not flutter too much. In our view, proponents of RBC theories are not claiming that monetary policy cannot or has never had a significant impact on the fluctuation of real output, investment, or consumption. Rather we subscribe to the second interpretation of RBC analyses as investigations of real allocations under the assumption that, to a good approximation, monetary policy shocks have played an insignificant role in determining the behavior of real variables.

The assumption in equilibrium RBC models that monetary shocks have not been an important source of aggregate fluctuations is similar to the basic premise of certain early Keynesian models. According to these models, interest rates affected at most long-lived fixed investments, so the interest elasticity of aggregate demand was preceived as being low. Furthermore, the principal shocks impinging on the economy had their direct effects on aggregate demand. In particular, investment was thought to be influenced capriciously by "animal spirits." Thus, aggregate fluctuations were associated primarily with real shocks. Indeed, the economic environment was assumed to be such that changes in the money supply (both systematic and current unanticipated shocks) had small impacts on real economic activity. The latter feature of these models led to the conclusion that fiscal policy was preferred to monetary policy for stabilizing output fluctuation.

More recent Keynesian-style models share some common features with both early Keynesian and equilibrium RBC models, but they are also fundamentally different in several important respects. Proponents of modern Keynesian models often argue that monetary policy shocks have not been a significant source of "instability" in the U.S. economy. For example Modigliani (1977, p. 12) states that "there is no basis for the monetarists' suggestion that our post war instability can be traced to monetary instability." Thus on this feature of the economy, proponents of modern Keynesian models and of equilibrium RBC theories are often in agreement.

However, for at least two reasons, it would be misleading to argue that equilibrium RBC models and Keynesian models are simply different versions of business cycle models in which only (or primarily) real shocks matter for fluctuations in real quantities. First, the propagation mechanisms by which exogenous shocks impinge on the endogenous variables are typically very different in the two classes of models. As noted, equilibrium RBC models focus on such technological frictions as gestation lags in building capital or intertemporal nonseparability of preferences in generating endogenous sources of dynamics. Contingent claims markets are assumed to be complete and goods and asset prices adjust freely in competitive markets. In contrast, Keynesian models typically emphasize various frictions that prevent perfectly flexible goods prices and wages (e.g., Modigliani 1958, Taylor 1980). The sources of these rigidities may be frictions associated with incomplete markets, contractual arrangements, or imperfect competition among firms. These differences in propagation mechanisms may imply very different reactions of the equilibrium RBC and Keynesian economies to the same type of shock.

Second, and closely related to the first consideration, the potential roles for stabilization in these economic environments may be very different. The inflexible prices and incomplete markets in Keynesian models have been used to justify activist fiscal *and* monetary policies designed to stabilize output fluctuation. Of particular relevance for our analysis is the important role often attributed to monetary policy in affecting the cyclical behavior of real variables in Keynesian models. While exogenous monetary policy shocks may not be important sources of aggregate fluctuations, activist monetary policies are often deemed to have had significant effects on the propagation of nonmonetary shocks. Hence, though the sources of uncertainty may be real, it seems clear that money plays a central role in modern Keynesian models. This interpretation of modern Keynesian models was made explicitly by Modigliani (1977, p. 1): "Milton Friedman was once quoted as saying 'We are all Keynesians, now, and I am quite prepared to reciprocate that 'we are all monetarists'—if by monetarism is meant assigning to the stock of money a major role in determining output and prices'."

In contrast, equilibrium RBC models typically assume that there is a complete set of contingent claims markets and that prices are perfectly flexible. One implication of these assumptions in the models that have been examined to date is that real allocations are Pareto optimal. This in turn implies that there is no role for a central policy authority. Thus, equilibrium RBC theories assume both that exogenous monetary shocks have not been an important source of fluctuations, and that the policy rules followed by the monetary authorities have not had an important role in propagating nonmonetary shocks. Only under this joint hypothesis does it seem likely that an equilibrium RBC model would accurately characterize the economy.

This article presents and interprets some new evidence on the validity of the RBC approach to business cycle analysis. Particular attention is given to: (1) the question of whether monetary policy shocks were an important determinant of real economic activity during the postwar period, and (2) several potentially important pitfalls in interpreting the available evidence as supporting or refuting the validity of RBC models. The analysis of the first question bears on the validity of any business cycle model that assumes such shocks have been important. Certain aspects of our findings can be viewed as being consistent with both early Keynesian and equilibrium RBC models. However, the extreme assumptions that underlie the former models have been largely rejected in the recent literature (see, e.g., Modigliani 1977).[1] Accordingly, in discussing potential interpretations of our empirical findings we shall focus primarily on the properties of what we call equilibrium business cycle models—monetary and nonmonetary models that are specified at the level of preferences and technology. This allows us to address directly the strengths and weaknesses of equilibrium RBC models as explanations of fluctuations in the U.S. economy during the postwar period.

To date, empirical investigations of RBC models have typically proceeded by fitting these models to the data and evaluating the extent to which the cycles implied by the models match those exhibited by the data. Virtually without exception, studies of RBC models have not considered explicitly the conditions under which RBC models emerge approximately or exactly as special cases of monetary models of the business cycle. In contrast, we begin our analysis in section 3 by setting forth an explicit monetary business cycle model. The presentation of this model serves three purposes. First, we are able to make precise one potential link between monetary policy actions and real allocations in an equilibrium model. Money matters in this model because agents face a cash-in-advance constraint. Therefore the money-output linkages in our model are very much in the spirit of those in the recent models of Lucas and Stokey (1983, 1984), Townsend (1982), and Svensson (1985) among others. Within the context of this model, we provide sufficient conditions for an RBC model to provide an accurate characterization of real fluctuation in the monetary economy. The conditions discussed are, of course, specific to the model examined. Nevertheless, we feel they are

1. After we completed this paper, Bennett McCallum pointed out that an important implication of early Keynesian business cycle models with sticky prices and a horizontal *LM* function is that money should not Granger cause nominal income. This implication is, of course, counterfactual. The equilibrium real business cycle models that we examine do not have this implication.

suggestive of the type of strong restrictions on monetary policy rules that will be required for RBC models to accurately approximate other, more complicated, monetary models.

Second, we use this model to interpret Granger causal relations between nominal and real aggregates. Anticipating our results in sections 4 and 5, we find little empirical support for the proposition that money growth or inflation Granger cause output growth. Interpreted within the context of the monetary model of section 3, these results suggest that exogenous shocks to the monetary growth rate were not an important independent source of variation in output growth during the postwar period in the United States. Admittedly, this conclusion emerges from considering a model with very simple specifications of the production and monetary exchange technologies, as well as a specific market structure. However, introducing more complicated market structures that lead to sticky prices and wages as in Fischer (1977) or overlapping nominal contracts as in Taylor (1980) would only increase the complexity of the interaction between monetary growth and real economic activity. This added complexity would make it more difficult to reconcile the absence of Granger causality of output growth by monetary growth with the belief that exogenous monetary policy shocks were an important source of variation in output. More generally, our empirical evidence suggests that monetary models which imply that money growth rates Granger cause output growth are inconsistent with postwar U.S. data.

Third, for certain monetary policy rules, our monetary model implies that the failure to find Granger causality from money to output is not sufficient for an RBC model to accurately characterize the economic environment. More precisely, we argue that even if real shocks are the predominant source of variation in real quantities over the cycle, one may be seriously misled using an RBC model to evaluate the implications of alternative government policies. Essentially, monetary feedback policies can be set in a manner that affects the time-series properties of output even though exogenous monetary shocks are not important determinants of output. This may be true even though RBC models appear to fit the data for the sample period by the usual criteria.

The remainder of the article is organized as follows. Section 2 presents a brief review of the literature on equilibrium RBC models, and our equilibrium monetary business cycle model is presented in section 3. In section 4, the laws of motion for the quantity variables implied by an RBC model are compared to those of the monetary model. These two models are used to interpret bivariate vector autoregressive representations (VARs) of money and output. A more extensive set of empirical results is presented in section 5. "Variance decompositions" for output are displayed for several multivariate time-series models of output, monetary growth, inflation, and asset returns. Concluding remarks are presented in section 6.

2. *Overview of Equilibrium Business Cycle Models*

A primary goal of business cycle analysis is to explain the recurrent fluctuations of real aggregate economic quantities about their trends and the co-movements among different aggregate economic time series. A key assumption of real business cycle theories is that monetary policy actions are unimportant for explaining either the amplitude or frequency of business cycles. In the words of King and Plosser (1984), RBC theories view "business cycles as arising from variations in the real opportunities of the private economy, which include shifts in government purchases or tax rates as well as technical and environmental conditions." (p. 363). In this section we briefly summarize some of the sources of variations in private market economies that have received the most attention in the literature on RBC models.

In modeling aggregate fluctuations, RBC theorists often distinguish between the exogenous sources of uncertainty impinging on economic decisions and the endogenous propagation mechanisms for the exogenous shocks. Adopting this taxonomy, we shall consider, first, the various exogenous sources of uncertainty that have typically been emphasized in the recent literature. In modern economies, many types of shocks impinge on the decisions of agents in different sectors. For the purpose of aggregate business cycle analyses, it is typically assumed implicitly or explicitly that idiosyncratic sector or agent-specific shocks "average out" and have no effect on aggregate quantities. On the other hand, the common components of individual shocks that remain after aggregation are interpreted as the aggregate sources of uncertainty in business cycle models. The number of these aggregate disturbances is typically assumed to be small; often the number does not exceed the number of real quantity variables appearing in the model.

Furthermore, when using RBC models to describe economic data, attention has been restricted almost exclusively to exogenous shifts in the production technologies of goods. See, for example, Kydland and Prescott (1982), Long and Plosser (1983), King and Plosser (1984), Altug (1985), and Hansen (1985). Notably absent from these models are aggregate shocks to preferences and to the fiscal policy rules of governments. The omission of shocks to preferences seems to be simply a matter of taste. Apparently, an implicit assumption in many of the RBC theories is that large technology shocks are more likely than large aggregate stochastic shifts in tastes. We relax this assumption in constructing our illustrative monetary and real business cycle models in sections 3 and 4.

The absence of shocks to government purchases or tax rates can be explained by the nature of the models that have been developed to date. Kydland and Prescott (1982), and many others since, have examined economies in which there is a complete set of markets for contingent claims to future goods, there is no private information, and there are no public goods. Therefore, real allocations are Pareto optimal in these economies and there is no welfare-improving role for a central government. The absence of incomplete insurance and market failures from these models can in part be attributed to the difficulties involved in analyzing aggregate fluctuations in general equilibrium when such "frictions" are present. However, in some cases, their absence also seems to be a manifestation of the belief that aggregate fluctuation in output that approximates that observed historically can be generated by equilibrium models without introducing these frictions. Long and Plosser (1983), for example, state, regarding their model, "We believe that major features of observed business cycles typically will be found in the kind of model economy outlined above." (p. 42) A similar view has recently been expressed by Prescott (1986): "Given the people's ability and willingness to inter- and intra-temporally substitute consumption and leisure and given the nature of the changing production set, there would be a puzzle if the American economy did not display the business cycle phenomena. By display the business cycle phenomena, I mean that the amplitudes of fluctuations of the key economic aggregates and their serial correlation properties are close to that predicted by theory." (p. 1)

Although RBC models have relied on unobserved technology shocks to induce fluctuations in output, investment, consumption, and hours worked, these models typically adopt quite parsimonious time-series representations of these shocks. Parsimony is important if these models are to have refutable implications. It has long been known that low-order stochastic difference equations can generate recurring irregular cyclical fluctuations not unlike those exhibited by aggregate time series. Thus, the covariogram of a given set of variables implied by a model can be matched to the sample covariagram of the data by specifying sufficiently rich laws of motion for the unobserved shocks in a model. But clearly, profligately parameterized specifications of unobserved shock processes do not yield interesting explanations of business cycles. RBC models lead to overidentifying restrictions on the autocovariance functions by allowing for only a small number of shocks with parsimonious time-series representations. More complicated patterns of autocorrelations and patterns of cross-correlations among the variables are then induced by endogenous sources of dynamics. It is these endogenous sources of dynamics (what King and Plosser (1985) refer to as the propagation mechanisms) that are the centerpieces of equilibrium RBC theories.

To date, RBC theorists have stressed the role of technology and agents' preferences in magnifying the response of economic systems to exogenous impulses. For example, Kydland and Prescott (1982) assume that it takes time to build capital goods (i.e., more than one period or decision interval). This time-to-build technology has an important effect on the time-series properties of investment and output. They also assume that consumers' utility from leisure in the current period depends on past leisure decisions. Specifically, the marginal utility of an additional unit of leisure today is larger (smaller) the smaller (larger) is the amount of leisure consumed in previous periods. This specification of preferences leads to substantially more intertemporal substitution of leisure than the comparable time-separable specification of preferences. Since hours worked are more sensitive to a given change in the real wage rate with this specification of preferences, they are better able to capture the fluctuation in aggregate hours than the corresponding model with time-separable utility. Nevertheless, their model falls short of providing an adequate explanation of the time-series behavior of hours worked. Efforts are currently under way to enrich the specification of the labor market in their model in an attempt to improve the fit of the model (Hansen 1985).

Although the models examined by Kydland and Prescott (1982) and Kydland (1984) fail to fully explain fluctuation in hours worked, it is nevertheless striking that they do so well in attempting to replicate the time-series behavior of several of the economic aggregates considered. As the authors emphasize, their results are certainly encouraging, for they show that fairly simple dynamic equilibrium models are capable of generating the types of cycles that are similar to those that have been observed historically. Moreover, these examples provide a useful reminder of the fact that fluctuation in real quantities per se need not reduce social welfare; real allocations are Pareto optimal in their model.

Those economists who believe firmly that monetary fluctuations and the actions of the monetary authority are central to an understanding of business cycles may be inclined to dismiss these models outright because of their omission of monetary considerations. Yet there seems to be both indirect and direct evidence that such a dismissal is difficult to support. Indirect evidence is provided by Kydland and Prescott (1982), Long and Plosser (1983), and Kydland (1984), among others. These authors have shown that, for plausible values of the parameters characterizing preferences and technology, the variances of the shocks to technology can be chosen such that equilibrium RBC models imply empirical second moments for certain real aggregates that approximately match the corresponding sample second moments.

More formal evidence is provided in the provocative studies by Sims (1980a, 1980b). He found that monetary shocks had little explanatory power for industrial production during the post–World War II period when lagged values of industrial production and nominal interest rates were included. Sims interpreted the contribution of nominal interest rates in predicting industrial production as capturing expectations about the future productivity of capital, which is very much in the spirit of real business cycle analysis. Litterman and Weiss (1985) corroborate Sims's findings and also give an RBC interpretation to their findings.

The models considered by Kydland and Prescott (1982) and Long and Plosser (1983) are representative agent models with complete markets so that credit does not enter prominently in the determination of real quantities. King and Plosser (1984) have discussed an extended version of an equilibrium RBC model in which there is a role for organized credit markets. Their model can be interpreted as a RBC model in which certain (perhaps informational) frictions in private markets lead to the creation of institutions that specialize in issuing credit. King and Plosser proceed to argue that, while credit may have an important influence on the nature of aggregate fluctuations, the actions of the Federal Reserve's Open Market Committee may not be an important independent source of fluctuations in real quantities and relative prices. As evidence for this proposition, they note that real output seems to be significantly correlated with inside money but is only weakly correlated with outside money.

More recently, critics of the view that RBC theories are accurate characterizations of the postwar experience have noted that these findings are also consistent with comparably simple business cycle models in which monetary policy plays an important role. For instance, McCallum (1983a) has shown that if the Federal Reserve followed an interest rate rule (or mixed interest rate–monetary aggregate rule) for most of the postwar period, then the interest rate innovation in Sims's regressions may be a proxy for the innovation in the policy rule of the Fed. For the same reasons, the analysis by King and Plosser (1984) may not accurately capture the effects of monetary policy shocks on real output (McCallum 1985).

Critics of RBC models have provided several additional challenges to the conclusion that the RBC models studied to date explain the postwar experience in the United States Most of the studies purporting to provide evidence in support of RBC models have examined only a limited set of own- and cross-correlations of aggregate quantity variables. In particular, cross-correlations of relative prices and asset returns with aggregate real quantities have typically not been studied. There is no a priori reason why the restrictions examined should be given more weight than other restrictions on cross-correlations in evaluating the performance of these models. When cross-correlations of asset returns and output are examined there is substantially more evidence against RBC models (see, for example, Mehra and Prescott (1985)). Moreover, when particular RBC models are subjected to formal methods of estimation and inference which incorporate a fairly comprehensive set of moment restrictions, the results are not supportive of the models (e.g., Altug (1985), Eichenbaum, Hansen, and Singleton (1985), and Mankiw, Rotemberg, and Summers (1985)).

The acceptance or rejection of previous RBC models must be based in part on an assessment of the plausibility of the variances and autocorrelations of the technology shocks.[2] Kydland and Prescott (1982) take their structure of preferences and technology as given and then determine the values of the variances of the shocks to technology that are consistent with particular second moments of observed variables. Prescott (1986) provides an estimate of the standard deviation of the shock to technology in a simple growth model, but this measure is in effect the standard error of the residual from regressing the growth rate of output on the growth rates of capital and labor. This measure is justified by his assumption of a Cobb-Douglas production function defined over labor and capital and thus is clearly model dependent in the same manner that the Kydland-Prescott estimates of standard deviations were model dependent. In a manner that attempts to account for measurement errors, Prescott estimates the ratio of the standard deviations of the percentage changes in the technology shock and output to be approximately .40. It seems difficult to assess the plausibility of this estimate and related estimates provided by Kydland and Prescott (1982), especially in light of the highly aggregated nature of their models.

Furthermore, we have little independent evidence about the absolute magnitudes of these second moments, since the theories do not lead us to specific sources for these disturbances. Hamilton (1983) provides some descriptive evidence that oil price shocks were an important source of aggregate fluctuations in the United States during the postwar period. Also, Miron (1985) argues that weather shocks are an important source

2. See McCalllum (1985) for a related criticism of the Kydland-Prescott analysis.

of variation in aggregate consumption. This strategy of attempting to quantify the various shocks impinging on the economy may yield important insights into the nature of real shocks underlying business cycles.

A complementary strategy is to assess empirically the relative importance of alternative types of shocks in the context of models that accommodate various types of shocks. RBC theorists have not attempted to assess the relative importance of monetary versus technology shocks, for example. A comparison of the stochastic properties of these shocks may lead to more convincing conclusions about RBC models than statements about the absolute magnitudes of technology or preference shocks. In models that accommodate monetary shocks, it would be possible to decompose the variation in output into variation attributable to monetary and real shocks (assuming the model is identified). Then the theoretical problem of characterizing the classes of economies and monetary policies for which real allocations are well described by RBC models could be addressed. To our knowledge, King and Plosser (1984) have come closest to attempting such an exercise. However, they stop short of constructing a monetary model and evaluating the relative importance of alternative shocks. Constructing a model at a plausible level of generality and performing these calculations is admittedly a formidable task. Recent work is just beginning to provide the necessary tools needed to solve for the stochastic equilibria of monetary models (e.g., Lucas and Stokey 1984). Nevertheless, simple illustrative monetary models can be constructed, and it is this task to which we turn next.

3. *An Equilibrium Business Cycle Model*

Here we present an equilibrium business cycle model and discuss some of its properties. The model is that of a monetary economy in which anticipated monetary growth has real economic effects. Money is introduced into the model using the construct of a cash-in-advance constraint and this constraint is the only source of monetary nonneutrality in this model. In particular, we abstract from frictions that might lead to sticky prices or wages, and agents are assumed to have rational expectations. The exclusion of these and other sources of frictions from the economic environment should not be interpreted as necessarily reflecting a view that other frictions are absent from modern economies. Rather, we are intentionally constructing an economic model that is simple to analyze and which allows us to discuss several pitfalls in interpreting the time-series evidence that purportedly supports or refutes RBC models. Many of our observations are valid for a much larger class of real and monetary models than those examined explicitly.

The monetary business cycle model that we consider is an extended version of the RBC model discussed by Garber and King (1983) (which is closely related to the model in Long and Plosser (1983)). Suppose that a representative, competitive firm produces a nondurable consumption good y_t using the input x_t. The production function for y_t is given by

$$y_t = x_t^{\alpha}\lambda_t, 0 < \alpha < 1, \quad (3.1)$$

where λ_t is a shock to the consumption good technology at date t. The intermediate good x_t depreciates at the rate of 100 percent when used in production. The firm buys x_t from consumers in a competitive market at the unit real price of w_t. Acquisitions of the input are made so as to maximize the expected discounted value of future profits. For our model, this optimum problem simplifies to the following static optimum problem: at each date t the firm chooses x_t to maximize

$$x_t^{\alpha}\lambda_t - w_t x_t. \quad (3.2)$$

Profits of the firm are returned each period to the shareholders in the form of dividends, d_t.

The intermediate good, x_t, is storable. The representative consumer has an initial endowment of the intermediate good of k_0. The law of motion for the consumer's holdings of the intermediate good at the beginning of period t is given by

$$k_t = \theta_t [k_{t-1} - x_{t-1}]. \quad (3.3)$$

In equation (3.3), θ_t represents a stochastic shock to the storage technology.

In addition to holdings of the intermediate good, the wealth of the representative consumer includes holdings of claims to the future cash flows of the firm and money holdings. We shall let z_t denote the number of shares in the firm held by the consumer and q_t^s (Q_t^s) denote the ex-dividend real (money) price per share in the firm.

There are a variety of ways in which to generate valued fiat money in theoretical models (see, e.g., the volume edited by Kareken and Wallace (1980)). Following Lucas (1980, 1984), Townsend (1982), Lucas and Stokey (1984), and Svensson (1985), we adopt the construct of a cash-in-advance constraint. While this construct is known to have some undesirable characteristics, it is analytically convenient and can be interpreted as arising from a very special shopping time technology (e.g., McCallum 1983b). The timing conventions for monetary transactions in this economy are assumed to be as follows. The consumer enters the period t with a predetermined cash balance M_t, and a predetermined share, z_t, of claims to the dividends of the representative firm. He learns the realization of all time t random variables and then chooses the quantity of intermediate goods (x_t) to sell to the firm and the amount of consumption goods (c_t) to purchase at the dollar price P_t. Payment for the sale of x_t to the firm is received in cash after the consumption decision. Therefore, the money received (if any) cannot be used to relax the cash-in-advance constraint in period t. It follows that goods purchases must obey the cash-in-advance constraint

$$P_t c_t \leqslant M_t. \quad (3.4)$$

After the goods market is closed, the consumer receives in cash his share of dividends, $D_t z_t$, where D_t is the money value of dividends at date t. In addition, the consumer receives a lump sum monetary transfer from the policy authority in the amount J_t. Finally, at the end of period t, money and equity shares in the firm are traded. Thus, the evolution of the nominal money holdings by the consumer are described by the equation

$$M_{t+1} + Q_t^s z_{t+1} \leqslant [M_t - P_t c_t] + [Q_t^s + D_t]z_t + W_t x_t + J_t, \quad (3.5)$$

where W_t is the per unit cash payment from the firm to the consumer for supplying the intermediate good. Dividing both sides of equations (3.4) and (3.5) by P_t yields the real relations

$$M_{t+1}/P_t + q_t^s z_{t+1} \leqslant [m_t - c_t] + [q_t^s + d_t]z_t + w_t x_t + \tau_t, \quad (3.6)$$

$$c_t \leqslant m_t, \quad (3.7)$$

where lowercase letters denote real quantities and $\tau_t = J_t/P_t$. We shall henceforth assume that the constraint (3.7) is always binding. The consistency of this assumption with the specification of other aspects of the model will be discussed after we derive the equilibrium law of motion for x_t.

The consumer is assumed to choose contingency plans for c_t, x_t, M_{t+1} and z_{t+1} so as to maximize the logarithmic intertemporal objective function

$$E_0 \sum_{t=0}^{\infty} \beta^t v_t \ell n c_t, \quad (3.8)$$

subject to the constraints (3.3) and

$$M_{t+1}/P_t + q_t^s z_{t+1} = [q_t^s + d_t]z_t + w_t x_t + \tau_t. \quad (3.9)$$

In (3.8), E_t denotes the expectation conditioned on agents' information set at date t and the disturbance ν_t is a taste shock, which is assumed to follow the process

$$\nu_t = \nu_{t-1}^a \, \varepsilon_t, \ |a| \leqslant 1, \quad (3.10)$$

where $\ell n \varepsilon_t$ is normally distributed with mean zero, variance σ_ε^2, and is not serially correlated.

The first-order conditions for this optimum problem are

$$E_t \left\{ \frac{\beta \, \nu_{t+1}}{M_{t+1}} \right\} - \xi_t/P_t = 0, \quad (3.11)$$

$$-w_t\xi_t + \beta \, E_t\{w_{t+1} \, \theta_{t+1} \, \xi_{t+1}\} = 0, \quad (3.12)$$

$$-q_t^s\xi_t + \beta \, E_t\{\xi_{t+1} \, (q_{t+1}^s + d_{t+1})\} = 0, \quad (3.13)$$

where ξ_t is the Lagrange multiplier associated with the constraint (3.9). Substituting equation (3.11) into equation (3.12) gives

$$E_t\{W_t \, \nu_{t+1}/M_{t+1}\} = E_t\{\beta \, W_{t+1} \, \nu_{t+2} \, \theta_{t+1}/M_{t+2}\}. \quad (3.14)$$

Using (3.4), an equivalent way of writing (3.14) is

$$E_t \left[\frac{W_t \, \nu_{t+1}}{P_{t+1} \, c_{t+1}} \right] = E_t \left[\frac{\beta \, W_{t+1} \, \theta_{t+1} \, \nu_{t+2}}{P_{t+2} \, c_{t+2}} \right], \quad (3.14')$$

which has the following interpretation. By selling a unit of the intermediate good to the firm at date t the consumer receives W_t dollars, which can be used to acquire the consumption good at date $t + 1$. Therefore, the benefits from providing x_t are evaluated using the marginal utility of consumption at date $t + 1$ (ν_{t+1}/c_{t+1}). On the other hand, postponement of the sale of x for one period yields the physical rate of return of θ_{t+1} from storage. At date $t + 1$ the consumer can then sell x for θ_{t+1} W_{t+1} dollars, and these dollars can be used to purchase consumption goods at date $t + 2$. Equation (3.14') states that in equilibrium the consumer is indifferent between these two strategies. Notice that the timing convention of our model implies that, in supplying the intermediate good to the firm at date t for a per unit nominal price W_t, consumers are effectively contracting for an uncertain per unit real price of W_t/P_{t+1} at date $t + 1$.

Equation (3.14) can be used to determine the equilibrium law of motion for x_t, once a money supply rule has been specified. We assume that M_t follows the process

$$M_{t+1} = M_t f(s_t), \quad (3.15)$$

where s_t is a vector of state variables that are known at date t. (Recall that M_{t+1} is known at the end of date t and M_t is determined at date $t - 1$.) Substituting equation (3.15) into equation (3.14) and using the cash-in-advance constraint leads to

$$E_t \left\{ \frac{w_t \nu_{t+1}}{f(s_t) c_t} \right\} = E_t \left\{ \frac{\beta w_{t+1} \theta_{t+1} \nu_{t+2}}{f(s_{t+1}) c_{t+1}} \right\}. \quad (3.16)$$

In equilibrium, $z_t = 1$ (all equity claims are held) and $c_t = y_t$ (consumption equals output). Also, the first-order conditions to the firm's optimum problem imply that the real price of the intermediate good equals the marginal product of the good in production:

$$w_t = \alpha x_t^{\alpha - 1} \lambda_t. \quad (3.17)$$

Imposing these equilibrium conditions and using equation (3.16) gives

$$E_t \left\{ \frac{\nu_{t+1}}{x_t f(s_t)} \right\} = E_t \left\{ \frac{\beta \theta_{t+1} \nu_{t+2}}{x_{t+1} f(s_{t+1})} \right\}. \quad (3.18)$$

Given that $f(s_t)$ is in agents' information set at date t, it is straightforward to verify that

$$x_t = \beta \exp[\tfrac{1}{2}\sigma_\varepsilon^2]\, x_{t-1} \nu_t^{\alpha - 1} \theta_t f(s_{t-1})/f(s_t) \quad (3.19)$$

satisfies equation (3.18).[3] Therefore, equation (3.19) is the equilibrium law of motion for x_t. Taking logarithms of both sides of equation (3.19) gives

$$\ell n x_t = \tfrac{1}{2}\sigma_\varepsilon^2 + \ell n[\beta \nu_t^{\alpha - 1} x_{t-1} \theta_t] + (\ell n f(s_{t-1}) - \ell n f(s_t)). \quad (3.20)$$

3. In solving for x_t we have followed the common practice of not imposing non-negativity constraints on the capital stock k_t. Whether or not this constraint is binding in practice will depend on the distribution of the shocks and the particular realizations in the cur-

More general linear time-series representations for $\ell n\nu_t$ could easily be accommodated; they would only complicate the manner in which preference shocks enter equation (3.20).

Before proceeding with our discussion of equation (3.20), it will be instructive to discuss briefly whether the assumption that the cash-in-advance constraint is always binding is consistent with our assumptions about the distributions of the exogenous shocks. In the context of our model, the cash-in-advance constraint is binding if and only if the nominal interest rate on a one-period pure discount bond that pays off one dollar is positive. Thus, to check for consistency we must verify that, having imposed the constraint, the nominal rate implied by the model is in fact positive. The rate of return on a one-period nominal bond in this environment is given by[4]

$$r^b_{t+1} = \nu_t^{1-a} f(s_t) \exp\{\tfrac{1}{2}\sigma^2_\varepsilon\}/\beta - 1.$$

In the absence of preference shocks, a necessary and sufficient condition for r^b_{t+1} to be positive is that the growth rate of money, $f(s_t)$, exceed β. We used the growth rate of M1 as a measure of $f(s_t)$ in our empirical analysis. Interestingly, for the sample period 1949:1 through 1983:6, this measure of $f(s_t)$ exceeds .995 (a plausible value of β for monthly decision intervals) in all but five months. More generally, the assumption that $r^b_{t+1} > 0$ imposes restrictions on the joint distribution of the taste shock, ν_t, and $f(s_t)$.[5]

From equation (3.15) we see that the growth rate in the money supply, $(\ell nM_{t+1} - \ell nM_t)$, is equal to $\ell nf(s_t)$. It follows that changes in the growth rate of the money supply affect the consumer's decision rule for

rent period. One way of obtaining a solution for which the constraint never binds is to assume that in equilibrium x_t is proportional to k_t with the proportionality factor being in the interval (0,1). This is the approach taken by Garber and King (1983) for their real economy. It turns out that the two approaches yield the same law of motion for x_t for the real economy in the absence of taste shocks, but they differ when taste shocks are present. In practice, neither solution may be strictly correct for the chosen distributions of the shocks under a non-negativity constraint. Fortunately, our key points about the properties of real versus monetary business cycle models emphasized subsequently are not sensitive to which solution is studied.

4. This relation is derived by introducing one-period bond holdings into the consumer's budget constraint and deducing the first order conditions for this modified optimum problem without assuming that the cash-in-advance constraint is always binding.

5. Throughout this paper the assumption that $\ell n\varepsilon_t$ is lognormally distributed is made only for convenience; none of our qualitative conclusions depend on this assumption. The expression for r^b_{t+1} implied by our model when the distribution of ε_t is left unspecified is identical to the expression in the text, except that $\exp\{\tfrac{1}{2}\sigma^2_\varepsilon\}$ is replaced by $E_t\{1/(\varepsilon_{t+1})\}$.

supplying the intermediate good. The dependence of x_t on monetary growth, in turn, implies that equilibrium output and dividends are also affected by monetary policy. As is typical of models with cash-in-advance constraints, increases in the growth rate of money decrease output. A similar property often emerges in corresponding models in which money is introduced directly as an argument of the agent's utility function or through a shopping time transactions technology. Lucas (1985) has conjectured that a positive relation between money growth and output growth may obtain with the addition of informational imperfections to models with cash-in-advance constraints. The qualitative nature of the major conclusions drawn subsequently from equation (3.20) and our empirical findings are not sensitive to whether the sign of the effect of money on output is positive or negative. What is crucial is that money affect real activity through more than just the current innovation in money.

Notice that real allocations in our monetary economy are unaffected by permanent and proportional increases in either the level or the growth rate of the money supply. Thus, this monetary model displays the property of superneutrality. The result that a once-and-for-all change in the level of the money stock has no effect on output was derived in a more general setting by Lucas (1984). The stronger result that money is superneutral will typically not obtain in models in which consumers make nontrivial labor supply decisions as well as consumption decisions.

Examination of the logarithms of equations (3.1), (3.17), and (3.19) reveals several interesting characteristics of the model set forth above:

$$\ell n x_t = \ell n \beta + \tfrac{1}{2}\sigma_\varepsilon^2 + \ell n x_{t-1} + (a - 1)\ell n \nu_t + \ell n \theta_t + \ell n f(s_{t-1}) - \ell n f(s_t), \quad (3.21)$$

$$\ell n c_t = \alpha \ell n x_t + \ell n \lambda_t, \quad (3.22)$$

$$\ell n w_t = \ell n \alpha + (\alpha - 1)\ell n x_t + \ell n \lambda_t. \quad (3.23)$$

Notice first of all that output ($\ell n c_t$) is a function of both θ_t (through x_t) and λ_t. This is an illustration of the more general principle that sectoral shocks associated with the production of intermediate goods will have a cumulative effect on final output. Furthermore, if these shocks are positively correlated, then the variance of the sum will exceed the sum of the own variances. That the "aggregate" technological shock impinging on final output represents such a combination of shocks may affect what is perceived to be a plausible value for the variance of the shock to final output.

Equations (3.21)–(3.23) also illustrate the well-known, but often ignored, fact that trends in the endogenous variables may be intimately related. Simply put, this is because all of the endogenous variables are functions of subsets of the same set of taste and technology shocks and trends enter the model primarily through these shocks. It turns out that many of our statistical results using VARs are *not* insensitive to the assumptions about the nature of trends in the variables examined. The sensitivity of estimates from multivariate autoregressive representations to the method of detrending has been noted previously by Kang (1985) and Bernanke (1985). In section 5 we use equations (3.21)–(3.23) to interpret the sensitivities of our results to the specifications of trends.

Having deduced the equilibrium laws of motion for the real quantities in our monetary model, we turn next to an investigation of conditions under which an RBC model provides an accurate approximation to this economy.

4. *Interpreting Bivariate VARs using Monetary and RBC Models*

As background information for comparing the properties of the monetary and RBC models, it is instructive to examine some empirical evidence. Accordingly, we begin with a discussion of the findings from estimating bivariate autoregressive time-series representations of output and money growth. A much more comprehensive set of empirical results is discussed in section 5.

The Granger causality relations between output and money were investigated using monthly data for the U.S. economy over the sample period February 1949 through June 1983. Output was measured by the Industrial Production Index constructed by the Federal Reserve Board. Money was measured by M1 and was obtained from the CITIBASE data tape. Table 4.1 displays the results for the growth rate of output (the difference in the logarithm of industrial production) and the second difference in the logarithm of M1. The second difference of the money stock was used, because this is the empirical counterpart to the construct appearing in the expression for $\Delta \ell n y_t$ in section 3. Both $\Delta \ell n y_t$ and $\Delta^2 \ell n M_{t+1}$ were assumed to be covariance stationary stochastic processes. (The issue of trends is discussed in more detail in section 5.) All VARs included twelve lags of each variable and a constant. In none of the five sample periods considered does $\Delta^2 \ell n M_{t+1}$ Granger cause $\Delta \ell n y_t$ at the one percent level. And only in the sample period 1959:2–1983:6 does $\Delta^2 \ell n M_{t+1}$ Granger cause $\Delta \ell n y_t$ at the five percent level. Though not reported in table 4.1, the corresponding results obtained with $\Delta \ell n M_{t+1}$ in place of $\Delta^2 \ell n M_{t+1}$ were virtually identical.

These results could plausibly be interpreted as evidence in favor of the view that RBC models provide accurate characterizations of the behavior of real quantity variables for this sample period. The remainder of this section explores ways in which this interpretation of the evidence can be reconciled with economic theory and ways in which advocates of various models can be misled by this evidence. In subsection 4.a we study a version of the model from section 3 in which no cash-in-advance constraint is imposed. In addition, we deduce conditions under which real allocations from this RBC model correspond to those in the cash-in-advance economy. Subsection 4.b explores the possibility of RBC models providing an accurate, though not exact, approximation to the monetary economy.

4.a. AN RBC MODEL

Consider the following version of the economy of section 3 in which agents do not face a cash-in-advance constraint. Suppose that agents face the period budget constraint

$$c_t + q_t^s z_{t+1} = (d_t + q_t^s) z_t + w_t x_t. \quad (4.1)$$

Table 4.1 DECOMPOSITION OF VARIANCE OF $\Delta \ln y_t$[a]

	49,2–83,6	*52,1–79,12*	*52,1–83,6*	*59,2–79,12*	*59,2–83,6*
$\Delta \ln y_t$[b]	93	94	92	92	87
	(4)	(4)	(4)	(5)	(6)
$\Delta^2 \ln M_{t+1}$	7	6	8	8	13
	(4)	(4)	(4)	(5)	(6)
	Probability Values: Granger causality of $\Delta \ln y_t$[c]				
$\Delta \ln y_t$	0.00	0.00	0.00	0.00	0.00
$\Delta^2 \ln M_{t+1}$	.158	.189	.185	.230	.029
	Probability Values: Granger causality of $\Delta^2 \ln M_{t+1}$[d]				
$\Delta \ln y_t$	.035	.024	.025	.079	.028
$\Delta^2 \ln M_{t+1}$	0.00	0.00	0.00	0.00	0.00

a. Entries give the percentage of the forecast error in the error variance accounted for by the orthogonalized innovations in the listed variables. The order of orthogonalization is as listed. Standard errors are displayed in parentheses.
b. $\Delta \ln y_t$ denotes the growth rate of industrial output at time t and $\Delta^2 \ln M_{t+1}$ denotes the change in the growth rate of the stock of money at time t.
c. Probability values for the null hypothesis that the lagged coefficients of the given variable in the regression equation for $\Delta \ln y_t$ are zero.
d. Probability values for the null hypothesis that the lagged coefficients of the given variable in the regression equation for $\Delta^2 \ln M_{t+1}$ are zero.

In this economy the consumption good is the numeraire and agents are paid in consumption goods for supplying the intermediate good to the firm. Payments during period t are available for immediate consumption during period t. Also suppose that the representative consumer chooses contingency plans for c_t, x_t, and z_{t+1} so as to maximize the logarithmic intertemporal objective function (3.8) subject to the constraints (3.3) and (4.1). In equilibrium, $z_t = 1$ (share market clears), $y_t = c_t$ (consumption equals output),

$$w_t x_t + d_t = y_t \quad (4.2)$$

(dividends plus factor costs exhaust output), and the supply and demand of the intermediate good are equilibrated, so that equation (3.17) holds. Imposing these equilibrium conditions and using arguments similar to those leading to equation (3.19) yields the following laws of motion for the quantity variables:

$$x_t = \beta \exp[\tfrac{1}{2}\sigma_\varepsilon^2]\, x_{t-1}\, \nu_{t-1}^{a-1}\, \theta_t, \quad (4.3)$$

$$c_t = x_t^\alpha \lambda_t, \quad (4.4)$$

$$d_t = (1 - \alpha)\, x_t^\alpha \lambda_t, \quad (4.5)$$

where the last expression follows from equation (4.2).

The equilibrium laws of motion for x_t in the monetary and nonmonetary economies, given by equations (3.19) and (4.3) respectively, differ by the multiplicative term $[f(s_{t-1})/f(s_t)]$ and the dating of the preference shock ν. The latter difference arises because cash payments received at date t from the sale of the intermediate good to the firm cannot be used to acquire the consumption good until date $t + 1$ in the monetary model.

When will the real allocations be identical in the monetary and nonmonetary models described above? The difference between the dating of the preference shock in the law of motion for x_t will trivially be inconsequential if preference shocks are absent from the model. Most of the RBC models that have been studied to date do exclude preference shocks. Alternatively, if the preference shock follows a logarithmic random walk ($a = 1$), then again this shock will not appear in the law of motion for x_t. Additionally, the monetary term in equation (3.19) must be zero. This will be the case if the monetary authorities follow a constant growth rate rule. Under these circumstances, equations (3.19) and (4.3) give the same equilibrium laws of motion for x_t. This, in turn, implies that the real equilibrium for the real and monetary models are identical, since d_t

and c_t are proportional to x_t in both economies. Given that $a = 1$, a constant monetary growth rate is both necessary and sufficient for the real allocations to be identical in these economies. In addition, it can be shown that formulas for asset prices and relative prices of goods are identical in the monetary and RBC models under these assumptions.

4.b. COMPARING MONETARY AND REAL BUSINESS CYCLE MODELS

Now, in fact, the monetary growth rate has not been constant over the postwar period. In our view, this observation alone is not sufficient to dismiss an RBC explanation of aggregate fluctuations. The extreme case of monetary policy having no impact on real allocations, what we will refer to as the strong RBC hypothesis, is presumably not what most proponents of RBC theories have in mind when arguing that RBC models fit the data. Instead, such claims are more plausibly interpreted as statements about the insensitivity of real allocations to the current structure of financial institutions, and the insignificance of exogenous shocks to the money supply relative to exogenous real shocks. We refer to this latter interpretation as the weak RBC hypothesis. Initially we discuss conditions under which measures of monetary growth are not likely to Granger cause the growth rate of output under the weak RBC hypothesis. Then, circumstances under which measures of monetary growth Granger cause the growth rate of output are discussed.

In our illustrative monetary model, the equilibrium quantities will be approximately unaffected by exogenous money supply shocks if the *change* in the growth rate of money is not too variable relative to preference and technology shocks. Under this condition, the last term in expression (3.21),

$$\begin{aligned} \ell n x_t = {} & \ell n\beta + \tfrac{1}{2}\sigma_\varepsilon^2 + \ell n x_{t-1} \\ & + (a - 1)\ell n\nu_t + \ell n\theta_t - \Delta^2 \ell n M_{t+1}, \quad (4.6) \end{aligned}$$

can be ignored. The corresponding expression from the RBC model set forth in section 4.a is

$$\ell n x_t = \ell n\beta + \tfrac{1}{2}\sigma_\varepsilon^2 + \ell n x_{t-1} + (a - 1)\ell n\nu_{t-1} + \ell n\theta_t. \quad (4.7)$$

Comparing equations (4.6) and (4.7) we see that when technology and taste shocks predominate the two laws of motion are nearly identical, the only difference being the dating of the preference shock. Thus, whether or not $a = 1$, the RBC model will provide a reasonably good approximation to the monetary economy under this assumption about monetary growth. Furthermore, for the sample sizes typically considered in macroeconomic time-series analyses, money may not Granger cause output in this system due to statistical power considerations.

It seems difficult to reconcile the absence of Granger causality from money to output with the opposing view that monetary policy shocks contributed significantly to the variability of output during our sample period. Within the model of section 3, one such reconciliation is achieved by assuming that $\Delta^2 \ell nM_{t+1}$ is serially uncorrelated (monetary growth follows a random walk). Then the last term in equation (4.6) is serially uncorrelated. Consequently, money will not Granger cause output in the bivariate system $[\Delta \ell ny_t, \Delta^2 \ell nM_{t+1}]$.This will be the case even though money shocks affect output and may have a large variance relative to real shocks. The assumption that the change in the monetary growth rate is serially uncorrelated is counterfactual, however (see table 4.1).

More generally, suppose that the monetary growth rate is chosen by the policy authorities to follow the process

$$\begin{aligned}\Delta \ell nM_{t+1} &= \gamma_1\, \ell ny_{t-1} + \gamma_2\, \ell ny_{t-2} + \gamma_3\, \Delta \ell nM_t + \psi_t,\\ &= (1-\gamma_3 L)^{-1}[\gamma_1 \ell ny_{t-1} + \gamma_2 \ell ny_{t-2}] + (1-\gamma_3 L)^{-1}\, \psi_t \qquad (4.8)\end{aligned}$$

where $|\gamma_3| < 1$, ψ_t is a random shock to the policy rule in period t that is independent of the preference and technology shocks, and L is the lag operator. Taking the first difference of the output equation (3.22) and substituting equation (4.8) for $\Delta^2 \ell nM_{t+1}$ and ignoring constant terms gives the following equations:

$$\begin{aligned}\Delta \ell ny_t = \alpha[(a-1)\ell n\nu_t + \ell n\theta_t - (1-\gamma_3 L)^{-1}\{\gamma_1\, \Delta \ell ny_{t-1}\\ + \gamma_2\, \Delta \ell ny_{t-2}\}] + \Delta \ell n\lambda_t - \alpha(1-\gamma_3 L)^{-1}\, \Delta\psi_t, \qquad (4.9)\end{aligned}$$

$$\Delta^2 \ell nM_{t+1} = (1-\gamma_3 L)^{-1}[\gamma_1\, \Delta \ell ny_{t-1} + \gamma_2\, \Delta \ell ny_{t-2} + \Delta\psi_t]. \qquad (4.10)$$

In this example, $\Delta^2 \ell nM_{t+1}$ will not Granger cause $\Delta \ell ny_t$ only under the special assumptions that $\gamma_3 = 0$ in equation (4.8) and the composite shock $[(a-1)\ell n\nu_t + \ell n\theta_t + \Delta \ell n\lambda_t + \Delta\psi_t]$ is serially uncorrelated. The assumption that the projection of $\Delta^2 \ell nM_{t+1}$ onto its own history and the past history of $\Delta \ell ny_t$ is not a function of $\Delta^2 \ell nM_{t-j}$, $j \geq 0$, is counterfactual. Also, we are not aware of any compelling scientific evidence that strongly suggests that either the changes or levels of the taste and technology shocks are white-noise processes.

Of course, if the variance of the monetary policy shocks are small relative to the variances of the real shocks, then money may not Granger cause output even though $\Delta^2 \ell n M_{t+1}$ is highly variable. In particular, suppose that the variance of $(1 - \gamma_3 L)^{-1} \Delta\psi_t$ is small relative to the variances of the terms involving the other shocks, so that the monetary policy shock is not an important independent source of variation of output in this model. Then inspection of equation (3.22), (3.23), and (4.9) reveals that monetary growth may fail to Granger cause output in the multivariate system $[\ell n x_t, \ell n c_t, \ell n w_t, \Delta^2 \ell n M_{t+1}]$. This scenario presumably motivates RBC analyses.

While it is necessarily true that real shocks should be the focal point of business cycle analyses if monetary shocks are relatively unimportant, as the bivariate VARs suggest, it is premature to conclude that RBC models correctly represent the *structure* of the economy. The economic environment leading to the use of fiat money as a medium of exchange may be very different from the economic environment underlying RBC models. That is, modern institutional arrangements are associated with market structures very different from the structures adopted in RBC models and hence monetary models may have very different sources of endogenous dynamics.

To illustrate this point, consider again the output equation (4.9) associated with the money supply rule (4.8). Suppose that the linear combination of the taste and technology shocks in equation (4.9) is serially uncorrelated. The persistence in output is then due entirely to the fact that the monetary policy rule feeds back on lagged output growth; there is nothing technological about this persistence. Yet an RBC theorist might explore non-time-separable specifications of technology and preferences in order to induce autocorrelations similar to those implied by equation (4.9). It seems likely that RBC models could be developed with sufficiently rich specifications of preferences and technology to match the autocorrelations of output quite closely. For, as we have noted, low-order stochastic difference equations are often acceptable representations of economic aggregates. But inferences about the structure of the economy using an RBC model could be very misleading. It follows that policy analysis using the RBC formulation of the economy could lead to misguided policy prescriptions.

As a second example of this phenomenon, suppose that $\Delta^2 \ell n M_{t+1}$ is set so as to substantially attenuate (or completely offset) the impact of certain shocks on $\Delta \ell n y_t$. Then the time-series properties of $\Delta \ell n y_t$ will be determined by the remaining shocks in equation (4.6) and money growth may not Granger cause output growth. Nevertheless, the properties of $\Delta \ell n y_t$ are clearly affected by the particular feedback rule adopted by the monetary authorities. We suspect that a version of this scenario could be developed in which lagged values of $\Delta^2 \ell n M_{t+1}$ also were useful in predicting $\Delta^2 \ell n M_{t+1}$.

Up to this point we have focused on situations in which money growth does not Granger cause output growth. In anticipation of empirical results using linearly detrended data reported in section 5, we briefly explore structural interpretations of a Granger causal relation from money to output. The most straightforward interpretation of such a statistical relation is that in fact monetary policy actions are important determinants of aggregate real activity. On the other hand, a statistical relation between money and output may reflect the fact that money is proxying for unobserved shocks to tastes and technologies. That is, if there are more aggregate shocks to preferences and technology than real variables included in the VAR, then in general $\Delta^2 \ell n M_{t+1}$ will Granger cause the real variables. This is the interpretation of money-output correlations adopted by Litterman and Weiss (1985).

To illustrate a signaling role for money, consider a trivariate VAR of $\Delta \ell n y_t$, $\Delta \ell n x_t$, and $\Delta^2 \ell n M_{t+1}$. In our model, when $a \neq 1$ there are three real shocks, so if monetary growth follows a feedback rule like equation (4.8), then $\Delta^2 \ell n M_{t+1}$ will convey information about $[\Delta \ell n y_t, \Delta \ell n x_t]$ that is not embodied in the past histories of the quantity variables. Thus, money will Granger cause output in this setting even if monetary policy shocks are absent from the model. On the other hand, when $a = 1$, there are only two real shocks so that the vector of quantities will not be Granger caused by monetary growth if the variance of the monetary shock is small.

We now examine the question of what proportion of the variance of output is accounted for by innovations in nominal aggregates. Attempts to answer this question raise additional questions regarding the interpretation of VARs. We begin by describing a procedure proposed by Sims (1980b) for calculating variance decompositions and then review an important objection to the procedure which has been raised by Blanchard and Watson (1984) and Bernanke (1985), among others. These issues are intimately connected with the set of circumstances under which Granger-causality tests can be used to shed light on structural, rather than statistical, issues.

Let $\mathbf{S}'_t = [\mathbf{S}'_{1t}, \mathbf{S}'_{2t}]$, where $\mathbf{S}_{1t}$ is a $j \times 1$ vector of real variables and $\mathbf{S}_{2t}$ is a $(k - j) \times 1$ vector of nominal variables. We suppose that $\mathbf{S}_t$ has the vector autoregressive representation,

$$\mathbf{G}(L)\mathbf{S}_t = \varepsilon_t, \quad (4.11)$$

where $\mathbf{G}(L)$ is a $k \times k$ matrix polynomial in the lag operator L, $I + G_1L + G_2L^2 + \ldots$ which satisfies the invertibility conditions, and ε_t is a $k \times 1$ vector of serially uncorrelated disturbances which may be contemporaneously correlated. In general the elements of the vector ε_t will be nonlinear functions of the innovations to agents' preferences, productivity shocks and nominal disturbances. Suppose that the analyst estimates the parameters of $\mathbf{G}(L)$ and the contemporaneous covariance of ε_t,

$$E\varepsilon_t\varepsilon_t' = \Sigma_\varepsilon. \quad (4.12)$$

The analyst wishes to partition the variance of the T-step ahead forecast error of a particular element of $\mathbf{S}_t$ into the portions attributable to innovations in the different components of $\mathbf{S}_t$.

Suppose that the forecast error variance of interest is that of the first component of $\mathbf{S}_t$, $\mathbf{S}_{1t}$. Let $\mathbf{L}_1$ be the $1 \times k$ row vector with 1 in the first place and zero elsewhere. Also let $\mathbf{S}_t = \mathbf{M(L)}\varepsilon_t$ denote the moving average representation of $\mathbf{S}_t$ where $\mathbf{M(L)}$ is a $k \times k$ matrix of polynomials in the lag operator which satisfies the invertibility conditions and $\mathbf{M(L)G(L)} = \mathbf{I}$, with $\mathbf{I}$ being the $k \times k$ identity matrix. Then the T-step ahead forecast error of $\mathbf{S}_{1t}$ can be written as

$$\mathbf{S}_{1t+T} - \mathbf{E}_t\mathbf{S}_{1t+T} = L_1\{\varepsilon_{t+T} - M_1\varepsilon_{t+T-1} \ldots -M_{T-1}\varepsilon_{t+1}\}. \quad (4.13)$$

The variance of the T-step forecast error of $\mathbf{S}_{1t}$, is equal to

$$E\{[S_{1t+T} - E_tS_{1t+T}]^2\} = \sum_{\tau=0}^{T-1} \sum_{j=1}^{k} \sum_{l=1}^{k} M_\tau(1,j)\, M_\tau(1,l)\sigma_{jl}, \quad (4.14)$$

where $M_\tau(i,j)$ is the ij^{th} element of the matrix $\mathbf{M}_\tau$.

If Σ_ε is diagonal, then the percentage of the variance in the T-step forecast error of $\mathbf{S}_{1t}$ due to innovations in the ℓth variable, $S_{\ell t}$, is

$$\frac{100 \sum_{\tau=0}^{T-1} M_\tau^2(1,\ell)\sigma_\ell^2}{\sum_{\tau=0}^{T-1} \sum_{j=1}^{k} M_\tau^2(1,j)\sigma_j^2} \quad (4.15)$$

As T approaches infinity the variance of the T-step ahead forecast error of $\mathbf{S}_{1t}$ converges to the unconditional variance of $\mathbf{S}_{1t}$. Accordingly, the percentage of the unconditional variance of $\mathbf{S}_{1t}$ which is attributable to innovations in $S_{\ell t}$ is well approximated by calculating (4.15) for large values of T.

In general, the matrix Σ_ε is not diagonal, so that some set of normalizations or identifying restrictions must be imposed on the system before a decomposition of $\mathbf{S}_{1t}$ can be calculated. More precisely, we define a new set of error terms ζ_t,

$$\zeta_t = F^{-1} \varepsilon_t, \quad (4.16)$$

with F chosen such that

$$E\varepsilon_t\varepsilon_t' = \Sigma_\varepsilon = FE\zeta_t\zeta_t'F' = F\Sigma_\zeta F', \quad (4.17)$$

and Σ_ζ is a $k \times k$ diagonal positive definite matrix. Then equation (4.11) and

$$\mathbf{G}(L)\mathbf{S}_t = F\zeta_t, \quad (4.18)$$

are observationally equivalent representations of $\mathbf{S}_t$. In general there are an infinite number of matrices $\mathbf{F}$ that satisfy equation (4.17), so normalizations must be imposed before calculating variance decompositions.

The method suggested by Sims (1980b) for decomposing the vector ε_t into orthogonal components (i.e., for choosing a particular matrix $\mathbf{F}$) is to proceed with a particular ordering of the elements of $\mathbf{S}_t$ and restrict attention to the class of matrices $\mathbf{F}$ which are lower block triangular. This amounts to setting the off-diagonal elements of the jth row of $\mathbf{F}^{-1}$ equal to minus the coefficient on ε_{lt} from the projection of the jth element of ε_t on elements 1 through $j - 1$ of ε_t, $(l = 1, \ldots, j - 1)$. In general the matrix $\mathbf{F}$ depends on the ordering of the variables. Once the matrix $\mathbf{F}$ has been chosen we can substitute $\varepsilon_t = \mathbf{F}\zeta_t$ into (4.15) to achieve the desired decomposition. Notice that if Σ_e is diagonal then there is a unique matrix $\mathbf{F} = \mathbf{I}$ which satisfies equations (4.16) and (4.17). As Sims (1980b), Blanchard and Watson (1984), Bernanke (1985), and Cooley and LeRoy (1985) have noted, this procedure for choosing the matrix $\mathbf{F}$ presumes that the structural model for $\mathbf{S}_t$ is recursive when Σ_e is not diagonal.

In the context of the following example, we discuss the pitfalls of Sims's procedure when applied to our problem. Consider again the representation (4.9) for $\Delta\ell ny_t$. Relation (4.9) implies that the innovation to the growth rate of output will be a linear combination of the innovations to agents' preference shocks, sector-specific technology shocks, and the change in the growth rate of money. In order to make our example as simple as possible we concentrate on a bivariate time series representation for $\Delta\ell ny_t$ and $\Delta^2\ell nM_{t+1}$, and simplify the stochastic structure of the model. Suppose that preference shocks follow a random walk ($a = 1$), $\theta_t = 1$, and the law of motion for the technology shock is given by

$$\Delta\ell n\lambda_t = D(L)^{-1}\varepsilon_{\lambda t}, \quad (4.19)$$

where $D(L) \equiv 1 - Ld(L)$ is an invertible polynomial in the lag operator, $d(L) = (d_1 + d_2L + d_3L^2 + \ldots)$, and $\varepsilon_{\lambda t}$ is a serially uncorrelated random variable. It is convenient to modify relation (4.6) by replacing the term $\Delta^2\ell nM_{t+1}$ by $z\Delta^2\ell nM_{t+1}$ where $z\varepsilon\{0,1\}$. When $z = 1$, we obtain the monetary model of section 3. When $z = 0$, we obtain the RBC model discussed in section 4.a that imposes the strong RBC hypothesis. Under these assumptions, (again ignoring constant terms), the law of motion of $\Delta\ell ny_t$ becomes

$$\Delta\ell ny_t = \Delta\ell n\lambda_t - z\alpha\mu_t, \quad (4.20)$$

where $\mu_t \equiv \Delta^2\ell nM_{t+1}$. Substituting equation (4.19) into equation (4.20) and rearranging, gives

$$\Delta\ell ny_t = d(L)\Delta\ell ny_{t-1} - z\alpha\mu_t + z\alpha d(L)\mu_{t-1} + \varepsilon_{\lambda t}. \quad (4.21)$$

Next, suppose that the monetary authority sets the change in the monetary growth rate according to the feedback rule

$$\mu_t = e(L)\Delta\ell ny_{t-1} + f(L)\mu_{t-1} + \varepsilon_{\mu t} + x\varepsilon_{\lambda t}, \quad (4.22)$$

where $e(L)$ and $f(L)$ are scalar invertible polynomials in the lag operator L, x is a scalar constant, and $\varepsilon_{\mu t}$ is a serially uncorrelated random variable. We assume that $\varepsilon_{\lambda t}$ and $\varepsilon_{\mu t}$ are contemporaneously uncorrelated.

Relations (4.21) and (4.22) imply that $\Delta\ell ny_t$ and μ_t have the bivariate VAR representation

$$\begin{bmatrix} \Delta\ell ny_t \\ \mu_t \end{bmatrix} = \begin{bmatrix} 1 & -z\alpha \\ 0 & 1 \end{bmatrix} \begin{bmatrix} d(L) & z\alpha d(L) \\ e(L) & f(L) \end{bmatrix} \begin{bmatrix} \Delta\ell ny_{t-1} \\ \mu_{t-1} \end{bmatrix} + \begin{bmatrix} \varepsilon_{1t} \\ \varepsilon_{2t} \end{bmatrix}, \quad (4.23)$$

where

$$\begin{bmatrix} \varepsilon_{1t} \\ \varepsilon_{2t} \end{bmatrix} = \begin{bmatrix} 1 - z\alpha x & -z\alpha \\ x & 1 \end{bmatrix} \begin{bmatrix} \varepsilon_{\lambda t} \\ \varepsilon_{\mu t} \end{bmatrix}. \quad (4.24)$$

Suppose the analyst estimates the VAR equation (4.23) and has in hand estimates of the three parameters of $\sum_e$. For this economic model $\sum_e$ is a function of four parameters: $z\alpha$, x, σ_ε^2, and σ_λ^2, where the last two parameters are the variances of $\varepsilon_{\mu t}$ and $\varepsilon_{\lambda t}$, respectively. It follows that the parameters of the innovation covariance matrix cannot be identified separately from the parameters of the regression equation. This, in turn, implies that the methods proposed by Blanchard and Watson (1984), Bernanke (1985), and Sims (1985) for analyzing innovation covariance matrices are in general not applicable to dynamic economic models. Put differently, proponents of this approach are implicitly ruling out a large and important class of dynamic economic models as candidates for explaining business cycles.

Pursuing this observation, suppose that the empirical evidence suggests that $\Delta\ell ny_t$ is not Granger caused by μ_t. Within the context of equation (4.23), this implies that $z\alpha = 0$ unless we are in the counterfactual case where $d(L)$ is identically equal to $f(L)$. Setting $z = 0$ leads to the structural model

$$\begin{bmatrix} \Delta\ell ny_t \\ \mu_t \end{bmatrix} = \begin{bmatrix} d(L) & 0 \\ e(L) & f(L) \end{bmatrix} \begin{bmatrix} \Delta\ell ny_{t-1} \\ \mu_{t-1} \end{bmatrix} + \begin{bmatrix} 1 & 0 \\ x & 1 \end{bmatrix} \begin{bmatrix} \varepsilon_{\lambda t} \\ \varepsilon_{\mu t} \end{bmatrix}. \quad (4.25)$$

The model (4.25) has three important features. First, it corresponds to the RBC model of section 4.a. Second, it exhibits a block recursive structure between the real and monetary sectors. Third, implementing Sims's procedures for orthogonalizing the covariance matrix of the innovations in a bivariate VAR by placing $\Delta\ell ny_t$ before μ_t would uncover the true orthogonal shocks of interest. It is worth emphasizing that the justification for the ordering of the variables in this example depends critically on the assumed pattern of Granger-causality results. For the RBC model in section 4.a, imposing the Granger noncausality of output by money identifies the parameters of the matrix $\sum_\varepsilon$. There is no natural way to separate the identification of $\sum_\varepsilon$ from the specification of the structure in this dynamic model.

Recall that the findings in table 4.1 provide little evidence that $\Delta\ell ny_t$ is Granger caused by $\Delta^2\ell nM_{t+1}$. Therefore, consistent with the previous discussion, we implemented Sims's procedure for decomposing the variance of $\Delta\ell ny_t$ by placing $\Delta\ell ny_t$ before $\Delta^2\ell nM_{t+1}$. All of the variance decompositions are for forty-eight-month-ahead forecast errors ($T = 48$). Table 4.1 displays the decompositions and their associated standard errors.[6] Notice that for all the sample periods considered the innovation in $\Delta^2 \ell nM_{t+1}$ accounts for very little of the variance of $\Delta \ell ny_t$. In four of the five sample periods considered the percentage of the variance of $\Delta \ell ny_t$ explained by innovations to $\Delta \ell ny_t$ is within one standard error of 95 percent. Even in the sample period 1959:2–1983:6, where $\Delta^2 \ell nM_{t+1}$ Granger causes $\Delta \ell ny_t$ at the 5 percent level, the percentage of the variance of $\Delta \ell ny_t$ accounted for by innovations in $\Delta \ell ny_t$ is within one standard error of 90 percent. Viewed as a whole, the empirical results emerging from the bivariate time series analysis yield very little evidence against the weak RBC hypothesis.

In section 5 we analyze VARs that include additional variables as a check on the robustness of the qualitative findings from the empirical analysis of the bivariate VARs. In decomposing the variance of the growth rate of output we proceed under the null hypothesis imposed by the strong RBC hypothesis that there is a block recursive structure between real and nominal variables.

5. *Interpreting the Evidence from Vector Autoregressions*

Much of the recent empirical evidence that has been used to support or refute RBC models has come from studying vector autoregressive or moving average representations of the variables comprising the models. See, for example, Sargent (1976), Sims (1980a, 1980b), King and Plosser (1984), Altug (1985), and Bernanke (1985). In this section we examine the empirical evidence from multivariate VARs in light of the discussion in section 4, using monthly data for the postwar U.S. economy.

At the outset of this discussion it is important to explore in detail the role of detrending in the empirical analysis. As noted in section 3, several authors have documented the sensitivity of the results from estimating unconstrained VARs to the assumptions about trends. At the same time, previous studies have virtually ignored the fact that the trends are determined both by the specification of the underlying uncertainty in the economy *and* the structure of the economic model itself. Therefore,

6. Standard errors of all variance decompositions reported in this paper were computed using the Monte Carlo procedure described in the RATS manual, page 17-3. Let **b** denote the estimated VAR coefficient vector and let **V** denote the estimated covariance matrix of the residuals in the VAR. Suppose that the VAR disturbances are i.i.d. and normally distributed. Then the posterior distribution of (**b**,**V**) is Normal-Wishart (see Zellner (1971)). Two hundred draws were taken from this distribution and the variance decomposition of the 48-month-ahead forecast error implied by each draw was calculated. The reported standard error is the square root of the sample variance of the estimated variance decompositions from the two hundred simulations.

how one detrends is in general not independent of one's view about the structure of the economy. This observation represents an additional reason why it is not possible to embark on an empirical analysis of business cycle models using VARs without implicitly or explicitly restricting the class of models being investigated. We briefly illustrate the nature of these restrictions using the models of section 3.

Different specifications of preferences and technologies, as well as the laws of motion for the exogenous shocks, will in general lead one to consider different autoregressive representations of the data. For instance, had we started with quadratic preferences and technologies, a linear representation of the levels of the variables, instead of their logarithms, would have emerged from the model. The question of whether trends are deterministic or stochastic would then have been addressed to the levels of the variables. Rather than working out in detail some of the many possible time-series representations that might emerge from alternative specifications of preferences and technologies, we continue to focus on the log-linear representation that emerges from the model in section 3. Even holding fixed the specifications of technology and preferences, it turns out that many possible trend specifications may arise in our model from alternative specifications of the structure of uncertainty.

To see this, it is convenient to work with a special case of the monetary model given by equations (4.9) and (4.10). Suppose the monetary policy rule is given by

$$\Delta^2 \ell nM_t = \rho \; \ell n x_{t-1} + \psi_t. \quad (5.1)$$

There is no deep economic significance to having monetary growth depend on the intermediate good. This specification allows us to make our points without extensive additional calculations using alternative specifications of the model. Substituting equation (5.1) into equation (3.21) gives (ignoring constants):

$$\ell n x_t = (1 - \rho)\ell n x_{t-1} + (a - 1)\ell n \nu_t + \ell n \theta_t - \psi_t. \quad (5.2)$$

The expressions (3.22) and (3.23) for ℓnc_t and ℓnw_t, respectively, are unchanged. Notice that the coefficient on ℓnx_{t-1} in equation (5.2) is determined both by the specifications of the storage technology for the intermediate good and the monetary feedback rule. If $\rho < 0$, then ℓnx_t will be an explosive process and so will ℓnc_t and ℓnw_t. In this case, neither the removal of a deterministic polynomial trend or first-differencing will render the logarithm of output stationary! Similar examples of potentially explosive processes for output are easily constructed by relaxing the assumption of independent taste and technology shocks. Also, we conjecture that an explosive output process may well emerge in models with increasing returns to scale in production. For instance, some specifications of learning-by-doing might generate such an increasing returns to scale technology.

If, on the other hand, $2 > \rho > 0$, then the trend in $\ell n x_t$ will be determined by the properties of $\ell n \nu_t$, $\ell n \theta_t$, and ψ_t. For instance, if a subset of these variables exhibits linear deterministic trends and the other variables are stationary stochastic processes, then the logarithms of output, consumption, and the price of the intermediate good will also exhibit linear trends. An assumption like this must implicitly underlie the common practice of removing linear trends. This result depends critically on the specification (5.1) of the money supply rule. If $\rho = 0$, then removing linear trends from $[\ell n x_t, \ell n c_t, \ell n w_t]$ will not render these variables stationary (see below). It would be necessary in this model to adopt an entirely different specification of the storage technology to preserve the linear trend assumption.

If $2 > \rho > 0$ and $\ell n \nu_t$, $\ell n \theta_t$, ψ_t, and $\ell n \lambda_t$ are all stationary, then $\ell n y_t$ will also be stationary. At least for the postwar period, the evidence seems not to support this assumption about trends.

Finally, returning to the original specification of the model, if $\rho = 0$, then there is a unit root in the process for $\ell n x_t$. If the technology shock $\ell n \lambda_t$ also has a unit root and $\ell n \nu_t$ and $\ell n \theta_t$ are stationary processes, then $\Delta \ell n x_t$, $\Delta \ell n c_t$, and $\Delta \ell n w_t$ are all stationary stochastic processes. This case is of particular interest since Prescott (1986) has argued that the technology shock in his model approximately follows a random walk. Also, Altug (1985) found that the estimated autoregressive parameter in her time-series representation of the technology shock was essentially unity. Third, Nelson and Plosser (1982) have argued that many real macroeconomic time series must be differenced to induce stationarity. In our work we consider only the possible need to first-difference output. However, the need for higher order differencing could be justified by introducing unit roots into the $\ell n \nu_t$ or $\ell n \theta_t$ processes.

With these observations in mind, we turn next to an empirical analysis of monthly data for the postwar period. Let $\mathbf{S}_t^*$ denote a $k \times 1$ vector of variables observed by the econometrician. In light of our previous discussion regarding trends, we assume that $\mathbf{S}_t^*$ is related to the $k \times 1$ covariance stationary stochastic process, $\mathbf{S}_t$, via one of the following two relations:

$$\mathbf{S}_t^* = \mathbf{S}_t + Ag(t), \quad (5.3a)$$

or

$$A[\mathbf{S}_t^* - \mathbf{S}_{t-1^*}] = \mathbf{S}_t, \quad (5.3b)$$

where $g(t)$ is a scalar valued deterministic function of time and $\mathbf{A}$ is a $k \times k$ matrix of constants, and $\mathbf{S}_t$ has the autoregressive representation (4.11). As before, we partition the vector $\mathbf{S}_t$ as

$$\mathbf{S}'_t = [\mathbf{S}'_{1t}, \mathbf{S}'_{2t}], \quad (5.4)$$

where $\mathbf{S}_{1t}$ is a $j \times 1$ vector of real quantity variables and $\mathbf{S}_{2t}$ is a $(k - j) \times 1$ vector of relative prices and nominal variables.

Initially, we address the question of whether nominal aggregates have predictive power for aggregate real output, once lagged outputs are accounted for. Trivariate VARs, including measures of aggregate real output, the rate of inflation, and the stock of money were examined. That is,

$$\mathbf{S}_t^{*\prime} = [\ell n y_t, \pi_t, \ell n M_{t+1}], \quad (5.5)$$

where π_t denotes the rate of inflation between time $t - 1$ and time t. (Recall that M_{t+1} is chosen at date t.) Similar VARs were studied by Sims (1980a) and Litterman and Weiss (1985). In order to allow comparisons with the latter study, the components of $\mathbf{S}_t^*$ were taken to be monthly versions of the data used by Litterman and Weiss over the sample period 1949:2–1983:6. The variable y_t was measured as industrial production, M_{t+1} was measured as M1, and π_t was measured as the monthly change in the logarithm of the consumer price index less shelter. Seasonally adjusted versions of the money, price, and output series were used.

Recall that Sims and Litterman and Weiss estimated their VARs using levels of variables. Sims does not discuss the trend issue, while Litterman and Weiss note that their findings are largely insensitive to whether or not linear trends are removed. Their approach amounts to running a VAR using data on $\mathbf{S}_t^*$ rather than $\mathbf{S}_t$. Here we investigate the sensitivity of Litterman and Weiss's Granger-causality findings to both changes in the sample period, and the removal of linear deterministic trends or first-differencing the data.

Five sample periods were considered: 1949:2–1983:6; 1952:1–1979:12; 1952:1–1983:6; 1959:2–1979:12; and 1959:2–1983:6. All VARs included twelve lagged values of each variable and a constant. Table 5.1 displays the test results for the null hypotheses that the coefficients on lagged values of π_t and $\ell n M_{t+1}$ (H_π and H_M, respectively) in the $\ell n y_t$ equation are zero in the context of the trivariate VAR for $\mathbf{S}_t^*$ (equation

(5.5)). The null hypothesis H_M is rejected at the 1 percent level for the sample periods 1949:2–1983:6 and 1959:2–1983:6, but not for the other three sample periods. The null hypothesis H_π is rejected at the 1 percent level only for the period 1959:2–1979:12. There is substantially more evidence against the null hypothesis H_M at the 5 percent level; H_M is rejected at this level for all five sample periods.

Table 5.2 reports the corresponding tests for ℓny_t with $\mathbf{S}_t^*$ given by (5.3a). The matrix **A** was chosen to be the 3×3 identity matrix, and the function $g(t)$ was given by

$$g(t) = a + bt. \quad (5.6)$$

Thus the inputs into the VAR were the linearly detrended values of ℓny_t, π_t and ℓnM_{t+1}, denoted by $\ell ny'_t$, π'_t, and $\ell nM'_{t+1}$, respectively. Let $H'_M(H'_\pi)$ denote the null hypothesis that the coefficients on lagged values of $\ell nM'_{t+1}$ (π'_t) in the $\ell ny'_t$ equation are zero. It is interesting that the strongest evidence against H'_M comes from the post-1959 sample periods. For these subperiods, H'_M is rejected at the 1 percent level. The null hypothesis H'_π is not rejected at the 5 percent significance level for any of the subperiods.

The results of table 5.2 are based on a decomposition of the movements in $\mathbf{S}_t^*$ into secular and cyclical components. Secular movements

Table 5.1 DECOMPOSITION OF VARIANCE OF $\ln y_t$[a]

	49,2–83,6	*52,1–79,12*	*52,1–83,6*	*59,2–79,12*	*59,2–83,6*
$\ln y_t$[b]	41	27	28	12	20
	(13)	(11)	(13)	(8)	(11)
π_t	25	64	59	79	67
	(14)	(14)	(16)	(12)	(14)
$\ln M_{t+1}$	34	9	13	9	13
	(12)	(7)	(8)	(8)	(8)
			Probability values for H_x[c]		
$\ln y_t$	0.00	0.00	0.00	0.00	0.00
π_t	.414	.201	.578	.009	.127
$\ln M_{t+1}$	.003	.019	.017	.032	.006

a. Entries give the percentage of the forecast error in the error variance accounted for by the orthogonalized innovations in the listed variables. The order of orthogonalization is as listed. Standard errors are displayed in parentheses.
b. $\ln y_t$ denotes the ln of industrial output at time t, π_t denotes the inflation rate between time $t-1$ and time t, and $\ln M_{t+1}$ denotes the ln of the stock of money at time t.
c. Probability values for the null hypothesis that the coefficients of lagged values of variable x in the regression equation for $\ln y_t$ are zero.

were modeled as deterministic functions of time. A number of authors like Nelson and Plosser (1982) have argued, on statistical grounds, that many macroeconomic time series display stochastic rather than deterministic time trends. Given the weak power of existing statistical tests for detecting the presence of unit roots in time-series processes, it is not clear that these issues can be settled on purely statistical grounds (see for example the discussion of Nelson and Plosser (1982) in McCallum (1985)). However, we are sympathetic to the possibility that a variety of aggregate time series are members of what Nelson and Plosser (1982) call the class of difference stationary stochastic processes. Moreover, several of the models in sections 3 and 4 are consistent with the presence of a unit root in the autoregressive component of the time-series representation for the logarithm of real output. Therefore, we reestimated the trivariate VARs, allowing for the possibility that the data display stochastic trends. However, we made no attempt to decompose the movements in real output (or the other components of $\mathbf{S}_t^*$) into secular and cyclical components, because we did not wish to impose the a priori restriction that nominal disturbances affect only the cyclical component of real output.

Table 5.3 displays the results of testing the null hypotheses that the coefficients on lagged values of $\Delta \ell n M_{t+1}$ and $\Delta \pi_t$ in the $\Delta \ell n y_t$ equation ($H_{\Delta M}$ and $H_{\Delta \pi}$, respectively) are zero. The trivariate VARs were estimated using observations on $\mathbf{S}_t$, with $\mathbf{S}_t$ and $\mathbf{S}_t^*$ related via equation (5.3b). The

Table 5.2 DECOMPOSITION OF VARIANCE OF $\ln y'_t$[a]

	49,2–83,6	*52,1–79,12*	*52,1–83,6*	*59,2–79,12*	*59,2–83,6*
$\ln y'_t$[b]	83	45	62	29	42
	(10)	(12)	(12)	(9)	(11)
π_t'	6	36	22	48	25
	(8)	(13)	(12)	(14)	(13)
$\ln M_{t+1}'$	11	19	17	23	33
	(7)	(10)	(9)	(10)	(10)
	Probability values for the null hypothesis H_x'[c]				
$\ln y_t'$	0.00	0.00	0.00	0.00	0.00
π_t'	.912	.246	.703	.090	.342
$\ln M_{t+1}'$	.171	.010	.117	.004	.001

a. Entries give the percentage of the forecast error in the error variance accounted for by the orthogonalized innovations in the listed variables. The order of orthogonalization is as listed. Standard errors are displayed in parentheses.
b. $\ln y_t'$ denotes the detrended ln level of industrial output at time t, π_t' denotes the detrended rate of inflation between time $t-1$ and time t, and in M_{t+1}' denotes the detrended ln level of the stock of money at time t.
c. Probability values for the null hypothesis that the coefficients of lagged values of variable x′ in the regression equation for $\ln y_t'$ are zero.

matrix **A** was chosen to be the 3 × 3 identity matrix so that $\mathbf{S}_t$ is simply equal to $\Delta\mathbf{S}_t^*$. A striking feature of the results is that neither $H_{\Delta M}$ or $H_{\Delta\pi}$ is rejected at the 5 percent level for any of the postwar sample periods. These results stand in sharp contrast to those reported in tables 5.1 and 5.2.

To summarize this portion of our empirical analysis, the test results were most sensitive to changes in the sample period when the VARs were estimated using data that were not detrended in any way (as in Sims (1980a) and Litterman and Weiss (1985)) and least sensitive when the VARs were estimated using first-differenced data. In addition, the strongest evidence against the null hypothesis that real output is exogenous with respect to measures of inflation and the stock of money was obtained when the VARs were estimated using nondetrended data. There is no evidence against this null hypothesis from VARs estimated using first-differenced data.

Next, we examine the consequences of adding asset returns to the joint time-series representation for output, inflation, and money. Sims (1980a) and Litterman and Weiss (1985) report that the role of money in VARs is very sensitive to the inclusion of rates of return on Treasury bill securities. For this reason, several VARs that included the ex post real value-weighted return on stocks listed on the New York Stock Exchange, r_t^s, and the ex post real rate of return on one-month Treasury bills, r_t^b, were estimated. Real rates of return were studied instead of nominal re-

Table 5.3 DECOMPOSITION OF VARIANCE OF $\Delta\ln y_t$[a]

	49,2–83,6	*52,1–79,12*	*52,1–83,6*	*59,2–79,12*	*59,2–83,6*
$\Delta\ln y_t$[b]	93	92	93	86	85
	(3)	(4)	(4)	(6)	(6)
$\Delta\pi_t$	1	3	1	8	5
	(2)	(3)	(2)	(5)	(3)
$\Delta\ln M_{t+1}$	6	5	6	6	11
	(3)	(3)	(4)	(4)	(5)
			Probability values for $H_{\Delta x}$[c]		
$\Delta\ln y_t$	0.00	0.00	0.00	0.00	0.00
$\Delta\pi_t$	.979	.937	.957	.197	.319
$\Delta\ln M_{t+1}$	.314	.259	.421	.238	.724

a. Entries give the percentage of the forecast error in the error variance accounted for by the orthogonalized innovations in the listed variables. The order of orthogonalization is as listed. Figures in parentheses are corresponding standard errors.

b. $\Delta\ln y_t$ denotes the growth rate of industrial output at time t, $\Delta\pi_t$ denotes the growth rate in inflation rate at time t, and $\Delta\ln M_{t+1}$ denotes the growth rate in the stock of money at time t.

c. Probability values for the null hypothesis that the coefficients on lagged values of variable Δx in the regression equation for $\Delta\ln y_t$ are zero.

turns, because the nominal rate of return on Treasury bills, R_t^b, displays a marked trend in the postwar period. This trend is far less pronounced for the real rate of return, r_t^b.

The reasons for including stock returns in the empirical analysis are threefold. First, we agree with Fischer and Merton (1984) that macroeconomists have unduly neglected the role of the stock market as a determinant of aggregate output. Second, there are good theoretical reasons to believe that stock returns are useful statistical predictors of real output. Changes in stock prices reflect both revised expectations about future corporate earnings and revisions in the discount rate at which these expected earnings are capitalized. Revisions in both of these variables may be induced by the shocks impinging on output. Third, a number of authors, including Doan, Litterman, and Sims (1983), report that stock returns are, in fact, important indicators of movements in real output.

In estimating the VARs with asset returns, attention was restricted to the post-1959 period, because tables 5.1 and 5.2 suggest that this period was the least likely to be consistent with RBC theories. Table 5.4 reports

Table 5.4 DECOMPOSITION OF VARIANCE OF $\Delta \ln y_t$[a]

	59,2–83,6	*59,2–79,12*		*59,2–83,6*	*59,2–79,12*
$\Delta \ln y_t$[b]	81	80	$\Delta \ln y_t$	70	66
	(6)	(7)		(7)	(6)
r_t^b	3	11	r_t^s	24	27
	(3)	(5)		(7)	(6)
$\Delta \pi_t$	12	3	$\Delta \pi_t$	3	4
	(5)	(4)		(2)	(3)
$\Delta \ln M_{t+1}$	4	6	$\Delta \ln M_{t+1}$	3	3
	(3)	(4)		(3)	(3)
		Probability values for $H_{\Delta x}$[c]			
$\Delta \ln y_t$	0.00	0.00	$\Delta \ln y_t$	0.00	.005
r_t^b	.765	.608	r_t^s	.087	.004
$\Delta \pi_t$	.659	.970	$\Delta \pi_t$	.758	.628
$\Delta \ln M_{t+1}$	.108	.127	$\Delta \ln M_{t+1}$	.633	.282

a. Entries give the percentage of the forecast error in the error variance accounted for by the orthogonalized innovations in the listed variables. The order of orthogonalization is as listed. Figures in parentheses are corresponding standard errors.

b. $\Delta \ln y_t$ denotes the growth rate of industrial output at time t, $\Delta \pi_t$ denotes the growth rate in inflation rate at time t, $\Delta \ln M_{t+1}$ denotes the growth rate in the ln of the stock of money at time t, r_t^b denotes the ex post real rate of return on Treasury securities at time t, and r_t^s denotes the real rate of return on stocks at time t.

c. Probability values for the null hypothesis that the coefficients of lagged values of variable Δx in the regression equation for $\Delta \ln y_t$ are zero.

results from four-variate VARs including $\{\Delta \ell ny_t, r_t^b, \Delta\pi_t, \Delta \ell nM_{t+1}\}$ and $\{\Delta \ell ny_t, r_t^s, \Delta\pi_t, \Delta \ell nM_{t+1}\}$. In neither of the two sample periods can we reject at the 5 percent level the null hypotheses H_{r^b}, $H_{\Delta M}$, or $H_{\Delta\pi}$. However, the null hypothesis H_{r^s} can be rejected at the 1 percent level for the period 1959:2–1979:12.

Table 5.5 displays the results from four-variate VARs including $\{\ell ny_t', r_t^b, \pi_t', \ell nM_{t+1}'\}$ and $\{\ell ny_t', r_t^s, \pi_t', \ell nM_{t+1}'\}$. Somewhat surprisingly, only lagged values of $\ell ny_t'$ helped predict future values of $\ell ny_t'$ for the sample periods examined.

Table 5.6 displays results from five-variate VARs including $\{\Delta \ell ny_t, r_t^s, r_t^b, \Delta\pi_t, \Delta \ell nM_{t+1}\}$ and $\{\ell ny_t', r_t^s, r_t^b, \pi_t', \ell nM_{t+1}'\}$. Only lagged values of $\Delta \ell ny_t$ help predict future values of $\Delta \ell ny_t$ at the 1 percent level. Similarly, only lagged values of $\ell ny_t'$ help predict $\ell ny_t'$ at the 1 percent level. However, there is some evidence that ex post real stock returns have predictive power for both $\Delta \ell ny_t$ and $\ell ny_t'$ in the period 1959:2–1979:12. As with the trivariate VARs, there is somewhat more evidence that nominal aggregates help predict real variables when detrended data are used, but overall there is very little evidence of predictive power for nominal vari-

Table 5.5 DECOMPOSITION OF VARIANCE OF $\ln y_t'$[a]

	59,2–83,6	59,2–79,12		59,2–83,6	59,2–79,12
$\ln y_t'$[b]	27	34	$\ln y_t'$	27	23
	(8)	(8)		(10)	(7)
r_t^b	4	27	r_t^s	14	17
	(4)	(11)		(9)	(10)
$\ln\pi_t'$	22	20	$\ln\pi_t'$	7	21
	(11)	(9)		(6)	(9)
$\ln M_{t+1}$	48	19	$\ln M_{t+1}'$	52	39
	(12)	(11)		(14)	(14)
		Probability values for H_x[b,c]			
$\ln y_t'$	0.00	0.00	$\ln y_t'$	0.00	0.00
r_t^b	.111	.646	r_t^s	.148	.061
π_t'	.096	.408	π_t'	.612	.194
$\ln M_{t+1}'$	.074	.060	$\ln M_{t+1}'$	.224	.060

a. Entries give the percentage of the forecast error in the error variance accounted for by the orthogonalized innovations in the listed variables. The order of orthogonalization is as listed. Figures in parentheses are corresponding standard errors.

b. $\ln y_t'$ denotes the detrended ln level of industrial output at time t, π_t' denotes the detrended rate of inflation rate at time t, $\ln M_{t+1}'$ denotes the detrended ln level of the stock of money at time t, r_t^b denotes the ex post real rate of return on Treasury securities at time t, and r_t^s denotes the real rate of return on stocks at time t.

c. Probability values for the null hypothesis that the coefficients of lagged values of variable x' in the regression equation for $\ln y_t'$ are zero.

ables. Finally, table 5.7 reports the results of replacing real rates of return by first differences of nominal rates of return and linearly detrended nominal returns. The qualitative conclusions from these tests are essentially the same as those from using real returns.

The results using differenced data provide little support for the view that monetary policy actions were important determinants of real output over the sample periods considered. The absence of Granger causality from money to output suggests that exogenous policy shocks were not a major source of output variability. Overall, the pattern of results from the VARs are not inconsistent with an RBC interpretation of the postwar aggregate time-series data.

There is perhaps one puzzling feature of these results. Recall from the discussion in section 4.b that monetary growth might be expected to

Table 5.6 DECOMPOSITION OF VARIANCE OF:

	$\Delta \ln y_t$			$\ln y_t'$	
	59,2–83,6	59,2–79,12		59,2–83,6	59,2–79,12
$\Delta \ln y_t^b$	66	64	$\ln y_t'$	18	23
	(7)	(6)		(6)	(6)
r_t^s	24	24	r_t^s	18	26
	(6)	(5)		(9)	(10)
r_t^b	3	6	r_t^b	3	23
	(3)	(5)		(4)	(11)
$\Delta \pi_t$	4	4	π_t'	16	16
	(3)	(3)		(9)	(7)
$\Delta \ln M_{t+1}$	3	3	$\ln M_{t+1}'$	46	12
	(2)	(2)		(11)	(7)
	Probability values for $H_{\Delta x}$			Probability values for H_x'	
$\Delta \ln y_t$	0.00	.006	$\ln y_t'$	.000	.000
r_t^s	.051	.011	r_t^s	.071	.013
r_t^b	.554	.800	r_t^b	.053	.217
$\Delta \pi_t$	.627	.857	π_t'	.049	.067
$\Delta \ln M_{t+1}$	.493	.266	$\ln M_{t+1}'$	.295	.047

a. Entries give the percentage of the forecast error in the error variance accounted for by the orthogonalized innovations in the listed variables. The order of orthogonalization is as listed. Figures in parentheses are standard errors.

b. $\Delta \ln y_t$ denotes the growth rate of industrial output at time t, $\Delta \pi_t$ denotes the growth rate in inflation rate at time t, $\Delta \ln M_{t+1}$ denotes the growth rate in the stock of money at time t, y_t' denotes the detrended ln level of industrial output at time t, $\ln M'_{t+1}$ denotes the detrended ln level of the stock of money, r_t^b denotes the ex post real rate of return in Treasury securities at time t, π_t' denotes the detrended level of inflation, and r_t^s denotes the real rate of return on stocks at time t.

c. Probability values for the null hypothesis that the coefficients of lagged values of variables Δx and x' in the regression equations for $\Delta \ln y_t$ and $\ln y_t'$ respectively are zero.

Granger cause output growth in an RBC model when the number of aggregate real shocks impinging on the economy is large relative to the number of real variables in $\mathbf{S}_{1t}$. Here we have found little evidence that $\Delta \ell n M_{t+1}$ Granger causes $\Delta \ell n y_t$ in several multivariate VARs including bivariate representations. At the same time, stock returns evidently do Granger cause $\Delta \ell n y_t$, which suggests that there were at least two significant aggregate real shocks impinging on the postwar economy. Money is evidently not proxying for unobserved taste or technology shocks in these VARs, even though the number of real shocks exceeds the dimension of $\mathbf{S}_{1t}$. These findings raise interesting questions about the links between money and output in the U.S. economy that warrant further

Table 5.7 DECOMPOSITION OF VARIANCE OF:

	$\Delta \ln y_t$			$\ln y_t'$	
	59,2–83,6	59,2–79,12		59,2–83,6	59,2–79,12
$\Delta \ln y_t^b$	75	72	$\ln y_t'$	18	23
	(6)	(6)		(6)	(6)
ΔR_t^s	10	12	$R_t^{s\prime}$	18	25
	(4)	(4)		(9)	(8)
ΔR_t^b	7	7	$R_t^{b\prime}$	12	16
	(4)	(4)		(9)	(8)
$\Delta \pi_t$	4	4	π_t'	7	24
	(3)	(3)		(6)	(9)
$\Delta \ln M_{t+1}$	3	4	$\ln M_{t+1}'$	46	12
	(3)	(3)		(13)	(8)
	Probability values for $H_{\Delta x}$			Probability values for $H_x'^c$	
$\Delta \ln y_t$	0.00	0.00	$\ln y_t$	0.00	.000
ΔR_t^s	.641	.037	$R_t^{s\prime}$	.080	.013
ΔR_t^b	.416	.348	$R_t^{b\prime}$	.049	.218
$\Delta \pi_t$	.463	.584	π_t'	.213	.200
$\Delta \ln M_{t+1}$	.240	.238	M_{t+1}'	.295	.047

a. Entries give the percentage of the forecast error in the error variance accounted for by the orthogonalized innovations in the listed variables. The order of orthogonalization is as listed. Figures in parentheses are corresponding standard errors.

b. $\Delta \ln y_t$ denotes the growth rate of industrial output at time t, $\Delta \pi_t$ denotes the growth rate in inflation rate at time t, $\Delta \ln M_{t+1}$ denotes the growth rate in the stock of money at time t, $\ln y_t'$ denotes the detrended ln level of industrial output, π'_t denotes the detrended level of inflation, $\ln M'_{t+1}$ denotes the detrended ln level of the stock of money, ΔR_t denotes the first difference of the monthly nominal return on Treasury securities at time t, $R_t^{b\prime}$ denotes the detrended monthly nominal rate of return on Treasury securities at time t, ΔR_t^s denotes the first difference of the nominal rate of return on stocks at time t and $R_t^{s\prime}$ denotes the monthly detrended nominal rate of return on stocks at time t.

c. Probability values for the null hypotheses that the coefficients of lagged values of the variables Δx and x' in the regression equation for $\Delta \ln y_t$ and y_t', respectively, are zero.

investigation and that are not easily addressed within the context of many recent monetary models or the model in section 3.

Proceeding under the null hypothesis that a real business cycle view is correct, the variance decompositions of output were also calculated. Sims's method for orthogonalizing the error terms from the VAR was used, with real variables appearing before the nominal variables in the vector $\mathbf{S}_t$. Under this ordering, the innovations in the real variables are interpreted as linear combinations of the innovations to agents' preference and technology shocks. In all of the decompositions we chose an ordering of variables in which output appeared first. It would be equally consistent with the RBC model of section 4.a to choose an ordering in which either of the two asset returns appeared prior to output. In practice, we encountered very little sensitivity to permutations of the orderings within the real block $\mathbf{S}_{1t}$. In part this reflects the fact that monthly data were used. For monthly data, the contemporaneous correlations among the innovations in the VAR are small.

All reported variance decompositions are based on 48-month-ahead forecast errors. Table 5.1 reports the decomposition of the variance of $\ell n y_t$ based upon trivariate VARs including $\ell n y_t$, π_t and $\ell n M_{t+1}$. The reported variance decompositions of $\ell n y_t$ are sensitive to changes in the sample period. For example, in the sample period 1949:2–1983:6, the innovations to $\ell n M_{t+1}$ and π_t account for 34 and 25 percent, respectively, of the error variance of $\ell n y_t$. When the sample period is 1952:1–1979:12 these percentages are 9 and 64, respectively. Most dramatically, in the sample period 1959:2–1979:12, innovations in π_t account for 79 percent of the forecast error variance of $\ell n y_t$, while monetary innovations account for only 9 percent of the forecast error variance in $\ell n y_t$.

The decompositions of the variance of output in table 5.2, which are based on trivariate VARs including $\ell n y_t'$, π_t' and $\ell n M_{t+1}'$, are also quite sensitive to changes in the sample period. Again innovations in the inflation rate account for the largest proportion of the variance of output in the post-1959 period. However, comparing tables 5.1 and 5.2 we see that innovations in the inflation rate play a relatively more important role in the variance decomposition of output based on VARs estimated with nondetrended data. Nevertheless, nominal variables accounted for fairly large proportions of the variance of $\ell n y_t'$ in all of the sample periods.

The decompositions of the variance of output reported in table 5.3 are based on trivariate VARs which included $\Delta \ell n y_t$, $\Delta \pi_t$ and $\Delta \ell n M_{t+1}$. These results differ in two important respects from those reported in tables 5.1 and 5.2. First, the results display very little sensitivity to changes in the sample period and the reported standard errors are smaller. Second, innovations in $\Delta \pi_t$ and $\Delta \ell n M_{t+1}$ account for only a small proportion of the error variance of $\Delta \ell ny_t$. Overall the most unfavorable sample periods from the point of view of RBC theories are the post-1959 periods.

Consider next the decompositions of the variance of output based on VARs that included asset return data. As before, attention is restricted to the post-1959 period. Table 5.4 displays the decomposition of the variance of output based on four-variate VARs including $\{\Delta \ell ny_t, r_t^b, \Delta\pi_t, \Delta \ell nM_{t+1}\}$ and $\{\Delta \ell ny_t, r_t^s, \Delta\pi_t, \Delta \ell nM_{t+1}\}$. As in table 5.3, the reported decompositions are largely insensitive to changes in the sample period. In both cases the output innovations account for a large proportion of the variance of $\Delta \ell ny_t$. Innovations in r_t^b account for a very small proportion of the variance of $\Delta \ell ny_t$, while innovations in r_t^s account for approximately 25 percent of the variance of $\Delta \ell ny_t$.

Table 5.6 reports the variance decomposition of $\Delta \ell ny_t$ based on a five-variate VAR including $\{\Delta \ell ny_t, r_t^b, r_t^s, \Delta\pi_t, \Delta \ell nM_{t+1}\}$. The results are again insensitive to the choice of the sample period. Together, innovations in real variables account for over 90 percent of the variance of the growth rate in output. Innovations in $\Delta\pi_t$ and $\Delta \ell nM_{t+1}$ play an insignificant role in the decomposition. Both tables 5.4 and 5.6 indicate that ex post real stock returns play a far more important role that ex post real Treasury bill returns in the time-series behavior of $\Delta \ell ny_t$. This is reflected both in the Granger causality tests and the decomposition of the variance of $\Delta \ell ny_t$.

Finally, table 5.6 displays the decomposition of the variance of output based on a five-variate VAR which included $\{\ell ny_t', r_t^b, r_t^s, \pi_t', \ell nM_{t+1}'\}$. Innovations in π_t' and $\ell nM_{t+1}'$ account for a significant proportion of the variance of $\ell ny_t'$. However, the results are sensitive to the choice in the sample period. For example, $\ell nM_{t+1}'$ accounts for 46 percent of the variance of $\ell ny_t'$ when the sample period is 1959:2–1983:6, but only 12 percent when the sample period is 1959:2–1979:12. A similar instability of the variance decompositions is displayed in table 5.5 for the four-variate VARs, including $\{\ell ny_t', r_t^b, \ell n\pi_t', \ell nM_{t+1}'\}$ and $\{\ell ny_t', r_t^s, \ell n\pi_t', \ell nM_{t+1}'\}$, and in table 5.7 for the five-variate VARs which included $\{\ell ny_t', R_t^{s\prime}, R_t^{b\prime}, \pi_t', \ell nM_{t+1}'\}$. Not surprisingly, standard errors are larger for the decompositions based on linearly detrended data than those based on the differenced data.

6. Concluding Remarks

A striking finding from our empirical analysis is that, for all sample periods considered and for various multivariate VARs, lagged values of the monetary growth rate are *not* helpful in predicting the current and future growth rates of output, after conditioning on the other variables in the VARs. Interpreted within the context of the monetary model of section 3, these results suggest that exogenous shocks to the monetary growth rate were not an important independent source of variation in output growth during the postwar period in the U.S. More precisely, statistical representations of the monetary growth rate suggest that the monetary policy rule involves feedback on both lagged monetary growth and output. This observation, combined with the dependence of output on monetary growth through our transactions technology, suggests that if monetary shocks were an important source of output variability, then monetary growth would have Granger caused the growth rate of output in VARs. Adding sticky wages and prices, overlapping nominal contracts, or entering money directly in agents' utility functions seems likely to reinforce the conclusion that monetary growth will Granger cause output growth if exogenous shocks to the money supply were an important source of business cycle fluctuation.

We hasten to add that the design of our empirical analysis is such that infrequent monetary shocks that had an important effect on output growth may not have been detected by our statistical procedures. All of the sample periods examined covered several different political administrations, and in several cases there were significant changes in the structure of financial institutions. Additionally, specific events that are widely viewed as being monetary in nature occurred during sample periods that may also have included numerous real shocks. Put differently, our results do not rule out the possibility that particular movements in output were largely due to monetary shocks. Our results only indicate that such shocks were not sufficiently frequent and large to be statistically significant over the entire sample period. More thorough study of specific events seems worthwhile.

There are several other considerations that we feel make a real business cycle interpretation of our findings premature. First, the empirical results are not insensitive to the assumptions about the nature of trends. The virtual absence of Granger causality from money to output was obtained when both of these variables were first-differenced. In contrast, when linear deterministic trends were removed from the logarithms of output and money, there was much more evidence that money Granger caused output. Even with linear trends, however, the evidence was mixed. For the sample period 1959:2 through 1983:6, and in a five-variate VAR including real stock and bond returns, money innovations accounted for 46 percent of the variation in detrended output. (Interestingly, this finding is not consistent with Sims's finding that monetary shocks explain little of output variation in the presence of interest rates.)

For the sample period 1959:2 through 1979:12, monetary innovations accounted for 12 percent of the variation in detrended output. A comparison of the results for these two sample periods suggests that monetary shocks may have been important for output fluctuation during the early 1980s. But the standard errors for the estimated variance decompositions are quite large and detrended money did *not* Granger cause detrended output for the longer sample period. Also, recall that money accounted for an insignificant percentage of the variation in output over both sample periods when these series were time-differenced.

We wish to reemphasize the potential importance of investigating the role of technological factors in generating business cycles within models that explicitly incorporate monetary exchange. Market structures in monetary economies are very different from the market structures that have been assumed in the literature on real business cycle models. Our example economies show that one could be seriously misled in characterizing the structure of a monetary economy, despite obtaining a good statistical fit using a real business cycle model.

Finally, it is perhaps possible to reconcile our empirical findings with modern Keynesian or non-Keynesian monetary business cycle theories. However, to accomplish this reconciliation, these models must be formulated so as to be consistent with *both* the findings that money growth does not Granger cause output growth and that money growth depends on lagged output growth and money growth. We conjecture that in constructing such models researchers will be led to reexamine the relative importance of various channels through which monetary factors affect real economic activity. In particular, the importance of financial institutions in the propagation of real shocks may be more pronounced in monetary models in which the structure of financial contracts emerges from a more thorough treatment of frictions.

We have benefited from helpful discussions with Lars Hansen, Bennett McCallum, Allan Meltzer, Dan Peled, Michael Woodford, and our discussants Robert Barro and Greg Mankiw. Research assistance was provided by Kun-hong Kim and David Marshall.

REFERENCES

Altug, S. 1985. Gestation lags and the business cycle: An empirical analysis. University of Minnesota. Manuscript.

Bernanke, B. S. 1985. Alternative explanations of the money-income correlation. *Carnegie-Rochester Conference on Public Policy,* ed. K. Brunner and A. Meltzer. Forthcoming.

Bernanke, B. S., and M. Gertler. 1985. Banking in general equilibrium. NBER Working Paper no. 1647.

Blanchard, O., and M. Watson. 1984. Are business cycles all alike? NBER Working Paper no. 1392.

Cooley, T. F., and S. F. Leroy. 1985. Atheoretical macroeconometrics: A critique. *Journal of Monetary Economics* 16:283–308.

Doan, T., R. Litterman, and C. Sims. 1983. Forecasting and conditional projection using realistic prior distributions. NBER Working Paper no. 1202.

Eichenbaum, M. S., L. P. Hansen, and K. J. Singleton. 1985. A time series analysis of representative agent models of consumption and leisure choice under uncertainty. Carnegie-Mellon University. Manuscript.

Fischer, S. 1977. Long-term contracts, rational expectations, and the optimal money supply rule. *Journal of Political Economy* 85:191–205.

Fischer, S., and R. C. Merton. 1984. Macroeconomics and finance: The role of the stock market. In *Essays on macroeconomic implications of financial and labor markets and political processes,* ed. K. Brunner and A. Meltzer. Carnegie-Rochester Series on Public Policy, Vol. 21:57–108.

Garber, P. M., and R. G. King. 1983. Deep structural excavation? A critique of Euler equation methods. NBER Technical Working Paper no. 31.

Hamilton, J. D. 1983. Oil and the macroeconomy since World War II. *Journal of Political Economy* 91:228–48.

Hansen, G. 1985. Indivisible labor and the business cycle. *Journal of Monetary Economics* 16:309–28.

Kang, H. 1985. The effects of detrending in Granger-causality tests. *Journal of Business and Economic Statistics* 3:344–49.

Kareken, J. H., and N. Wallace, eds. 1980. *Models of Monetary Economies.* Federal Reserve Bank of Minneapolis.

King, R., and C. Plosser. 1984. Money, credit, and prices in a real business cycle economy. *American Economic Review* 74:363–80.

———. 1985. Nominal Surprises, Real Factors and Propagation Mechanisms, Department of Economics, University of Rochester.

Kydland, F. E. 1984. Labor-force heterogeneity and the business cycle. In *Essays on macroeconomic implications of financial and labor markets and political processes,* ed. K. Brunner and A. Meltzer. Carnegie-Rochester Series on Public Policy, Vol. 21:173–208.

Kydland, F. E., and E. F. Prescott. 1982. Time to build and aggregate fluctuations. *Econometrica* 50:1345–70.

Litterman, R., and L. Weiss. 1985. Money, real interest rates, and output: A reinterpretation of postwar U.S. data. *Econometrica* 53:129–56.

Long, J., and C. Plosser. 1983. Real business cycles. *Journal of Political Economy* 91:39–69.

Lucas, R. E., Jr. 1980. Equilibrium in a pure currency economy. *Economic Inquiry* 18:203–20.

———. 1984. Money in a theory of finance. In *Essays on macroeconomic implications of financial and labor markets and political processes,* ed. K. Brunner and A. Meltzer. Carnegie-Rochester Series on Public Policy, Vol. 21:9–46.

———. 1985. Models of business cycles. University of Chicago. Manuscript.

Lucas, R. E., Jr., and N. L. Stokey. 1983. Optimal fiscal and monetary policy in an economy without capital. *Journal of Monetary Economics* 12:55–93.

———. 1984. Money and interest in a cash-in-advance economy. CMSEMS Discussion Paper no. 628, Northwestern University.

Mankiw, N. G., J. J. Rotemberg, and L. H. Summers. 1985. Intertemporal substitution in macroeconomics. *Quarterly Journal of Economics* C:225–52.

McCallum, B. T. 1977. Price-level stickiness and the feasibility of monetary stabilization policy with rational expectations. *Journal of Political Economy* 85:627–34.

———. 1983a. A reconsideration of Sims' evidence concerning monetarism. *Economic Letters* 13:167–71.

———. 1983b. The role of overlapping-generations models in monetary economics. In *Money, Monetary Policy and Financial Institutions,* ed. K. Brunner and A. Meltzer. Carnegie-Rochester Series on Public Policy, Vol. 18:9–44.

———. 1985. On 'real' and 'sticky-price' theories of the business cycle. Carnegie-Mellon University. Manuscript.

Mehra, R., and E. C. Prescott. 1985. The equity premium: A puzzle. *Journal of Monetary Economics* 15:145–62.

Miron, J. A. 1985. Seasonal fluctuations and the life cycle-permanent income model of consumption. Manuscript.

Modigliani, F. 1958. New development on the oligopoly frontier. *Journal of Political Economy* 66:215–33.

———. 1977. The monetarist controversy or, should we forsake stabilization policies? *American Economic Review* 67:1–19.

Nelson, C. R., and C. I. Plosser. 1982. Trends and random walks in macroeconomic time series: Some evidence and implications. *Journal of Monetary Economics* 10:129–62.

Prescott, E. C. 1986. Theory ahead of business cycle measurement. *Carnegie-Rochester Conference on Public Policy,* ed. A. Meltzer and K. S. Brunner. Forthcoming.

Sargent, T. J. 1976. A classical macroeconometric model for the United States. *Journal of Political Economy* 84:207–37.

Sims, C. A. 1980a. Comparison of interwar and postwar business cycles: Monetarism reconsidered. *American Economic Review* 70:250–57.

———. 1980b. Macroeconomics and reality. *Econometrica* 48:1–48.

Svensson, L. E. O. 1985. Money and asset prices in a cash-in-advance economy. *Journal of Political Economy* 93:919–44.

Taylor, J. 1980. Aggregate dynamics and staggered contracts. *Journal of Political Economy* 88:1–23.

Townsend, R. 1982. Asset return anomalies: A choice-theoretic, monetary explanation. Carnegie-Mellon University. Manuscript.

Zellner, A. 1971. *An introduction to Bayesian inference in econometrics.* New York: Wiley.

Comment

ROBERT J. BARRO
The University of Rochester

My expectation was that this paper would deal with the empirical role of real business cycle theories (henceforth RBC theories). In fact, the empirical analysis focuses on the issue of whether variations in the quantity of money (M1) influence output. Apparently if the real effects of money are strong (weak), the RBC theories are to be viewed as unimportant (important). Eichenbaum and Singleton conclude from monthly post–World

War II U.S. data that M1 is not a major causal factor for industrial production, which, if correct, is an important finding. But I do not see what this result would say about the empirical significance of RBC theories. It seems inadequate to conclude that whatever is not monetary (i.e., related to M1) must be real in the sense of the real disturbances that appear in RBC theories. Even if the monetarists are wrong, the realists may not be right.

Consider as an example the model of Keynes's *General Theory*. The model implies that variations in the quantity of money are relatively unimportant for the behavior of output and employment (because of a peculiar-looking demand-for-money function). Yet the model contains nominal rigidities, for wages at least, perhaps also for prices. The aggregates of output and employment are determined inefficiently, in the sense that (perceived) mutually advantageous trades do not occur. As a consequence there is a desirable role for activist governmental policies, especially of the fiscal variety. From a positive standpoint, the Keynesian model says that the major driving element for business fluctuations is animal spirits—that is, exogenous changes in optimism or pessimism by business investors. (I doubt that animal spirits could ever be seen directly in the data.) These shifts are then multiplied by the endogenous elements of the model—hence relatively small disturbances can create substantial changes in output and employment.

For present purposes the important issue is not the empirical validity of this fine theory; rather, the point is that data generated by this model would accord with Eichenbaum and Singleton's finding that money has a minor causal role in industrial production. Hence, they would look at this data and find support for RBC theories (at least in the sense of failing to reject such theories). Yet most economists would not regard the Keynesian model as an example of RBC theory—at least not the "equilibrium"-style theory that is now popular.

The equilibrium versions of RBC theory focus on technological shifts as key disturbances to the economy. These shifts could involve innovations in technique, introduction of new products, changes in comparative advantage across regions or countries, natural disasters, and so on. The models can also accommodate shifts in preferences, although these are generally regarded as less important. In any event, the economy responds efficiently to the various disturbances, taking account of mobility costs, incomplete information, and the like. Although phenomena that resemble aggregate business fluctuations can arise in these models, there is no role for activist stabilization policies. (There would be the usual issues of optimal taxation and provision of public goods.) Overall, these kinds of models bear little resemblance to Keynes's *General Theory*.

Some RBC models (such as Long and Plosser 1983) show that, given some initiating real disturbances, it is possible to reproduce the standard business cycle pattern with respect to persistence over time and comovements across industries. Also the endogenous response of inside money (as in King and Plosser 1984) can explain some positive correlation in the data between a monetary aggregate such as M1 and measures of real economic activity. Further, variations in financial intermediation can be modeled as one of the real disturbances that matters for output, investment, and so on. This interpretation is consistent with Bernanke's (1983) analysis of nonmonetary factors during the Great Depression. That is, RBC theories are consistent with real effects from a collapse in credit institutions.

Despite these favorable aspects, economists' main skepticism about RBC theories reflects the doubt that real disturbances are large and frequent enough to account for much of observed business fluctuations. It is important to note here that RBC models—although they can account for dispersion across industries and propagation over time—lack important multipliers. Basically the models need big disturbances to get big movements in output. Thus, I would have preferred the focus of Eichenbaum and Singleton's empirical work to be on the question of whether real shocks are large and frequent enough to account for a major part of the business cycle. As a dividend, it would also be nice to identify some of the initiating real disturbances with observable variables.

The events that got macroeconomists interested in real disturbances—sometimes referred to as "supply shocks"—were the oil crises of 1973–74 and 1979–80 (and presumably with the opposite sign for 1985–86). Hamilton's (1983) detailed study finds a regular pattern whereby increases in oil prices are followed by declines in real GNP. Remarkably, this pattern applies even before the celebrated oil crises of recent years—for example, to the Suez crisis of 1956–57 (which preceded the recession of 1957–58) and to the Iranian nationalization of its oil fields in 1952–53 (which came before the recession of 1953–54). The evidence is especially impressive because the changes in the (relative) price of oil can often be related to observable, exogenous events.

An obvious question is why oil, and not an array of other commodities, as the source of supply shocks? The crises of 1973–74 and 1979–80 can be interpreted as exogenous changes in market structure that reduced the supply of a major input to production. In this respect the disturbance would tend to lower world output, perhaps especially in the short run when producers are motivated to adjust their capital stocks to a new configuration of relative prices. (There would also be distributional effects on world income—but these may be less important for the effects on production.) Disturbances that affect the supply of other inputs could also be important in principle, although they may be difficult to isolate in the aggregate data. In any case it is unclear what general research strategy to follow in applying the results for oil (or energy) to other areas.

Lilien's (1982) approach to intersectoral shifts seemed promising because it avoided the need to isolate a detailed array of supply shocks. His idea was that many—mostly unobservable—disturbances to technology and preferences motivate reallocations of resources across sectors. Because of the costs of matching workers to new jobs and of accumulating new types of capital, the transition tends to involve temporary reductions in aggregate production and employment. Also, the increase in job separations leads to a temporary rise in the unemployment rate (which shows up as more people searching for jobs). This theory has since been extended by Topel and Weiss (1985) and Rogerson (1986).

Two attractions of the Lilien-style analysis were, first, that the dispersion of changes in employment and production across industrial sectors seemed to be positively correlated with the overall unemployment rate (or other measures of economic contraction), and second, that the method did not require the isolation of observable supply shocks, such as oil crises. But further empirical research brought out some problems. Abraham and Katz (1986) showed that the correlation of Lilien's dispersion variable with the business cycle could reflect purely aggregate disturbances that had differential effects on the various sectors. Also, models that stress sectoral shifts imply that a high sectoral dispersion of changes in production and employment would create high vacancies as well as high unemployment. Hence this analysis predicts a positive relation between vacancies and unemployment, which Abraham and Katz show is inconsistent with the evidence. (The negative association between vacancies and unemployment is often called a Beveridge curve, although given Lord Beveridge's work (1945) it is not clear why a curve should be named after him.)

Loungani (1986) brings out another problem with Lilien's analysis. When the relative price of oil is held fixed, it turns out that there is no remaining association between Lilien's dispersion variable and the unemployment rate or other measures of aggregate business fluctuations. Oil shocks would create a dispersion across sectors in the changes in employment and production, and this dispersion may be part of the story behind oil's effect on aggregate output. But Loungani's results show that Lilien's method fails to isolate other, unobservable supply shocks that were important in historical business cycles. Thus one major attraction of the sectoral approach seems to have been illusory. (As an aside,

Loungani shows that there was an oil shock in 1920, which matches up well with the sharp economic contraction in 1921. Apparently, oil shocks were important even before oil was very important. But perhaps it is energy shocks that are being isolated, which accords with the significance attached much earlier by Jevons (1865) to the supply of coal in Britain.)

My conclusion is that real business cycle theories represent promising ideas for explaining business cycles. Given the weak state of alternative ideas (such as animal spirits and monetary shocks), it would be a mistake to dispense too readily with this line of theory. But at this stage the main empirical support for RBC theories concerns the role of oil shocks. Thus, the available evidence is not very satisfying.

REFERENCES

Abraham, K. G., and L. F. Katz. 1986. Cyclical unemployment: Sectoral shifts or aggregate disturbances? *Journal of Political Economy* 94:507–22.

Bernanke, B. S. 1983. Nonmonetary effects of the financial crisis in the propagation of the Great Depression. *American Economic Review* 73:257–76.

Beveridge, W. H. 1945. *Full Employment in a Free Society.* New York: Norton.

Hamilton, J. D. 1983. Oil and the macroeconomy since World War II. *Journal of Political Economy* 91:228–48.

Jevons, W. S. 1865. *The Coal Question.* London: Macmillan.

King, R. G., and C. I. Plosser. 1984. Money, credit and prices in a real business cycle. *American Economic Review.* 74:363–80.

Lilien, D. M. 1982. Sectoral shifts and cyclical unemployment. *Journal of Political Economy* 90:777–93.

Long, J. B., and C. I. Plosser. 1983. Real business cycles. *Journal of Political Economy* 91:39–69.

Loungani, P. 1986. Oil price shocks and the dispersion hypothesis, 1900–1980. Rochester Center for Economic Research. Working paper no. 33.

Rogerson, R. 1986. Sectoral shifts and cyclical fluctuations. Unpublished. Rochester, N.Y.: University of Rochester.

Topel, R., and L. Weiss. 1985. Sectoral uncertainty and unemployment. Unpublished. Los Angeles: University of California/Los Angeles.

Comment

N. GREGORY MANKIW
Harvard University and NBER

Real business cycle theory is one of the currently "hot" topics in macroeconomics, especially among those who live closer to lakes than to oceans. Eichenbaum and Singleton take on the difficult, but obviously very important, question of whether the economic fluctuations observed during the past forty years can be reconciled with these theories. In particular, they examine the interaction between the variation in the quantity of money and fluctuations in real economic activity, using the now-standard techniques of vector autoregression, Granger causality, and variance decomposition. The primary empirical finding, which in light of Sims's celebrated work comes as a complete surprise, is that money appears not to Granger cause output, even in bivariate systems.

Vector autoregressions and Granger causality tests are, to my mind, difficult to interpret. Eichenbaum and Singleton's analysis, however, in contrast to much previous empirical work of this kind, is not completely atheoretical. They begin with a simple theory, in particular a model in which money enters by virtue of a cash-in-advance constraint. They show that money will, in general, matter in this economy. If, however, fluctuations in money are relatively small, then a real business cycle model could provide a good approximation to this monetary economy. While the model provides one framework within which the empirical work can be interpreted, Eichenbaum and Singleton argue that the absence of Granger causality from money to output appears inconsistent with more complex monetary models as well, including those in which wages and prices are sticky.

The central question of the article, "Does Money Matter?", is of course a long-standing one. The novelty of the article is the answer. While Eichenbaum and Singleton prudently refrain from jumping to the broad conclusion that money does not matter, they do argue, in essence, that money has not mattered, at least over the past forty years, and that their findings are problematic for many prominent theories of the business cycle.

The question for a commentator of course is, "Are they right?" I will argue, first, that Eichenbaum and Singleton are not obviously wrong. It is not absurd to entertain the notion of monetary neutrality. Second, I will argue that Eichenbaum and Singleton are not obviously right. In particular, the failure of money to Granger cause output might not have implications as far-reaching as they suggest.

Questioning the Non-neutrality of Money

Let me begin with the first issue: Might money be neutral?

To many economists, especially among those who live close to oceans, the non-neutrality of money is simply common sense. One only needs to look out at the world or to read the newspaper, I am often told, to convince oneself that money matters.

I must confess that I am suspicious when one side of a hotly contested issue lays claim to common sense as an argument. Albert Einstein once said that "common sense is the collection of prejudices acquired by age eighteen." I suspect that Einstein was not talking about the non-neutrality of money at the time, because if he had been, he likely would have chosen age twenty-six, when one leaves graduate school. The thought, however, appears appropriate here.

Many people believe that the stock market exhibits regular patterns and that they can forecast price movements using these regular patterns. We call them chartists; they call themselves technical analysts. To these chartists, the patterns in the stock market are also a matter of common sense; they have been observing these patterns for years.

Most economists are quick to ridicule chartists; the primary reason is that there is no firm statistical evidence that chartist techniques are effective. The stock market appears to follow a random walk, or nearly so. Economists remain unconvinced about the chartists' claims because they do not hold up against formal hypothesis testing.

Yet if economists are to require that chartism pass the test of formal inference, our own cherished beliefs must be subject to similar rigor. For this reason, the empirical results of Eichenbaum and Singleton should give pause to believers in the non-neutrality of money.

One might argue, and in fact I will, that testing the neutrality of money is a very difficult task, given the problems of simultaneity. Yet appealing to common sense and anecdotal evidence does not avoid the identification problem. The difficulty of the task should only make economists less confident about whether money is neutral or not.

Interpreting Granger Causality

I should probably disclose my own prejudices regarding the central question of this paper. After spending most of my adult years hanging around Princeton, MIT, and Harvard, I of course see the world through the lens of wage and price stickiness. Eichenbaum and Singleton assert that their results are difficult to reconcile with this sort of model. If so, much of my human capital would be made obsolete. Let me therefore turn to the second issue: Do Eichenbaum and Singleton correctly interpret their finding that money does not Granger cause output?

It is now well known that Granger causality has nothing to do with causality as the term is usually used. My own favorite example is the permanent income hypothesis, as presented in Hall's 1978 paper. The model is one in which consumption depends only on current and future income. Hence, fluctuations in income "cause" fluctuations in consumption. Yet the theory implies that income does not "Granger cause" consumption, since changes in consumption are not forecastable. It would of course be ridiculous to interpret Hall's empirical findings on

Granger causality as evidence that income is not a causal determinant of consumption.

How, then, can we interpret Eichenbaum and Singleton's finding that money does not Granger cause output? As the authors are aware, we cannot jump directly to a conclusion about actual causality. Instead, they interpret this finding using the cash-in-advance model presented in the paper. In the context of this model, if money were important to the path of economic activity, then money would appear to Granger cause output. They *suggest* that other popular monetary models would also have the feature that money should Granger cause output.

It is this last suggestion with which I disagree. I suspect that money need not Granger cause output for money to be a fundamental determinant of output. The following two examples, which are based on a stylized variant of Fischer's model of nominal wage contracts, illustrate this possibility.

Suppose that workers sign contracts two periods ahead of the transaction date. That is, at $t - 2$, workers agree on a nominal wage at which they will sell labor to firms; the contracted wage is of course based on their expectation of the price level. It is straightforward to show that this leads to the aggregate supply function:

$$Y_t = \alpha (P_t - E_{t-2} P_t), \quad (1)$$

where Y is the log of output and P is the log of the price level. For simplicity, I use the quantity theory of money as my aggregate demand equation:

$$M_t + V_t = P_t + Y_t, \quad (2)$$

where velocity V_t is an exogenous random variable. Equations (1) and (2) trivially imply that

$$Y_t = \beta (M_t - E_{t-2}M_t) + \beta (V_t - E_{t-2}V_t), \quad (3)$$

where $\beta = \alpha/(1 + \alpha)$.

Monetary policy potentially plays an important role in this economy. But would one find that money Granger caused output? The answer is, not necessarily, as the following two special cases illustrate:

Example 1: Suppose that velocity is constant, and the money supply follows an AR(1) process:

$$M_t = \rho M_{t-1} + \nu_t. \quad (4)$$

Equation (3) implies that

$$Y_t = \beta(\nu_t + \rho\,\nu_{t-1}), \quad (5)$$

which in turn implies

$$(1 + \rho L)^{-1}\beta^{-1}Y_t = \nu_t. \quad (6)$$

In this economy, the innovation in output and the innovation in money are perfectly correlated contemporaneously. Past values of money, however, have no additional explanatory power once we have controlled for past values of output. That is,

$$E[Y_t|Y_{t-1}, Y_{t-2}, \ldots, M_{t-1}, M_{t-2}, \ldots] = E[Y_t|Y_{t-1}, Y_{t-2}, \ldots].$$

Hence, even though exogenous monetary shocks are the sole driving force of output fluctuations, money does not Granger cause output.
Example 2: Suppose velocity follows a random walk:

$$V_t = V_{t-1} + \varepsilon_t, \quad (7)$$

implying

$$Y_t = \beta(M_t - E_{t-2}M_t) + \beta(\varepsilon_t + \varepsilon_{t-1}). \quad (8)$$

Suppose further that the money supply is set one period ahead in an attempt to stabilize output. Clearly, the Fed cannot offset the demand shock realized at time t. It can, however, offset the demand shock realized at time $t - 1$. An optimal policy is therefore

$$M_t = -\varepsilon_{t-1}, \quad (9)$$

which implies that output is

$$Y_t = \beta\varepsilon_t. \quad (10)$$

Note that $\text{corr}(Y_t, M_{t-j}) = 0$ for $j \geq 0$, but $\text{corr}(Y_t, M_{t+1}) \neq 0$. In this economy, therefore, money does not Granger cause output, but output does Granger cause money.

These two examples are highly stylized, and I would not begin to claim that they well approximate the actual economy. Nor would I claim that the absence of Granger causality would arise generically in this sort of sticky-wage model. These examples do illustrate, however, that the absence of Granger causality from money to output is not itself sufficient to conclude that money has not mattered. In both of these examples, variation in the quantity of money plays an important role for output fluctuations, yet an observer would fail to detect Granger causality.

One might argue, and correctly so, that in my second example, money is not an exogenous source of shocks causing output fluctuations. Instead, money partly accommodates the exogenous changes in liquidity preference. This feature of the example is probably not too unrealistic. During much of the postwar period, the Fed's stated goal was to allow the money supply to fluctuate in order to stabilize interest rates. My guess is that during such a regime, the failure of money to Granger cause output is probably not a problem for standard "saltwater" theories of the business cycle. That the monetary regime may play a key role in interpreting the results is given some support by Eichenbaum and Singleton's finding that money appears to start Granger causing output in the post-1979 period.

While these two examples convince me that it is not yet time to discard my prejudice for models with nominal rigidities, the Eichenbaum and Singleton results do leave me uneasy. To determine more fully whether their findings provide evidence for real business cycle theories against Keynesian alternatives, one might consider the following exercise. Take some clearly Keynesian model, together with empirically plausible reaction functions for the monetary and fiscal authorities. Use the model to generate forty years of artificial data. Then run the Granger causality tests on this data. If, as I suspect, one could obtain the Eichenbaum and Singleton results with this artificial Keynesian data, then one would conclude that the absence of Granger causality in the actual data provides no evidence in favor of real business cycle models.

Unfortunately, I do not have the results from such an experiment to report. That would be the task of an entirely new paper. It is not even clear that such a paper could be written, given that there is no model widely accepted even among Keynesians. I therefore suspect that the absence of Granger causality from money to output will become another stylized fact without an obvious interpretation.

In summary, I would like to applaud Eichenbaum and Singleton for addressing one of the most important and difficult questions dividing macroeconomics today. Their discussion is thoughtful, and their empirical work is carefully done. My main difference with them is one of interpretation. I doubt that the question of monetary neutrality can be usefully addressed by tests of Granger causality.

REFERENCES

Fischer, S. 1977. Long-term contracts, rational expectations, and the optimal money supply rule. *Journal of Political Economy* 85:191–210.

Hall, R. E. 1978. The stochastic implications of the life cycle-permanent income hypothesis: Theory and evidence. *Journal of Political Economy* 86:971–87.

Sims, C. A. 1972. Money, income, and causality. *American Economic Review* 62:540–52.

Discussion

Answering the discussants, Kenneth Singleton commented that policy may be useful even if the business cycle is an equilibrium real phenomenon. He agreed with Mankiw that there are ways to reconcile their results with the belief that money matters. To do this, further work is needed on the simultaneous modeling and estimation of trends and cycles.

Robert Hall questioned the existence of the extensive intertemporal substitution associated with real interest rate shocks that is needed in equilibrium real business cycle theory. He also questioned whether there was in fact enough persistence in technology shocks to drive observed serial correlation or persistence in the business cycle.

John Taylor doubted that the importance of oil shocks could be taken as support for real business cycle models. Prolonged adjustment after an oil shock is the result of wage stickiness, not of real business cycle phenomena.

The use of M1 in the empirical investigation was questioned by Lawrence Summers. First, M1 may not have much to do with aggregate demand. And second, if M1 is used to stabilize future output, then M1 will not Granger cause output. Summers also remarked that the fact that announcements about monetary policy have immediate effects on asset prices is difficult to reconcile with models in which money does not matter. One of the questions raised by the Eichenbaum-Singleton paper might be why effects that do occur are so difficult to detect with existing statistical techniques.

Julio Rotemberg questioned the strong restrictions implied by the use of the first-differenced data. Under the stationarity assumption, even if money Granger causes output in the level, it will not do so in first differences.

Lawrence Weiss suggested that causality results might change if quarterly rather than monthly data were used. He noted that the data sample in the Eichenbaum-Singleton paper contains two episodes, 1966 and 1981, in which the Fed is supposed to have caused a recession, and that these should affect the results. He thought it significant that the standard models used in macroeconomics imply causal structures with which the data are inconsistent.

Robert Gordon suggested that Granger causality tests might show that money Granger causes nominal GNP, even though it might appear not to Granger cause either real GNP or inflation. Bennett McCallum said that empirical work in fact typically shows that money Granger causes output. The use of first-differenced data may be the cause of its failure to do so in the Eichenbaum-Singleton data, for only a small fraction of systematic variability may be left in the data after first-differencing. James Stock agreed, noting that he and Mark Watson had been unable to detect common variations that exist in level data when using first-differenced or detrended data.

Albert Ando pointed out the fragility of Granger causality. Using the MPS (MIT-Penn-SSRC) model, in which there is a powerful role for money, he could easily generate data in which money does not Granger cause output.

Singleton concluded the discussion by stressing the importance of building models that explicitly include money, in order to be able to detect and evaluate the importance of both monetary and real shocks. The very fact that it is possible to construct examples of monetary models in which money does not Granger cause output further highlights the importance of their explicit modeling approach.

Fumio Hayashi
OSAKA UNIVERSITY, JAPAN

Why Is Japan's Saving Rate So Apparently High?

1. *Introduction*

The huge U.S. trade deficit with Japan, which totaled $50 billion in 1985 and accounts for a thumping one-third of the total U.S. trade deficit, has worried policy makers and economists alike for some time. The widening trade gap has cost jobs in the United States, particularly in the manufacturing sector, providing ample ammunition for protectionists. The identity in the national income accounts states that the excess of saving over investment equals the trade surplus. The blame for Japan's large trade surplus with the United States must therefore fall on Japan's high saving or her slumping investment. The widespread sentiment that the Japanese save too much was even echoed in a 1985 speech by the U.S. Secretary of State.[1] The sentiment has some empirical grounds. In 1984 the most widely mentioned saving rate—the rate of personal saving—was 16 percent for Japan, a full 10 percentage points higher than that in the United States.

The purpose of this article is to explore possible factors that contribute to Japan's high saving rate. That Japan's saving rate is high by international standards has been recognized in Japan for more than two decades, yet the reason for it is poorly understood: I quote the last sentence of a recent survey in the Japanese literature. "In any event . . . Japan's high personal saving rate remains a mystery to be resolved."[2] It is not that empirical investigations have been hampered by a scarcity of data. Although consistent time series in the Japanese national income accounts do not start until 1965, a large amount of micro data on house-

1. George Shultz's speech at Princeton University attracted widespread attention in the Japanese press.
2. Kurosaka and Hamada (1984).

holds is available from various surveys that have been conducted regularly by the Japanese government. Perhaps the issue of Japan's high saving rate has not attracted enough of the empirical attention it deserves.

I will begin with very down-to-earth facts about aggregate saving in Japan and the United States. Those are contained in section 2, which tries to see if the perception of high savings in Japan has any empirical basis. It will be argued that some conceptual differences between U.S. and Japanese national accounting explain a substantial portion of the observed differences in the saving rates. Section 3 summarizes the explanations that have been offered in the literature. (I will examine them further in later sections.) The first theory of saving, to be taken up in section 4, is the life-cycle hypothesis. After rejecting the life-cycle explanations, I turn in section 5 to micro data on households analyzed by age group to locate possible deviations from the life-cycle hypothesis of the actual Japanese saving behavior. It turns out that the cross-section age profile of saving in Japan appears to defy any simple life-cycle explanation, including an explanation based on the high housing-related saving by younger generations. Continuing the theme at the end of section 5 that bequests might be an important factor, section 6 digresses somewhat to calculate the aggregate flow of intergenerational transfers that can be inferred from the cross-section saving profiles. Other aspects of household behavior, including the impact of social security, relevant to assessing the importance of bequests will be analyzed in section 7. Section 8 then takes up a separate issue, tax incentives for saving. The Japanese tax system does seem to be geared to promote saving. Taxes, however, are probably not the main factor behind the high saving rate, I argue, because saving does not appear to be responsive to interest rates.

2. *Facts about Japan's Aggregate Saving Rates*

2.1. WHICH SAVING RATE?

When comparing saving behavior between the two countries, we must first decide which saving rate to use. The choice of the saving rate has several dimensions. The first is the boundary of the relevant sector. Should we look at the household sector, the private sector, or the nation as a whole? The focus on *personal* (household) saving is unwarranted if undistributed profits (corporate saving) are fully reflected in the capital gains in stock prices that are recognized by households as part of income, or if corporations are just an accounting device for individuals to receive corporate tax treatment on their income.[3] We should then look at *private* saving (the sum of personal and corporate saving). But even private saving is inappropriate if the private sector can see through the government veil and internalize the government budget constraint. The Ricardian Equivalence Thorem states that a government budget deficit is recognized by the private sector as a tax of the same amount because the public debt is just a signal of future increased taxes. The relevant notion of saving then is *national* saving (the sum of private and government saving). The question of the relevant boundary is one of the basic issues in economics yet to be resolved, and in this article we will not commit ourselves to any one particular saving rate. We should, however, bear in mind that the substance of the corporate sector in the Japanese National Accounts is somewhat different from corporate business in the U.S. National Income and Product Accounts. At one end of the corporate sector in the Japanese national accounts there are numerous token corporations that are essentially a disguised form of the household sector. At the other end lie most government enterprises (including the central bank as well as institutions that are not corporations in the legal sense).[4]

The second dimension in the choice of the saving rate is the definition of income. Should we include in income, and hence in saving, revaluation (capital gains/losses) of assets? Perhaps fully anticipated revaluation should be included, but that is difficult to identify. If revaluation is recognized as part of income, private saving is a more meaningful saving concept than personal saving.

The third dimension is the scope of assets, which is where the treatment of consumer durables is relevant. In principle, any commodity that is durable should be regarded as an object of saving. But measurement of the durability of commodities in general is a difficult task.[5] The impor-

3. The top combined national and local personal tax rate is currently 88 percent in Japan. (However, we are told, there is a footnote in the personal tax code that reduces the top marginal rate to 75 percent.) People in high-income tax brackets can spread their income over their spouses and relatives by setting up a token corporation. By paying them high wages and by taking advantage of the more generous tax deductibility provisions in the corporate tax codes, they can understate corporate income and thus avoid double taxation at the corporate and personal levels. In 1983 there were about 1.8 million corporations in Japan. The largest 1.2 percent paid close to 70 percent of the total corporation tax. About 60 percent of all corporations reported negative taxable income.

4. The Japanese national accounts also divide the nation into private and public sectors. Government enterprises are included in the public sector. In retrospect, the focus on private sector might have been more appropriate. Fortunately, as we shall see later, the difference between the national and the private saving rates is small compared to the difference of the personal rate from the private and the national saving rates.

5. A good example is dental services. It is classified as services in the national accounts but

tance of consumer durables will be touched upon when we compare the personal saving rate between the two countries in figure 2. Depending on the stand one takes in each of the three dimensions, there can be multitudes of saving rates. Only a subset of the possible saving rates will be discussed in the text. The data appendix to this paper provides information necessary for calculating not only the saving rates discussed in the text but also several others that the reader might care to entertain.

2.2. DATA COMPARABILITY

Even after the choice of the saving rate is made, there is a measurement problem that makes international comparison tricky. There are (at least) four major conceptual differences between the United States and Japan in the compilation of national accounts.

1. A very surprising fact about the Japanese national income accounts is that depreciation is valued at *historical costs*.[6] This means that personal saving is overstated during and after the inflationary period of the 1970s.[7] Remember that personal disposable income is a *net* concept—it excludes depreciation of household assets. Since personal saving is defined as personal disposable income minus consumption, it is net of depreciation. Corporate saving is severely overstated for the same reason. There must, however, be an official estimate of replacement-cost depreciation floating around within the Economic Planning Agency, the statistical mill of the Japanese national accounts data, since the stock of assets is valued at replacement costs in the capital accounts (balance sheets and stock-flow reconciliations) of the Japanese national accounts. Although the official estimate is neither published nor released, we can recover it fairly accurately from the numbers published in the *Annual Reports on National Accounts*. Detailed descriptions of our calculation procedure and our estimate of capital consumption adjustments (the excess of depreciation at replacement costs over depreciation at historical costs) are given in the data appendix. The basic idea is to separate out the revaluation component from the reconciliation accounts and identify the residual as capital consumption adjustments. The calculation can be done only for the post-1969 period because the capital accounts start in 1970. Since investment goods prices were more or less stable until the

in essence it is a purchase of a durable good of good teeth. Hayashi (1985a) reports using Japanese data that food is almost the only commodity that exhibits no durability. Recreational expenditures are found to be more durable than consumer durables.

6. Inventory valuation adjustments are incorporated in the Japanese national accounting.

7. Investment goods prices more than doubled in the 1970s.

first oil crisis of 1973–74, the capital consumption adjustment is not significant for that period. However, the size of the adjustment to private depreciable assets has increased rapidly since then, reaching as much as 30 percent of reported private saving in several recent years. (See table A2.)

2. Unlike most other countries (including Japan), the U.S. National Income and Product Accounts compiled by the Bureau of Economic Analysis (BEA) treat all types of government expenditure as consumption and fail to credit the government for the value of its tangible assets. The BEA definition of government saving is therefore the government's budget surplus, while government saving in the Japanese national accounts includes in addition the net increase in government tangible assets. This conceptual difference also means that even GNP and NNP are not directly comparable because the BEA definition does not include output service flows from government tangible assets.

To make matters even more complicated, the Japanese national accounts do not depreciate government depreciable assets except buildings. Thus reported depreciation of government assets is very substantially understated: it is valued at historical costs and it covers only buildings. In the data appendix we constructed time series on the stock of government depreciable assets by the perpetual inventory method and the associated depreciation at replacement costs, so that the saving rate series for which government assets are included as components of assets can be constructed for Japan. We decided not to construct such saving rate series for the United States. When we compare the Japanese to the U.S. data, we will recalculate the Japanese saving rates according to the BEA convention.

Readily available data sources on U.S. government capital accounts are Ruggles and Ruggles (1982) and Eisner (1985).[8] The definition of government assets in Ruggles and Ruggles appears comparable to that in the Japanese national accounts, but the data do not extend beyond 1980. The ratio to NNP of net government capital formation for the United States was roughly around 1 percent in the 1970s. Eisner's data encompass a much broader spectrum of assets and are thus not directly comparable. According to our estimate of government assets, the ratio to NNP of net government capital formation is about 3–5 percent (see table A5). Thus the exclusion of government capital alone makes a 2–4 percent difference to the BEA definition of the national saving rate. However, it is not clear that all government capital formation should be counted as saving. Government investment projects in Japan, often politically motivated

8. The estimates of government capital in Boskin, Robinson, and Roberts (1985) are for the federal government only.

and not necessarily justifiable on economic grounds, may be viewed by the private sector as wasteful and incapable of yielding any useful service flows. It could even be argued that government capital is inherently unobservable, in which case it would be difficult to estimate the useful (as viewed by the private sector) asset lives for municipal buildings, highways, dams, and tunnels.

3. The Japanese national accounts do not adjust after-tax income for "capital transfers" (wealth taxes and lump-sum transfers), so in the capital transactions (saving/investment) accounts the sum of saving, depreciation, and capital transfers equals the sum of investment in tangible and financial assets plus a statistical discrepancy. In what follows we include transfers as part of saving, which is consistent with the U.S. practice. For the household sector, capital transfers are negative because they are mainly bequest and gift taxes. In 1984 these are about 5 percent of reported personal saving. Almost all of the reduction of personal saving is transferred to corporate saving, making little difference to national saving.

4. (very minor) In the U.S. national accounts personal consumption and saving do not add up to personal disposable income because interest paid by households to business and to foreigners is included in personal disposable income. In what follows that interest component will be subtracted from U.S. personal disposable income.[9]

All the saving rates to be presented are adjusted as described above. The data source for Japan is the *1986 Annual Report on National Accounts* (which incorporates the latest benchmark revision). For the U.S. National Income and Product Accounts data we use the *1985 Economic Report of the President* (which does not incorporate the January 1986 benchmark revision). It is supplemented by the *Balance Sheets for the U.S. Economy, 1945–84* (compiled by the Board of Governors of the Federal Reserve System) for balance sheet information, without addressing the question of compatibility between the two sets of U.S. data.

2.3. A LOOK AT AGGREGATE SAVING RATES

The most widely cited evidence in support of the notion that the Japanese like to save far more than Americans do is Japan's exceptionally high personal saving rate (the ratio of personal saving to personal disposable income). Is it still higher than the U.S. personal saving rate after the needed adjustments? Figure 1 shows the adjusted personal saving rate for Japan and the United States. Japan's personal saving rate in 1984 was

9. If the principal is reduced as a consumer repays loans, that reduction in principal is part of saving.

Figure 1 PERSONAL SAVING AS PERCENT OF PERSONAL DISPOSABLE INCOME

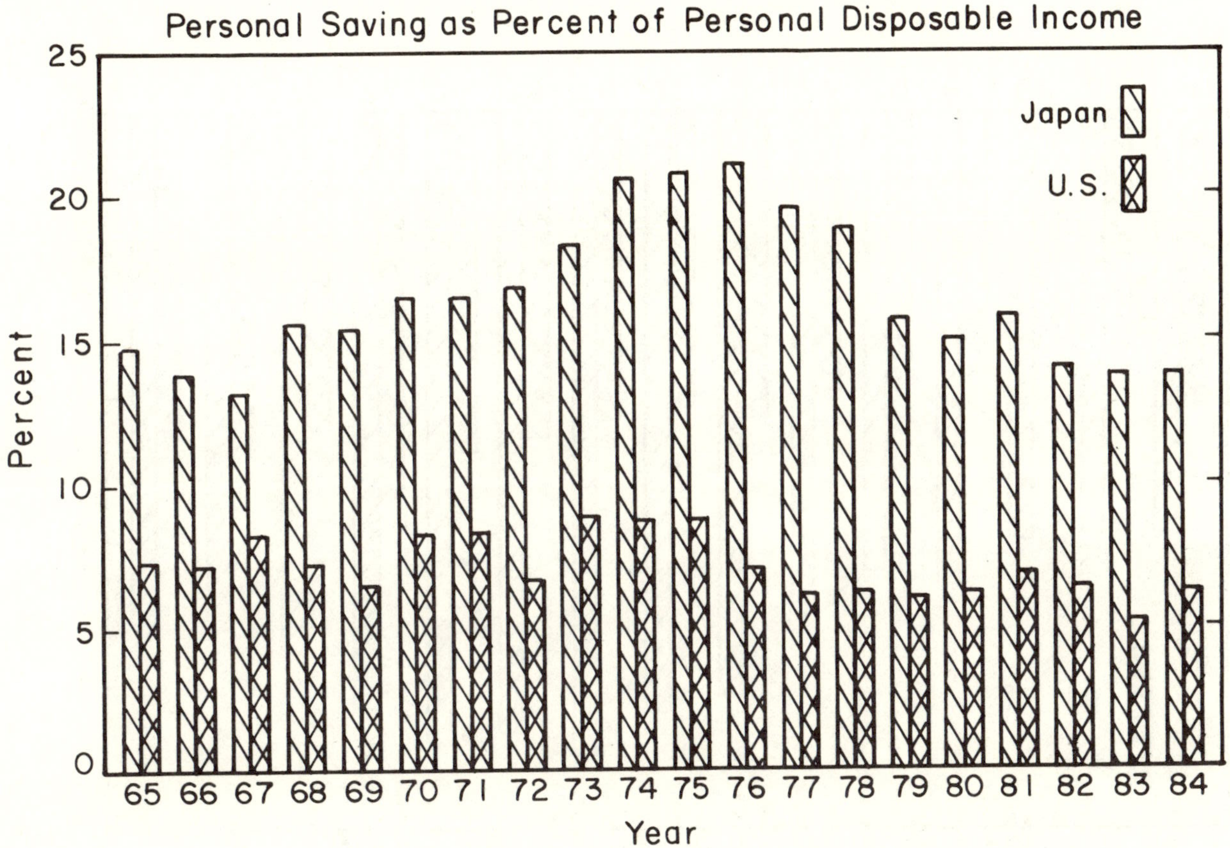

Figure 2 PERSONAL SAVING RATE WITH CONSUMER DURABLES

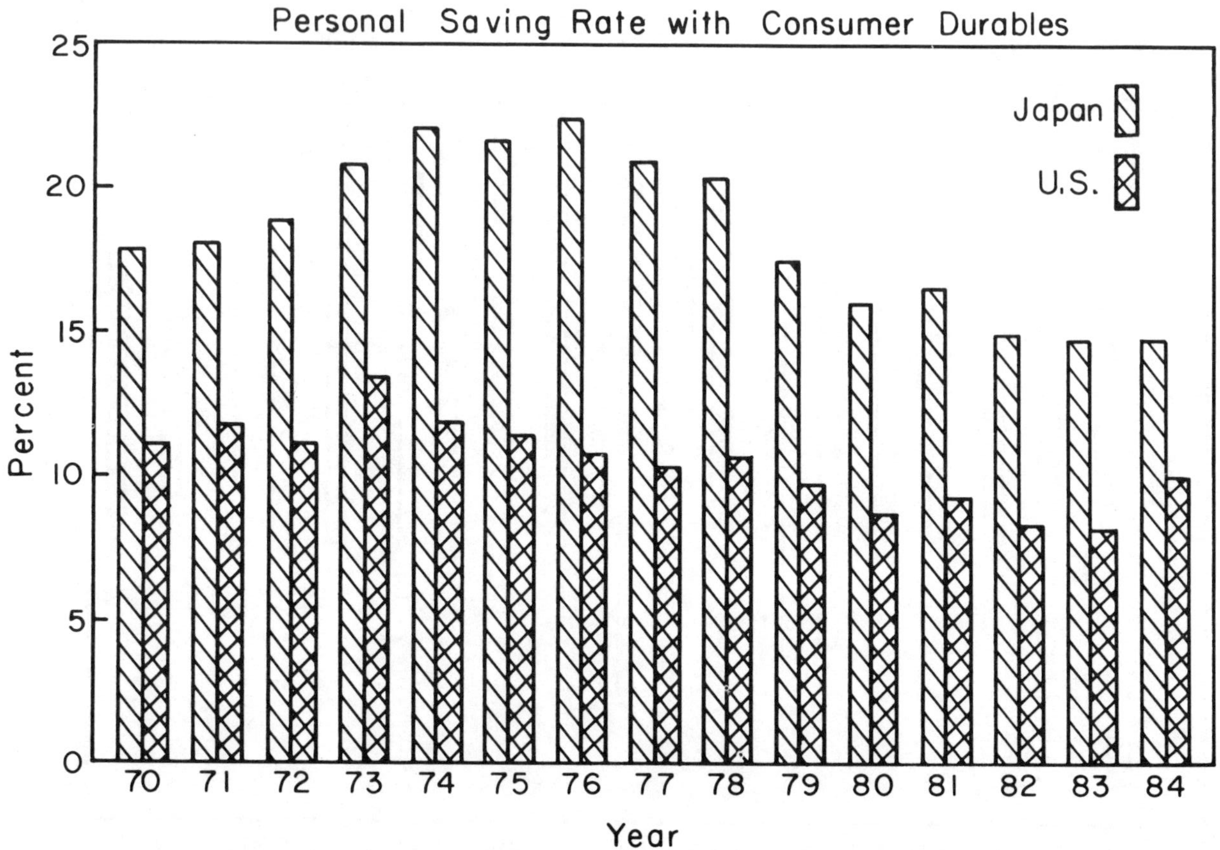

13.7 percent, about 2.5 percent lower than the personal saving rate reported in the national accounts and about 7 percent higher than the U.S. rate. The difference between the adjusted and the reported rate is mainly due to the capital consumption adjustments. The adjusted personal saving rate still exhibits the same basic pattern: it surges after the first oil crisis of 1973–74 to a peak in 1976 of 21.1 percent. The U.S. personal saving rate is stationary and has been fluctuating around 6 percent. It is clear that even after the needed adjustments Japan's personal saving rate is substantially higher.

Figure 2 shows the effect of including consumer durables as assets. Personal consumption thus excludes expenditures on durables but includes gross service flows from consumer durables. Personal disposable income now includes net service flows from consumer durables. A depreciation rate for consumer durables of 19 percent and a constant real rate of 4 percent are used for imputation. (See the data appendix for a detailed description of the imputation process.) It is well known in the United States that inclusion of consumer durables raises the personal saving rate by a few percent. That is not the case for Japan—the personal saving rate is little affected, thus narrowing the gap between the two countries for 1984 to about 4 percent.

Figure 3 (and column (1) of table 1) displays the private saving rate (the ratio of private saving to NNP, where Japan's NNP is calculated according to the BEA convention of not including net service flows from government assets). It does not include consumer durables. The U.S. rate is more or less stationary. For Japan the behavior of the private saving rate is very different from that of the personal rate. It *declines* during and after the first oil crisis and has a declining trend since 1970. This is brought about by the sharp drop in corporate saving depicted in figure 4 which shows the ratios of personal, corporate, and government saving to NNP for Japan. (The NNP here includes service flows from government capital.) The corporate saving rate declined by 9 percent points from 1973 to 1974 in the face of stagnant earnings, increased dividend payments, and increased depreciation at replacement costs.

The BEA definition of the national saving rate, which excludes government net capital formation from national saving, is compared in figure 5 for the two countries. It reveals a surprising fact about Japan—though one that is already apparent from a look at Japan's private saving rate in figure 3—that the national saving rate has declined quite sharply since 1970. In the late 1970s there was only a small difference between the national saving rates in the two countries. If one takes the view that private, not national, saving is the relevant saving concept, a good part of the de-

Figure 3 PRIVATE SAVING AS PERCENT OF NNP

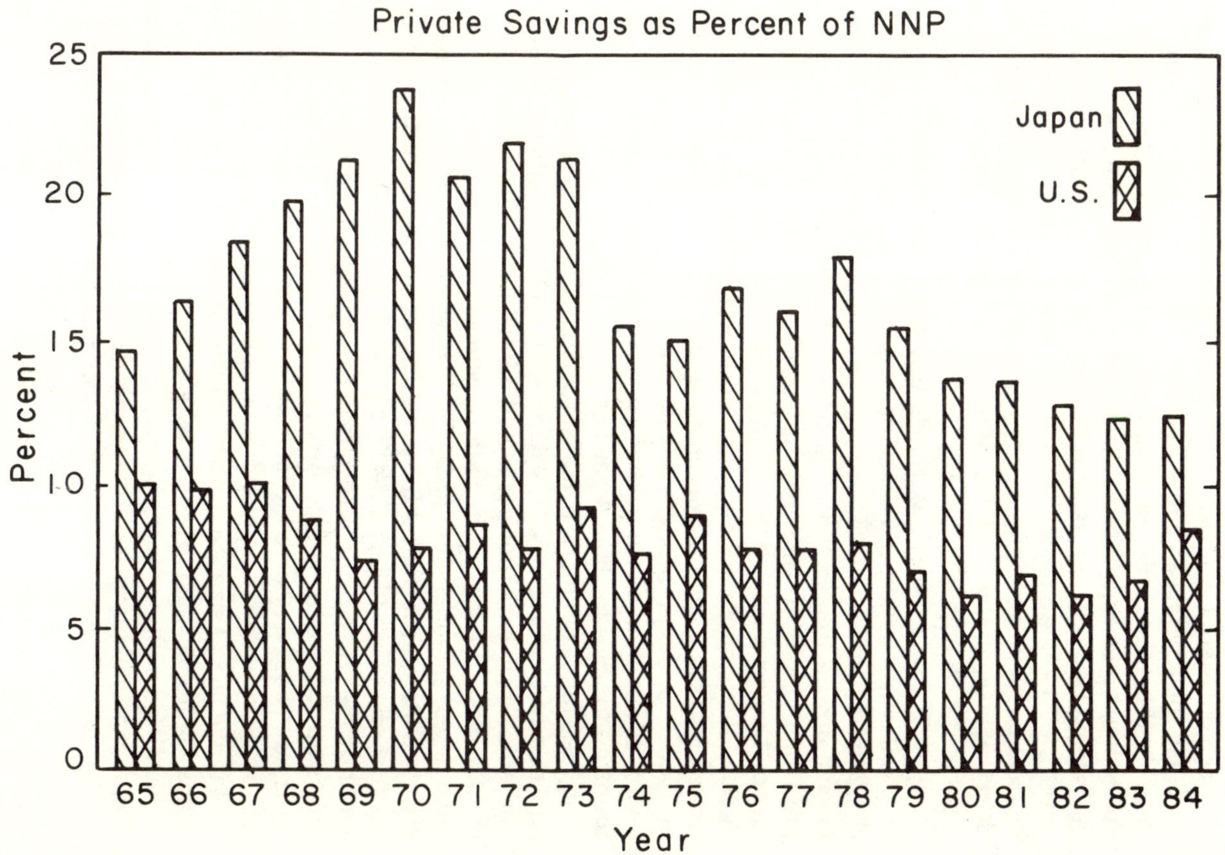

Table 1 NET SAVING AS PERCENT OF NNP WITH AND WITHOUT REVALUATION

	Japan					*United States*				
Year	*(1)*	*(2)*	*(3)*	*(4)*	*(5)*	*(1)*	*(2)*	*(3)*	*(4)*	*(5)*
1970	23.8	25.6	2.1	−.4	51.2	7.8	−3.1	−1.2	1.6	5.2
1971	20.8	28.7	2.0	−.9	50.6	8.6	.4	−2.0	1.3	8.3
1972	21.9	96.5	.1	−.3	118.2	7.7	7.6	−.3	1.3	16.2
1973	21.4	57.8	1.0	−1.0	79.2	9.2	9.4	.6	2.4	21.6
1974	15.6	−89.2	.4	−1.6	−74.7	7.6	4.1	−.4	3.4	14.7
1975	15.2	−13.1	−3.5	−.4	−1.8	8.9	−.2	−4.6	1.8	5.9
1976	17.0	−8.8	−4.7	−.2	3.4	7.7	7.8	−2.4	1.6	14.8
1977	16.1	−.8	−4.8	.2	10.7	7.6	15.2	−1.0	2.1	23.9
1978	18.0	23.5	−7.3	−.2	34.0	7.9	21.1	.0	2.3	31.3
1979	15.5	52.3	−5.4	.4	62.8	7.0	7.3	.7	2.8	17.8
1980	13.8	31.4	−4.9	1.7	42.0	6.1	1.2	−1.3	3.0	8.9
1981	13.7	29.6	−5.5	.5	38.3	6.8	1.8	−1.0	2.1	9.8
1982	12.9	17.4	−4.4	.5	26.3	6.1	−9.0	−4.3	1.5	−5.7
1983	12.4	1.9	−4.9	.5	9.9	6.7	−1.0	−4.6	1.0	2.0
1984	12.5	2.0	−2.6	.6	12.4	8.4	−7.5	−3.8	1.1	−1.8
Average	16.7	17.0	−2.8	−.0	30.8	7.6	3.7	−1.7	1.9	11.5

(1) Private saving.
(2) Net revaluation (adjusted for general inflation) of private tangible and financial assets. The general inflation rate during the year is represented by the rate of change of the deflator for consumption expenditure from the last quarter of the previous year to the last quarter of the current year.
(3) Government budget surplus.
(4) Net revaluation of government net financial assets.
(5) Sum of (1), (2), (3), and (4).

NNP is net of service flows from government tangible assets.

Source: Data Appendix.

Figure 4 SAVING RATE TO NNP BY SECTOR (JAPAN)

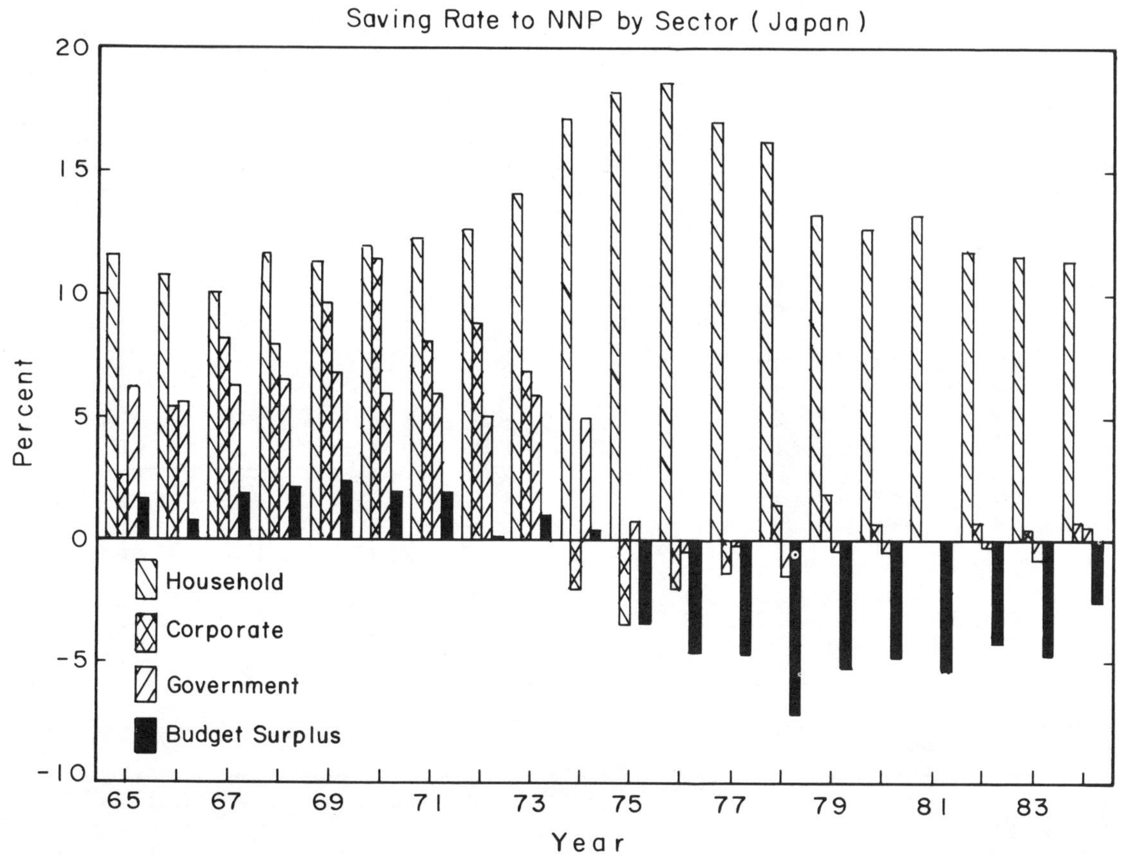

Figure 5 NATIONAL SAVING (BEA DEFINITION) AS PERCENT OF NNP

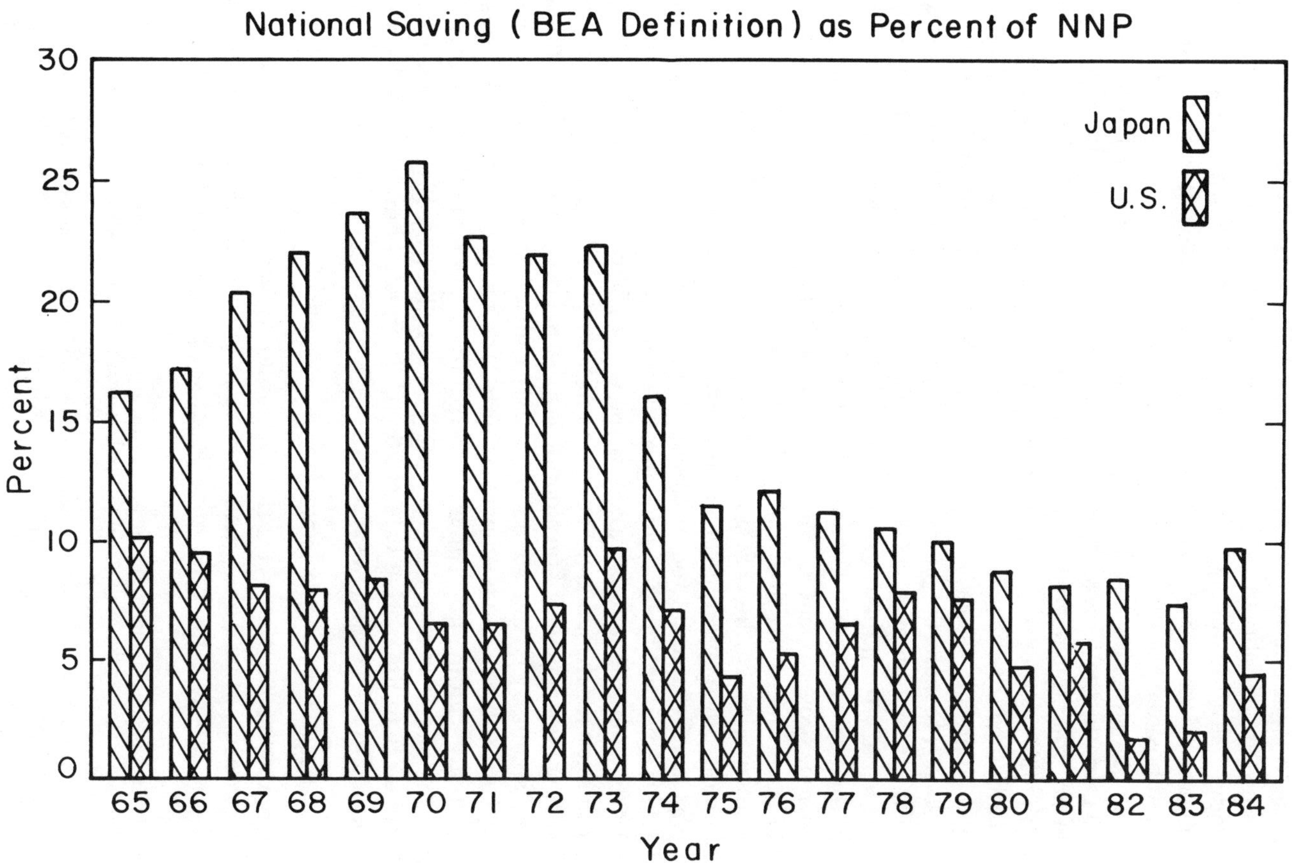

cline in Japan's national saving rate after 1974 is attributable to the large budget deficit shown in figure 4. Government saving, the sum of the budget surplus and net government capital formation, has also been negative since 1976, while reported government saving (not shown) has been positive for all years.

The saving rates displayed thus far do not allow for revaluation or capital gains/losses. This leads to an understatement of saving by net debtors in an inflationary environment. Column (2) in table 1 reports net revaluations—that is, changes in nominal values minus changes in value attributable to changes in the general price level—on private (tangible and financial) assets as a percent of NNP for Japan and the United States.[10] (To make the Japanese data comparable to the U.S. data, I use the BEA convention here.) The huge capital gains and losses for Japan come principally from the value of land, which is over 75 percent of the value of total private assets. Column (3) in table 1 reports the size of the budget surplus (government saving under the BEA definition). Net revaluation of government net financial assets is in column (4). It shows the well-known fact that the U.S. government has gained substantially as a net debtor. Since the ratio of net government financial liabilities to NNP was low in Japan in the inflationary period of the 1970s (the ratio was *minus* 6 percent in 1974) and since the inflation rate has been low in the 1980s when the ratio is rapidly rising (it was 30 percent in 1984), net revaluation for the Japanese government has been small. The total national saving rate inclusive of revaluation is reported in column (5). The number for Japan may be overstated, as it is strongly dependent on the estimate of land value in the national accounts. The value of land in the private sector (excluding government enterprises) at the end of 1984, according to the Japanese national accounts, is 858 trillion yen. It is substantially higher than the market value of the U.S. private land of $3.3 trillion reported in the Federal Reserve's *Balance Sheets*.

2.4. MEASUREMENT OF DEPRECIATION

Coming back to the saving rates without revaluation, the impact of capital consumption adjustments for Japan is most dramatically shown in figure 6 where the ratio of national saving to NNP (with government

10. The household and corporate sectors are already consolidated in table 1, because the data on the market value of equity in the Japanese national accounts seem wholly unreliable. The value of Tobin's q (the ratio of the value of tangible assets at replacement cost to the market value of net financial liabilities) for the corporate sector at the end of 1984 is 0.38 (see table A4). The reported market value of net financial liabilities is less than the reported value of inventory. This low estimate is due to the fact that stocks that are not publicly traded are valued in the Japanese national accounts at their "par" value (a mere 50 yen). By consolidating the household and corporate balance sheets, the prob-

Figure 6 NATIONAL SAVING RATE AND CAPITAL CONSUMPTION ADJUSTMENTS

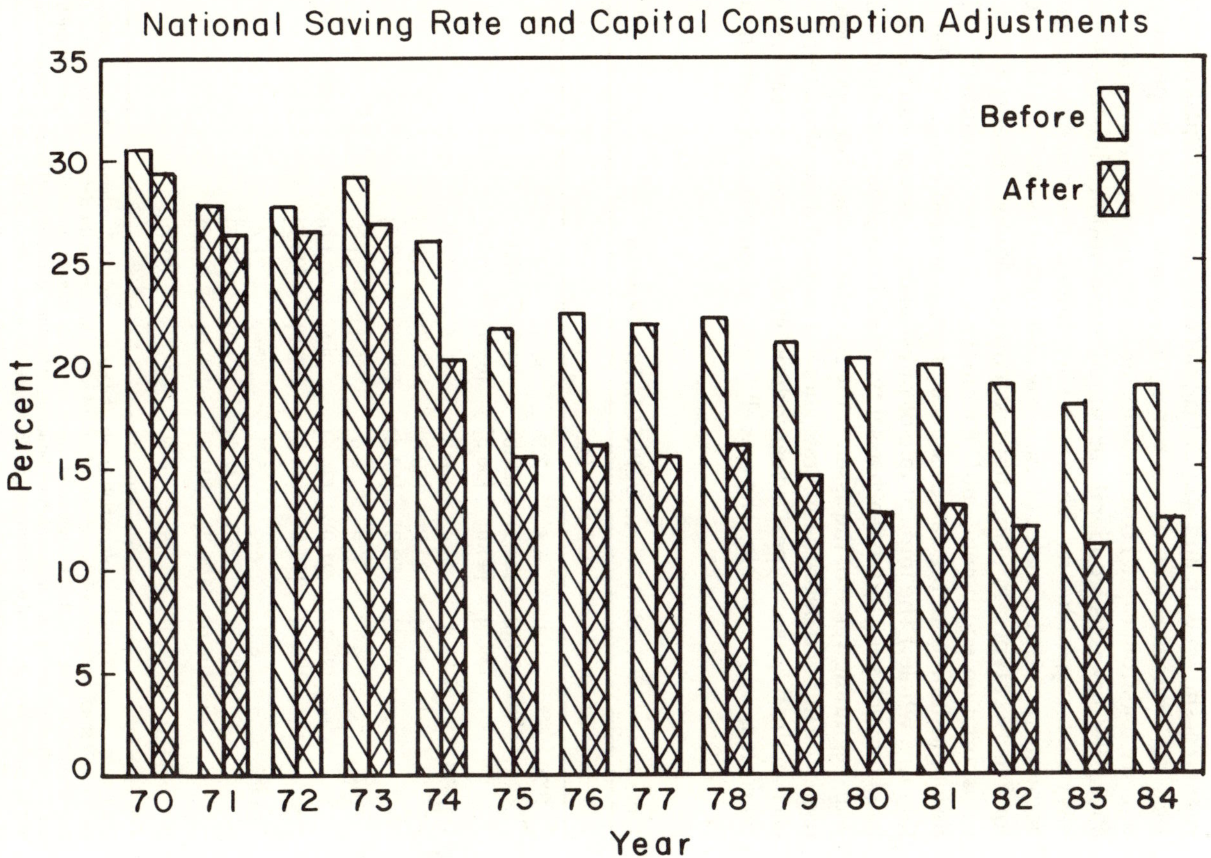

capital) is shown with and without capital consumption adjustments. In 1984 the difference was over 6 percentage points, about 60 percent of which came from capital consumption adjustments on private assets. Its sheer size makes us wonder if our capital consumption adjustments may have been carried too far. The capital accounts in the Japanese national accounts provide estimates of the value of the nation's depreciable assets for five asset types: housing, nonresidential buildings, other structures, transportation equipment, and machinery and other equipment. (The decomposition of depreciable assets by type is available only for the nation as a whole.) The implicit rate of physical depreciation can be calculated for each year and for each asset type as a ratio of depreciation to the year-beginning value of the asset. If the reported value of depreciation is used, the implicit depreciation rate shows a marked downward trend for each of the five asset types, a clear indication that depreciation at historical costs is inappropriate. The overall (asset-weighted) depreciation rate

Table 2 IMPLICIT PHYSICAL DEPRECIATION RATES

Year	*(1)*	*(2)*	*(3)*	*(4)*	*(5)*	*(6)*	*(7)*
1970	9.8	6.8	7.8	54.6	22.8	12.5	13.9
	(20.6)	(24.9)	(29.8)	(4.2)	(20.6)		
	[39.5]	[40.0]	[36.5]	[69.4]	[64.6]		
1975	8.8	6.4	6.3	31.2	20.5	7.3	11.0
	(23.5)	(22.7)	(30.0)	(4.7)	(19.1)		
	[70.1]	[70.3]	[67.4]	[91.0]	[93.7]		
1980	9.1	6.8	6.3	31.8	21.9	6.5	10.6
	(26.1)	(21.9)	(34.6)	(3.4)	(14.0)		
	[95.7]	[94.0]	[93.3]	[96.6]	[95.7]		
1984	8.5	6.4	5.7	30.6	21.4	6.6	9.9
	(23.5)	(22.7)	(37.1)	(3.0)	(13.6)		
	[103.0]	[106.3]	[107.3]	[99.0]	[95.5]		
Average	9.0	6.5	6.6	33.5	21.6		

The first row for each year is the depreciation rate, the second row in parentheses is the value share in the nation's stock of depreciable assets, and the third row in brackets is the deflator for the asset at the beginning of the year. Depreciation rates and shares are in percents. Columns (1)–(5) represent the five asset types: (1) housing, (2) nonresidential buildings, (3) other structures, (4) transportation equipments, and (5) machines and other equipment. The depreciation rates reported in these five columns are net of our capital consumption adjustments. Column (6) shows the overall depreciation rate as reported in the Japanese national accounts. Column (7) is the overall depreciation at replacement costs and government depreciable assets.

Source. Columns (1)–(6) from the *1985 Annual Report on National Accounts* (with our capital consumption adjustment procedure applied to columns (1)–(5)). Column (7) from the Data Appendix.

is reported for selected years in column (6) of table 2. It clearly shows the impact of the 1973–74 inflation.

If our procedure for capital consumption adjustments, briefly described above, is applied to the five asset types to obtain depreciation at *replacement cost*, we obtain the implicit depreciation rates reported in columns (1)–(5) of table 2 along with the asset shares in parentheses and asset price indexes in brackets. The depreciation rate for other structures still shows a downward trend, but it may be attributable to the practice in the Japanese national accounts of not depreciating government assets other than buildings, which also distorts the asset shares in table 2 in favor of structures. (The depreciation for transportation equipment shows a steep downward trend for the first three or four years after 1970. We suspect that the 1970 value of the stock of transportation equipment is understated.) The average depreciation rates in the last rows of columns (1)–(5) do not seem totally out of line with, for example, the average implicit BEA rates reported in Hulten and Wykoff (1981, table 2).[11] Column (7) reports the overall depreciation rate implied by our capital consumption adjustment procedure and implicit in all the saving rates displayed so far. It is not strictly the asset-weighted average of columns (1)–(5) because it is based on our estimate of government capital where the depreciation rate is constrained to be 6.5 percent. It still shows a clear but mild downward trend. This downward trend, which is not apparent in asset-specific depreciation rates in columns (1)–(5), is attributable to the shift in asset value shares in favor of longer-lived assets. This shift in turn is due mainly to the large-scale change in relative asset prices that has continued since at least 1970, shown in brackets. It appears that our capital consumption adjustments are of reasonable magnitude.

We conclude that Japan's aggregate saving rate—however defined—is indeed higher than the comparable U.S. saving rate, but not by as much as is commonly thought. Not only is the level different, but the pattern over time of Japan's saving rate with large peaks and well-defined trends is in sharp contrast to the stationary U.S. pattern. We now turn to the question of how one might explain the difference.

---

lem of a correct valuation of equity can be avoided. This amounts to valuing corporate capital at replacement cost rather than at the market value observed in the financial markets.

11. The average depreciation rates obtained in table 2 are close to the asset life reported in the *1970 National Wealth Survey*. Almost all the available estimates of the capital stock in Japan are based on this periodic official sampling survey of the net capital stock of the nation. The survey has not been conducted since 1970.

3. *A Catalogue of Explanations*

That Japan's personal saving rate is one of the highest in the world was recognized in Japan as early as 1960. A concise survey of the early literature can be found in Komiya (1966). The most recent and most exhaustive survey is Horioka (1985b) which lists over thirty possible factors that might contribute to Japan's high personal saving rate. A striking feature of the Japanese literature is its lack of a neoclassical perspective: the personal saving rate as a fraction of personal disposable income is the center of attention. Also, no attention has been given to the measurement of depreciation which, as we have seen, is very important. This section is a catalogue of explanations of Japan's high saving rate that have been offered in the literature and still enjoy some currency. They will be examined later.

High Income Growth An association of the income growth rate and the saving rate is consistent with several alternative hypotheses of saving. Both the life-cycle hypothesis (with finite lives) and the permanent income hypothesis (with infinite horizon) imply that a temporary rise in the growth rate raises the saving rate. For a permanent increase in the growth rate, the permanent income hypothesis would predict a lower saving rate (if the real interest rate is unchanged). In the life-cycle hypothesis, the initial impact of a permanent increase in the growth rate on the saving rate is probably to lower it, but the long-run impact is a higher saving rate, because older and dissaving generations are, in the long run, outweighed by younger and wealthier generations. The habit persistence hypothesis predicts a positive response of the saving rate to either a permanent or a temporary increase in productivity growth. For Japan the relation between the growth rate and the saving rate is far from clear-cut. Figure 7 contains the graph of the GNP growth rate and the personal saving rate. They tend to move in opposite directions, especially during and shortly after the first oil crisis. This is inconsistent with the habit persistence hypothesis. Comparing figure 7 with figures 3, 5, and 6, we see that the private and the national saving rates are more closely related to GNP growth than the personal rate.

The correlation of the saving rate with the growth rate is actually difficult to interpret because there can be a reverse causation running from saving to growth through capital accumulation. However, the clear prediction by the life-cycle hypothesis that a secularly high growth rate should be associated with a high saving rate could explain Japan's higher saving rate. This will be examined in the next section where we perform a saving rate simulation based on the life-cycle hypothesis.

Figure 7 PERSONAL SAVING RATE, BONUS RATIO AND GNP GROWTH RATE

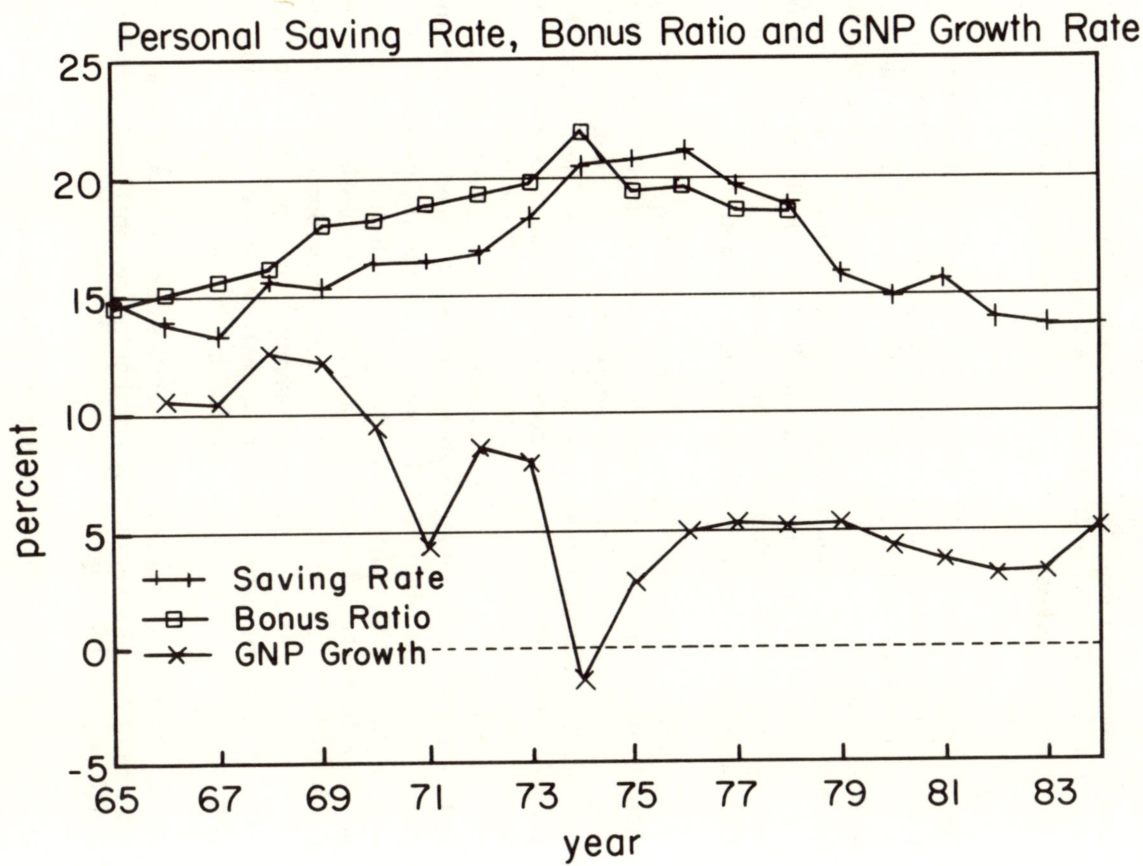

Demographics The proportion of the aged has historically been small in Japan. Also, the life expectancy of the Japanese is now the longest in the world. According to the life-cycle hypothesis, these demographic factors should raise the aggregate saving rate. This, too, will be taken up in the next section.

Underdeveloped Social Security System The reasoning is that because Japan's social security system is underdeveloped people have strong needs to provide for old age by themselves. Japan's social security system has expanded rapidly since 1973. If the household sector is the relevant boundary, this explanation is inconsistent with the data because the personal saving rate actually increased after 1973. The decline in the private saving rate could be explained by the enlarged social security system. The role of social security will be taken up in section 7.

Bonus System In postwar Japan, workers receive large lump-sum payments twice a year. The bonus system originated in large firms and has spread to smaller ones. The amount depends on the profitability of the firm and the industry, although less so in recent years. The evidence that appears to support this bonus hypothesis is that the ratio of bonuses to regular employee compensation is closely related to the personal saving rate, as shown in figure 7. (The data on the bonus ratio is from Ishikawa and Ueda (1984)). The bonus hypothesis was advanced very early and gained popularity when both the bonus ratio and the personal saving rate rose after 1973 and then slowly started to decline. This fact can, however, be explained straightforwardly by a neoclassical perspective that households can see through the corporate veil. Bonuses are a transfer of corporate saving to personal saving. If it is private saving that matters, the bonus ratio should raise personal saving. The bonus hypothesis cannot be an explanation of a high private saving rate.[12]

Tax Incentives The Japanese tax system encourages saving because income from capital is very lightly taxed at the personal level. This issue will be examined in section 8.

High Housing/Land Prices As Horioka (1985a) reports: "The annual Public Opinion Survey on Saving . . . has consistently found that the five most important motives for household saving in Japan are those relating to illness/unexpected disaster, education and marriage, old age, land/

12. Those who receive bonuses and those who own the company's stock are often different. The neoclassical reasoning is that they are linked with operative bequest and gift motives.

housing purchases, and peace of mind. Moreover, a comparison of the Japanese findings and those of a similar U.S. survey shows that the biggest differences are that the motives relating to education and marriage and land/housing purchases are far more important in Japan, while the old age motive is far more important in the United States." As documented in Hayashi, Ito and Slemrod (1985, incomplete), the Japanese had to accumulate probably as much as 40 percent of the purchase price of a house while borrowing the remaining fraction from government loans (subsidized and therefore rationed) and from private financial institutions. The high down-payment ratio and the nondeductibility of interest expense for mortgage borrowing may contribute to high savings by younger generations. Like the first three explanations above, this explanation has life-cycle considerations in mind. Some evidence will be presented in section 5 to gauge the relevance of high housing prices.

Bequests This is probably the least popular explanation in Japan. There is a casual discussion in Shinohara (1983) to the effect that perhaps the Japanese may like to leave large bequests. Horioka (1984), after rejecting the standard life-cycle hypothesis on the basis of household survey data and various opinion surveys, also notes at the end the importance of bequests and their connection to the prevalence of the extended family in Japan. To anticipate, my conclusion is that bequests are probably the most important factor.

Cultural Factors If all else fails, there is a cultural explanation. The Japanese are simply *different*. They are more risk-averse and more patient. If this is true, the long-run implication is that Japan will absorb all the wealth in the world. I refuse to comment on this explanation. Horioka (1985b), after examining various studies that address the cultural issue, concludes that the available evidence is mixed.

4. *Explanation by the Life-cycle Hypothesis*

The life-cycle hypothesis of saving (Modigliani and Brumberg (1954), Ando and Modigliani (1963)) asserts that people's saving behavior is strongly dependent on their age. Aggregate saving can be explained by such demographic factors as age distribution and life expectancy, and such economic factors as the age profile of earnings. The hypothesis is attractive because it generates very specific empirical predictions about aggregate saving if data are available on demographics, the age profile of earnings, and asset holdings. This section performs a standard "steady-state" simulation of aggregate saving under the life-cycle hypothesis.

The steady-state assumption allows us to impute rather than observe the age profile of asset holdings. The profile of asset holdings by the age of a person (rather than by the age of a head of household) is difficult to observe for the case of Japan because of the prevalence of the extended family.

Before getting into the actual simulation, however, a precise definition of the life-cycle hypothesis is in order. Its essential feature, eloquently expounded by Modigliani (1980), is that people are selfish and do not plan to leave bequests. It is this feature which, coupled with the single-peaked age-earnings profile, leads to the prediction that people save to prepare for their retirement. An equally important, but often implicit, assumption is that people can purchase annuities and life insurance at actuarially fair prices. This means (see Barro and Friedman (1977)) there is only one constraint, the lifetime budget constraint, faced by the consumer:

$$\sum_{i=0}^{\infty} q(t,v,i)(1 + r)^{-i}c(t + i,v + i)$$
$$= \sum_{i=0}^{\infty} q(t,v,i)(1 + r)^{-i}w(t + i,v + i) + A(t,v), \quad (1)$$

where $c(t,v)$, $w(t,v)$ and $A(t,v)$ are, respectively, consumption, earnings and initial assets of a consumer aged v at time t. $q(t,v,i)$ is the probability at time t that the consumer of age v survives into period $t + i$. r is the real rate of return. This version will be referred to as the strict life-cycle model.

In the absence of complete annuity markets, perfect insurance, as represented by equation (1), against living "too long" is not available. Involuntary bequests are the price to be paid to self-insure against longevity risk. But, as Kotlikoff and Spivak (1981) point out, longevity risk can be partially insured against if selfish parents "purchase," in exchange for bequests, a promise by children to provide assistance in old age. This class of models may be called the selfish life-cycle model with imperfect insurance.

Other models of saving include the strategic bequest model recently proposed by Burnheim, Shleifer, and Summers (1985) and the model of dynastic altruism of Barro (1974) and Becker (1981). In the latter model parents care about the welfare of their children and thus behave as if their planning horizon is infinite. In the former model, parents are not necessarily altruistic toward their children but use bequests to influence their children's action. I do not here intend to confront all these models with the Japanese data in a formal fashion. Since most of the explanations surveyed in the previous section have the strict life-cycle model in mind, the first order of business is to test it on Japanese data by a simulation technique.

If the strict life-cycle model is applicable to Japan, it should for realistic values of relevant parameter values generate the aggregate saving rate and the wealth-income ratio as observed in Japan. If we take seriously the numbers in the capital accounts of the Japanese national accounts, the ratio of national wealth (including land) to (capital consumption-adjusted) NNP was about 4 in 1970 and about 6 in 1980 (see figure 8, where the inverse of the wealth-NNP ratio is plotted). The inputs to the simulation are: (i) the actual age-earnings profile ($w(t, v)$), (ii) the actual age distribution of the population, (iii) survival probabilities (q), and (iv) a constant annual real rate of return of 4 percent.[13] There are two parameters: the longitudinal consumption growth rate (h) implicit in the age-consumption profile and the secular productivity growth rate (g). Thus the longitudinal consumption profile is assumed to be

$$c(t + i, v + i) = c(t, v)(1 + h)^i, \quad (2)$$

and the prospective earnings profile is

$$w(t + i, v + i) = w(t, v)(1 + g)^i. \quad (3)$$

The potential lifespan is represented by seven ten-year periods. The first period corresponds to ages 20–29 and the last to 80–89. Under the steady-state assumption that earnings and assets of a consumer of given age v grow at a constant rate g over time, we can calculate for each combination of h and g the aggregate saving rate and wealth-NNP ratio.[14]

13. The age-earnings profile is constructed as follows. Earnings by age are taken from the *Basic Survey of Wage Structure* (the Ministry of Labor). They are multiplied by the labor force participation rate taken from the Labor Ministry's *Labor Force Survey*. The earnings for 50–59-year-olds are then multiplied by a factor of 1.18 to accommodate the retirement payments. This factor is calculated from the age-earnings profile displayed in Table 3-24 of the *1985 White Paper on Japanese Economy* (Economic Planning Agency). The survival probability for a cohort in year t in a ten-year age group is calculated as the ratio of the number of the cohort in year $t + 10$ to year t. For 1980, the survival probability is assumed to be the same as in 1970, except for cohorts over 60. For the 60–69-year-olds it is set at (1 − 0.01483)**10, where the number 0.01483 is the death probability for 60–69-year-olds reported in a Ministry of Health and Welfare publication. Similarly for the 70–79-year-olds the survival probability is set at (1 − 0.046045)**10.

14. Our "steady-state" simulation is a mere replication of the analysis in the second half of Tobin's (1967) paper but using Japanese data on the age-earnings profile and the age distribution. To be more concrete, equations (1)–(3) are sufficient to give the prospective consumption and asset holdings profile ($c(t + i, v + i)$ and $A(t + i, v + i)$ for all i)

Table 3 displays the actual age profile of earnings for 1970 and 1980 with the sum normalized to unity, along with the U.S. earnings profile.[15] For lack of data, earnings for those aged 70 and over are set at zero. The share of earnings for ages 20–29 has declined in Japan, mainly due to a decline in the labor force participation rate brought about by the increase in college enrollment. Earnings in Japan peak in the 50–59 age group because of lump-sum retirement payments. It may be argued that the high earnings by those aged 50–59 do not reflect productivity; rather the earnings are a return from implicit saving whose amount equals the excess of true productivity over actual earnings at younger ages. Without the retirement payment adjustment, earnings for groups 40–49 and 50–59 are nearly the same, but the steady-state calculations do not change

for those aged $v = 0$ in period t because for $v = 0$ we have $A(t,0) = 0$ under the selfish life-cycle hypothesis. The steady-state assumption implies that assets held by v-year-olds in period $t + i$ are $(1 + g)^{**}i$ times as large as assets held by v-year-olds in period t. That is, $A(t + i,v) * ((1 + g)^{**}(- i)) = A(t,v)$. This allows us to calculate prospective consumption and asset holdings profile for those who are v years old in period t because their initial assets $A(t,v)$ can be set at $A(t + v,v) * ((1 + g)^{**}(-v))$. The simulation is partial equilibrium in nature, because what is generated is the supply of saving, that is not guaranteed to equal changes in the capital stock. Also note that the aggregate output growth rate depends on the age distribution as well as on the productivity growth rate g. Our simulation does not take taxes and transfers into account. Proportional income taxes will not affect the saving and wealth-income *ratios*. We also do not consider social security, because assumptions about future expected benefits are inevitably arbitrary. If social security is actuarially fair, then it is clear that the size of the social security system does not affect our steady-state calculations of the national saving rate.

15. The U.S. earnings profile is taken from the 1972–73 Consumer Expenditure Survey. It would have been preferable to obtain it from labor market data.

Table 3 AGE DISTRIBUTION OF EARNINGS AND POPULATION

	Earnings						
	20–29	30–39	40–49	50–59	60–69	70–79	80–89
Japan, 1970	0.12	0.22	0.26	0.28	0.13	0.0	0.0
Japan, 1980	0.09	0.22	0.28	0.29	0.13	0.0	0.0
United States, 1972–73	0.17	0.24	0.26	0.22	0.11	0.0	0.0
	Population (Fraction of total population)						
	20–29	30–39	40–49	50–59	60–69	70–79	80–89
Japan, 1970	0.19	0.16	0.11	0.09	0.06	0.03	0.01
Japan, 1980	0.14	0.17	0.14	0.11	0.07	0.04	0.01

See footnote 13 for the source of the Japanese data. The U.S. earnings profile is obtained from the *Consumer Expenditure Survey, 1972–73*, Bureau of Labor Statistics Bulletins 1992 and 1997, Table 3.

Table 4 STEADY-STATE SIMULATION RESULTS

Panel A. Japanese Earnings Profile, Japanese Age Distribution of Population

1970	Saving rate (%)			Wealth-income ratio		
Annual consumption growth (h)	Annual productivity growth			Annual productivity growth		
	0%	5%	10%	0%	5%	10%
h = 0%	3	−81	−680	−0.5	−7.8	−30.4
5%	32	28	−87	6.6	1.2	−4.1
10%	52	66	53	10.0	5.0	1.9

1980	Saving rate (%)			Wealth-income ratio		
Annual consumption growth (h)	Annual productivity growth			Annual productivity growth		
	0%	5%	10%	0%	5%	10%
h = 0%	8	−64	−596	−0.9	−8.9	−35.1
5%	33	27	57	7.0	1.5	−3.9
10%	52	68	60	10.5	5.5	2.3

Panel B. U.S. Earnings Profile, Japanese Age Distribution of Population

1970	Saving rate (%)			Wealth-income ratio		
Annual consumption growth (h)	Annual productivity growth			Annual productivity growth		
	0%	5%	10%	0%	5%	10%
h = 0%	7	−50	−400	1.1	−5.0	−17.9
5%	34	30	−47	7.5	2.2	−2.3
10%	54	70	61	10.6	5.4	2.3

1980	Saving rate (%)			Wealth-income ratio		
Annual consumption growth (h)	Annual productivity growth			Annual productivity growth		
	0%	5%	10%	0%	5%	10%
h = 0%	10	−35	−330	1.6	−5.2	−19.7
5%	34	36	−23	8.5	2.2	−1.9
10%	53	72	67	11.6	6.1	2.8

In Panel B, the actual 1970 Japanese age distribution of population is used for 1970, and the actual 1980 Japanese age distribution of population is used for 1980.

significantly.[16] Table 3 also shows the actual age distribution of the population over the seven age groups. The postwar baby boom generation is now approaching the prime earning ages. There are now more 40–59-year-olds, which should increase the aggregate saving rate.

The steady-state values of the aggregate saving rate and wealth-income ratio expressed at annual rates are shown in table 4. The table suggests several conclusions: Consumption must rise very rapidly through life for the selfish life-cycle model to be consistent with the observed values of the aggregate saving and wealth-income ratios, because the Japanese age-earnings profile is much steeper. To isolate the effect of the earnings profile, Panel B of table 4 displays the simulation result which uses the 1972–73 U.S. earnings profile for both the 1970 and 1980 simulations, but still uses the same actual Japanese age distribution of population. Comparing the saving rates in Panel B with those in Panel A for the same year for each combination of the consumption growth rate and the productivity growth rate, we can see that with the age structure fixed the difference in the earnings profile between the United States and Japan should make the U.S. saving rate *higher*. Looking at Panel B for 1970 and 1980 and thus holding the age profile of earnings fixed, we see that the Japanese demographics also work against the life-cycle hypothesis: it predicts a rising aggregate Japanese saving rate.

Another surprising conclusion is that the saving rate generally *declines* with the productivity growth rate under the Japanese age-earnings profile and demographics. This has a clear and simple explanation. Since earnings are highly skewed toward older ages, quite contrary to the usual textbook picture of hump saving, saving is done primarily by older generations. As the secular productivity growth rate goes up, aggregate saving becomes dominated by a younger and wealthier generation whose saving rate is lower than the saving rate for older generations. It is still true that the *very* old are dissaving, but their weight in the actual age distribution is tiny.

Since a primary source of the failure of the life-cycle model to mimic the observed saving and wealth-income ratios is dissaving by younger generations, the introduction of liquidity constraints may alter the conclusion. The result (not shown) of a simulation in which consumption is constrained not to exceed the sum of income and initial assets indicates that the saving and wealth-income ratios are now higher because the negative saving by the young is constrained from below, but that the de-

16. This is because what is crucial in the simulation turns out to be the steepness of the Japanese age-earnings profile. See Hashimoto and Raisian (1985) for a full documentation on the effect of tenure on earnings in Japan and the United States.

mographics still works clearly against the model and the inverse relation of the aggregate saving rate with the productivity growth rate remains.

5. *Evidence from Household Survey Data*

5.1. HOUSEHOLD SURVEYS

The failure of the steady-state life-cycle simulation to mimic the aggregate saving rate and wealth-income ratio means that the actual Japanese age profiles of consumption and asset holdings differ greatly from the life-cycle predictions. We now examine them in order to locate possible deviations of the Japanese saving behavior from the life-cycle models. To this end, survey data on households grouped by age of head of household are essential. Several household surveys in tabulated form are publicly available in Japan. The *Family Income and Expenditure Survey* (FIES) is a monthly diary survey of about 8,000 households. It has no information on assets and imputed rents and no information on income for households other than the so-called *worker household* (namely, households whose head is on a payroll). The *Family Saving Survey* annually collects data on balances and changes in financial assets and liabilities and pretax annual income. It has no information on expenditures and physical assets. The sample size is less than six thousand, insufficient to give reliable tabulations by age. These two surveys do not cover one-person households. The *National Survey of Family Income and Expenditure* (hereafter National Survey), conducted every five years since 1959, is a very large sample (over 50,000) and covers most types of households (the exceptions are agriculture and fishing). It obtains information through biweekly collection of diaries on expenditures on various items, imputed rent, income, taxes, and financial assets. The shortcoming of this survey is that it covers only three months (September, October, and November) and that except for the pretax income for the twelve-month period ending in November no information is available on monthly income and taxes for nonworker households, which are about 30 percent of the sample. The 1974 and 1979 tapes on individual households have been extensively analyzed by Ando (1985). Our present study uses only the published tabulations in the National Survey Reports.

Table 5A displays some cross-section information for the United States, taken from the *1972–73 Consumer Expenditure Survey.* Table 5B contains similar information for Japan taken from the 1974 National Survey Report. One-person households are counted as a half household in the tabulation for Japan. Since average monthly income and taxes are not available for nonworker households, we show disposable income, consumption expenditure and the saving rate separately for worker households. In-

Table 5A SELECTED FAMILY CHARACTERISTICS, INCOME AND EXPENDITURE BY AGE OF FAMILY HEAD, U.S., 1972–73

	<24	*25–34*	*35–44*	*45–54*	*55–64*	*65+*	*Implied average*	*NIPA average*
Households in the universe (millions)	6.3	14.2	12.0	13.0	11.5	14.3	71.3 (total)	
Family size	1.8	3.2	4.3	3.5	2.3	1.7	2.9	
Persons 65 and over	.0	.0	.0	.1	.1	1.3	.3	
Percent homeowners	9	40	68	73	74	66	59	
Disposable income (thousands)	$5.6	$9.9	$12.2	$13.3	$10.6	$6.3	$9.9	$12.4
Consumption expenditure (thousands)	$6.5	$9.4	$11.0	$11.1	$8.5	$5.4	$8.8	$10.9
Saving rate (%)	−15	5	10	17	20	13	12	8
Market value of owned home (thousands)	$2.2	$11.3	$18.7	$19.4	$17.1	$12.1	$14.3	$11.1

The NIPA averages are the averages implied by the National Income and Product Accounts and the U.S. Balance Sheets for the total number of households of 71.3 million. They are averaged over 1972 and 1973.

Source: Consumer Expenditure Survey, 1972–73, Bureau of Labor Statistics, Bulletins 1992 and 1997, Table 8. *1985 Economic Report of the President*. *Balance Sheets for the U.S. Economy, 1945–84* (Board of Governors of the Federal Reserve System).

Table 5B SELECTED FAMILY CHARACTERISTICS, INCOME AND EXPENDITURE BY AGE OF FAMILY HEAD, JAPAN, 1974

	<24	25–34	35–44	45–54	55–64	65 +	*Implied average*	*NIPA average*
Households in the universe (millions)	1.0	5.4	6.7	4.9	2.5	1.1	21.6 (total)	
Family size	2.2	3.5	4.3	3.9	3.6	3.5	3.8	
No. of older parents	.06	.17	.25	.27	.32	.27	.24	
Percent homeowners	8	37	62	75	81	85	60	
1974 pretax income (millions)	¥2.1	¥2.2	¥2.6	¥3.2	¥3.1	¥2.5	¥2.7	¥3.1
Consumption expenditure (millions)	¥1.6	¥1.7	¥2.0	¥2.2	¥2.0	¥1.7	¥2.0	¥2.3
Net financial assets (millions)	¥.7	¥.9	¥1.3	¥2.2	¥3.3	¥3.6	¥1.7	¥3.3
Market value of owned home (millions)	¥.4	¥1.9	¥3.1	¥3.6	¥3.8	¥3.8	¥2.9	¥9.8
For worker households:								
Disposable income (millions)	¥2.2	¥2.3	¥2.5	¥3.0	¥2.7	¥2.2	¥2.5	
Consumption expenditure (millions)	¥1.6	¥1.8	¥2.0	¥2.3	¥2.1	¥1.7	¥2.0	
Saving rate (%)	25	21	21	21	21	21	21	

As the National Survey does not cover households in agriculture and fishing, the number of households in the universe is 21.6 million (where singles are counted as a half). It is used to calculate the NIPA averages. The 1974 pretax income is for the period from December 1973 to November 1974. The number of older parents living with the head is for worker households.

Source: 1974 National Survey, vol. 1, part 1, Table 6. *1986 Annual Report on National Accounts.*

come and expenditure variables are at annual rates.[17] The value of owned homes (which includes the value of land) is obtained from data on imputed rent assuming that the annual real rate of return is 4 percent and the depreciation rate 1 percent. The definition of disposable income and consumption expenditure is brought closer to the national income definition by using the following formulas:

consumption expenditure = total consumption expenditure
+ income in kind (including imputed rent), (4)

disposable income = total income (including social security benefits and pensions)
+ income in kind (including imputed rent)
− depreciation on owned home (20 percent of imputed rent)
− interest part of loan repayments (6 percent times financial liabilities outstanding). (5)

Unless otherwise stated, this is the definition of disposable income and consumption that we employ throughout the article. Although the remaining conceptual differences make the comparison with the national accounts data more or less meaningless (see Ando (1985) for detailed discussion) it appears from the last two columns of table 5B that the National Survey severely underreports asset values.

From the viewpoint that the private sector or the nation is the relevant boundary, the definition of income should include anticipated capital gains on stocks. We should bear in mind that the saving rate displayed in the tabulations is the personal saving rate, exclusive of revaluations. We know from table 1 that there were large capital losses on private assets in 1974 and large capital gains in 1979. To the extent that some components of revaluation were anticipated, the saving rate for 1974 in table 5B is overstated.

Several differences between the United States and Japan are clearly noticeable from tables 5A and 5B. First, the share in the total universe of households headed by persons 65 and over is very small in Japan. Second, the average number of old people living with younger households is much higher. Third, home-ownership does not decline after the house-

17. Monthly figures averaged over the three-month period of September through November are converted to annual rates by using the seasonality factors reported in the *Annual Reports of the Family Income and Expenditure Survey.*

hold head retires. These are just different aspects of the same important fact about Japan, emphasized in Ando (1985), that elderly parents often invite one of their children (usually the eldest son) and his family to move into their house or, less frequently, the parents move into the younger household. According to the *Basic Surveys for Welfare Administration,* over 80 percent in 1960 and 67 percent in 1983 of persons 65 or over lived with their children. For persons 80 years or over, the proportion was 90 percent in 1983. Thus data such as those given in table 5B organized by age of head of household give only a mixture of the saving behavior by the young and the old. This certainly makes the interpretation of the data less straightforward. We will come back to this issue of household merging shortly.

5.2. HIGH HOUSING/LAND PRICES?

The fourth difference is that the saving rate does not depend very much on age.[18] This could be explained by the saving behavior of the elderly living with younger families, but, as we will see (in table 9, Panel A), the pattern is clearly observed for nuclear families as well. This is why the life-cycle models fail to explain the Japanese saving rate. Fifth, unlike the United States, there is no indication of dissaving by very young households. This can be explained by a combination of liquidity constraints, the extremely high Japanese housing prices, and the high downpayment required to purchase a house.

This brings us to the explanation mentioned in section 3 that the Japanese saving rate is high because the Japanese have to save a great deal to purchase a house whose price is several times their annual income. The National Survey Reports since 1974 have separate tabulations for the three largest metropolitan areas. We can therefore calculate the saving rate separately for urban and rural areas. Since housing prices are much higher in urban areas, the saving rate must be higher as well. We can actually get more information from the National Survey Reports because since 1979 the tabulations are further broken down to three household types: homeowners; renters *without* a plan to purchase a house within the next five years; and renters *with* such a plan.

Table 6 displays the saving rate by region and household type for 1979 and 1984. (As disposable income is not available for nonworker house-

18. This pattern shows up consistently in almost any household survey in Japan for every year. We must, however, be careful about the saving rate for the old. The saving rate is for worker households, which automatically excludes retirees. But table 5B indicates that, for all households whose head is 65 or over, average annual income is 2.5 million yen and average expenditure 1.7 million yen. For those households the average tax rate would be at most 15 percent. Thus their personal saving rate must be over 20 percent.

holds, the saving rate is calculated for worker households only.) As predicted by the housing price hypothesis, the saving rate for renters with purchase plans is several percent over that for other types of households in 1979. However, the saving rate for those who plan to purchase a house in urban areas is about the same as that in rural areas, which suggests that the elasticity of substitution between housing and other forms of consumption may be close to unity. It is not the price of houses per se that is driving the saving rate up. More important are the unavailability of housing loans and the tendency of the Japanese to own, rather than rent, houses despite no tax advantages on mortgage payments. Another piece of evidence in the table unfavorable to the housing-price hypothesis is that the saving rate averaged over household types is, if anything, higher for rural areas, where houses are much cheaper. This underscores the general principle that a high saving rate for the young population by itself does not translate into a high aggregate saving rate. If for some reason or other the young are forced to save more than they otherwise would, the life-cycle hypothesis implies that the involuntary saving will be spent in the later stages of life and thus reduce the saving rate for older generations. The high housing price does not seem to have any relevance in very recent years, because the table shows that for 1984 saving rates are not at all affected by the intent to purchase a house.

5.3. ASSET HOLDINGS BY THE AGED

The prevalence of children living with parents creates two problems that must be borne in mind in analyzing Japanese household survey data. First, as already mentioned, tabulation by age of the household head does not fully reveal the life cycle of a typical person, because of

Table 6 SAVING RATES BY AGE, TYPE AND REGION, WORKER HOUSEHOLDS

	1979		*1984*	
	Urban	Rural	Urban	Rural
1. Homeowners	18	19	18	20
2. Renters without purchase plans	19	19	18	20
3. Renters with purchase plans	25	24	19	21
Average	19	19	18	20

Source: 1979 National Survey Report, vol. 1, part 1, Table 26, and vol. 1, part 2, Table 18. *1984 National Survey Report*.

the presence of the elderly in the extended family. Second, since the household survey defines the head of a household to be the main income earner, there is a sample selection bias, in that heads of extended families in older age groups are high-income people whose earnings are greater than the earnings of their adult offspring in their prime earning ages.

This sample selection bias is particularly relevant when we examine the issue of asset decumulation by the aged, a popular test of the selfish life-cycle models. Table 7 combines two of the tabulations given in Ando's (1985) study. The table is arranged to make it easy to trace over the five-year period of 1974–79 the asset holdings by cohorts defined by five-year age groups. The tabulation is for two-or-more-person households whose head was over 56 in 1974, so both nuclear and extended families are included. Assets here consist of financial assets (excluding the present value of social security benefits), the market value of any owned home (whose main component, of course, is the value of land), and consumer durables. They are stated in 1979 prices. The mean asset holdings do not decline as cohorts age. The essential aspect of the life-cycle models does not seem to hold. This, however, is a premature conclusion, for three reasons. The first is probably familiar to American researchers, while the other two are specific to the prevalence of the extended family. First,

Table 7 AGE PROFILE OF ASSET HOLDINGS BY OLDER TWO-OR-MORE-PERSON HOUSEHOLDS, 1974 AND 1979

	Age of head in 1974			
1974	56–60	61–65	66–70	71–75
Sample size	1572	1418	927	553
Mean	1946	1936	1815	1813
First quantile	1185	1153	1095	1107
Second quantile (median)	1760	1755	1662	1660
Third quantile	2455	2456	2293	2323
	Age of head in 1979			
1979	61–65	66–70	71–75	76–80
Sample size	1623	1187	615	245
Mean	1971	1839	1865	1847
First quantile	1160	1038	1080	965
Second quantile (median)	1785	1565	1636	1515
Third quantile	2512	2351	2398	2291

In ten thousands of 1979 yen.

Source: Ando (1985).

poor people at the lower end of the 1974 asset distribution are more likely to die and thus disappear from the asset distribution for 1979. Second, of old nuclear families, poor ones may be more likely to disappear as they are merged into younger households. Third, by the very design of the survey, older household heads of extended families are the ones who still dominate their sons in terms of income. This is the sample selection bias mentioned above.

For these reasons the lower end in the 1974 asset distributions becomes tapered as time goes on. However, it should still be the case that if the old are decumulating, the upper ends of the asset distribution shift to the left. For those who were 56–60 years old in 1974, there is no attrition in the first place because the sample sizes for 1974 and 1979 are about the same. Thus simply comparing the mean is enough to conclude that there is no asset decumulation. For the 61–65-year-olds in 1974, there is a slight reduction in the sample size (from 1,418 to 1,187), and the whole upper end seems to have shifted to the left between 1974 and 1979. But the shift is very small—averaging across quartiles less than 10 percent over five years. For the 66–70-year-olds the sample size declines by a third over the five-year period. If assets were neither accumulated nor decumulated, the 1979 second quantile should be somewhere between the 1974 second and third quantiles. But in the table the 1979 second quantile is actually less than the 1974 quantile, indicating that asset decumulation may have occurred. We get the same conclusion for the 71–75-year-olds. Thus, there is some evidence of slight asset decumulation by the old. We hasten to add, however, that the conclusion is based on the assumption of no attrition for the upper end of the asset distribution. Also, the sample size for the very old may not be large enough to deem the quantile estimates reliable.

5.4. IMPORTANCE OF BEQUESTS

Thus, the evidence on old persons maintaining independent households with or without their children is not very favorable to the selfish life-cycle models. Does the same conclusion apply to the elderly living with younger generations—the majority of the older population in Japan? Ando (1985) claims that there is strong evidence that they decumulate assets. He drew this conclusion from an equation explaining asset holdings for preretirement households. The equation shows a positive effect on household assets of the presence of the elderly in the household. This by itself is not surprising because when older parents retire they bring previously accumulated assets to younger households. What is significant is that the positive effect rapidly declines as the age of the older person increases. However, it seems that Ando's conclusion is premature because it ignores the role of bequests.

The saving behavior of the elderly living with younger generations can be inferred from a comparison of the nuclear family with the extended family. Table 8 displays the age profile of pretax income, expenditure, and financial asset holdings for 1979 and 1984. Because the tabulation in the 1979 and 1984 National Survey Reports by family type (nuclear and extended) do not show income in kind and imputed rent by age, consumption expenditure and income in the table are not adjusted for it. The market value of owned homes cannot be estimated, either. Taxes also are not shown because the National Surveys have no data on taxes for nonworker households. The profiles for nuclear families are in Panel A, and the profiles for extended families (households with adults of more than one generation) are in Panel B. One-person households are counted as half a nuclear household.[19] If entries in Panel A are subtracted from the corresponding entries in Panel B, we obtain Panel C. It therefore contains the difference in income, expenditure, and assets brought about by the presence of older parents. Consistent with Ando's conclusion, financial assets attributable to the elderly start to decline as we move to the right across age groups in Panel C.[20] This pattern of asset *decumulation* by the elderly, however, is inconsistent with the low expenditure relative to income shown in Panel C. Although table 8 shows pretax income, similar tabulations (not shown) based on disposable income for worker households indicate that the average tax rate is somewhere between 13 percent and 17 percent depending on age and family type and is somewhat higher for nuclear families. Thus if the pretax income is multiplied by 0.85 it serves as a lower bound for the difference in personal disposable income (though not adjusted for income in kind). Comparison of this estimate of disposable income and consumption expenditure

19. At the time of writing, the 1984 National Survey Report was not yet published, but I was given access to the 1984 tabulations in computer printout form. The tabulation for 1984 in table 8 does not take single-person households into account. It would make little difference to the results.

20. The difference in financial assets for the 20–29 age group in Panel C is small for the sample selection bias I have mentioned. Because the survey defines the household head to be the main income earner, older persons in a young extended family where the household head is the son tend to be low-income people, unable to earn more than 20–29-year-olds do. Their contribution to household assets is therefore small. Because table 8 is a cross-sectional tabulation of assets, we must also be aware of the cohort effect due to economic growth that asset holdings by v-year-olds in year $t + i$ are $(1 + g)^{**}i$ times as large as asset holdings by v-year-olds in year t, where g is the long-term growth rate. The cross-sectional decline in asset holdings reported in Panel C of the table is too steep to be accounted for by the growth factor, however.

Table 8 AGE PROFILE OF INCOME, EXPENDITURE, AND ASSET HOLDINGS BY FAMILY TYPE, ALL HOUSEHOLDS, 1979 AND 1984

1979, Panel A (nuclear)	*20–29*	*30–39*	*40–49*	*50–59*	*60+*
Households in the universe (millions)	1.7	6.1	5.3	3.1	1.1
Family size	3.0	3.8	3.9	3.2	2.5
Pretax income	3545	4278	5356	6243	4917
Consumption expenditure	2614	2917	3515	3863	2865
Net financial assets	2086	1247	3052	6512	8604
Panel B (extended)					
Households in the universe	0.1	1.3	1.5	0.8	0.4
Family size	4.6	5.4	5.3	4.5	5.5
Pretax income	4792	5188	5999	6728	7179
Consumption expenditure	3016	3314	3954	4005	3794
Net financial assets	1851	3148	4753	7326	8860
Panel C (Panel B – Panel A)					
Family size	1.6	1.6	1.4	1.4	2.9
Pretax income	1247	911	643	485	2262
Consumption expenditure	401	397	439	142	929
Net financial assets	765	1901	1701	814	256

1984, Panel A (nuclear)	*20–29*	*30–39*	*40–49*	*50–59*	*60+*
Households in the universe	1.3	6.2	6.0	4.2	1.5
Family size	2.9	3.8	3.9	3.1	2.5
Pretax income	3650	4555	5740	6446	5550
Consumption expenditure	2625	2955	3565	3843	3148
Net financial assets	1088	829	1967	6177	10174
Panel B (extended)					
Households in the universe	0.1	1.4	1.9	1.4	0.6
Family size	4.6	5.4	5.4	4.6	5.3
Pretax income	4842	5662	6452	6960	6915
Consumption expenditure	3249	3348	3887	4085	3447
Net financial assets	1304	3224	4489	7124	7841
Panel C (Panel B – Panel A)					
Family size	1.7	1.7	1.5	1.5	2.8
Pretax income	1191	1108	712	513	1365
Consumption expenditure	624	393	321	243	309
Net financial assets	215	2395	2522	947	−2334

Income, expenditure and assets in thousands of 1984 yen. Income and expenditure are not adjusted for income in kind. Pretax income is for the period from December of the previous year to November of the current year.

Source: 1979 National Survey Report, vol. 1, part 1, Table 23. *1984 National Survey Report*.

in Panel C indicates that the elderly in younger extended households are *accumulating*. Put differently, then, how is it that nuclear families are accumulating assets so rapidly without the help of parents?

Our answer is that nuclear families do receive help from their parents—in the form of *bequests*. As we move to the right across age groups in Panel C, both parents and children (heads of household) get older. More and more parents die as they get older. If parents in an extended family leave bequests, the extended family turns into a nuclear family with additional assets. Furthermore, as the head of a nuclear family gets older, more and more parents who maintain independent households die and leave bequests, not to extended families, but to the nuclear family. In short, for middle-aged and older families, being an extended family is more like a signal of not yet having received bequests. The next section formalizes this argument to arrive at the flow of intergenerational transfers.

6. *Calculation of Intergenerational Transfers*

The sharp contrast between positive saving and declining assets shown in Panel C suggests a substantial amount of intergenerational transfers. We digress in this section to evaluate the quantitative importance of bequests. Since saving and asset holdings by age in 1979 are given in table 8, we can calculate asset holdings by age in 1984 that would have been obtained through saving accumulated over the five-year period 1979–84 in addition to the 1979 asset were it not for intergenerational transfers. (This calculation becomes rather complicated because within each age group there are inflows and outflows of households between the nuclear and extended families.) The difference between the actual and predicted 1984 asset holdings is then attributable to transfers. Aggregating transfers over age groups of recipients, we arrive at an estimate of the aggregate flow of transfers over the 1979–84 period. Clearly, this procedure captures only *intergenerational* rather than *intragenerational* transfers. It is the former that we are most interested in. And the captured flow of transfers would include bequests as well as gifts *inter vivos*.

This simple idea cannot be implemented for the 1979–84 period, though. For one thing, table 8 presents data by ten-year age groups, whereas we need tabulations organized by five-year groups. Second, the table gives no information on real assets. The value of owned homes is by far the most important household wealth in Japan. Fortunately, the 1969 and 1974 National Survey Reports do give such needed information, albeit only for worker households.[21] The age profiles of disposable income, consumption expenditures, and the sum of financial assets and the market value of owned homes are displayed in table 9 for 1969 and 1974. As in table 7, the tabulation for the second year in table 9 is shifted to the left by five years for tracking cohorts. For example, the saving rate for a typical nuclear family whose head was 25 to 29 years old in 1969 is 17 percent. Moving down vertically in the same column across panels, we see that five years later its saving rate is 21 percent. To eliminate the sample selection bias that parents (who are also the household heads) in older extended families are rich while parents (who are not the household heads) in younger extended families are relatively poor, extended families in the 55–59 group are put into the 25–29 group, the 60–64 group into the 30–34 group, and the 65-and-over group into the 35–39 group. This is why data for 1974 for cohorts in the 50–54 age group in 1969 get lost and are not shown in table 9. This means that we cannot calculate transfers going to the households in the 1969 50–54 group.

A somewhat detailed description of the calculation of the flow of intergenerational transfers is as follows. Households are classified into three categories:

(a) young nuclear, whose head was under 55 in 1969 (and under 60 in 1974),
(b) young extended, whose younger generation was under 55 in 1969 (and hence under 60 in 1974),
(c) old independent, whose head was 55 or over in 1969 (and 60 or over in 1974, or may have disappeared due to death or household merging by 1974).

As one-person households are counted as a half of (a), all households except for single-parent households (whose number is small and which are ignored in our calculation) fall into one of the three categories. Households in (a) and (b) are further classified by five-year age groups according to the age in 1969. Thus table 9 contains the income, consumption and asset information for (a) and (b). Let $W(i,j,t)$ and $S(i,j,t)$ be the average total wealth and saving (at 1974 prices) of households of type i

21. The tabulations by age and family type (nuclear and extended) in the 1969 and 1974 National Survey Reports have no separate listing of imputed rent, although income in kind is listed. The tabulation by age alone does list imputed rent, which shows a more or less stable proportion to food expenditure across age. This proportion is used to separate out imputed rent from income in kind. Disposable income and consumption expenditure are then calculated by the formulas (4) and (5) in section 5.

Table 9 AGE PROFILE OF INCOME, EXPENDITURE, AND ASSET HOLDINGS BY FAMILY TYPE, WORKER HOUSEHOLDS, 1969 AND 1974

	Age in 1969					
1969, Panel A (nuclear)	*25–29*	*30–34*	*35–39*	*40–44*	*45–49*	*50–54*
Households in the universe	1.4	1.6	1.7	1.4	0.9	0.7
Family size	2.7	3.4	3.8	3.9	3.8	3.6
Percent homeowners	15	29	41	51	56	63
Disposable income	1765	1729	1913	2133	2302	2432
Consumption expenditure	1460	1460	1606	1786	1945	2039
Saving rate (%)	17	16	16	16	16	16
Total assets	1640	2574	3124	3805	4027	4894
Panel B (extended)						
Households in the universe	0.2	0.3	0.4	0.4	0.2	0.1
Family size	4.6	5.1	5.3	5.3	5.2	5.1
Percent homeowners	79	76	79	78	78	80
Disposable income	2033	2100	2158	2348	2570	2695
Consumption expenditure	1791	1899	1867	2016	2271	2319
Saving rate (%)	12	10	13	14	12	14
Total assets	4921	4844	4866	5209	6073	5799
Panel C (Panel B – Panel A)						
Family size	1.9	1.7	1.5	1.5	1.4	1.4
Disposable income	268	371	244	215	269	262
Consumption expenditure	331	439	261	230	326	280
Saving rate (%)	−24	−18	−7	−7	−21	−7
Total assets	3282	2270	1742	1404	2046	905

	Age in 1969					
1974, Panel A (nuclear)	*25–29*	*30–34*	*35–39*	*40–44*	*45–49*	*50–54*
Households in the universe	2.2	2.1	1.8	1.5	0.9	—
Family size	3.6	3.9	3.9	3.7	3.3	—
Percent homeowners	33	46	56	67	70	—
Disposable income	2218	2393	2641	2916	2954	—
Consumption expenditure	1746	1887	2064	2320	2291	—
Saving rate (%)	21	21	22	20	22	—
Total assets	2480	3048	3770	4732	5237	—
Panel B (extended)						
Households in the universe	0.5	0.5	0.5	0.4	0.3	—
Family size	5.2	5.5	5.4	5.1	4.8	—
Percent homeowners	88	89	90	91	89	—
Disposable income	2854	2759	2888	3205	3209	—
Consumption expenditure	2206	2260	2324	2554	2528	—
Saving rate (%)	23	18	20	20	21	—
Total assets	6473	6226	6528	6750	7018	—
Panel C (Panel B − Panel A)						
Family size	1.6	1.6	1.5	1.4	1.4	—
Disposable income	636	366	248	289	255	—
Consumption expenditure	459	373	260	234	237	—
Saving rate (%)	28	−2	−5	19	7	—
Total assets	3993	3178	2757	2019	1782	—

Income, expenditure and assets in thousands of 1974 yen. The number of households in millions. Income and expenditure are adjusted for income in kind and imputed rent. Total assets are the sum of net financial assets and the market value of owned homes. Data for the 50–54 age bracket for 1974 are not given, because they are added to the 25–29 bracket.

Source: 1969 National Survey Report, vol. 1, Table 17. *1974 National Survey Report*, vol. 1, Tables 6 and 21.

($i = a,b$) in age group j ($j = 1$ for the 25–29 group, $j = 2$ for the 30–34, and so forth) in year t. Let $N(i,j,t)$ be the number of such households. If $p(i,k;j)$ is the fraction of households in the (i,j) cell in year t (= 1969) moving into the $(k,j + 1)$ cell in $t + 1$ (= 1974), we have, for each age band j,

$$N(a,j + 1,t + 1) = N(a,j,t)p(a,a;j) + N(b,j,t)p(b,a;j), \quad (6)$$

where we assume that young households never disappear. We assume that the flow of saving in real terms is constant over the five-year period for each type of household. If $L(i,j,t)$ is the predicted wealth (stated at 1974 prices) of a typical household in the (i,j) cell in year t that can be accounted for by accumulated saving on top of initial assets in year t, it can be written as[22]

$$L(i,j,t) = 5.0 * S(i,j,t) + W(i,j,t). \quad (7)$$

Thus the aggregate flow of intergenerational transfers is

$$\begin{aligned} TR = & \sum_j N(a,j + 1,1974)W(a,j + 1,1974) \\ & - \sum_j N(a,j,1969)p(a,a;j)L(a,j,1969) \\ & - \sum_j N(b,j,1969)p(b,a;j)L(b,j,1969), \quad (8) \end{aligned}$$

where all the wealth variables $W(a,j + 1,1974)$, $L(a,j,1969)$ and $L(b,j,1969)$ are stated in 1974 prices. The first sum is actual aggregate wealth held in year $t + 1$ (= 1974) by all households of type (a). The second sum is the wealth accumulated through saving by households that stayed in (a), and the third sum represents the wealth of households which moved from (b) to (a) during the 1969–74 period. Here $S(b,j,t)$ and $W(b,j,t)$ are those that are attributable to the younger generation in the extended family. Note that intergenerational transfers occur only from (c) to (a) or from (b) to (a).

22. In equation (7) it is not necessary to multiply $S(i,j,t)$ or $W(i,j,t)$ by $(1 + r)$, where r is the real rate of return, because $S(i,j,t)$ already incorporates the return from assets as it is defined as disposable income less consumption. If $S(i,j,t)$ were defined as after-tax labor income less consumption, then the interest rate adjustment would have been necessary. During the early 1970s revaluation of assets was substantial (see table 1). In the actual calculation of $L(i,j,t)$, we multiplied $S(i,j,t)$ by a factor of 2.13. This factor translates net saving to saving inclusive of net revaluation. To calculate this factor, we first calculate annual personal net saving and net revaluation at 1974 prices, and then take the averages over the 1970–74 period. The factor is the ratio of the sum of average real net saving (14.5 trillion in 1974 yen) and average real net revaluation (16.4 trillion) to the average real net saving.

Table 9 gives data on: $N(i,j,t)$ ($i = a,b$; $t = 1969, 1974$), $S(a,j,1969)$ and $W(a,j,t)$ ($t = 1969, 1974$) for each j. To estimate $S(b,j,1969)$ and $W(b,j,1969)$, we have to divide the saving and wealth of the extended family between the younger generation and the older generation. We assume the elderly neither accumulate nor decumulate. Thus their saving is zero (so that $S(b,j,1969) = S(a,j,1969)$ for all j). For the 25–29 age group $W(b,j,1969)$ equals $W(a,j,1969)$, so that from Panel C for 1969 we see the asset holdings by the elderly in the 25–29 group to be 3,282 thousand yen (in 1974 prices). Assuming a productivity growth rate of 5 percent, asset holdings by the elderly in the 30–34 group are then this 3,282 thousand multiplied by (1 − .05)**5, which enables us to calculate $W(b,j,t)$ for this age group, and so forth. Finally, the values for S and W are blown up to agree with the implied aggregate averages to account for the underreporting noted in table 5B. Data on $p(b,a;j)$ can be obtained from the 1969 mortality table assuming that parents are thirty years older than their children. (If there are two parents in the extended family, $p(b,a,j)$ should be the probability that *both* parents die within five years.) We are thus assuming that an extended family becomes a nuclear family only when the dependent elderly die. Using equation (6), $p(a,a;j)$ can be calculated from $p(b,a;j)$. This completes the description of the calculation procedure.

There is one problem of head counting: the number of nuclear families in the 30–39 age group in 1974 is too large to be accounted for by the number of extended and nuclear families in the 25–34 group in 1969. (We see from table 8 that the same phenomenon happened between 1979 and 1984.) Without further information, it is impossible to resolve the question of where those extra nuclear families came from. We decided to ignore this 1969 25–34 group in the summation in equation (8). We have already discarded the 1969 50–54 age group. This leaves only three age groups for 1969: 35–39, 40–44 and 45–49. Thus our aggregation captures only a part of aggregate flow of transfers.

The result is that aggregate wealth held by worker nuclear households in 1974 in the 40–54 age group stood at 78.0 trillion yen.[23] Of that, the amount that was accumulated by saving by those households since 1969 in addition to their 1969 wealth holdings was 70.0 trillion yen. The flow

23. From Panel A for 1974 in table 9 the stock of aggregate total assets for the 1974 40–54 age group (i.e., the 1969 35–49 group) is: 1.8 * 3.770 + 1.5 * 4.732 + 0.9 * 5.237 = 18.6. If this is multiplied by a factor of 3.55, we arrive at 66 trillion yen. The factor of 3.55 is to adjust for the underreporting already mentioned. If we compare this factor with the information given in the last two columns of table 5B, the factor seems a bit too large. The factor one can calculate from table 5B for financial assets is 3.3/1.7 = 1.9 and for houses it is 9.8/2.9 = 3.4. But table 5B is for all households. If the similar calculation is done for worker households and the asset-weighted average over financial assets and houses is taken, one comes out with the factor of 3.55.

of transfers was thus 8 trillion yen. If this is adjusted by the fraction of worker households in the universe, we arrive at an annual flow of 11.5 trillion. Compared with the 1974 year-end aggregate private wealth of 598 trillion, it looks small. Our calculation thus captures only a part of the total flow of intergenerational transfers. Moreover, looking at the tabulation for 1969 in table 9, we note from Panel C negative savings and not-so-rapidly declining total assets. Thus the year 1969 might have been a poor (though inevitable) choice. Our calculations also rely on the average total asset holdings for the 25–29 age group in 1969. But that average may be unreliable, since the estimated number of households in that cell is small. Thus, our estimate should be taken as a very loose lower bound for the true aggregate flow of intergenerational transfers.

7. *Intergenerational Transfers*

The evidence already presented points to the importance of intergenerational transfers. Their implication for the aggregate saving rate, however, depends critically on whether or not they are based on intergenerational altruism. Even if parents are not altruistic toward their children, they still leave bequests if they die prematurely (accidental bequests); bequests are used as payments to children for their service rendered to care for older parents; or parents hold wealth in bequeathable form to influence their children's action. In any of the three models the implications of the standard life-cycle model for the saving rate would still hold. Although it is difficult to draw a firm conclusion from the data at our disposal about the nature of bequests, the following pieces of evidence seem largely consistent with intergenerational altruism.

Saving by Retirees Japan's social security system was greatly expanded in 1973. It is now essentially a pay-as-you-go system. Quite likely, this large-scale transfer of resources from the young to the old engineered by the government was not anticipated. The average annual old age benefit per person covered by the annuity benefit program for those employed in the private sector (*Kosei Nenkin*, the largest public annuity program) is 538 thousand yen in 1974 and 1,360 thousand in 1983, an increase in real terms of 53 percent. The model of dynastic altruism predicts that this increase will be entirely saved by the old to offset the government-engineered transfer. It is supported by the fact observable from a comparison of income and consumption in Panel C of table 9 with Panel C of table 8 that the saving attributable to the elderly in extended families appears to have increased in several recent years. This is inconsistent with the selfish life-cycle models, which predict that the increase in annuities will be consumed.

Does this conclusion favorable to dynastic altruism also apply to older persons maintaining independent households? Since 1969 the National Survey Reports have data on pretax annual income, consumption expenditure, and assets of retired couples where the husband is 65 or over and the wife is 60 or over. They are shown in table 10. The personal saving rate shows no tendency to increase, which appears inconsistent with dynastic altruism. But for older households revaluation of assets may be an important component of income. For 1974 and 1979, there is a great deal of uncertainty in estimating net revaluation (revaluation excluding change in value attributable to general inflation) that might have been perceived by the households over the three-month period of September through November, because as reported in the table (and also in table 2) price changes were so large. The real price of housing was more or less

Table 10 SAVING BEHAVIOR OF RETIRED OLDER COUPLES

	1969	*1974*	*1979*	*1984*
Sample size	242	407	653	951
Percent homeowners	80	81	81	86
Percent of pension recipients	n.a.	n.a.	n.a.	94
Pretax income	1494	1907	2278	2457
Consumption expenditure	1082	1468	1872	1899
Income in kind (incl. imputed rent)	285	302	n.a.	n.a.
Value of owned home	4581	5059	n.a.	n.a.
Net financial assets	4934	5566	6934	8684
General inflation rate (%)	5.1	22.9	4.7	2.4
Rate of change of deflator for the stock of houses	n.a.	7.7	13.7	2.2
Rate of change of deflator for housing investment	4.1	19.8	12.8	2.3
Saving rate (%)	28	23	18	23
Saving rate with revaluation	13	?	?	16

Income, expenditure and assets in thousands of 1984 yen. Income and expenditure are not adjusted for income in kind. Pension recipients are defined as couples whose main source of income is a public or private pension. The saving rate does not take taxes into account. The saving rate with revaluation includes in income net revaluation of net financial assets. It is not calculated for 1974 and 1979 because of the uncertainty about the size of net revaluation of owned homes.

Source: 1969 National Survey Report, vol. 1, Table 24. *1974 National Survey Report,* vol. 1, Table 27. *1979 National Survey Report,* vol. 7, Table 16. *1984 National Survey Report. 1986 Report on National Accounts.*

constant in 1969 and 1984, so that net revaluation of an owned home can be ignored. If only the net revaluation of financial assets is taken into account, the saving rate is 13 percent in 1969 and 16 percent in 1984. Still, the sharp increase in saving predicted by dynastic altruism is absent.

It may be that, as conjectured in Ando (1985), the saving behavior of older persons who maintain independent households is different from that of older persons living with their children. This is perhaps not surprising. It is hard to imagine that social security has any big impact on the consumption behavior of the elderly in the extended family, because there must be some in-house sense of proportion regarding consumption within the extended family. If social security benefits for older parents are raised with a simultaneous increase in the social security tax on their children living under the same roof, older parents, even without a strong sense of altruism toward their children, would find it morally hard to raise their spending at their children's expense.

Euler Equation There is another way to examine the impact of social security on the consumption behavior by the aged. Every five years since 1959 the National Survey Reports have tabulations by age where the age groups are also five years. As we did in table 9, we can track from year t to $t + 1$ a cohort in the jth 5-year age group in year t by looking at the $(j + 1)$th age group in year $t + 1$. For example, a cohort in the 20–24 age group in 1969 was in the 25–29 age group in 1974. If $C(j,t)$ and $Y(j,t)$ are consumption and disposable income of a representative cohort in age group j in year t, we can get from the National Survey Reports data on $C(j,t)$ and $Y(j,t)$ for $j = 1$ (20–24-year-olds), 2 (25–29-year-olds), . . . , 9 (60–64-year-olds) (nine age groups) and for $t = 1959, \ldots, 1984$ (six time points). Thus the synthetic cohort analysis as done by Browning, Deaton and Irish (1985) is feasible here. For each cohort, we assume that the Euler equation applies:

$$\ell nC(j + 1,t + 1) - \ell nC(j,t) = a + b\, r_t + e(j,t). \quad (9)$$

Here, the left-hand side is the growth rate of consumption from year t to $t + 1$. When interest rates are high, it pays to reduce consumption now relative to future consumption. Thus the consumption growth rate should increase with the expected real rate r_t. This r_t is the expectation as of year t of $\ell n[(1 + R_t)P_t/P_{t+1}]$, where R_t is the nominal rate on a 5-year bond and P is the price index. The sum of the first two terms on the right-hand side, $a + br_t$, is the planned rate of consumption growth. But actual growth can differ from the planned rate, perhaps because the interest rate forecast proved to be wrong, or because earnings change unexpectedly over the period t through $t + 1$. The last term $e(j,t)$ represents those unexpected developments happening to cohort j. As the 1973 expansion of Japan's social security system was an unexpected development that transferred resources from younger generations to older generations, the selfish life-cycle hypothesis predicts that consumption growth from year 1969 to 1974 for older cohorts should be greater than $a + br_t$ and their $e(j,t)$ positive.

As we have data on $C(j,t)$ for six time points (1959, 1964, 1969, 1974, 1979, and 1984), the consumption growth rate can be calculated for five consecutive periods. Thus the sample size for estimating equation (9) is 45 (five times nine age groups). Growth rates and interest rates are stated at annual rates. Because the Euler equation presupposes that expenditure is perishable, we use food expenditure for consumption. Table 11 reports various regression results. In all regressions, AGE (1 for 20–24-year-olds, 2 for 25–29-year-olds, and so forth) and AGE squared are included to account for possible age differences in the intercept term a in equation (9). Equation (9) is estimated in Regression 1. The actual real rate is used in place of r_t. It picked a wrong sign. In Regression 2, to

Table 11 ESTIMATION OF EULER EQUATION ON SYNTHETIC COHORT DATA

Regression #	*Real rate of interest*	*Social security dummy*	*Log of real disposable income*	R^2	*Other included variables*
1	−0.14	—	—	0.55	AGE, AGE^2
	(1.8)				
2	−0.29	−0.024	—	0.61	AGE, AGE^2
	(3.0)	(2.4)			
3	−0.027	—	−0.043	0.79	AGE, AGE^2
	(0.5)		(6.8)		
4	−0.098	−0.011	−0.041	0.80	AGE, AGE^2
	(1.3)	(1.4)	(6.2)		
5	—	−0.013	—	0.84	AGE, AGE^2,
		(1.9)			time dummies
6	—	—	−0.13	0.89	AGE, AGE^2,
			(4.9)		time dummies
7	—	−0.010	−0.12	0.90	AGE, AGE^2,
		(1.8)	(4.7)		time dummies

All variables are stated at annual rates. The dependent variable is the growth rate of real food expenditure over five-year periods. Real disposable income is the ratio of nominal disposable income to the food component of the CPI. The nominal rate used to construct the real rate is the rate on 5-year discount bonds issued by financial institutions. The price index used to calculate the real interest rate is the food component of the CPI. See the text for the definition of the social security dummy. Numbers in parentheses are the t values. The data source is the National Survey Reports.

examine the impact of the unexpected 1973 expansion of the social security system, a dummy variable which takes a value of unity for cohorts over 44 years of age for the 1969–74 period is added to the equation. It also has a negative coefficient, which means, contrary to the life-cycle prediction, that the 1973 change *reduced* consumption by older generations.

In regressions 3 and 4, the log of disposable income, $\ell n Y(j,t)$, is included to test for liquidity constraints with or without the social security dummy. If people wish to borrow to finance current consumption but are prevented from doing so, a higher level of disposable income leads to an increase in current consumption, thereby reducing the consumption growth over the following five years. Thus if there are liquidity constraints, the disposable income variable should pick up a negative coefficient, which is what is happening in regressions 3 and 4. The social security dummy still picks up negative coefficients.

For the expected real rate r_t, we have used the actual real rate. This amounts to conferring on consumers perfect foresight about future prices and thus may be unrealistic. Regressions 5–7 use time dummies in place of the actual real rate. Thus the $a + br_t$ term in equation (9) can change its value over the five periods, reflecting changes in the expected real rate and possibly economywide shocks that affect all generations uniformly. Again, the disposable income coefficients are significantly negative and the social security dummy picks up the "wrong" sign.

The Extended Family and Bequests Finally, the fact that most older parents invite their children to move in has two further implications for theories of bequests. First, because if older parents get sick or incapacitated children would feel obliged to take care of them, accidental bequests are clearly less important. Second, the merging of older and younger households means that long before older parents' death there is a de facto transfer from older parents to the children of housing—by far the most important component of wealth.[24] The strategic aspect of bequests looks less significant for Japan.

24. The actual transfer of ownership does not usually occur until the death of the parents. In 1983 taxable bequests were valued at 5.0 trillion yen, while taxable gifts were 0.6 trillion (see *Annual Statistical Report of the Tax Bureau,* the only official source of data on taxes in Japan). A standard guidebook on Japanese bequest and gift taxes indicates that bequests are taxed slightly less heavily. The effective bequests tax rate is much lower on houses than on financial assets, because the assessed value of real estate is often less than half the market value. This may explain why the Japanese prefer owning a house to renting.

8. The Role of Taxes

To examine the only remaining major issue, the effect of taxes on saving, we need to address two issues. One is the effective marginal tax rate on income from saving, and the other is the so-called (after-tax) interest elasticity of saving. A good deal of work has been done on the first issue. A comprehensive official description of Japan's tax system can be found in *An Outline of Japanese Taxes* (various years) by the Ministry of Finance. A good economist's description is in Horioka (1985b, section 4), Shoven and Tachibanaki (1985) and Makin (1985). The treatment of personal interest and dividend income in the Japanese tax system differs considerably from that in the United States. The notorious *Maruyu* system implies that interest income from a principal of up to 6 million yen (about $30 thousand) for "nonsalaried" workers and 12 million yen for "salaried" workers is nontaxable. Because abuse of this system is so common, it is difficult to estimate the marginal tax rate on interest income. Capital gains on stocks are not taxed if the gain is less than a certain amount and if the number of transactions is not large (less than fifty transactions a year). But this provision, too, can be avoided by trading stocks through several different brokers. The tax rate on dividend income is at most 35 percent, as high-income taxpayers can elect to have interest and dividends taxed separately at that rate, and for many middle- and low-income earners it is substantially less. Since the return from Japanese stocks has been mainly in the form of capital gains, the average tax rate on income from equity capital is very low. These facts led Shoven and Tachibanaki (1985) to assume very low marginal personal tax rates on interest income and income from equity (9.6 percent and 18.1 percent respectively). The very generous tax treatment of income from capital at the personal level is in sharp contrast to taxes on labor income whose top combined national and local statutory marginal rate is close to 80 percent.

At the corporate level, it appears that income is more heavily taxed in Japan than in the United States.[25] Although there is not much difference in the statutory corporate tax rate, the U.S. treatment of depreciation allowances and investment tax credits is more generous, at least in the 1980s. So the marginal tax rate on income from new capital at the corporate level in Japan is higher. The generous tax treatment at the personal level coupled with a relatively heavy tax burden at the corporate level must at least in part be responsible for the recent capital outflow from Japan to the United States.

25. See Ando and Auerbach (1985) for a comparison of the cost of capital in Japan and the United States.

The present Japanese tax system is thus geared to encourage saving. The other issue is whether it has been effective in promoting saving. The conventional approach to analyzing the response of saving to changes in the after-tax rate of return to saving is the saving function, which relates aggregate saving to the after-tax interest rate. Because of many serious problems, including the Lucas critique, the saving function approach seems to have been discredited by now. The modern approach that replaces it is the Euler equation approach, discussed in the previous section, which looks at the relation between consumption growth and the real interest rate. If saving is elastic to the interest rate, it should show up as a positive relation of the real interest rate with the growth rate of consumption from one period to the next, because increased current saving makes the level of current consumption relative to future consumption lower. The evidence presented in table 11, however, shows no such relation; in fact the sign of the real rate coefficient is the opposite of the theoretical prediction. Saving does not seem sensitive to the interest rate.

To check the robustness of this conclusion, the same form of the Euler equation (9) is estimated on monthly aggregate data on food expen-

Table 12 ESTIMATION OF EULER EQUATION ON MONTHLY AGGREGATE DATA

Equation #	*Real rate of interest*	*Log of real disposable income*	*Estimation technique*	*Durbin-Watson statistic*
1a	0.10 (1.1)	—	forward filtering	—
1b	0.11 (4.3)	—	OLS	1.3
2a	0.08 (0.96)	−0.003 (1.3)	forward filtering	—
2b	0.12 (4.5)	−0.014 (3.6)	OLS	1.4

The dependent variable is the growth rate of real food expenditure from the month to the month one year ahead, namely, $\ell n(c_{t+12}) - \ell n(c_t)$. The nominal rate used for constructing the real rate is the rate on one-year time deposits. The food component of the CPI is used to calculate the real rate. The log of real disposable income is $\ell n(y_t)$ where y_t is disposable income of month t divided by the food component of the CPI. Because the consumption growth rate is over one-year periods while the sampling interval is a month, the error term will be a moving average of order 11. The forward filtering technique proposed in Hayashi and Sims (1983) is used for equations 1a and 2a. Because the ex-post real rate is potentially correlated with the error term, it is instrumented in equations 1a and 2a by the current one-year nominal rate, current and 12 lags of the monthly food inflation rate, and current and 12 lags of the log of monthly disposable income. They explain about 39 percent of monthly variations in the real rate. The data period is from January 1963 through October 1985. Numbers in parentheses are the t values. The data on monthly food expenditure and disposable income for worker households are taken from the *Annual Reports of the Family Income and Expenditure Survey*.

diture. The *Annual Reports of the Family Income and Expenditure Survey* contain data since 1963 on average monthly expenditure and disposable income for worker households. For reasons explained in the previous section, food expenditure is used for the estimation. (For details of the estimation see the note to table 12.) The real rate coefficient is now positive (the right sign), but still insignificantly different from zero. The negative effect of disposable income suggests the presence of liquidity constraints, but it too is insignificant. The wrong sign of the real rate coefficient found in table 11 may be explainable by the correlation between the ex-post real rate (used for the expected real rate) and the error term that represents unexpected developments (over the five-year periods). On the other hand, the real rate coefficients in table 12, while corrected for the correlation with the error term, suffer from the possible aggregation bias. The Euler equation holds for each individual. Since each year the oldest generations are replaced by new younger generations, it is not necessarily true that the Euler equation holds for aggregate consumption. On the whole, then, there is no strong evidence for a high interest elasticity of saving or for the effectiveness of the tax incentives for saving.

9. *Concluding Comments*

If one subscribes to the dynastic view of Barro (1974) and Becker (1981), it seems that all the evidence presented in this article—the insensitivity of the aggregate saving rate to demographics, saving rates that are independent of age, the possibly significant flow of intergenerational transfers, the insignificance of the social security dummy, and certainly the prevalence of the extended family—are parsimoniously explainable, although we must hasten to add that no direct and formal test of the dynastic model against other theories of bequests was given in the article.[26] A large flow of bequests by itself does not lead to high saving rates. One can easily construct a stationary economy with a zero saving rate in which assets are passed on from one generation to the next and in which each generation consumes all of its income. The existence of a significant flow of bequests does, however, imply that the infinite horizon assumption may be a good approximation. Add to this the fact that Japan had to

26. The existence of liquidity constraints is not inconsistent with the dynastic model. Suppose that people do not come to realize the linearity of the family until they reach middle age. Until then the only limits on their consumption are liquidity constraints. Their parents *do* think about the family. Because of liquidity constraints they can determine their impatient son's consumption through transfers. Thus family consumption is effectively controlled by the parents. Also, liquidity constraints do not necessarily invalidate the Ricardian doctrine of the equivalence of taxes and deficits. See Hayashi (1985b).

Figure 8 NNP—WEALTH RATIO AND SAVING AND INVESTMENT RATES

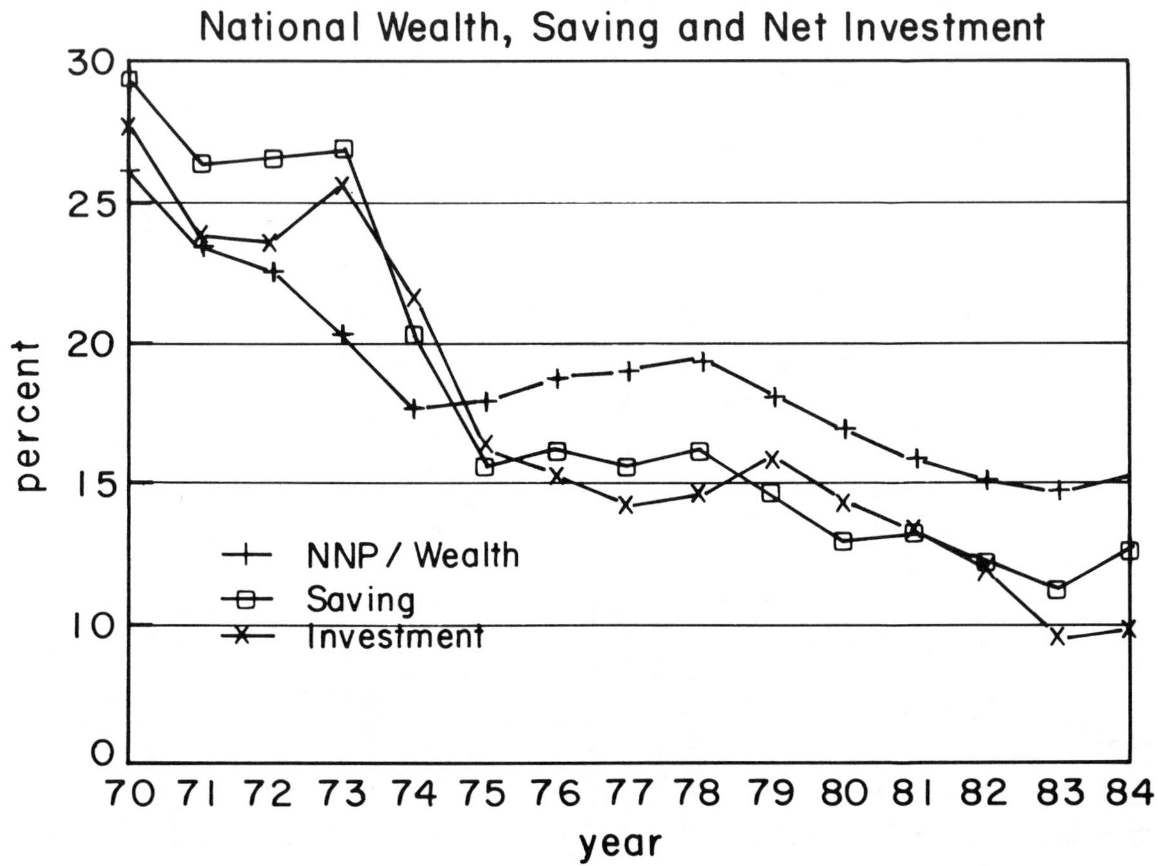

start with a low level of wealth. The infinite horizon optimal growth model implies that the economy's response to the low initial wealth is a high saving rate that gradually stabilizes to a lower level as wealth approaches its steady-state value. Japan's saving rate has been high because the Japanese desire to accumulate wealth in order for their children to live as well as Americans do.

That this simplistic view is consistent with Japan's experience in the last fifteen years (though not in the 1960s, which are not included in the figure) can be seen from figure 8, which includes a plot of the national saving rate and the (reciprocal of) the national wealth–NNP ratio. (If private saving and private wealth are used one gets a similar picture.) Japan has come a long way toward the steady state. She still has some room to accumulate faster than the United States because her per capita income at a current yen/dollar exchange rate is about 85 percent of the U.S. level. Given Japan's track record, it will not take long to fill the gap. If the infinite horizon view is correct, the rise in the national saving rate that occurred in 1984 is not likely to persist. The plot in the figure of net national investment in tangible assets indicates that Japan's large trade surplus in the 1980s is due more to slumping investment than to saving, which is not high by historical standards.

The author is grateful to Tsuneo Ishikawa, Takatoshi Ito, Paul Romer, and other conference participants for discussions and comments on earlier drafts, and especially to Albert Ando, whose detailed written comments helped to improve the final version of the paper.

REFERENCES

Ando, A. 1985. The savings of Japanese households: A micro study based on data from the National Survey of Family Income and Expenditure. University of Pennsylvania. Mimeo.

Ando, A., and A. Auerbach. 1985. The corporate cost of capital in Japan and the U.S.: A comparison. NBER Working Paper 1762.

Ando, A., and F. Modigliani. 1963. The life cycle hypothesis of saving: Aggregate implications and tests. *American Economic Review* 53:55–84.

Barro, R. 1974. Are government bonds net wealth? *Journal of Political Economy* 82:1095–1117.

Barro, R., and J. Friedman. 1977. On uncertain lifetimes. *Journal of Political Economy* 85:843–49.

Becker, G. 1981. *A treatise on the family.* Cambridge: Harvard University Press.

Boskin, M., M. Robinson, and J. Roberts. 1985. New estimates of federal government tangible capital and net investment. NBER Working Paper 1774.

Browning, M., A. Deaton, and M. Irish. 1985. A profitable approach to labor supply and commodity demands over the life-cycle. *Econometrica* 53:503–44.

Burnheim, D., A. Shleifer, and L. Summers. 1985. The strategic bequest motive. *Journal of Political Economy* 93:1045–76.

Eisner, R. 1985. The total incomes system of accounts. *Survey of Current Business* 55:24–48.

Hashimoto, M., and J. Raisian. 1985. Employment tenure and earnings profiles in Japan and the United States. *American Economic Review* 75:721–35.

Hayashi, F. 1985a. The permanent income hypothesis and consumption durability: Analysis based on Japanese panel data. *Quarterly Journal of Economics* 100:1083–1113.

———. 1985b. Tests for liquidity constraints: A critical survey. NBER Working Paper 1720.

Hayashi, F., and C. Sims. 1983. Efficient estimation of time-series models with predetermined, but not exogenous, instruments. *Econometrica* 51:783–98.

Hayashi, F., T. Ito, and J. Slemrod. 1985. Housing finance imperfection: A simulation analysis for a comparison of the U.S. and Japan. University of Minnesota. Incomplete mimeo.

Horioka, C. 1984. The applicability of the life-cycle hypothesis to Japan. *Kyoto University Economic Review* 54 (2): 31–56.

———. 1985a. Household saving in Japan: The importance of target saving for education and housing. Kyoto University. Mimeo.

———. 1985b. A survey of the literature on household saving in Japan: Why is the household saving rate so high in Japan? Kyoto University. Mimeo.

Hulten, C., and F. Wykoff. 1981. The measurement of economic depreciation. In *Depreciation, inflation and the taxation of income from capital,* ed. C. Hulten, 81–125. Washington, D.C.: Urban Institute.

Ishikawa, T., and K. Ueda. 1984. The bonus payment system and Japanese personal savings. In *The economic analysis of the Japanese firm,* ed. M. Aoki, 133–92. (Contributions to Economic Analysis Series no. 151). Amsterdam: North-Holland.

Komiya, R. 1966. The supply of personal savings. In *Postwar economic growth in Japan,* ed. R. Komiya, 157–86. (trans. Robert Ozaki). Berkeley: University of California Press.

Kotlikoff, L., and A. Spivak. 1981. The family as an incomplete annuities market. *Journal of Political Economy* 89:372–91.

Kurosaka, Y., and K. Hamada. 1984. Why is the personal saving rate so high? In *Macro Keizaigaku to Nihon Keizai* [Macroeconomics and the Japanese economy]. Tokyo: *Nihon Hyoronsha.*

Makin, J. 1985. Saving rates in Japan and the United States: The roles of tax policy and other factors. Washington, D.C.: American Enterprise Institute. Mimeo.

Modigliani, F. 1980. The life cycle hypothesis of saving twenty years later. In *Contemporary Issues in Economics,* ed. M. Parkin, 2–36. Manchester: Manchester University Press.

Modigliani, F., and R. Brumberg. 1954. Utility analysis and the consumption function: An interpretation of cross-section data. In *Post-Keynesian economics,* ed. K. Kurihara, 388–436. New Brunswick, N.J.: Rutgers University Press.

Ruggles, R., and N. Ruggles. 1982. Integrated economic accounts for the United States, 1947–80. *Survey of Current Business* 52 (5): 1–53.

Shinohara, M. 1983. The determinants of post-war savings behaviour in Japan. In *The Determinants of National Saving and Wealth,* ed. F. Modigliani and R. Hemming, 143–80. London: Macmillan.

Shoven, J., and T. Tachibanaki. 1985. The taxation of income from capital in Japan. Stanford University. Mimeo.

Tobin, J. 1967. Life cycle saving and balanced growth. In *Ten economic studies in the tradition of Irving Fisher*, ed. W. Fellner, 231–56. New York: Wiley.

DATA APPENDIX

This appendix describes and presents the Japanese aggregate time-series data used in the text. All the raw data come from the *1986 Annual Report on National Accounts* and the *Report on Revised National Accounts on the Basis of 1980*. The former includes the most recent (1985) benchmark revision with the base year of 1980. The latter is a companion volume that extends the benchmark revision back to either 1965 or 1970 depending on the series. The series in the capital transactions (saving/investment) accounts and the capital accounts (balance sheets and reconciliations) currently starts in 1970. The variable labels and their values are displayed in tables A1 through A5. They are stated in trillions of current yen. As a general rule, variable labels with "_H" are for the household sector (including private nonprofit institutions serving households), "_C" for the corporate sector (nonfinancial corporations and financial institutions), and "_G" for government. The value of the stock of assets is at the beginning of the year. Revaluations are gross (that is, without adjustments for general inflation). As mentioned in the text, the Japanese national accounts report depreciation in the capital transactions accounts at historical costs, do not adjust after-tax income for capital transfers (wealth taxes and lump-sum transfers), and do not depreciate government depreciable assets either in the capital transactions accounts or in the capital accounts (except for buildings). Data necessary for correcting these are available only for the period after 1969. The data presented in this appendix for 1970–84 are all corrected values unless otherwise noted. The variables listed in the tables can therefore be grouped into four categories: (1) those that are directly available from the National Accounts Reports, (2) those that require capital consumption adjustments, (3) those that also require adjustments for capital transfers, and (4) those that are influenced by our estimate of government depreciable tangible assets.

(1) The following variables are available directly from the Reports after consolidating five sectors into the three sectors (household, corporate and government.)

GNP = gross national product.
CON = personal consumption expenditure.
PCON = deflator for CON.
SVG_BEA = government budget surplus, or net investment in government net financial assets. "_BEA" is placed in the label because if we

take the U.S. Bureau of Economic Analysis (BEA) convention of ignoring government tangible assets it should equal government net saving. This is available directly from the government capital transactions accounts after 1969. For 1965–69 it is defined as: government net saving + depreciation − gross government capital formation. This should equal net investment in financial assets up to statistical discrepancy.

DEPH_x = reported depreciation in the capital transactions accounts of sector x (x = H,C,G).

DFA_x = net investment in financial assets in the capital accounts of sector x (x = H,C,G). After 1969 DFA_G equals SVG_BEA.

FA_x = stock (at the beginning of the year) of net financial assets for sector x (x = H,C,G).

RFA_x = gross revaluation of net financial assets (x = H,C,G).

GCD = expenditure on consumer durables.

CD = stock of consumer durables at the beginning of the year.

KD_B_G = reported value of government depreciable tangible assets.

As the Japanese national accounts has data on the stock of depreciable tangible assets at replacement costs in the capital accounts of the corporate and household sector (but not for the government sector), the following stock variables are also directly available from the Reports:

TA_x = stock of tangible assets (depreciable tangible assets, nonreproducible tangible assets, and inventories) for sector x (x = H,C).

KD_x = stock of depreciable tangible assets (x = H,C).

(2) As assets are valued at replacement cost in the capital accounts, depreciation at replacement cost implicit in the Japanese National Accounts can be estimated as follows. Because depreciation in the capital transactions accounts are at historical cost, reconciliations in the capital accounts consist of: revaluation, capital consumption adjustments (i.e., the excess of depreciation at replacement cost over depreciation at historical cost), and some other minor items (e.g., accidental loss/gain of assets). If $KD(t)$ is the nominal stock of depreciable assets at the beginning of the year, $P(t)$ its associated deflator, and $N(t)$ nominal net investment, then revaluation in the National Accounts is calculated as:

$$\text{revaluation} = \frac{P(t+1) - P(t)}{P(t)} KD(t) + \frac{PA(t) - P(t)}{P(t)} N(t), \quad \text{(A1)}$$

where $PA(t)$ is an average of the deflator over the year (see *A Guide to the Use of the National Economic Accounting*, p. 233, Economic Planning

Agency, 1978). Thus capital gains/losses are conferred on assets acquired during the year. In our calculation $PA(t)$ is taken to be the simple average of $P(t)$ and $P(t + 1)$. It is unclear whether nominal net investment $N(t)$ is before or after capital consumption adjustments. We use reported net investment (before capital consumption adjustments) for $N(t)$.

CCAJ_x, our estimate of capital consumption adjustments for the household and the corporate sector ($x = H,C$), is calculated from the relationship that should hold if the other minor items in reconciliation are ignored:

CCAJ_x = (A1) for sector x − reconciliation on depreciable assets for sector x.

For 1965–69, *CCAJ_x* is set at zero (for lack of data on the capital accounts). With this estimate of capital consumption adjustments, the following variables can be calculated for the household and the corporate sector ($x = H,C$).

DTA_x = net investment in tangible assets, equals the reported value less *CCAJ_x*.
DKD_x = net investment in depreciable tangible assets similarly calculated.
RTA_x = gross revaluation of tangible assets, equals the reported value of reconciliation plus *CCAJ_x*.
RKD_x = gross revaluation of depreciable tangible assets similarly calculated.

For consumer durables, a different procedure is used because depreciation is not reported at all. We first calculate using data on the nominal stock (*CD*) and nominal gross investment (*GCD*), the depreciation rate $\delta(t)$ for each year implicit in the perpetual inventory method:

$$(P(t)/P(t + 1)) * CD(t + 1) = CD(t) + GCD(t) - \delta(t) * CD(t), \quad \text{(A2)}$$

where $P(t)$ here is the deflator for the stock of consumer durables available from the Reports. The implicit depreciation rate for 1970–84 turned out to be stable over years with a mean of 19.0 percent. Depreciation at replacement costs on consumer durables is thus calculated as 0.19 times *CD*. Gross revaluation of consumer durables is:

RCD = (A1) with *KD* replaced by *CD*, *N* by $GCD - 0.19 * CD$, and *P* by the deflator for *CD*.

(3) To arrive at net saving, we have to subtract from reported net saving capital consumption adjustments and then add capital transfers. The variables

SVG_x = net saving by the household sector ($x = H$) and by the corporate sector ($x = C$)

are thus calculated. Capital transfers are positive for the corporate sector and negative for the household sector for all years since 1970.

(4) As shown in table 2, the average physical rate of depreciation implicit in the capital accounts for buildings is 6.5 percent. Using the beginning of 1970 value of government depreciable assets as the benchmark and using reported government gross investment series and the reported value of deflator for the stock of government depreciable tangible assets, we generate the stock of depreciable assets by the perpetual inventory method (A2). Namely,

KD_G = government depreciable tangible assets generated by perpetual inventory with a depreciation rate of 6.5 percent.

The benchmark 1970 value in the National Accounts is based on the *1970 National Wealth Survey* which is a sampling survey on the replacement value of assets by type, industry and institutional sector.

The remaining variables for the government sector are now easy to calculate:

TA_G = stock of government tangible assets, equals KD_G plus reported value of the stock of inventories and nonreproducible assets.
$CCAJ\_G$ = capital consumption adjustments, equals $0.065 * KD\_G$ minus reported depreciation.
DKD_G = net investment in depreciable tangible assets as reported in the capital accounts of the government minus $CCAJ\_G$.
DTA_G = net investment in tangible assets, equals DKD_G plus reported net investment in inventories and nonreproducible assets.
RKD_G = gross revaluation of depreciable assets calculated by (A1) with KD replaced by KD_G, N by DKD_G and P by reported deflator for government depreciable tangible assets.
RTA_G = gross revaluation of government tangible assets, equals RKD_G plus reported reconciliation on inventories and nonreproducible assets.

SVG_G = government net saving, equals reported net saving minus $CCAJ\_G$ minus capital transfers to other sectors.

This leaves GNP_A, NNP_A, GNP_BEA and NNP_BEA. Since in the National Accounts the value of government output is taken to be equal to the costs of producing it, GNP must be adjusted for the discrepancy between the reported value (KD_B_G above) and our estimate of the government depreciable assets (KD_G) and depreciation. NNP (net national product) then is this adjusted GNP less national depreciation at replacement costs. We use a rate of return of 4 percent to impute net service flows from government tangible assets. Thus:

$$GNP\_A = \text{reported GNP} + 0.04 * (KD\_G - KD\_B\_G) + CCAJ\_G.$$

$$NNP\_A = GNP\_A - (DEPH\_H + DEPH\_C + DEPH\_G) - (CCAJ\_H + CCAJ\_C + CCAJ\_G).$$

Neither $CCAJ$ nor KD_G is available for 1965–69. Thus for this period GNP_A and NNP_A are equal to respective reported values. The definition of GNP and NNP should be altered if government tangible assets are to be ignored. The BEA definition of Japan's NNP would be:

$$GNP\_BEA = GNP\_A - 0.04 * TA\_G - DEPH\_G - CCAJ\_G.$$

$$NNP\_BEA = NNP\_A - 0.04 * TA\_G.$$

For 1965–69 data on TA_G and $CCAJ\_G$ are not available. We use the 1970 ratio of GNP_A to GNP_BEA to extrapolate GNP_BEA for 1965–69. The same extrapolation method is used for NNP.

Table A1 OUTPUT, EXPENDITURE AND PRICES

Year	*GNP*	*GNP__A*	*NNP__A*	*GNP__BEA*	*NNP__BEA*	*CON*	*PCON*
1965	32.71	32.71	28.35	31.70	27.86	19.17	32.8
1966	37.99	37.99	32.97	36.82	32.40	22.06	34.1
1967	44.53	44.52	38.64	43.15	37.98	25.30	35.6
1968	52.77	52.77	45.83	51.15	45.05	28.92	37.6
1969	62.10	62.10	53.82	60.19	52.90	33.33	39.5
1970	73.19	74.06	63.23	71.78	62.15	38.33	41.5
1971	80.59	81.65	69.34	78.94	68.05	43.23	45.0
1972	92.40	93.65	79.56	90.47	78.05	49.90	47.8
1973	112.52	114.14	95.87	110.10	93.92	60.31	50.5
1974	134.00	136.43	110.00	130.77	107.32	72.91	57.7
1975	148.17	151.33	122.63	144.28	119.40	84.76	70.9
1976	166.42	169.81	137.84	162.08	134.31	95.78	76.3
1977	185.53	189.44	153.97	180.56	149.95	107.08	83.2
1978	204.47	208.84	170.34	198.82	165.84	117.92	87.8
1979	221.82	226.81	183.93	215.32	178.75	130.08	91.3
1980	240.10	245.93	196.69	232.44	190.60	141.32	95.6
1981	256.82	263.41	211.25	248.00	204.26	149.38	102.3
1982	269.70	276.76	221.77	259.97	214.11	159.61	105.9
1983	280.57	287.92	230.32	270.15	222.19	167.81	107.9
1984	298.59	306.17	245.81	287.59	237.32	176.14	109.9
1985	n.a.	n.a.	n.a.	n.a.	n.a.	n.a.	112.5

GNP = gross national product,
GNP__A = gross national product with our estimate of government depreciable tangible assets,
NNP__A = net national product with our estimate of government depreciable tangible assets,
GNP__BEA = gross national product without government tangible assets,
NNP__BEA = net national product without government tangible assets,
CON = personal consumption expenditure,
PCON = price index for CON at the 4th quarter of previous year.

In trillion yen except for PCON. For 1965–69 the numbers do not incorporate capital consumption adjustments.

Table A2 DEPRECIATION AND NET SAVING

Year	*DEPH__H*	*CCAJ__H*	*DEPH__C*	*CCAJ__C*	*DEPH__G*	*CCAJ__G*	*SVG__H*	*SVG__C*	*SVG__G*	*SVG__BEA*
1965	n.a.	n.a.	n.a.	n.a.	n.a.	n.a.	3.34	.83	1.79	.47
1966	n.a.	n.a.	n.a.	n.a.	n.a.	n.a.	3.54	1.81	1.85	.25
1967	n.a.	n.a.	n.a.	n.a.	n.a.	n.a.	3.87	3.17	2.42	.73
1968	n.a.	n.a.	n.a.	n.a.	n.a.	n.a.	5.34	3.65	2.99	.97
1969	n.a.	n.a.	n.a.	n.a.	n.a.	n.a.	6.08	5.20	3.68	1.30
1970	2.36	.47	7.05	−.24	.33	.87	7.57	7.24	3.78	1.29
1971	2.71	.56	7.83	−.22	.37	1.06	8.56	5.59	4.16	1.36
1972	3.19	.66	9.22	−.65	.42	1.25	10.10	7.01	4.06	.07
1973	3.87	1.58	10.96	−.23	.47	1.63	13.54	6.60	5.68	.93
1974	4.79	2.79	12.42	3.45	.55	2.42	18.88	−2.11	5.52	.46
1975	5.77	2.48	12.59	4.05	.67	3.15	22.31	−4.19	1.00	−4.13
1976	6.80	3.00	13.12	4.86	.79	3.42	25.62	−2.76	−.63	−6.28
1977	7.79	3.21	14.33	5.29	.90	3.96	26.14	−1.98	−.22	−7.16
1978	8.77	3.33	15.18	5.71	1.05	4.45	27.48	2.39	−2.40	−12.12
1979	9.68	4.27	16.77	5.85	1.20	5.12	24.33	3.40	−.83	−9.63
1980	10.63	5.38	18.71	7.11	1.39	6.01	25.02	1.30	−.92	−9.41
1981	11.46	5.07	21.02	6.20	1.60	6.83	27.86	.03	−.07	−11.26
1982	12.11	5.05	22.34	6.36	1.75	7.38	25.98	1.58	−.54	−9.43
1983	12.67	5.24	23.83	6.21	1.89	7.75	26.61	.91	−1.81	−10.78
1984	13.28	4.99	25.44	6.56	2.02	8.07	27.91	1.65	1.31	−6.27

DEPH__x = depreciation at historical costs as reported in the Japanese national accounts ($x = H$ for household, C for corporate, and G for government),
CCAJ__x = excess of depreciation at replacement costs over depreciation at historical costs ($x = H,C,G$).
SVG__x = net saving in sector x after capital consumption adjustments,
SVG__BEA = government saving in net financial assets, i.e., budget surplus. The difference between *SVG__G* and *SVG__BEA* is net government capital formation.

In trillion yen. The data on saving for 1965–69 incorporate neither capital consumption adjustments nor adjustments on capital transfers.

Table A3 HOUSEHOLD CAPITAL ACCOUNTS

Year	*TA_H*	*KD_H*	*FA_H*	*DTA_H*	*DKD_H*	*DFA_H*	*RTA_H*	*RKD_H*	*RFA_H*	*GCD*	*CD*	*RCD*
1970	119.15	20.61	40.03	1.93	3.97	5.39	24.29	1.29	−1.12	2.35	8.74	.35
1971	145.37	25.86	44.31	.95	4.11	7.08	27.88	.82	1.36	2.69	9.76	.16
1972	174.20	30.79	52.75	1.02	5.37	10.52	69.65	6.40	12.48	3.34	10.70	.20
1973	244.88	42.56	75.74	.66	6.95	8.80	71.57	9.89	4.00	4.15	12.09	2.29
1974	317.10	59.40	88.55	3.49	6.61	13.28	10.54	6.43	−4.28	4.55	15.90	3.47
1975	331.14	72.44	97.54	4.92	7.22	14.09	20.30	1.81	−3.47	5.02	20.46	.17
1976	356.35	81.47	108.16	6.58	8.39	17.12	28.43	7.61	4.78	5.87	21.99	.49
1977	391.37	97.47	130.06	6.45	7.83	18.47	26.70	2.58	−.40	6.34	24.17	.49
1978	424.52	107.87	148.13	8.41	8.38	19.89	49.11	4.62	6.21	7.38	26.64	.56
1979	482.04	120.88	174.23	6.42	8.62	18.94	88.27	14.92	3.84	8.23	29.34	.84
1980	576.73	144.42	197.01	3.50	7.07	16.93	88.44	7.32	−.55	8.10	32.82	.96
1981	668.67	158.80	213.39	2.20	6.09	25.13	79.07	2.74	1.65	8.60	36.20	.44
1982	749.94	167.64	240.16	2.11	5.34	25.63	43.65	2.06	−3.23	9.27	38.87	−.30
1983	795.70	175.04	262.57	.64	3.93	25.84	25.19	.19	7.56	10.07	41.15	−.18
1984	821.53	179.16	295.97	.54	3.56	26.45	26.56	3.56	8.21	10.44	43.91	.00
1985	848.63	186.29	330.63	n.a.	n.a.	n.a.	n.a.	n.a.	n.a.	n.a.	46.96	n.a.

TA = stock at year beginning of tangible assets,
KD = stock of depreciable tangible assets,
FA = stock of net financial assets,
DTA = net investment in tangible assets,
DKD = net investment in depreciable tangible assets,
DFA = net investment in net financial assets,
RTA = gross revaluation (without adjustment for general inflation) of tangible assets,
RKD = gross revaluation of depreciable tangible assets,
RFA = gross revaluation of net financial assets,
GCD = durables expenditure,
CD = stock of consumer durables,
RCD = gross revaluation of consumer durables.

In trillion yen.

Table A4 CORPORATE CAPITAL ACCOUNTS

Year	*TA_C*	*KD_C*	*FA_C*	*DTA_C*	*DKD_C*	*DFA_C*	*RTA_C*	*RKD_C*	*RFA_C*
1970	94.78	38.85	−42.86	13.35	9.17	−5.97	9.16	2.24	1.40
1971	117.30	50.26	−47.43	12.36	8.58	−6.44	8.19	1.12	−1.74
1972	137.85	59.96	−55.61	13.52	8.68	−8.59	23.93	5.31	−13.30
1973	175.31	73.95	−77.50	18.81	11.45	−9.76	42.52	18.11	−4.14
1974	236.64	103.51	−91.40	15.13	9.62	−15.07	19.58	17.38	4.47
1975	271.35	130.51	−102.01	9.88	8.19	−10.17	10.08	2.12	3.06
1976	291.30	140.82	−109.12	8.97	7.20	−9.76	18.57	9.58	−5.06
1977	318.84	157.60	−123.94	8.50	7.27	−8.47	10.83	4.47	1.20
1978	338.17	169.34	−131.21	7.45	8.25	−4.28	21.97	5.35	−7.25
1979	367.59	182.94	−142.74	12.99	10.96	−11.29	46.88	13.29	−4.09
1980	427.47	207.19	−158.11	15.02	12.24	−10.09	45.99	12.81	−.91
1981	488.48	232.24	−169.12	16.18	13.47	−12.72	25.02	2.86	−2.93
1982	529.68	248.56	−184.77	14.89	13.10	−14.42	17.13	2.05	4.86
1983	561.70	263.72	−194.33	12.75	11.85	−10.10	7.30	−.28	−9.43
1984	581.75	275.29	−213.85	15.68	13.99	−11.83	12.94	3.95	−7.87
1985	610.37	293.24	−233.55	n.a.	n.a.	n.a.	n.a.	n.a.	n.a.

See note to table A3.

Table A5 GOVERNMENT CAPITAL ACCOUNTS

Year	*TA__G*	*KD__G*	*FA__G*	*DTA__G*	*DKD__G*	*DFA__G*	*RTA__G*	*RKD__G*	*RFA__G*	*KD__B__G*
1970	27.01	18.40	3.47	2.51	2.08	1.29	2.52	1.45	.05	18.40
1971	32.12	22.01	4.81	3.23	2.63	1.36	2.25	1.04	−.29	21.97
1972	37.66	25.74	5.88	4.18	3.38	.07	6.59	2.99	.09	25.84
1973	48.62	32.30	6.03	5.09	4.27	.93	12.74	8.57	−.10	32.51
1974	67.04	45.73	6.87	5.04	4.03	.46	8.36	8.55	−.11	45.49
1975	80.83	58.71	7.22	5.11	4.02	−4.13	2.16	1.85	.03	58.34
1976	88.16	64.65	3.12	5.52	4.39	−6.28	6.59	5.55	−.01	65.18
1977	100.45	74.77	−3.17	6.85	5.41	−7.16	5.22	4.33	.17	76.07
1978	112.68	84.67	−10.16	8.82	7.02	−12.12	7.64	5.31	−.74	86.93
1979	129.36	97.22	−23.02	9.68	7.71	−9.63	12.72	8.67	−.33	100.53
1980	152.11	113.95	−32.97	9.67	7.28	−9.41	12.60	8.17	.90	118.60
1981	174.65	129.65	−41.48	9.80	7.22	−11.26	6.92	3.46	−.37	135.55
1982	191.47	140.43	−53.10	9.18	6.55	−9.43	1.51	1.40	.04	148.24
1983	203.20	148.41	−62.49	8.44	5.83	−10.78	0.65	1.02	−.01	158.36
1984	212.31	155.28	−73.29	7.74	5.05	−6.27	2.82	3.03	−.35	167.46
1985	222.91	163.41	−79.91	n.a.	n.a.	n.a.	n.a.	n.a.	n.a.	178.03

KD__B__G = stock of government depreciable tangible assets as reported in the National Accounts. For definition of other variables, see note to table A3.

Comment

ALBERT ANDO
University of Pennsylvania

Fumio Hayashi has produced a very large article which deals with a number of complex issues including data problems that arise in the course of attempting to understand whether or not the Japanese savings rate is indeed unusually high, and if so, what may be the reasons for it. Since his discussion is so wide-ranging, I comment on only a few of these issues.

How High Is the Japanese Savings Rate?

It is a curious fact that, as Hayashi demonstrates, there is substantial uncertainty on the magnitude of the Japanese saving rate. I believe, for example, that the saving rate based on the national income and product accounts of Japan is more subject to doubt than, say, the corresponding United States figures. I have no serious disagreement with Hayashi on the selection of adjustments undertaken to make Japanese figures comparable to those of the United States. I would be inclined, however, to rely mostly on the concept of private saving rather than on national saving for the purposes of characterizing Japanese savings and for comparing it with the U.S. case. We can always add net government saving to private saving to obtain national saving if the latter concept is needed for some specific purpose, but I believe that private saving is the more behaviorally meaningful concept than national saving, especially after recent U.S. history indicated that sudden and very large changes in government saving were not in any way compensated by changes in private saving.

It is also helpful to keep in mind the order of magnitude of the aggregate net worth–income ratio of the private sector. In table 1, I present the adjusted net worth of the household and its ratio to disposable income of the household sector in Japan for selected years between 1970 and 1983. The net worth reported in Japanese national income and product accounts was adjusted for two reasons. First, an extraordinarily large proportion of the total net worth is the value of land, which is, of course, nonreproducible and hence does not at the aggregate level result from accumulation of savings. For our purposes, it seems better to exclude the value of land from consideration. Second, for reasons that are too complex to go into here, the value of corporate shares owned by the household sector is grossly understated. Since I know of no reliable estimate of the market value of shares owned by households, I have replaced figures reported in the national income and product accounts by the net reproduction value of capital owned by nonfinancial corporations less the value of shares owned by financial institutions.

The ratio of adjusted net worth to disposable income rises dramatically from 2.5 in 1970 to 4.0 in 1983. Unfortunately, we do not have data to compute the same ratio for earlier years, but I offer a conjecture that this ratio declined during the 1960s, at least partly because even the high rate of saving of Japan was not quite enough to generate sufficient accumulation of net worth to keep pace with the high rate of growth of income in the 1960s. The comparable figure for the United States is a little higher than 4, so that Japan has just caught up with the United States in terms of this ratio. So long as adjustments for the value of land and the value of corporate shares are made, this result qualitatively remains for a wide variation in choices of the definition for ratios of this type. This immediately establishes two points. First, the high saving rate in Japan is not due to the very high asset-income ratio maintained by the Japanese household sector. Second, during the 1970s at least, the high saving rate assisted the recovery of the net worth–disposable income ratio of the household sector from a very low level to the level comparable to that in the United States, and indications are that the increase of the net worth–disposable income ratio has now stopped.

This fact and Hayashi's adjustments to figures in Japanese national income and product accounts which lowers the private savings rate noticeably from those reported in official data should place the whole problem in better perspective. The Japanese savings rate is still significantly higher

Table 1 ADJUSTED NET WORTH OF THE HOUSEHOLD SECTOR AND ITS RATIO TO DISPOSABLE PERSONAL INCOME IN JAPAN, SELECTED YEARS (Beginning of the year)

	Reported net worth	*Less value of land*	*Plus adj. for value of corp. shares*	*Adjusted net worth*	*Ratio of adjusted net worth to disposable income*
1970	167.3	104.0	52.3	115.6	2.5
1975	411.0	235.6	162.7	338.1	3.1
1980	744.0	394.3	249.1	598.8	3.5
1981	849.7	466.7	283.9	666.9	3.7
1982	954.4	535.5	306.3	752.2	3.9
1983	1031.6	577.3	321.1	775.4	4.0
1984	1082.0	600.5	312.0	793.5	

Source: Annual Report on National Accounts, 1985, Economic Planning Agency of the Government of Japan.

than that for the United States, but it does not appear to be very much higher than comparable ratios for at least some European countries, although figures for European countries, too, must be carefully reviewed before our comparisons are meaningful. Even Hayashi's figures may be subject to further adjustments, and I mention here one item that immediately comes to mind: In the nonfinancial corporate sector, where most of investment takes place, it should be the case that total gross investment less depreciation and retained earnings after taxes should equal the excess of borrowing over acquisition of financial assets, with a few well-defined adjustments. It turns out, however, that in the Japanese national income accounts the former has been substantially larger than the latter since 1970, and the discrepancy is quite often larger than the total of retained earnings plus dividends. I have never been able to resolve this puzzle, but it is possible that there is substantial underestimation of savings by the corporate sector in Japan.

I believe that there is an urgent need for the Japanese national income and product accounts to be thoroughly examined, and most importantly, much closer communication and exchange of information between officials in charge of these statistics and outside economists.

Hayashi's Theses

After reviewing a number of suggested causes of the high saving rate in Japan, Hayashi analyzes two of them seriously. First, he notes that the life-cycle theory with its hump-shaped asset accumulation pattern over life for families would make the saving rate dependent on the rate of growth of average productivity per manhour and the population structure; it is conceivable that the high saving rate in Japan can be explained by the high growth rate and an unusual demographic structure. The second hypothesis is the possibility that Japanese families tend to leave very large bequests relative to their lifetime earnings. Hayashi arrives at a tentative conclusion that the life-cycle hypothesis does not apply to Japan, and that bequests are the dominant motive for saving in Japanese families.

Based on his evidence as well as on my own research on this subject, I am sympathetic to the view that the life-cycle theory appears to be on shaky empirical ground in Japan, although I am inclined to say that it probably has somewhat stronger support in Japan than in other countries. I would agree with Hayashi in recognizing strong indications from various data sources for a substantial portion of accumulated assets by households being passed along to the next generation, either as intervivos gifts or as bequests. I find it hard to interpret the evidence as indicating that Japanese families are consciously motivated by the desire to leave bequests, any more than families in the United States or in Europe.

In any case, I believe the high rate of growth of real income in Japan since 1950 was an important factor contributing to the high saving rate, independent of the validity of the life-cycle hypothesis.

Hayashi bases his first conclusion on the result of his micro simulation analysis, reported in table 4 of his article. In particular, he observes that the aggregate savings-income ratio and the wealth-income ratio generated by his simulations have little relation to observed values of these ratios.

In the "steady state", if such a state exists, one would expect that the rate of growth of aggregate income and of aggregate wealth would be the same, and the aggregate wealth-income ratio, a, and the aggregate saving-income ratio, s, would satisfy the relationship $s = ga$, where g is the rate of growth of aggregate real income. From Hayashi's discussion of his "steady state" simulations given in footnote 14 of his paper, we can see that he is not requiring results of his simulations to satisfy a condition such as above. It is still somewhat surprising, however, that the pattern of his result is so far from this condition, and understanding the reasons for this divergence is a key to interpreting the result of his simulation analysis correctly.

Most of the results reported in table 4, especially some of the more startling values, are consequences of combining the observed age profile of earnings with the pattern of consumption assumed to grow at a constant rate for the entire life of the household. Given the age profile of earnings presented in table 3 of Hayashi's paper, when the optimal consumption growth rate is fairly low, there would be large dissavings by younger households, substantial savings by the middle-aged households, and dissavings by the elderly. Also the higher productivity growth means that younger persons have much larger lifetime earnings than their older counterparts, so that their dissavings would be greater and savings of the middle-aged would be smaller, thus reducing the level of aggregate savings. This mechanism explains the curious result that the savings rate in table 4 appears to decline when the growth rate of productivity increases, contrary to my proposition in the preceding paragraph. The dissaving by the oldest group matters relatively little, both because there are relatively few older persons and because their lifetime earnings are smaller than those of younger persons.

The above consideration hints that the problem might be alleviated if the dissaving by younger households is eliminated. Hayashi recognizes this possibility, and reports at the end of the section 4 of his paper that he repeated the simulation experiments with the constraint on consumption not to exceed the algebraic sum of income in the same period and the initial value of wealth. He further reports briefly a surprising result that even with such a constraint, the simulation fails to generate the value of the wealth-income and saving-income ratios that are even remotely close to observed aggregate ratios, and that the negative relationship between the rate of growth of productivity and the savings-income ratio persists. This is surprising since others have found it fairly easy to generate the wealth-income and saving-income ratios close to observed values through similar simulation experiments once dissavings by younger families are eliminated.

To gain some insights into what is going on, consider an extreme case in which the rate of real interest is zero and the optimal consumption path is to consume the same amount throughout the life of a household. Let us suppose also that the rate of growth of productivity is quite high, say between 5% and 10% per year as it has been in Japan since 1950. The cross-section earnings profile given in table 3 of Hayashi's paper would add another 5% to 10% to the growth rate of income, so that the family's longitudinal growth rate of income is between 10% to 20% per year. If such a growth rate of income is matched against the zero growth rate of consumption; in the absence of the liquidity constraint, the family would make very large dissaving at the beginning of its life, expecting to eliminate debts through later savings. When it is subject to the liquidity constraint, however, it begins its life consuming all its income, maintaining net wealth position of zero. When it reaches the age at which unconstrained families would have switched from dissaving to saving, it will continue to consume all its income since it has no debts to eliminate.

The liquidity constrained family, under these assumptions, would therefore go through most of its life with zero net wealth, and only shortly before the retirement, would save a very large part of its income in order to acquire wealth to cover consumption after retirement. It is also clear from this description that the greater the rate of growth of productivity, the shorter the period in which such a family would maintain a positive net wealth position. Hence, the size of net worth held by families averaged over the entire population is very small because only those families just before retirement hold any assets, and most families hold zero assets. Furthermore, the greater the rate of growth of productivity, the fewer families there will be with any positive assets, and the smaller the size of net wealth averaged over the entire population. Consequently, provided that the rate of longitudinal growth of income is quite high to begin with (which is insured by the Japanese age-earnings profile), the negative relationship between the aggregate wealth and the rate of growth of productivity can be strong enough to make the relationship between the rate of growth of productivity and the saving rate negative.

These are interesting implications of the model that Hayashi simulates, but it is not at all surprising that the wealth-income and saving-income ratios generated by his model do not correspond to those observed in Japan. In Japan, contrary to the implication of this model, we observe that virtually all young families save, and the age profile of savings is quite even throughout the working life of the family. This does not necessarily mean that the savings behavior of Japanese households is contrary to the life-cycle theory, as I am not at all sure how much his simulation and its constantly rising consumption at a fixed rate (and others like it used by other authors in recent years) have to do with the life-cycle model visualized by those who originally formulated the model. Modigliani, for example, in his earlier works often used a utility function which is also separable but cornered like a Leontief production function, so that the allocation of total resources to each period in life is predetermined, reflecting what is considered to be a normal pattern of consumption needs by most families. Logically, I do not see that one is superior to another, and if the utility function used by Hayashi is so clearly contradicted by the data, then perhaps we should consider alternatives.

Hayashi seems to conclude from the simulations not only that the life-cycle theory does not apply to Japan, but also that the growth rate of productivity has little to do with the savings-income ratio. As I have indicated before, the relationship between the growth rate of productivity and the aggregate savings-income ratio is by no means unique to the life-cycle theory. Consider, for example, a society in which all households always aim to leave a fixed proportion of total resources available to them during their lives as bequests to the next generation, and save a fixed proportion of their income throughout their lives to do so, so that there is no dissaving at any point in their lives. In such a society, the aggregate savings-income ratio must be strongly and positively correlated with the sum of the rate of growth of productivity and the rate of growth of population. Indeed, provided that the growth rates are substantial, that is, the sum of the growth rate of productivity and that of population is 3 percent or more, the behavior of older persons, whether they dissave their wealth or leave it to the next generation, makes only a minor difference in the aggregate savings-income ratio and the aggregate wealth-income ratio.

I nevertheless accept the proposition that a critical test of the life-cycle theory is the presence or absence of some dissaving after retirement, although the life-cycle theory can certainly coexist with the presence of some bequests, and that the apparent total lack of dissaving by older households in Japan is clearly inconsistent with the life-cycle theory unless this observation is due to some serious biases of sampling or measurement. Much of the rest of the Hayashi article deals with this question, and since he contrasts his analysis with some earlier results I reported elsewhere, I would also like to make a few comments on this rather technical question.

There is no dispute between Hayashi and me that the majority of those older persons maintaining independent households continue to save, and therefore, they leave most of their accumulated wealth as bequests or gifts. (The exception is the small group of some elderly single-person families, mostly women, who are very poor and have virtually no wealth, and appear to subsist on welfare payments and gifts from others.) The behavior of this group is, therefore, not consistent with the life-cycle theory. The problem in Japan is that a larger and larger proportion of older persons become dependent members of younger households as they age. Hayashi reports that in 1983 some 67 percent of persons 65 and over lived with their children. It is generally supposed, and fairly easy to demonstrate, that those older persons remaining independent are likely to be more active economically as well as wealthier. The critical question therefore is what the wealth holdings of those older persons merged into younger households look like, but this is a very difficult question to answer because we do not have any direct observations on them. The only way to infer anything about their wealth-holding behavior is to compare features of those younger households which contain older persons with those of other younger households which do not contain older persons, and try to get at net contributions of older persons indirectly. This is what Hayashi tries to do in his tables 8 and 9.

He draws several conclusions. First, the net contribution of the presence of older persons in the younger family to the total financial assets of the extended family appears to decline as the age of the younger head of the household increases. One needs to be careful about this proposition. Net financial assets is not total net worth, and in Japan by far the most important item in a family's net worth is the value of the residence, and the incidence of house-ownership increases very significantly with the age of the head of household. Furthermore, the probability of a family owning a house is very strongly and significantly affected by the presence of older persons when the head of the family is very young, but is almost unaffected when the head of the family is over 50.

Second, Hayashi observes that the net contribution of the presence of older persons to a measure of savings available in his table 8 is always positive, for all age groups. Hayashi further infers from these two observations that the only possible way in which the positive savings by older persons and the decline in their net financial assets can be reconciled is to suppose that older persons are giving substantial amounts of their assets as bequests and gifts.

I have carried out a somewhat similar analysis in an earlier paper, but since I had access to individual observations with fairly extensive demographic information for the same survey, I tried to work with my own estimate of total net worth of families rather than financial assets, estimated lifetime earned income after taxes rather than current pretax income, and attempted to control for both the age of the younger head of household and the age of the older dependent member of the family. I observed a much clearer decline in total net worth than Hayashi does, which may be due to the differences in definitions used and the explicit control for the age of older persons. The size of the increase in consumption expenditure indicated by Hayashi due to the presence of older persons is considerably smaller than mine, but the difference will not make their positive contribution to saving into a negative one. I did not attempt to estimate income or savings of dependent older persons. The surprising feature of his table 8, it seems to me, is the large net contribution to the income of the family by the presence of retired, older persons, from 10 percent to as much as 30 percent of the income of younger households. Hayashi suggests that I did not take account of the possibility that a part of the net worth of a younger household without an older person living in it may have been contributed by older persons who once lived with them but are now deceased, and that this process is what he is observing. I must confess my skepticism on this very subtle point. I hope that a projected future project using additional data will help Hayashi and me to clarify this.

Hayashi then attempts, through an extremely ingenious scheme, to compute the size of intergenerational transfers implied by data at his disposal, as shown in table 9. He finds it surprising that the size of implied intergenerational transfers appears to him to be very small in the light of the size of total net worth held by all households in the economy.

I am not very surprised. I have found in my own analysis of the U.S. case that of the total existing assets held by the household at any given time, the part contributed by bequests from the previous generation is quite small, say less than a third or a quarter of the total, even when one works through a model in which *all* accumulated savings by households are left as bequests to the next generation, provided that the economy has a respectable rate of growth of total real income, say 3 percent per year or more. This is because, given the rate of growth, assets accumulated by the currently living generation at their higher level of income are much larger than the assets accumulated by the deceased generation at their much lower level of income. Given that the rate of growth of output for Japan has been extraordinarily high for the past thirty years, Hayashi's result is clearly in line with what I would have expected.

Some Final Observations

This brings me to the point that I find basic to the understanding of the differences in the aggregate savings rate among countries and also its secular (not cyclical) changes in a single country. As I have suggested, the aggregate savings rate does not depend all that critically on the savings behavior of the older, retired persons, simply because the amount of wealth these older persons control as a proportion of the total wealth of the society is not large, provided that the economy is growing at a respectable rate. It depends more critically on the standard pattern of asset accumulation by individual households while they are still income earners, on whether or not this pattern is fairly stable among individuals and over time, and also on the rate of growth of income.

The dependence of the saving rate on the rate of growth of income is not a unique feature of the life-cycle theory, certainly not of a very restrictive version of it. Even when all households in the economy intend to leave all their accumulated savings to the next generation as bequests and succeed in doing so, the saving rate must be positively related to the growth rate. If the bequest motive is to explain variations in the aggregate savings rate among countries independent of the growth rate of income, then countries with high bequest motives must have not only high saving rates but also a high wealth-income ratio. I do not believe that we observe a very strong relationship between the savings-income ratio and the wealth-income ratio among countries. For the explanation of the aggregate savings-income ratio, my view therefore is that we must first pay attention to the pattern of accumulation during the earning period of individuals and to the rate of growth of income, and only secondarily to the behavior of older, retired persons, independent of whether the life-cycle theory or the bequest model is used as the basic descriptive vehicle. This does not mean that the distinction between the life-cycle model and the bequest model is never important. For example, it still seems critical in analyzing the effects of a substantial expansion in social security programs on household behavior.

I still have difficulty in understanding a bequest model that leads to substantial intergenerational transfers in the context of continually rising productivity. Individuals in a particular generation know that their children will have very much larger resources. For example, if the rate of productivity growth is 2 percent per year, a generation thirty years younger would on average have roughly twice the income of the older generation. If the older generation has a utility function that is separable in time and treats consumption of current and future generations symmetrically, then the maximization of expected utility subject to the budget constraint with an infinite horizon must lead to the transfer of resources from the younger to the older generation, not the other way around. Introduction of a very large subjective rate of discount to alleviate the situation will not do, because it is, in effect, introducing the result as an assumption of the analysis. It seems to me, therefore, that we need to have a much better-formulated model of the bequest before we can take it seriously. I am personally more attracted to a model in which individuals' wealth-holding behavior near the end of their lives is strongly affected by the uncertainty of the timing of death, and by the possibility that they might face a catastrophic situation, and who, as a result, end up leaving a substantial portion of their wealth at the time of their death, although their interest in leaving a bequest to the younger generation is limited. In this context, we may also remember the well-known proposition that the behavior of individuals may substantially deviate from that predicted by expected utility theory when the probability of events involved is extremely small.

In the case of Japan, I also believe that the role of home ownership plays an important role in the asset accumulation process, because the value of land is so extraordinarily high, but I think we have only scratched the surface of this complex question.

I have disagreed with a number of analyses and propositions offered by Hayashi in his article. Especially because of this fact, I must stress here that his is a remarkable effort, assembling a vast body of information in a reasonably well-organized manner, and I have learned a great deal from it. Even when I did not like his analysis, it forced me to think through the problem a little more deeply than I would have done otherwise. Problems that I raised in my comments reflect serious difficulties faced by all of us trying to press on with empirical analysis beyond very general observations, and I look forward to learning more about the characteristics of the Japanese economy solidly based on empirical research from Hayashi's future work.

Comment

PAUL M. ROMER
University of Rochester

Fumio Hayashi's article on Japanese savings, (Hayashi 1986), starts with a detailed examination of data from the United States and Japan. Before moving on to possible explanations for the behavior of savings in Japan, he tries to gauge the accuracy of the widespread perception that the Japanese saving rate has been, and continues to be, two to three times higher than the U.S. rate. He concludes that a simple comparison of personal saving rates overstates the difference in true savings behavior and masks a steady decline in the Japanese saving rate since 1970. He then proceeds to examine possible explanations for the remaining difference between the U.S. and Japanese experience and the behavior of Japanese savings over time.

The first part of the article is valuable because it suggests caution about how one measures savings and raises questions about the reliability of the available data. I heartily agree, and conclude that these difficulties make any comparison of the saving rate in the two countries uninformative about the key questions of interest: What is the nature of intergenerational transfers? Does a budget deficit or a social security system reduce national savings? However, the time-series behavior of savings in Japan does raise interesting issues of its own, especially when compared to the growth of GDP. The period of high savings seems to coincide with an unprecedented period of high GDP growth rates, and this coincidence may deserve more attention than Hayashi gives it.

The conventional way to approach the definition of savings is through national income accounting. Following the usual notation, let Y represent gross domestic product, C private consumption, G government expenditure, and X net exports. We can also define government transfer payments R, taxes T, and the budget surplus, $B = T - G - R$. Let F denote the value of net foreign assets and let r denote the (domestic consumption good) coupon rate on foreign bonds. Finally, recall that the current account surplus CA is net receipts from foreigners, $CA = X + rF$.

The conventional definition of savings as given in a macroeconomics textbook is the difference between net private disposable income and private consumption. For simplicity, let K denote the aggregate capital stock and let δ denote the depreciation rate. Then

$$S = [Y - \delta K + rF + R - T] - C. \quad (1)$$

Using the usual income identity and the definitions given above, private savings can be written as the sum of net investment and the current account, minus the budget surplus:

$$S = (I - \delta K) + CA - B. \quad (2)$$

The level of savings can be converted into a saving rate by dividing by net national income.

This kind of measure of savings is the focus of standard open-economy macroeconomics, but it is only one of many possible measures of accumulation and may not be the one relevant for a given theory. One alternative measure is dismissed early in the article. Savings given in equation (2) is total private-sector savings, but data for the private sector is collected separately in the personal and corporate sectors. The personal saving rate in Japan is indeed two to three times as high as personal savings in the United States, but the difference between private-sector savings is smaller and has been steadily diminishing since 1970. A simple Modigliani-Miller argument suggests that the division of private-sector savings into corporate and personal savings is only a matter of accounting and should have no theoretical significance.

Having made this observation, it is natural to pursue this line one step further and consider net national savings, $S + B$. Adding the budget surplus to private savings reinforces the effects caused by the addition of corporate savings to personal savings. The net national saving rate in Japan is closer still to the rate in the United States, and the downward trend is more pronounced. However, the theoretical justification for choosing national savings over private savings is more controversial. The choice of the measure of savings now depends on the theoretical stand one takes on the nature of intergenerational altruism and transfers. As is now well understood, a Modigliani-Miller argument applies to an increase in government debt caused by a shift in tax liabilities from the present to the future only if the agents who receive the current tax reductions must also pay the increased future taxes. If one believes in a life-cycle theory of savings, a comparison of national saving rates will understate the true divergence between the actions of agents in the United States and in Japan. From this point of view, the question becomes not only why private individuals in Japan save more than those in the United States, but also why government fiscal policy is set to partially offset this difference.

As Hayashi goes on to point out, the measure of the budget surplus in the United States is misleading because it does not distinguish between expenditures on capital goods and consumption goods. Using estimates by private economists of government capital formation for the United States, the article offers an additional measure of savings which adds back net capital formation in the government sector. Comparable figures for Japan are available from the national accounts. At a theoretical level, it is not clear how to take account of the substantial differences in the nature of government expenditures in the two countries, especially with regard to the military. But at this point, problems with the data appear to overwhelm the theoretical issues. The official Japanese accounts do not attempt to measure depreciation on most forms of government capital, presumably because of the difficulty of doing so. The data for the United

States do include depreciation on the entire capital stock. The net result of the correction for government capital formation is to suggest that net capital formation by the government in the United States is around 1 percent of NNP, but is roughly 5 or 6 percent of NNP in Japan. In the absence of some other systematic difference between the activities of the two governments—and I am aware of no such difference—military expenditure alone should cause net capital formation in the United States to be higher. I suspect, and Hayashi seems to agree, that the apparent difference results from differences in the accounting conventions used to generate the estimates for the two countries. If my prior belief that the U.S. government has the higher rate of net capital accumulation is correct, this suggests that differences in accounting conventions concerning issues like the treatment of depreciation, or simple errors in the system of accounts, can lead to differences in reported rates of accumulation on the order of 5 percent of NNP.

There is direct evidence that issues of measurement extend beyond the government sector. Hayashi notes that the published savings numbers from Japan are derived from a measure of net national product that uses historical cost data to estimate depreciation. Using other data, he can construct a replacement cost estimate of depreciation and reduce the estimate of net national product accordingly. Since the level of savings is calculated as a residual, this causes a one-for-one fall in savings and a reduction of the savings rates by 2 percentage points during the 1970s.

The U.S. data should also give reason for concern. The national income accounts estimate of personal savings constructed by the BEA has for some time differed substantially from the estimate constructed by the Federal Reserve Board using balance sheet data. For example, for the years 1980 through 1983, the FRB measure of savings by individuals is more than twice the BEA measure of personal savings, at a level of roughly 10 percent of NNP versus 5 percent of NNP. (Data taken from Tables B19, B25, and B26 of the 1985 Economic Report of the President.) The influence of depreciation on the measured rate of savings in Japan is suggestive of general difficulties. Since the national income accounts measure of savings is a residual, small percentage errors in net income or consumption can cause large changes in estimated saving rates. One explanation that has been offered for the most recent decline in the personal saving rate in the United States is that the proliferation of deferred compensation plans (e.g. 401k or 403b plans) may have artificially reduced income reported to the government without affecting measured consumption.

In the case of capital accumulation by the government, skepticism about the data overwhelms any conceptual issues, and emphasis is placed on measures that do not contain any estimate of this effect. The treatment of the government is of course not the only source of suspicious data or theoretical ambiguity. Even in the absence of any government capital formation, a national income account measure of savings does not capture all changes in wealth, yet wealth is presumably what matters to individuals. This is true whether or not they are inclined to leave bequests. The article refers explicitly to changes in wealth associated with depreciation in the real value of outstanding U.S. government debt, but the issues here go far beyond this case. To make this point, consider a simple model that is capable of allowing for general gains and losses.

Let $k_s(t)$ denote the amount of capital of vintage s—that is, capital produced at date s—still in service at date t. Using the notation from above, $k_t(t)$ can be expressed as gross domestic product minus private consumption, government consumption, and net exports:

$$k_t(t) = Y - C - G - X. \quad (3)$$

Let $p_s(t)$ denote the price at time t of vintage s capital. By the nature of the technology, $p_t(t)$ must be equal to 1, but $p_s(t)$ can differ from 1. Using these prices as weights, define a measure of the aggregate capital stock K as:

$$K(t) = \int_{-\infty}^{t} p_s(t)k_s(t)ds.$$

Finally, suppose that all vintages suffer the same exponential rate of physical depreciation, δ. Differentiating K with respect to time yields

$$\dot{K}(t) = k_t(t) + \int_{-\infty}^{t} p_s(t)\dot{k}_s(t)ds + \int_{-\infty}^{t} \dot{p}_s(t)k_s(t)ds.$$

Because of the exponential depreciation, the second term is equal to $-\delta K(t)$. The last term represents capital gains on capital, and will be denoted as Γ_K. Thus, we can write

$$\dot{K} = k_t(t) - \delta K + \Gamma_K. \quad (4)$$

Measured private sector wealth is the value of all traded assets. Let L denote the stock of land (or of any other input in fixed supply), let F denote the net quantity of foreign bonds, and let q and m denote corresponding prices. Then marketable wealth is

$$W(t) = K(t) + q(t)L + m(t)F(t), \quad (5)$$

and the rate of change of wealth is

$$\dot{W}(t) = \dot{K}(t) + \dot{q}(t)L + \dot{m}(t)F(t) + m(t)\dot{F}(t). \quad (6)$$

Following the notation from above, let Γ_N denote capital gains on land, $\dot{q}(t)L$, and let Γ_F denote increases in the market value of foreign bonds, $\dot{m}(t)F(t)$. Using equation (4) and the fact that $m(t)\dot{F}(t)$ equals the current account surplus, equation (6) becomes

$$\dot{W} = k_t(t) - \delta K + CA + \Gamma_K + \Gamma_L + \Gamma_F. \quad (7)$$

Finally, using the expression from equation (2) for national savings $S + B$ and from equation (3) for $k_t(t)$, we have

$$\dot{W} = (S + B) + \Gamma_K + \Gamma_L + \Gamma_F. \quad (8)$$

Thus, national savings differs from the rate of accumulation of wealth because it neglects capital gains on marketable wealth.

Whether the rate of change of wealth should be used in place of a national income account measure of savings for normative or positive purposes is not clear. Even if the capital gains terms in equation (8) could be measured accurately, it is not necessarily the case that they should be included. The article motivates consideration of changes in wealth based on the observation that the fall in the real value of outstanding U.S. government debt represents a true increase in future national consumption possibilities. For economic purposes, the division of the returns from bond holding into coupon income and appreciation is irrelevant; yet under the accounting arrangements described here, if the U.S. government were to refinance the outstanding debt held by foreigners with zero coupon bonds, the budget surplus and the current account surplus would increase immediately. Thus gains such as Γ_F should surely be included.

An opposing accounting argument arises because the coverage of this measure of wealth is incomplete. Recent increases in, say, the value of land or of corporate assets in the United States may simply reflect changes in taxation like the reduction in the average effective tax rate for corporations or the introduction of the exemption from taxation of gains from the sale of owner-occupied housing. If the resulting reduction in tax revenue from these sources was recovered by an increase in the tax on labor income, the increase in the value of marketable assets will have been largely offset by a fall in the value of human capital. Since there are no market prices for human capital, it can not be included in W and $\dot{W}$ will show a net increase in wealth.

This is not to argue that all or most measured capital gains arise purely from accounting conventions. Simple arguments suggest that real gains may be quite important. Consider a production function for GDP that can be written as a stationary function f multiplied by a term e^{gt} which captures exogenous technological change. The function f will depend on land L, labor N, and all vintages of capital:

$$Y = e^{gt} f(k_s \text{ for } s \in (-\infty, t], L, N). \quad (9)$$

If all arguments of f stayed constant over time, the term e^{gt} would cause the marginal products, and hence the rental prices, of all inputs to increase, leading to capital gains that represent real increases in welfare. Of course, one would not expect all inputs to stay constant. New capital $k_t(t)$ would continue to be added over time. If different vintages of capital are sufficiently good substitutes, this will lead to a compensating decrease in the marginal product and price of older capital. Technological change that leads to the introduction of a new megabyte computer memory chip does not in and of itself reduce the marginal product of existing chips; but if the cost of the new chip is low, the total number of bytes of memory in use will increase and the old chips will indeed suffer a capital loss. In the classical case where all vintages are perfect substitutes, these effects will cancel, the price of all capital goods is always 1, and no capital gains on capital take place. But if $f(K,L,N)$ is homogeneous of degree one, the marginal product $D_K f(K,L,N)$ is homogeneous of degree zero and

$$-KD_{KK}f = LD_{KL}f + ND_{KN}f. \quad (10)$$

Thus, the decrease in the rental price of capital, caused by an increase in the stock of capital, is offset by an increase in the rental price of some other input. To the extent that this increases the marginal productivity of land (or of any other marketable factor in fixed supply), technical change will still be captured in changes in wealth. If different types of capital are not perfect substitutes, gains on capital could still be observed; think for example of the effect of cheaper computer memory chips on the value of all of the patents and proprietary software held by IBM. To the extent that the gains accrue to labor, they will not be captured in a measure of increases in wealth. If the size of the work force were truly fixed at some level N, increases in the value of human capital would show up in high rates of growth of productivity; but in the United States, for example, employment has increased dramatically in the last fifteen years, so this effect must be estimated as part of a larger simultaneous system.

A national income accounting measure of accumulation captures that part of growth in income that is explained by growth in the stock of inputs in a growth accounting exercise. Capital gains correspond to the unexplained residual. Most growth accounting type exercises suggest that the technology residual is relatively large. For example, Kendrick (1976) estimates that a large fraction of the increase in per capita growth of output over the period 1929 to 1969 can not be accounted for by growth in a broadly defined set of tangible and intangible inputs to production. If technological change occurred at a uniform rate across countries, this would be of little import for the kind of cross-country comparative analysis undertaken here, but given our level of ignorance about this residual, this kind of argument should not offer much comfort.

This exercise may partially help explain why the estimates like the FRB measure of private savings that are based on balance sheet data differ from national income account estimates. Balance sheet data will pick up capital gains; national income account estimates do not. The problem is that the discrepancy seems too large to be explained entirely by the influence of capital gains. The FRB measure of savings in 1982 is $296 billion, equal to 11 percent of NNP in that year. The personal saving rate from the BEA is only 5 percent, and the private saving rate is 6 percent (Hayashi, table 1). Even if all corporate savings in the BEA sense (e.g., undistributed profits) show up as capital gains for individuals and hence are captured in the FRB measure of savings by individuals, this leaves 5 percent attributable to true capital gains on tangible assets in a year that was not noted for the robust performance of asset markets.

Ultimately, the article focuses primarily on the behavior of national savings $S + B$ without making any correction for government capital accumulation. The choice seems to be based on a mixture of simple theory and the degree of confidence in the data. Personal savings is not used because it neglects the substantial differences between corporate savings behavior in the two countries. National savings is chosen over private savings on less clear grounds, but the qualitative behavior of these two series is similar. Government capital accumulation and capital gains are neglected, apparently because they cannot be measured with any accuracy.

There is clearly a limit to how much can be done in a study of this size to reconcile, evaluate, and correct official data. Hayashi's article does quite a lot, especially given that its main focus is on explaining the data, not uncovering them. Nonetheless, it is perhaps worth emphasizing how much room there is for improvement in the data and how much work remains to be done before we can confidently take them as given and use them to refine our theories. Reliable data on national income account savings and on the rate of accumulation of wealth that are internally consistent and consistent across countries would offer a far more complete picture of how rapidly different countries are accumulating, of how rapidly future consumption possibilities are expanding. Whether this kind of data would alter our perspective on relative rates of growth across different countries is an open question. In the comparison between the United States and Japan, it seems quite unlikely that such data would alter the perception that the Japanese are saving more and growing rich faster, although it could change our estimate of the magnitude of the difference. In a comparison between Western Europe and the United States, such a reversal could indeed take place. At the present time, policy discussions focus on the low rate of savings in the United States relative to Western Europe, with its ominous implications for low relative rates of growth and accumulation of wealth in the United States; and focus simultaneously on the contrast between robust employment growth in the United States and persistent stagnation in Europe. In the absence of better data, it seems highly unlikely that we will be able to use cross-country comparisons to learn anything useful about the major outstanding questions concerning the extent to which the government budgetary policies and transfer programs affect rates of accumulation and growth. The number of data points is too small and the amount of noise in the data too large.

Presumably there is some consistency to the way savings is calculated in each country, so that the time-series properties of official savings data are likely to contain useful information about the true behavior of accumulation. Thus, one can still ask why the private and national saving rates in Japan have fallen since 1970. Given that there is fragmentary evidence that the saving rate in Japan during the 1950s and 1960s was also high relative to historical levels, one can also ask why it rose as it did.

The one piece of evidence about which there seems to be little room for dispute is that growth rates in postwar Japan have been astonishingly high. As is illustrated in Figure 1, the postwar growth rates are unprecedented in the prewar era. The figure plots the logarithm of an index of the level of real GDP for Japan and the United States, with the logarithm of each index equal to zero in 1885. To give information about the levels, Figure 2 plots the ratio of total and per capita GDP in the two countries. Whether one uses total GDP or per capita GDP, growth in the two countries prior to World War II is very similar. If anything, growth in the United States is higher. Income in the two countries increases by virtually the same factor in the fifty years from 1885 to 1935; even then, Japanese growth catches up with growth in the United States only because Japan was not significantly affected by the slowdown in the first half of the 1930s. In the postwar period, Japanese growth is uniformly higher than U.S. growth, which continues at approximately its prewar rate. By 1960, Japanese GDP had returned to the level that one would predict from an extrapolation of prewar levels using the prewar growth rate, but rapid growth continues for the next twenty years, slowing somewhat during the 1970s. From 1960 to 1978, the ratio of Japanese to U.S. per capita GDP doubles from roughly .35 to .70.

Figure 3 plots the growth rates and the net national saving rate for Japan. The casual impression from this graph is that savings tracks the broad movements in GDP growth. Although the data in the article go back only to 1965, Albert Ando reports that a study done for the Bank of Japan (cited in Ando (1985)) indicates that savings in prewar Japan did not occur at the high postwar levels, and was not notably different from savings in other countries.

Taken together, this evidence suggests that the problem for theory is to explain why savings and growth are simultaneously high. One of the key contributions of Hayashi's article is to emphasize that in the context of the standard life-cycle model, the rapid growth rate cannot explain the

Figure 1 REAL GDP GROWTH, US AND JAPAN
Log of GDP index set to 0 for 1885

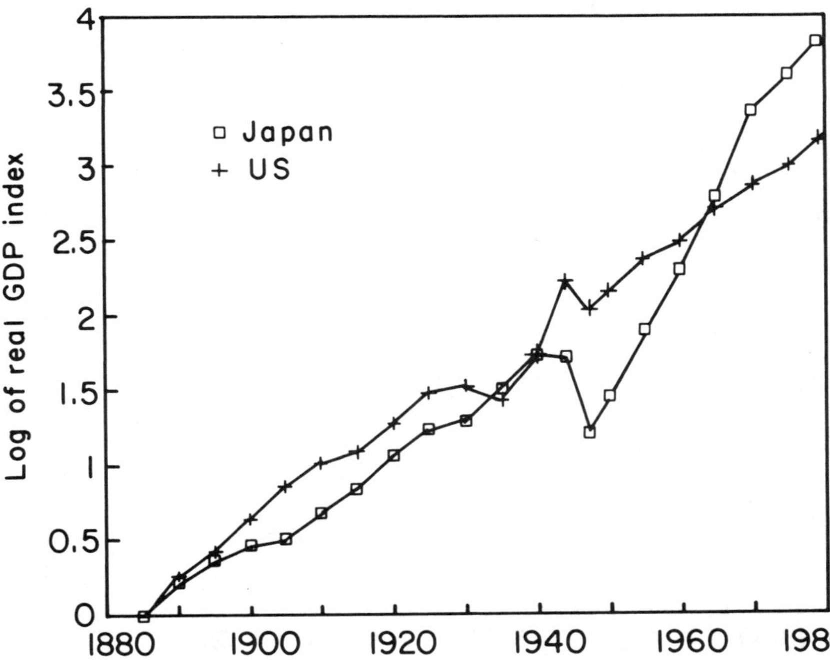

Raw data on GDP and prices for GDP comparisons are taken from Maddison (1982). Observations are taken every five years with two exceptions: observations for 1944 and 1947 are used in place of a 1945 data point, and 1979 is the last data point.

saving rate. His simulations show that the late peak in the age-earnings profile in Japan should cause the life-cycle saving rate to decrease with the productivity growth rate. (Moreover, it should cause the saving rate to be lower than the rate in the United States.) Demographic changes also suggest that in contrast to the observed downward trend, savings in Japan should be higher in 1980 than in 1970.

The article takes an ambivalent attitude toward one possible explanation for the coincidence of high growth and high savings. Under the standard optimizing growth model, the positive response of the saving rate to interest rates causes a country with low capital, hence high interest rates, to grow faster. This is the basis for the usual convergence to a steady-state level or to a steady-state growth rate driven by exogenous technological change. This argument can not offer a complete explana-

Figure 2 RATIO OF JAPANESE TO US GDP
Levels and Per Capita

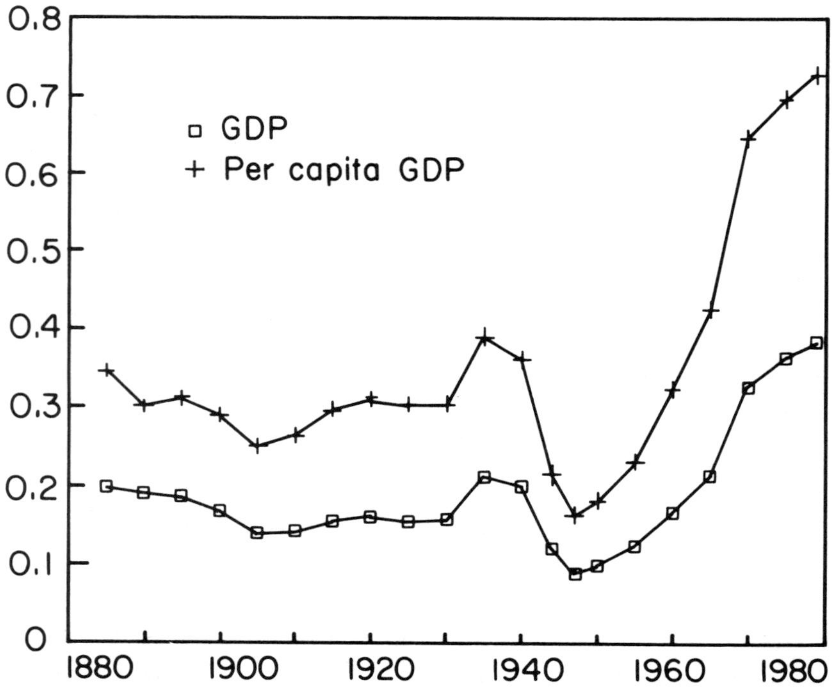

Raw data on GDP and prices for GDP comparisons are taken from Maddison (1982). Observations are taken every five years with two exceptions: observations for 1944 and 1947 are used in place of a 1945 data point, and 1979 is the last data point.

tion for the rapid growth after the war because it should apply with even more force to prewar Japan, and for that matter to all other countries starting from low levels of per capita capital. Something else is needed to explain the postwar acceleration in growth. But given that it took place, it must be true that ex post returns to investment were quite high during the 1950s and 1960s, falling somewhat since then. Assuming that these returns were foreseen and that the degree of intertemporal substitution of consumption was sufficiently large, growth and savings would have moved together. Given enough intertemporal substitution, this should be true in a model with either dynastic families or with life-cycle individuals. Note that the entire postwar era is roughly the time in the labor force for a single individual.

Hayashi suggests the classical theory of diminishing marginal productivity as an explanation for the recent slowdown, but also notes that his Euler equation estimates imply a very low degree of intertemporal substitution. Since these estimates are based only on consumption of food,

Figure 3 GROWTH AND SAVINGS IN JAPAN 1965 to 1979

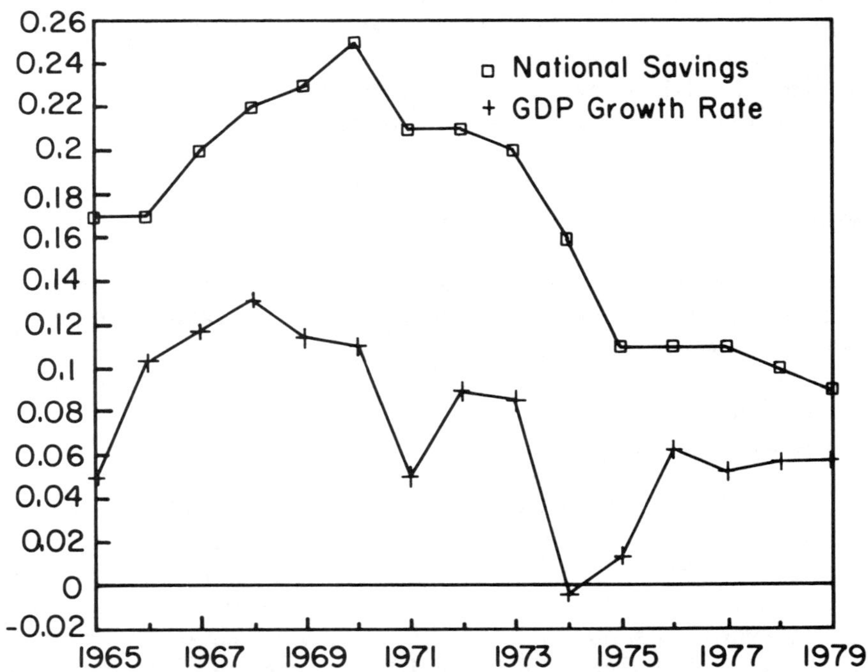

GDP data are from Maddison (1982). The saving rate is the national saving rate under the BEA conventions for government expenditure from table 1 in Hayashi (1986).

for which intertemporal subtitution may indeed be quite small, this does not offer decisive evidence about the overall degree of intertemporal substitution in consumption. Moreover, estimates of this kind have to be treated with caution because in any overall test of its implications, the underlying model is typically rejected by the data.

In addition to the qualification that the saving rate must be responsive to the interest rate, this explanation for the behavior of savings requires that the high postwar rates of return and growth were foreseen. (Note that this assumption of foresight is also made in the steady-state simulations given in the article for the life-cycle model.) Given the unprecedented nature of growth during this period, this is a very strong assumption. By 1960, it should have been clear to even the most naive that things were going extremely well, but the relevant question was how long this could be expected to last. An alternative line of attack on this problem might be to consider the effect of a long string of positive surprises in rates of return and in the rate of growth of labor income in either a life-cycle or infinitely lived agent model. Under the usual form of additively separable preferences, the entire consumption profile increases immediately in response to positive wealth shocks. But any added element in preferences or any adjustment cost that causes an agent to want to smooth the rate of change of consumption as well as the level of consumption will imply that the rate of growth of consumption will lag behind the rate of growth of income, especially if current rates of growth are not expected to be sustained indefinitely.

In summary, whether or not one believes in dynastic families or life-cycle individuals, it is possible to argue that high growth rates in Japan were responsible for high saving rates. What seems to be crucial is not the form of intergenerational transfers, but rather the degree of foresight that can be presumed in this extraordinary period, and the nature of intertemporal preferences for an individual—that is, whether the saving rate is responsive to the rate of interest and whether there is any tendency toward smoothing in the rate of growth of consumption as well as in the level.

This conclusion is based on the premise that causality runs from growth to savings rather than vice versa. Given the enormous cultural and social changes that took place in postwar Japan, one cannot completely dismiss the possibility of an exogenous increase in the saving rate, but I find it difficult to offer an explanation for why it might have taken place. It also seems implausible that double-digit rates of growth can be explained simply by an exogenously high rate of saving. From 1950 to 1970, GDP and population in Japan grew at annual average compound rates of 9.5 percent and 1.1 percent per year respectively. Using estimates of the relative share of capital in total income ranging from ⅓ to ¼, these growth rates imply that the net stock of capital in Japan had to grow at an average annual compound rate of between 25 and 30 percent per year; that is, by 1970, the stock of capital would have had to have increased to 150 times its level in 1950. I suspect that a growth accounting exercise for postwar Japan would find a large residual.

In principle, one must also allow for the possibility that there is no direct causal relationship between the time path for saving and growth rates, each being the result of some third influence; or for the possibility that there is no causal relation at all. But I would find it quite surprising if postwar savings and growth in Japan were not intimately linked.

REFERENCES

Ando, A. 1985. The savings of Japanese households: A micro study based on data from the National Survey of Family Income and Expenditure. University of Pennsylvania. Mimeo.

Hayashi, F. 1986. Why is Japan's saving rate so apparently high. (this volume)

Kendrick, J. 1976. *The formation and stocks of total capital*. New York: NBER.

Maddison, A. 1982. *Phases of capitalist development*. Oxford: Oxford University Press.

Discussion

Fumio Hayashi, in responding to his discussants, expanded on the difference between intentional and accidental bequests; in his article, he argued that bequests were intentionally large. The rapid expansion of the social security system in 1973 provided some evidence on whether the finite-life life-cycle model holds. If parents are not altruistic, then increased social security benefits would lead them to increase their consumption. If the dynastic view of the family is a good approximation, the elderly should increase their saving. The data show little change in the saving rate of the elderly.

James Poterba suggested that the savings behavior of the elderly received too much attention. The major difference between savings behavior in Japan and the United States appears to be in the behavior of the young, not the old, and it is that difference that should be the focus of the study.

Takatoshi Ito argued that much of Japanese saving may be for catastrophic events, despite the fact that the saving rate changed little after the introduction of the social security system. People may not trust the social security system very much, since many believe it will ultimately go bankrupt; they may be saving for the day the social security system breaks down. Ito also commented that Hayashi dismissed the life-cycle hypothesis too quickly. Hayashi tested the steady-state implications of the life-cycle hypothesis, but the Japanese economy may not have been in a steady state. Another possible explanation of the high Japanese saving rate is the target wealth hypothesis. This would explain the high saving rate from 1973 to 1975, since people have to increase their saving to maintain the target asset-income ratio in the presence of high inflation, which depreciates the assets. Finally, he questioned the validity of the data in the interest elasticity calculation. The nominal rate was regulated during the estimation period.

Lawrence Summers suggested cultural differences between Japanese and Americans as a possible explanation of the high saving rate in Japan. He cited a work based on survey data for Japanese-Americans by one of his students. The research showed that Japanese-Americans' saving rate is 5 percent higher than that of other groups, and that there is no systematic relation between the saving rate and the number of generations the Japanese-American has lived in this country. Albert Ando commented that the cultural difference explanation may not work, since the saving rate was not high in prewar Japan.

Martin Feldstein raised some questions. If the Japanese hide some of their assets for tax purposes using the Maruyu system, how honestly do they report the data in the survey used in Hayashi's article? How does the pattern of growth affect saving in the life-cycle hypothesis? What is the reason for the decline in national saving in Japan? For what purpose do Japanese accumulate bequests on the scale suggested by Hayashi?

Stephen Zeldes commented that the economy may exhibit altruistic characteristics even if not all of each bequest is intentional. He also pointed out that the current account deficit in Japan in the 1960s was consistent with an economy having effectively an infinite horizon: the low capital-output ratio in Japan meant that investment was highly profitable, so that investment may have driven the current account.

Paul Romer asked how one can reconcile the existence of systematic government transfers from the young to the old with the altruistic dynastic family view.

Lawrence F. Katz
UNIVERSITY OF CALIFORNIA, BERKELEY, AND NBER

Efficiency Wage Theories: A Partial Evaluation

1. Introduction

The question of why unemployed workers are unable to bid down the wages of seemingly comparable employed workers and gain jobs has long perplexed economists. A burgeoning literature on efficiency wage theories suggests that the answer may lie in the negative incentive effects of low wages. The basic efficiency wage hypothesis states that workers' productivities depend positively on their wages. If this is the case, firms may find it profitable to pay wages in excess of market clearing. This is possible because the wage that minimizes a firm's labor costs per efficiency unit of labor may not be the wage that clears the labor market. Employers may be quite reluctant to cut wages, even in the presence of an excess supply of labor, since reducing wages may actually lower productivity more than proportionately and increase labor costs. Equilibrium can therefore be consistent with persistent involuntary unemployment in some versions of these models.[1]

A variety of conceptually distinct, although potentially complementary, explanations for the direct relationship between wages and productivity have been analyzed in the literature. These approaches are based on the potential benefits to the firm of higher wages: increased

1. If efficiency wage considerations are equally important in all sectors of the economy, involuntary unemployment can arise—similar workers being treated differently—some employed and others unemployed and the unemployed preferring to be employed. If efficiency wage problems are not important in some sectors, jobs may always be available there. Jobs in the efficiency wage sector will still be rationed and offer a positive utility differential. Equivalent workers are treated differently even if there are always some (typically low-quality) jobs available. Unemployment may result from workers searching and waiting for the better, rationed jobs. See Mookherjee (1984b) for an interesting discussion of alternative concepts of involuntary unemployment.

effort level and reduced shirking by employees; lower turnover costs; a higher-quality labor force; and improved morale, more easily facilitated teamwork, and greater feelings of loyalty by workers to the firm. These economic gains to an employer of high-wage policies have long been stressed by institutional labor economists (Dunlop 1985; Reynolds 1978, chapter 9).

Alternative rationales for the payment of noncompetitive wage premiums relate to the presence of unions or threat of collective action by workers. Firms may find it profitable to pay greater than competitive wages to unionized workers to maintain industrial peace.[2] Industrial relations and human resource specialists and institutional economists have long argued that nonunion firms often pay higher wages than necessary to attract qualified labor for the purpose of avoiding unionization.[3] Dickens (1986) develops a model of the impact of the threat of collective action by workers on wages and employment which closely resembles efficiency wage models.

Efficiency wage models have been advanced in recent literature as providing a coherent explanation of normal unemployment. Some authors have even argued that these theories provide solid microfoundations for Keynesian propositions concerning the importance of wage rigidity and the existence of cyclically varying levels of involuntary unemployment.[4] Efficiency wage considerations also provide a potential explanation for large and persistent "noncompetitive" wage differentials across firms and industries for workers with similar productive characteristics. Bulow and Summers (1986) argue that wage differentials arising from efficiency wage reasons may provide a justification for trade and industrial policies designed to protect and subsidize sectors with high-wage jobs.

In this article, I survey recent developments in the efficiency wage literature and discuss theoretical and practical shortcomings of the models.[5]

2. Freeman and Medoff (1981) and Lewis (1982) provide detailed surveys of empirical studies of union relative wage impacts.
3. Foulkes (1980) presents numerous examples of large nonunion firms that maintain high wages as part of explicit union avoidance strategies. Freeman and Medoff (1984, chapter 10) provide a detailed discussion of the effects of unionization on nonorganized labor in the United States.
4. See, for example, Akerlof and Yellen (1984), Bulow and Summers (1986), Jones (1985), Stiglitz (1984), and Yellen (1984).
5. Stiglitz (1984) compares and contrasts the implicit contract and the efficiency wage theoretical literatures. Akerlof and Yellen (1984), Calvo (1979), and Yellen (1984) present excellent surveys of work on efficiency wage models. This article differs from earlier surveys in that it discusses new developments in the literature, analyzes the similarities of efficiency wage and union threat effect models, and focuses more explicitly on empirical evidence that can help in determining the consistency of the predictions of efficiency wage models with actual labor market behavior.

I review a wide variety of empirical evidence on wage patterns and cyclical properties of labor markets. The consistency of the models with this evidence helps provide a partial evaluation of the usefulness of the efficiency wage approach.

The paper is organized as follows. Section 2 presents a rudimentary efficiency wage model and discusses some of the basic implications of the efficiency wage hypothesis. Alternative models with efficiency wage structures, their empirical predictions, and theoretical shortcomings are analyzed in section 3. Efficiency wage models in which firms are assumed to be able to utilize only simple wage schemes as compensation mechanisms are shown to be capable of generating a number of important labor market phenomena including involuntary unemployment, dual (segmented) labor markets, and wage distributions for workers with identical productive characteristics. The same problems, such as the inability of firms to monitor worker performance costlessly and costly turnover, that give rise to efficiency wage payments above the market clearing level create incentives for the use of alternative incentive devices and the development of internal labor markets and long-term contractual relationships in the labor market. Alternative forms of labor contracts, typically involving the posting of performance bonds, can eliminate the job rationing that arises in versions of the models in which firms are limited to the use of simple wage policies. Practical problems arising from capital market imperfections and moral hazard problems on the part of firms may limit the potential for alternative compensation arrangements to eliminate efficiency wage problems.

A wide variety of evidence on interindustry wage differences is analyzed in section 4. Efficiency wage models make strong predictions concerning the existence of wage differentials arising from differences across industries in the wage-productivity relationship. Important systematic wage differentials across industries do not appear to be easily explained by the standard competitive rationales of differences in labor quality, compensating differentials, or transitory disturbances. Although no single efficiency wage model seems consistent with all the facts, efficiency wage models do appear useful in explaining the observed pattern of wage differentials. The consistency of efficiency wage theories with evidence on the cyclical behavior of labor markets and on labor market discrimination is also discussed in section 4.

Section 5 discusses the mechanisms through which efficiency wage models may help explain wage rigidity and cyclical fluctuations. The models explain why firms may not lose much if they fail to adjust wages to shocks. The addition of small costs of changing prices and wages, as emphasized by Mankiw (1985) and Blanchard and Kiyotaki (1985), or of near-rational inertial behavior, as analyzed by Akerlof and Yellen (1985a, 1985b), to efficiency wage models leads to a potential model of cyclical fluctuations in response to aggregate demand movements. Concluding remarks concerning the usefulness of the efficiency wage approach are presented in section 6.

2. *The Basic Efficiency Wage Hypothesis*

Some of the primary implications of efficiency wage models can be illuminated in a simple model in which a worker's physical health and therefore productivity is assumed to depend positively on the real wage paid. This formulation was advanced by Leibenstein (1957) to highlight the linkages among wages, nutrition, and health in less-developed countries. Firms, in this context, get healthier, more productive workers if they pay higher wages. Solow (1979) formulates a formally similar model for developed economies in which increased wages improve morale and thus directly affect productivity through an increase in worker effort.

Following Yellen (1984), I consider an economy with identical, perfectly competitive firms, each possessing a short-run production function of the form $Q = aF(e(w)L)$ where e is the effort (or efficiency) level of a worker, L is the number of employees, w is the real wage, a is a productivity shifter, and Q is output. The price of output is taken to be the numeraire. All workers are assumed to have identical wage-productivity relationships of the form $e(w)$ with $e' > 0$, $e(0) \leq 0$, and the elasticity of $e(w)$ with respect to w declining in w.[6]

A profit-maximizing firm, able to hire all the labor it wants at the wage it chooses to offer, solves the following problem:

$$\max_{w,L} aF(e(w)L) - wL \quad (1)$$

The solution to the problem yields

$$e'(w^*)w^*/e(w^*) = 1 \quad (2)$$

and

$$e(w^*)aF'(e(w^*)L) = w^*. \quad (3)$$

6. Akerlof and Yellen (1984) provide economic interpretations of these conditions required on the $e(w)$ function for a sensible solution to the firm's maximization problem.

The optimal wage w^* satisfies the condition that the elasticity of effort with respect to the wage is unity. The wage w^* is known as the efficiency wage since it minimizes wage costs per efficiency unit of labor. Each firm hires labor up to the point where its marginal product equals w^*.

If the aggregate demand for labor falls short of the aggregate labor supply at w^*, equilibrium will entail involuntary unemployment. Unemployed workers will strictly prefer to work at w^* rather than be unemployed, but firms will have no incentive to hire them at that wage or to lower wages. This simple version of the efficiency wage hypothesis can explain equilibrium involuntary unemployment. Real-wage rigidity also arises in this model. Changes in relative price to the firm or productivity shocks (shifts in a) do not affect the efficiency wage w^*, but lead to alterations in the level of employment.[7]

The simple efficiency wage model can easily be extended to provide potential rationales for wage differentials among workers with identical characteristics and the existence of dual labor markets. If the linkages between wages and effort differ across firms, then the optimal wage will differ across firms and a distribution of wages for workers with identical characteristics can arise in equilibrium. These wage differentials are not compensating differences for nonpecuniary aspects of work that directly affect workers' welfare. Dual labor markets of the type described by Doeringer and Piore (1971) can also arise if the wage-productivity relationship is more important in some sectors than in others. High wages and job rationing can arise in the sector where efficiency wage considerations are salient, while the secondary sector, where efficiency wage considerations are less important, acts as a competitive labor market.

The alternative efficiency wage models examined in the next section provide more explicit microeconomic foundations for the wage-productivity relationship in developed economies. A direct derivation of the wage-productivity relationship from assumptions concerning tastes, technology, and information structure is necessary to analyze the welfare implications of unemployment and labor market segmentation in these models.

7. Solow (1979) shows that wage rigidity of this type only arises when the real wage enters the production function in a labor-augmenting way. A general short-run production function of the form $Q = F(w,L)$ need not generate real wage rigidity with respect to these types of shocks.

3. *Variations on the Efficiency Wage Theme*

3.1. THE SHIRKING MODEL

3.1.1. The Basic Approach and Implications Employers typically have only imperfect information concerning the behavior of workers on the job. The supervision and monitoring of worker actions is costly. The punishments for substandard employee performance available to a firm are typically limited by legal constraints and social custom. Firms can suspend, demote, or fire an employee for inadequate performance or misbehavior, but imprisonment, physical torture, direct cash fines, or resort to tort or contract law for redress are simply not available options for many forms of worker malfeasance.

Under these conditions, employers must find mechanisms to elicit adequate effort from their employees. Piece rates and other direct pay-for-performance compensation schemes are often expensive to operate or impracticable since it may be difficult to observe an individual employee's contributions.[8] Firms may find it profitable in this situation to raise wages above the opportunity costs of workers. By increasing wages, firms raise the cost of job loss and encourage workers to put forth adequate effort. When workers are paid wages above their opportunity costs, they value their jobs, and the threat of termination for detected loafing creates an incentive for workers not to shirk. Models in which the need of firms to elicit effort from their workers can lead to the payment of wages in excess of market clearing and generate equilibrium involuntary unemployment have recently been examined by Bowles (1985), Bulow and Summers (1986), Calvo (1979, 1985), Calvo and Wellisz (1978), Eaton and White (1982, 1983), Foster and Wan (1984), Gintis and Ishikawa (1983), Jones (1985), Shapiro and Stiglitz (1984), and Stoft (1982).

In the Shapiro and Stiglitz (1984) version of the model, firms can only imperfectly monitor their workers' job performance, and workers make a discrete choice of whether to work or shirk. Workers and firms are assumed to be homogeneous. If all firms pay the same market clearing wage, there is full employment and no cost to shirking since workers, if fired, can immediately find another job at the same wage. This strong result of no costs of shirking requires no job switching or search costs and no adverse reputational effects on workers in the labor market if they develop a poor employment history. The homogeneous workers' assumption eliminates reputational effects on workers because all workers are assumed to act the same given the same incentives. If effort is costly, all workers shirk under these full-employment conditions. Thus it pays

8. Lazear (1983) and Pencavel (1977a) analyze the major issues arising in the choice of a piece rate as opposed to a salary or time-rate compensation system.

each firm to increase its wage to eliminate shirking. When all firms do this, the average wage rises and employment is reduced. In equilibrium, all firms pay a wage above the market clearing level, creating unemployment. Since jobs are scarce and rationed, the loss of a job can involve a lengthy spell of unemployment. The reserve army of the unemployed acts as a discipline device making shirking costly. Although some unemployment is optimal in this model since it plays a required role in creating work incentives, Shapiro and Stiglitz show that the equilibrium unemployment rate is not Pareto optimal.[9] Equilibrium unemployment is involuntary in this model since identical workers are treated differently and since the unemployed strictly prefer to be employed.

The shirking model postulates a variety of factors that affect the firm's ability to extract effort from workers and consequently yields some potentially testable predictions concerning the nature of wage differentials and unemployment. Firms should pay higher wages to a given quality worker where monitoring is costly or difficult so that the probability of detecting shirking is low. Higher wages may be required for positions in which poor employee performance can cause a great deal of damage. In fact, the job evaluation systems used in the design and maintenance of wage structures in many industries rate positions on a responsibility factor that is directly related to the probable damage that could be caused by improper job performance (Milkovich and Newman 1984). Workers in positions of trust and responsibility should receive wage premiums (Eaton and White 1982). The value to a worker of keeping a job is reduced if the likelihood of a future separation is great. This means firms with monitoring difficulties should avoid hiring workers from groups believed to exhibit high turnover and should attempt to maintain long-term employment relationships, perhaps through the use of work sharing or a layoff-recall process to deal with temporary downturns. Increased variability in labor demand across sectors (greater sectoral shift activity) directly increases unemployment through more separations to facilitate labor reallocation and indirectly raises the structural unemployment rate by requiring firms to pay higher wages to prevent shirking since it induces a greater likelihood of a future separation.[10]

9. The market equilibrium is generally not efficient since firms fail to adequately take into account the impacts of their wage and monitoring levels on the policies other firms must utilize to prevent shirking by employees (Shapiro and Stiglitz 1984, 1985).

10. Bulow and Summers (1986) analyze the impact of sectoral declines on wages and employment in a standard shirking model. Lilien (1982) presents evidence which he interprets as indicating that sectoral shifts are the main contributor to cyclical unemployment fluctuations in the postwar United States. Abraham and Katz (1986) show that his evidence is consistent with standard single-factor (or aggregate-demand-driven) business cycle models. Topel and Weiss (1985) argue that increased sectoral un-

The expected income from unemployment affects the wage needed to induce proper worker behavior. A higher unemployment insurance benefit raises the required wage and reduces employment. A higher unemployment rate and hence longer expected duration of unemployment for a worker fired for shirking reduces the needed wage. Finally, the level of wages offered by other firms affects the prospects of a discharged worker. The model suggests firms should be concerned with their position in the wage hierarchy (Bulow and Summers 1986).

3.1.2. Segmented Labor Markets The shirking model also provides a rationale for dual labor markets with a utility differential for similar workers across the primary and secondary sectors and rationing of primary sector jobs. The dual labor market hypothesis states that the labor market can be roughly divided into a primary sector that offers jobs characterized by high wages and internal labor markets and a secondary sector that offers low-paying, menial jobs with little room for advancement (Doeringer and Piore 1971).

Dickens and Lang (1985a, 1985b) find in two different micro data sets that the estimation of a switching model of wage determination with unknown regimes yields two distinct wage equations. The two equations closely resemble the predictions of dual market theory for the characteristics of earning functions in the primary and secondary sectors. The equation with which most workers are associated yields significant returns to experience and education. The other equation indicates little or no return from human capital variables. The estimation technique allows the simultaneous determination of the probability of each worker's attachment to each sector and each sector's earnings equation. The procedure allows a hypothesis test that can be interpreted as a test of the rationing of primary sector jobs. Their results indicate the presence of some job rationing (particularly for minority workers).

The basic objection to the dual labor market approach is based on the argument that if secondary workers envy primary workers and are as productive, then primary sector wages should be bid down to clear the market. One possibility is that wage differences across the sectors reflect unmeasured worker quality differences. Alternatively, the shirking model provides a coherent explanation for dual markets with job rationing of "good" primary jobs even in an economy populated by homogeneous workers.

---

certainty can explain the increase in the average (or natural) rate of unemployment in the United States since the mid-1970s. Altonji and Ham (1985) survey recent empirical work on sectoral shifts and unemployment.

Bulow and Summers (1986) and Jones (1985) analyze versions of the shirking model in which the detection of shirkers is difficult in one sector of the economy (the primary sector) and monitoring is costless in the other sector (the secondary sector). This roughly fits the empirical observation that the typical primary job entails a fair degree of responsibility and independent action on the part of the employee, while most secondary jobs involve assignments that are more easily supervised. Efficiency wages above market clearing arise in the primary sector, creating a utility differential between primary and secondary jobs that creates a cost to loss of a primary sector job.[11]

Wait unemployment (as in Hall 1975) can be generated if it is easier to get a primary sector job out of unemployment than out of the secondary sector and workers line up for primary sector jobs. This is likely if a history of secondary sector employment is a bad signal to primary sector employers. Workers with values of leisure greater than the secondary sector wage but lower than the primary sector wage may also enter unemployment to line up for primary sector vacancies. Wage differentials arising from differences in monitoring difficulties across firms create incentives for search unemployment.

Internal labor markets with internal promotion ladders are likely to arise in the primary sector to maintain long-term employment relationships. The development of internal labor markets and deferred payment schemes to induce effort in the primary sector may obviate the need for the use of efficiency wages with banishment to the secondary sector or unemployment as incentive devices. This type of alternative means to motivate workers is a basic difficulty with the efficiency wage models.

3.1.3. Objections to the Shirking Model: The Bonding Critique The predictions of the shirking model concerning job rationing and involuntary unemployment arise from the dual economic functions performed by the wage. The wage serves both to allocate labor and to provide incentives for adequate employee performance (Shapiro and Stiglitz 1984). The primary objection to the shirking model is that firms have other methods to enforce employee discipline in a more efficient manner than the use of a high wage plus threat of dismissal.

A variety of labor market bonding mechanisms can potentially eliminate the need for unemployment as a worker discipline device. One direct method is for workers to post performance bonds at the time of hiring that would be forfeited if they were caught shirking. Alternatively,

11. Bulow and Summers (1986) discuss the implications for industrial policy, trade policy, and antidiscrimination policy of the noncompetitive wage differentials arising in this shirking model.

firms can pay efficiency wages but charge workers an employment (or "entrance") fee (Becker and Stigler 1974). If firms use high wages to reduce incentives for workers to shirk or steal, unemployed workers should be willing to pay entrance fees or post bonds to gain employment at these firms. The threat of forfeiting a bond or paying a new employment fee to gain employment can create work incentives and enable the market for jobs to clear, thus eliminating involuntary unemployment.

Instances of workers posting direct performance bonds or purchasing their jobs are rare, although not entirely unknown. Employment arrangements that may implicitly perform bonding functions such as upward sloping age-earnings profiles, pensions and other deferred compensation schemes, and internal promotion ladders are observed in a large segment (the primary sector) of the labor market. These mechanisms appear in large establishments where monitoring problems are likely to be important. Lazear (1979, 1981) demonstrates that seniority wage systems in which workers post a bond against cheating by accepting wages below their marginal product initially and have it returned in the form of wages above the value of their marginal product later in their careers or in the form of a pension upon retirement can solve the effort elicitation problem. If workers are unable to post upfront bonds upon taking a job (pay an employment fee), optimal deferred payment schemes are likely to involve an efficiency wage premium above the market clearing level (Akerlof and Katz 1986).

Practical objections arise to the use of complete bonding schemes in the labor market. In the first place, workers, particularly early in their working lives, face capital market constraints and lack the liquidity required to post large bonds. If the probability of detecting shirking is low, the required bond or employment fee may be substantial. Carmichael (1985) argues that even if capital markets are imperfect, firms can charge a fee sufficient to make the expected utility of the job offer equal to the value of workers' reservation wages. Although this may eliminate the directly involuntary nature of unemployment, it does not lead to an efficient level of unemployment (Shapiro and Stiglitz 1985).

Since independent verification of detected shirking is difficult, firms have an incentive to say falsely that workers are shirking and claim the bonds; firms may collect employment fees and then dismiss workers. The firm's concern for its reputation as an employer may be able to overcome this problem (Lazear 1979, 1981). The difficulty of potential workers in verifying the honesty of a firm's behavior means that the reputation mechanism is quite fragile and may be a far-from-perfect enforcement mechanism (Kreps 1984). The likelihood of firm default on the bond can be reduced if the firm does not expect to gain from falsely claiming that the worker is shirking. For example, if the firm claims that a worker has shirked and discharges him or her, it is possible for the bond to be paid to a third party instead of to the firm. The worker is disciplined and the firm does not gain from cheating. We do not see the direct use of third-party systems like this in practice. Carmichael (1983) argues that seniority promotion rules with a fixed wage hierarchy can play this role. Additionally, tournament schemes (Bhattacharya 1983, Malcolmson 1984) may permit the firm to commit itself to a wage plan that creates the proper incentives for workers.

Reputational considerations are likely to be important precisely for the large, visible employers, such as IBM or General Motors, that provide high-paying, primary sector jobs. These large firms offer exactly the type of jobs that the shirking model indicates should pay efficiency wages and be rationed. Smaller, less visible secondary firms that may not stay in business long are unlikely to be able to get workers who will trust them not to renege on agreements concerning deferred compensation. Thus, the implication of considering possible bonding mechanisms and where they may be effective is that the secondary sector needs to pay efficiency wages while the primary sector can utilize deferred payments to reduce the required efficiency wage premiums. This unrealistic prediction of the model suggests that further work must be done on why full bonding schemes are not practicable for visible employers quite likely to value their reputations for keeping (implicit) promises to their employees.

If capital markets were perfect and third-party verification of shirking always possible, firms would spend next to nothing on raising the probability of detecting shirking and demand large bonds since monitoring is costly and the posting of bonds would be costless under these circumstances (Becker and Stigler 1974; Dickens, Katz, and Lang 1986). The empirical observation that firms devote substantial resources to monitoring workers suggests that a full bonding solution to the shirking problem is unattainable.[12] Thus, firms must be choosing one or both of two second-best alternatives to bonding: monitoring workers intensively or paying efficiency wages. The likely outcome is that firms utilize bonds to the ex-

12. Dickens, Katz, and Lang (1986) analyze these issues in far more detail. A caveat to this argument is that firms may monitor workers for reasons other than preventing shirking. Monitoring and supervision may be a way for firms to prevent costly, but honest, mistakes by workers. Monitoring may also help firms sort heterogeneous workers into tasks for which they are best suited. If firms cannot prevent mistakes and sometimes fire workers who were not actually cheating (make type II errors) and if workers are risk-averse, the firm may find it optimal to expend resources on monitoring to reduce the required bond and the wage differential needed to compensate workers for mistaken appropriations of their bonds. This is really a variation on the theme that third-party verification of detected shirking is not possible.

tent possible, and then choose the optimal combination of efficiency wages and monitoring required to prevent shirking in the presence of limited bonding ability.

Lazear (1979) argues that the existence and observed pattern of mandatory retirement provisions indicates that some bonding must be utilized in the labor market. Adverse selection problems provide an alternative rationale for the use of mandatory retirement policies. If individual performance is hard to observe, wage cuts for older workers may lead to the better workers moving to other jobs and the "lemons" remaining. Additionally, Medoff and Abraham (1980) provide evidence that experience-earnings and tenure-earnings profiles cannot be fully accounted for by rising productivity. The typical finding in cross-section wage equation estimates of a positive effect of years of tenure at current job (seniority) on earnings is often pointed to as evidence of these types of bonding arrangements, especially taken in conjunction with the Medoff and Abraham evidence. These estimates merely show that workers who have been on a given job for a longer period of time earn higher wages. This may reflect returns to seniority beyond those to general labor market experience as in the bonding stories, or it may reflect the fact that workers in good jobs or good matches earn higher wages throughout their job tenure and are less likely to quit these valuable jobs (Abraham and Farber 1986, Altonji and Shakotko 1985). Alternatively, better workers may earn more throughout their careers and have greater job tenure in any given cross-section since they may tend to be more stable. Nevertheless, pensions may be the primary labor force bonding mechanisms. Ippolito (1985) presents evidence indicating the importance of bonding through pensions.

Practical limitations on the use of alternative incentive mechanisms suggest that high wages and involuntary unemployment may be a profitable discipline device. However, the limitations on bonding devices appear least important in exactly the type of jobs the model predicts should pay efficiency wages (jobs in large, primary sector firms).

3.2. THE LABOR TURNOVER MODEL

Workers are likely to be more reluctant to quit a job the higher the (relative) wage paid by the current firm and the worse the prospects in the external labor market (e.g., the higher the aggregate unemployment rate). If firms must bear part of the costs of turnover and if quit rates are a decreasing function of wages paid, firms have an incentive to pay high wages to reduce costly labor turnover. Salop (1979) and Stiglitz (1974, 1985) formally analyze models based on these features. The formal structure of the labor turnover model is quite similar to that of the shirking model. Firms' attempts to pay high relative wages to minimize turnover costs can lead to an equilibrium with wages in excess of market clearing and involuntary unemployment serving to reduce quit rates.

The market failure in this model arises, as in the shirking model, because of the dual role played by the wage. The same wage is unable simultaneously to clear the market for new hires and the market for trained workers (Salop 1979). A seniority wage system in which new workers accept initial lower wages below their marginal product to pay for their training and hiring costs can solve the problem and eliminate involuntary unemployment. If training and hiring costs are large and are concentrated in a short initial period, employment or application fees need to be levied on new workers. Firms do not have an incentive to induce workers to quit if training must actually be provided or hiring costs entailed. Thus, the moral hazard problem on the firm's side is not as serious as in the shirking model. Capital market imperfections may make the payment of large fees impractical. Salop (1979) and Stiglitz (1984) point out that risk-averse workers are unlikely to be willing to post bonds and bear the risk of being unsuited to a job. These considerations indicate that it is realistic to assume that firms must bear part of the costs of turnover.

The model predicts that high wages will be found where hiring and training costs are formidable. These wage premiums should be associated with lower turnover rates. Stiglitz (1985) shows that the model provides an explanation for wage distributions within an industry for similar workers. Equally profitable high wage–low turnover and low wage–high turnover strategies can coexist for identical firms and workers for certain types of quit functions.[13]

3.3. THE ADVERSE SELECTION MODEL

Imperfect information by firms about the abilities of workers may provide a selection rationale for efficiency wage payments. If workers are heterogeneous in ability and if ability and reservation wages are positively correlated, firms that offer higher wages will attract higher-quality job applicants. If firms cannot observe applicant quality and lack devices to induce workers to reveal their true abilities, random hiring from the applicant pool must be done. A higher wage increases the expected ability of a worker hired randomly from the applicant pool. A wage above the market clearing level may minimize costs per efficiency unit of labor

13. See Stiglitz (1985) for a formal discussion.

under these circumstances (Stiglitz 1976, Weiss 1980). Institutional, legal, or sociological constraints preventing firms from differentiating wages across workers with different productive characteristics can lead to similar results.[14]

A basic objection to the model is that firms are likely to eventually learn a worker's ability. In this case, performance bonds can solve the adverse selection problem. The same moral hazard problem on the part of firms and capital market imperfections that limit the use of bonding for shirking problems apply in this context as well. If firms can measure performance on the job, pay-for-performance schemes eliminate the problem. Employment contracts with self-selection incentives (nonlinear wage-employment contracts) can also potentially ease adverse selection problems (Mookherjee 1984a).

3.4. SOCIOLOGICAL MODELS

Workers' effort levels may significantly depend on the extent to which they feel they are being treated fairly by their employers. The perceived justness of the wage may affect worker productivity if effort levels are linked to worker morale and feelings of loyalty to the firm.[15] Akerlof (1982, 1984) and Solow (1979) argue that wage rigidity in the face of unemployment may be due to the importance of social wage norms and other behavior not well captured by traditional individualistic utility functions. Akerlof (1984) discusses evidence from sociological studies indicating that a worker's effort level depends on the norms of his or her work group (peer pressure) and posits a number of sociologically based models with efficiency wage implications. Akerlof (1982) develops a model in which firms can raise group work norms by offering wages above the level necessary to attract a labor force. The firm's "gift" of high wages is rewarded by the "gift" of improved work norms and increased individual effort. Wages in excess of market clearing may be the outcome when wages play a dual role of both allocating labor across firms and of satisfying interpersonal and intertemporal wage norms that matter for worker performance.

Most firms pay careful attention to the perceived fairness and consistency of their internal wage structures. Doeringer and Piore (1971) find that firms devote far more resources to and place more weight in

14. The standard rate wage policies favored by many unions provide an example. Brown (1985) presents evidence on the prevalence and analyzes the implications of such policies.

15. Pencavel (1977b) presents an interesting analysis of the causes and effects of worker morale with an empirical application to British coal mining.

their wage policies on job evaluation programs designed to maintain or justify their internal wage structures than to market wage surveys used to keep wages in line with those of product or labor-market competitors. Richard Wing (1984, pp. 9–18), a former compensation director at Eastman Kodak, notes that "there is always some degree of conflict between internal and external pay equity. The position taken by most salary administrators is that internal relationships should be given first priority, and external pay relationships for certain jobs must be compromised on occasion." If certain wage relationships matter to a firm's work force, it is in the firm's interest to take those considerations into account.

The sociological models indicate that efficiency wages are likely to arise where work groups and teamwork are important. These models may also explain the direct impact of product market factors and the firm's "ability-to-pay" on wages. Worker morale and loyalty and consequently productivity may depend on the extent to which the firm shares its rents with its employees.

3.5. THE UNION THREAT MODEL

Firms are likely to face important diseconomies of scale in the hiring and training of workers. If there are costs to job search or relocation, a firm may have to increase its wage offer or reduce the quality of accepted applicants to replace a large number of workers quickly. If only a few workers leave a firm, their coworkers are likely to have overlapping firm- and job-specific knowledge and be able to train replacements. When many workers quit more or less at once, more valuable knowledge is lost per worker and no one may be left who is capable of training replacement employees. Since the costs of turnover to the firm rise rapidly as the number of workers needing to be replaced in a given interval increases, collective action can provide workers with more bargaining power than they have acting individually. Social norms, such as the willingness of customers and suppliers to boycott a struck firm, may in many settings prevent firms from doing business even if they can replace workers who attempt to act collectively. Collective action by workers may enable them to shut a business down. This bargaining power can potentially be used by workers to claim for themselves some part of the monopoly rents earned by an enterprise and (in the short run) a share of the returns on the fixed assets.

Dickens (1986) analyzes the effect of the threat of collective action by workers on wages and employment on firms that attempt to avoid collective bargaining with their employees (i.e., attempt to keep a union out). A firm can avoid unionization in the model by choosing wages and employment so that no coalition greater than or equal to a fixed fraction of the work force (in U.S. labor law a majority) can be formed around a feasible union contract. The organization of a union is assumed (realistically) to be costly to the work force. A firm can prevent collective action by paying its workers a wage as high as they would receive under a collective bargaining agreement minus the cost to the workers of organizing. Foulkes (1980) provides many examples of nonunion firms that try to keep wages close to the union wage level for comparable jobs. Dickens shows that the threat of collective action can explain why unemployed workers cannot bid down a firm's wages.[16] Unemployed workers who are hired and paid a lower wage will attempt to organize collectively. Firms may find it profitable to pay wages above the market clearing level to try to prevent unionization. Thus, the model can lead to job rationing and unemployment in a manner similar to efficiency wage models. The evidence presented by Ruback and Zimmerman (1984) that union organization drives reduce a firm's stock price and Freeman (1983) that unions are associated with lower profitability provides a strong rationale for firms to develop labor relations policies that help maintain a nonunion environment.

Firms may be able to avoid unionization in manners other than paying high wages. One possibility is the posting of a bond that is forfeited if a worker is involved in union activity. Jacoby (1983) notes that some firms in the late nineteenth century withheld some of workers' earnings. These withheld earnings were forfeited if workers went on strike. If a union were formed, the firm might extract the return of the bonds. Firms could also require workers to sign contracts barring them from engaging in collective action as a condition of employment. So-called yellow-dog contracts are not now enforceable in the United States.

The union threat model predicts that wage premiums should arise where the costs of organization are low for workers and where the potential gains from unionization are high. Product market power (larger monopoly rents per worker) and high capital/labor ratios increase the potential gains from collective action and should be associated with higher union wages and higher wages of nonunion workers with a credible threat to organize. Dickens (1986) provides a number of arguments within the framework of the model for the stability of real or nominal wages over the business cycle. International differences in labor law and the potential threat of unionization provide important identifying infor-

16. The "insider-outsider" theories of unemployment developed by Lindbeck and Snower (1984) and Solow (1985) also generate job rationing outcomes from the bargaining power of "insiders" (incumbent employees).

mation for the possible importance of collective action threats as a cause of unemployment and wage rigidity.

3.6. SUMMARY

There are several plausible explanations why firms may find it in their interest to pay wages in excess of market clearing. The mechanisms underlying these alternative efficiency wage theories are summarized in table 1. These models appear capable of explaining persistent involuntary unemployment, segmented labor markets, and wage differentials for similar workers that are not equalizing differences. The use of deferred payment schemes and internal promotion ladders within long-term employment relationships may be able to solve some efficiency wage problems without resort to job rationing. The empirical relevance of efficiency wage theories is examined in more detail in the next section.

Table 1 A SYNOPSIS OF ALTERNATIVE EFFICIENCY WAGE THEORIES

Theory	*Problems leading to efficiency wage payments*	*Benefits to firm of high wages*
Shirking	Imperfect observability of worker effort level and performance; monitoring is costly	Raise cost of job loss encouraging good performance; economize on monitoring costs
Turnover	Firms must bear part of turnover costs (hiring and training costs)	High wages reduce turnover costs if quit rate is decreasing function of wages
Adverse selection	Imperfect observability of worker quality and performance	Attract higher quality pool of applicants if more productive workers have better outside opportunities
Sociological	Morale and worker feelings of loyalty to firm depend on perceived fairness of wages	Improved work norms, morale, feelings of loyalty to firms which raise productivity
Union threat	Costs of replacing existing workforce gives employees bargaining power	Maintain industrial peace or prevent unionization

4. *Some Empirical Evidence Relating to the Usefulness of the Approach*

4.1. INTERINDUSTRY WAGE DIFFERENCES

4.1.1. Some Implications of Efficiency Wage Models for Wage Differentials It has long been noted that there are large differences in wages across industries for apparently similar work. Substantial industry wage differentials remain even after controlling for union status and observed worker and job characteristics (Bloch and Kuskin 1978, Dickens and Katz 1986, Krueger and Summers 1986, among others). In fact, large wage differences for essentially the same type of work in the same locality have invariably been uncovered by area wage surveys. Slichter (1950) observes that hiring rates paid for common labor by 85 plants in Cleveland in February 1947 ranged from $0.50 to $1.09 an hour. He notes that this spread persisted despite the fact that rates had been compiled and distributed to firms throughout the city by the Cleveland Chamber of Commerce for over twenty years. John Dunlop (1985, p. 18) summarizes the typical finding of studies of local wage variation: "It is a well-established fact that wage rates or average hourly earnings for a defined job classification, such as maintenance electrician or key punch operator, show very wide variation in a locality, particularly in a community with a variety of industries. The top wage rates for the same job classification are often two or three times the low ones. Differences in fringe benefit programs enlarge these differences." These wage differentials provide an empirical challenge to alternative labor market models. The ability of competitive and efficiency wage models of the labor market to meet this challenge is the focus of this section, which draws heavily upon the review and analysis presented in Dickens and Katz (1986).

A standard competitive labor market model implies that persistent industry wage premiums require industry-related differences in labor quality (skill) or nonwage dimensions of work requiring equalizing differences. Reder (1962, p. 276) summarizes these predictions as follows: "In the long run, under competitive conditions, any industry will pay the same price for a given grade of labor as any other industry hiring in the same location. This remark must be qualified for differences in nonpecuniary attractions of different industries and locations. . . Therefore, in the long run, the real wage differentials among industries will reflect differences in the skill mix." Alternatively, industry wage differences at any given time for similar work may reflect transitory differentials related to shifts in labor demand across sectors and imperfect short-run labor mobility.

On the other hand, a basic implication of efficiency wage models is that if the conditions necessitating efficiency wage payments differ across industries, then the optimal wage will differ among industries. This means that workers with identical productive characteristics are paid differently depending on their industry affiliation. These wage differences for similar workers reflect industry characteristics that do not directly affect the utility of workers and thus do not require compensating differentials. Intra-industry wage distributions for similar workers may arise from differences in the wage-productivity relationship across firms in an industry.

Each variant of the efficiency wage hypothesis potentially predicts that particular industry and firm characteristics should be associated with industry wage premiums. The shirking model leads to the prediction that wages should be high where monitoring costs are large. In these circumstances, high wages are likely to be substituted for intensive monitoring activities. Wage differentials may also be required where the costs of worker malfeasance are high. Oi (1983) suggests that higher wages are required in large establishments since monitoring is typically more difficult. The cost of foul-ups is likely to be large in industries with expensive equipment (possibly proxied by high capital/labor ratios) and for workers in positions where poor performance may affect many other workers' performances (e.g., workers in coordinating positions and workers involved in integrated production processes).

The turnover model implies that wage premiums should arise where turnover and training costs are large and that wage premiums should yield the benefit of lower quit rates. The adverse selection model predicts higher wages, after controlling for observables, where it is difficult to evaluate labor quality. The sociological (or normative) models are less specific but suggest that the importance of teamwork and ability to pay may be relevant. The importance of relative wage comparisons in some sociological models provides a rationale for long-term stability of wage differentials and for linkages in wage differentials across occupations within a firm or industry. Finally, the union threat model suggests that wage premiums arise where the costs of unionization are low to workers and where the firm has rents derived from market power or has large fixed capital investments. This means that product market power should be directly reflected in wages. Differences in industry wage premiums across occupations with important union threats (blue-collar occupations) and those with smaller threats or no possibility of unionization (managers and professional workers) provides further information on the importance of union-based models.

The primary point is that efficiency wage models predict that there should be important wage differentials not explained by compensating differentials, labor quality differences, or shifts in labor demand across sectors. An important approach to the assessment of the empirical relevance of wage models involves the determination of the importance of noncompetitive wage differences. Further relevant information can be gained by examining the nature of these wage premiums for consistency with the predictions of individual efficiency wage alternatives.

Some initial evidence on the nature and importance of industry wage differentials is provided through cross-section estimates of industry effects utilizing individual level data. Table 2 presents estimated wage differentials for broadly defined industries based on the results of a regression of log hourly earnings on industry dummies with human capital, demographic, and locational controls for a large sample of private-sector workers from the combined 1983 Current Population Sur-

Table 2 ESTIMATED OLS LOG WAGE DIFFERENTIALS FOR ONE-DIGIT INDUSTRIES AND UNION STATUS 1983 CPS—NONAGRICULTURAL PRIVATE-SECTOR WORKERS

Variable	*Coefficient (Standard Errors)*
Mining	.289
	(.009)
Construction	.127
	(.005)
Nondurables	.050
	(.004)
Durables	.098
	(.004)
Transportation and public utilities	.154
	(.005)
Wholesale trade	.042
	(.005)
Retail trade	−.161
	(.004)
FIRE	.052
	(.005)
Services	−.064
	(.003)
Union	.192
	(.003)
Sample size	134,928
$\bar{R}^2$	.546

Controls included are education (years of schooling) and its square; experience (age-education-5) and its square; married; sex; race; part-time work; SMSA; interaction terms for both experience and its square with married, race, sex, education, part-time work and SMSA; 11 occupation dummies; and 50 state dummies.

vey (CPS).[17] The employment-weighted average of the coefficients of the industry dummy variables from the regression was calculated with the omitted industry dummy treated as having a zero effect on wages.[18] The estimated differentials presented in table 2 are the differences between the actual industry coefficients and the weighted average. These differentials indicate the proportional difference in wages between an employee in a given industry and the average employee in the sample after controlling for individual characteristics, SMSA status, and state of residence. The industry variables have a sizable impact on wages. For example, workers in mining, transportation, and public utilities earn approximately 45 and 32 percent more than (observationally) equivalent workers in retail trade. The industry wage effects are comparable in magnitude to the effect of union status.

Krueger and Summers (1986) provide evidence on industry wage differentials for a more disaggregated industry breakdown. They report industry wage premiums that range from 38 percent above the average, for the petroleum industry, to 37 percent below the average, for private household workers. Their estimates are based on the May 1984 Current Population Survey that includes a wide variety of controls for individual characteristics, union status, and occupation. Krueger and Summers find that the employment-weighted standard deviation of industry wage premiums for two-digit industries ranges from 10 to 15 percent for different years of the CPS from 1974 to 1984.

Dickens and Katz (1986) find that the industry wage differentials persist when union and nonunion workers are analyzed separately. The patterns of industry wage premiums are extremely similar for union and nonunion employees. The raw correlation of three-digit industry wage premiums for union and nonunion workers in the combined 1983 CPS sample is 0.65.[19]

4.1.2. Competitive Explanations for Wage Differentials A number of explanations consistent with standard competitive labor market models are possible for the large impact of industry affiliation on wages even after

17. The data set is described in detail in Dickens and Katz (1986). The sample consists of private sector, nonagricultural employees, 16 years of age and older. The sample combines information on the outgoing rotation groups from all twelve months of the 1983 CPS. Workers with wages less than $1 an hour and greater than $250 an hour were treated as outliers and eliminated from the sample. The results do not change qualitatively when these observations are left in the data set.
18. In other words, the weights are the number of workers (observations) in an industry in the sample.
19. This raw correlation is a biased estimate of the true correlation since it is not corrected for the fact that the wage differentials are estimated rather than known.

controlling for measured human capital variables. The first explanation posits that differences in technology across industries make it profitable to hire higher-quality workers (and hence pay higher wages) in some industries. Estimated industry wage premiums in a cross-section may primarily reflect individual-specific components of earnings capacity that are unobservable (to the econometrician) and correlated with industry status. If unmeasured ability is highly correlated with observed labor quality variables, such as years of schooling and labor-market experience, then unmeasured labor quality cannot provide an explanation for the large estimated industry wage effects. Dickens and Katz (1986) show that the size of industry wage effects is not much altered if wage equations are first estimated without industry variables and then the residuals are used to determine the industry impacts. This approach credits observed quality variables with the impacts of unobserved variables correlated with both measured quality variables and industry status.

Longitudinal data provide a potential vehicle to control for time invariant, unmeasured labor quality. If high-wage industries simply have workers of high unobserved ability and if workers of a given quality are paid equally in different industries, wage changes should not systematically be linked to changes in industry status. Longitudinal data allow one to examine the wages of a given individual as he or she switches industries. First-difference (or fixed-effects) estimation allows one to eliminate the impacts of unchanging unobserved ability components (that are rewarded equally in all industries) on the industry wage effects estimates. Krueger and Summers (1986) estimate large effects of industry switches (for broadly defined industries) on wages in first-differenced regressions using a pooled sample of matched CPS May data for 1974–75, 1977–78, and 1979–80. The estimated industry effects from the first-differenced regression are similar in direction and magnitude to pooled regression estimates. Thus, workers moving from high- to low-wage industries appear to experience wage declines and workers moving from low- to high-wage industries appear to experience wage gains.[20] Vroman (1978) reports similar results for industry switchers in the 1964–71 period, using Social Security continuous wage-history data on individuals' annual earnings. Murphy and Topel (1986) find in matched CPS data for

20. These longitudinal results (industry switch effects) are potentially consistent with models in which worker quality is heterogeneous (multidimensional) and match quality varies. If match quality is not fully revealed at the start of a match, one could generate systematic relations of industry switches and wage changes of the type found by Krueger and Summers (1986). A matching model with costly renegotiation and uncertain match quality, such as the model analyzed in Antel (1985), may also be consistent with these results if the switches from high- to low-wage industries are primarily layoffs or discharges and the moves from low to high are primarily quits.

1977–1984 that industry switchers receive only 30 percent of the wage gains that would have been predicted from the industry differentials observed in cross-sectional data. The Krueger and Summers and Murphy and Topel studies differ substantially in their sample selection rules, procedures for the correction of measurement error in industry transitions, and other control variables included in the first-differenced regressions. The existing longitudinal evidence suggests that at least a moderate portion of the industry differentials found in cross-sectional analyses reflect "true" differentials rather than just unmeasured ability.

A second possible competitive explanation is that the industry wage differentials are compensating differentials for nonwage job attributes that directly affect the utility of workers.[21] In fact, this is often the justification for the inclusion of industry dummies in estimated wage equations with individual cross-section data. Krueger and Summers (1986) find that the inclusion of 10 working conditions variables in a standard wage equation barely affects the estimated industry wage premiums.[22] Many important nonpecuniary job attributes are unlikely to be captured by their control variables. Freeman (1981) and Krueger and Summers find that the fringe benefit differentials tend to expand wage differences. Murphy and Topel (1986) find that differences in unemployment risk across industries can account for only quite a small fraction of industry wage differentials.

If industry wage premiums reflect equalizing differences, then they do not reflect rents that make jobs especially valuable to workers. The implication is that the wage premiums should not be systematically related to quit rates. Industry and individual level studies both indicate that wage premiums are strongly associated with lower quit rates (Pencavel 1970, Freeman 1980, and Krueger and Summers 1986). This suggests that industry wage premiums reflect rents to good jobs or good matches and are not merely compensating differences.[23]

21. Rosen (1985) provides a comprehensive treatment of the theory of equalizing differences in the labor market and a review of empirical studies of compensating differentials.

22. Krueger and Summers (1986) use a sample derived from the 1977 Quality of Employment Survey. The working conditions variables included are weekly hours, variables indicating dangerous or unhealthy conditions on the job, commuting time, workshift dummies, dummies indicating extent of choice of overtime, and variables indicating whether working conditions are pleasant.

23. This interpretation is clean if workers have homogeneous tastes concerning nonpecuniary aspects of work. If workers have heterogeneous preferences, then it is possible to imagine distributions of worker preferences with respect to nonwage aspects of work in which wage differentials that reflect compensating wage differentials for marginal workers may be negatively correlated with average quit rates in an industry. This means that quit rates do not depend on wage differences for marginal workers but do for inframarginal workers. A particular contrived example is the case of one disamenity that some workers mind and others do not. If enough workers care about the disamenity, a

An additional competitive explanation for industry wage premiums observed at any particular time is that they largely reflect transitory differentials created by shifts in labor demand across sectors and maintained by incomplete labor mobility in the short run. The strong stability of industry differentials over time appears to rule out transitory factors as a major component of the explanation. Cullen (1956) presents data showing remarkable stability in the industry wage structure in the United States from 1899 to 1950. He finds the rank correlation of average annual earnings for 76 manufacturing industries for the years 1899 and 1950 to be .66. Cullen finds for a group of 84 manufacturing industries that 14 of the 21 industries in the highest-wage quarter in 1899 were still in the highest-wage quarter in 1947. Also, 15 of the 21 lowest-wage industries in 1899 remained in the lowest-wage quarter in 1947. Cullen furthermore provides evidence of stability in the extent of wage dispersion over the long term. The degree of dispersion across industries was approximately the same in 1950 as it was in 1899.

This long-term stability in industry average wages may reflect stability in skill mix differences. Industry differentials for any given grade of labor could reflect responses to sectoral labor demand or supply shifts. Limited evidence available from this time period suggest that industry wage differences for particular grades of labor were fairly stable. Slichter (1950) finds the rank correlation of males' unskilled average hourly earnings for 20 manufacturing industries between 1923 and 1946 to be .73.[24]

Strong stability in interindustry wage rankings is also evident for the postwar United States. Montgomery and Stockton (1985) report that the rank correlation of mean hourly wages for 20 two-digit manufacturing industries between 1951 and 1981 was .675. Bell and Freeman (1985) find strong stability in the rankings for a group of 53 industries (both manufacturing and nonmanufacturing) from 1948 to 1982. Both Bell and

compensating differential may arise to compensate the marginal worker for this disamenity. Workers who do not care about the disamenity take jobs at the high-wage firms with the disamenity and earn rents. These workers have lower quit rates and reduce the average quit rate in high-wage firms. Low-wage firms without the disamenity have no workers earning rents. In this example, more inframarginal workers are at the high-wage firm and average quit rates are negatively correlated with wages. One could also construct examples going in the other direction. Thus, if workers have heterogeneous preferences, the relationship among quit rate and wage differentials may be difficult to relate to the importance of equalizing differences in the labor market.

24. Slichter uses data from the National Industrial Conference Board surveys of establishments. The unskilled wage rate applies to jobs for which no previous job training is required. Similar stability is apparent in the industry rankings of the male skilled and semiskilled wage rate for this period. This may reflect stability in skill differences given the heterogeneity of the category. Katz (1986) provides a more detailed analysis of the stability and determinants of interindustry wage structure in the pre-1950 period.

Freeman and Montgomery and Stockton note that the dispersion (log standard deviation) of industry mean wages increased substantially during the 1970s. On the other hand, Krueger and Summers (1986) find that the estimated two-digit wage premiums using individual data from the CPS and controlling for individual characteristics did not appear to have grown from 1974 to 1984. Krueger and Summers find the correlation of the estimated industry wage premiums between 1974 and 1984 to be .970. These results indicate that the rising dispersion in average industry wages since the early 1970s may largely reflect changes in the composition of labor forces across industries and possibly also changes in union wage impacts.

A further possibility is that industry wage differences arise from differences in patterns of human capital accumulation across industries. Krueger and Summers (1986) find that industry wage differentials are approximately equal in magnitude and highly correlated for young (ages 20 to 35) and older (ages 50 to 65) workers. Furthermore, the 1979 Current Population Survey contains information on job tenure (years with current employer). I used this data set to see whether industry wage differences vary with job tenure. Estimates of log earnings equations for separate tenure groups for nonunion, private sector workers indicated that industry differentials are quite similar for different tenure groups. For example, the standard deviation of one-digit industry wage differentials for workers with less than one year of tenure and for workers with more than ten years of tenure was 0.11 and 0.12 respectively.[25] The correlation (corrected for sampling error) for the differentials of the two tenure groups was .74. Large industry wage effects were apparent for entry-level workers that are close in size and highly correlated with those of long-term employees. One exception was that the differentials of all other industries versus retail trade appeared to be substantially larger for workers with long job tenure than for entry-level workers.

4.1.3. The Occupational Structure of Industry Wage Premiums Although most explanations for wage differentials provide reasons why one would expect particular occupational groups to be highly paid in some indus-

25. These are standard deviations of the estimated industry differentials from separate regressions for each tenure group of log earnings on the same set of control variables as those listed in table 2 and one-digit industry dummy variables. The standard deviations listed are unbiased standard deviations corrected for sampling error in the estimates of the industry dummy variable coefficients. The sample is private sector, nonagricultural, nonunion workers, 16 years of age and older from the May 1979 CPS. Workers without tenure data and with earnings less than $1 an hour and greater than $250 an hour were deleted from the sample. The sample size for the less-than-one-year-of-tenure group is 2770 and for the ten-years-or-more is 1912.

tries relative to others, they do not lead one to expect the pattern of wage premiums to be the same across industries for diverse occupational groups. For example, a standard competitive model suggests that an industry with dangerous production jobs may pay its blue-collar workers high wages to compensate them for the risks their jobs entail, but it does not suggest that secretaries in this industry should earn a pay premium. Working conditions, skill requirements, and monitoring problems are quite likely to differ across occupations in a firm or industry.

Dickens and Katz (1986) estimate industry wage differentials by occupation (for a 12-occupation and three-digit Census of Population industry breakdown) for nonunion, private sector workers from the combined 1983 CPS sample. The effects of human capital variables, demographic characteristics, and locational variables were constrained to be the same across occupational groups. Industry wage effects were allowed to vary by occupation. This involves the estimation of an earnings function of the following form:

$$W_{ij} = \mathbf{X}_{ij}\boldsymbol{\beta} + \alpha_j + \varepsilon_{ij}, \quad (4)$$

where W_{ij} is log(hourly wage) of individual i in industry-occupation cell j, $\mathbf{X}_{ij}$ is a vector of individual and locational variables for individual i, $\boldsymbol{\beta}$ is a vector of parameters, α_j is a fixed effect (or differential) for industry-occupation cell j, and ε_{ij} is an error term. This is equivalent to a wage equation with industry dummies, occupation dummies, and a full set of interaction terms between the industry and occupation dummies. The large number of industry-occupational cells implies that the feasible approach to estimating the industry differentials for each occupation is first to run a de-meaned regression in which the industry-occupation cell means are subtracted off for the dependent variable and all the independent variables:

$$W_{ij} - \bar{W}_j = (X_{ij} - \bar{\mathbf{X}}_j)\beta + u_{ij}, \quad (5)$$

where $\bar{W}_j$ is the mean of the log of hourly earnings for workers in cell j, $\bar{\mathbf{X}}_j$ is the vector of the means of the individual and locational variables for workers in cell j, and u_{ij} is a regression error. This regression, assuming that the ε_{ij} in equation (4) are uncorrelated with the X_{ij}, yields a consistent estimate $\hat{\beta}$ of β. The mean residual for each cell j is then a consistent estimate of the industry-occupation j fixed effect:

$$\hat{\alpha}_j = \bar{W}_j - \bar{\mathbf{X}}_j\hat{\beta}. \quad (6)$$

Table 3 CORRELATIONS OF INDUSTRY WAGE DIFFERENTIALS ACROSS OCCUPATIONAL GROUPS—FIXED EFFECTS 1983 CPS PRIVATE-SECTOR NONUNION WORKERS

Position	*Manage*	*Prof.*	*Tech.*	*Super.*	*Sales*	*Cleric*	*Service*	*Crafts*	*Operate*	*Semi-skilled*	*Trans. oper.*	*Labor*
Managers	1.00	.99	.60	.85	.84	.99	.84	.90	.70	.67	.80	.81
Professionals		1.00	.72	.94	.74	.90	.73	.86	.82	.77	.74	.77
Technicians			1.00	.78	.61	.76	.70	.80	.63	.37	.45	.56
Supervisors				1.00	.88	.91	.97	.99	.78	.94	.79	.90
Sales					1.00	.79	.73	.78	.41	.46	.53	.69
Clerical						1.00	.86	.90	.76	.70	.78	.88
Service							1.00	1.00*	.98	.75	.74	.89
Crafts								1.00	.93	.95	.79	.78
Operatives									1.00	1.00*	.76	1.00*
Semi-skilled										1.00	.91	.90
Trans. equip. oper.											1.00	.91
Laborers												1.00

*The correction for sampling error in industry-occupation cell means causes some correlations to be greater than 1.00.

The regression from which the fixed effects were calculated contained education (years of schooling) and its square; experience (age-education-5) and its square; 50 state dummy variables; dummy variables for marital status, race, sex, part-time work, and whether or not an individual lives in an SMSA; and interaction terms for both experience and experience squared with all the other variables except the state dummies and education squared. The correlation coefficients are corrected for within cell sampling error. A detailed discussion of the correction procedure is available in Dickens and Katz (1986).

The estimated fixed effects were then grouped by occupation to analyze the relationships among industry impacts on wages in different occupations.

Correlations of these estimated industry wage differentials across occupations are presented in table 3. The correlations are corrected for sampling error.[26] Table 3 indicates that even after controlling for a wide variety of individual and geographic variables there are quite large correlations (most in the range .7 to 1) between average wages for workers in any two occupations within an industry. If one occupational group in an industry is highly paid, all categories of workers tend to be highly paid. This finding is hard to reconcile with views that the industry wage differences reflect unobserved ability or compensating differentials since skill requirements and working conditions are unlikely to be common to all occupations in an industry.

The results seem to support the union threat model since product market power or profitability is likely to raise worker bargaining power across occupations in an industry. Furthermore, the occupational structure of industry wage effects is quite similar for union and nonunion workers (Dickens and Katz 1986). The union threat model does not explain why groups of workers that do not pose a threat of collective action (e.g., managers) also share in the industry pay premiums.

The high correlation in industry differentials among different occupations is consistent with sociological models in which wage norms are linked in a firm or industry. The great efforts taken by firms to maintain their internal wage structure is quite consistent with these findings.

4.1.4. Industry Characteristics and Industry Wage Patterns An understanding of the empirical relevance of alternative theories of wage determination requires knowledge of the industry characteristics associated with high wages and low wages after controlling for worker characteristics. A considerable amount of empirical research has focused on the relationship between wages and industry structure. These studies (partially surveyed by Long and Link (1983) and Kwoka (1983)) have focused on the

26. Dickens and Katz (1986) provide further details on the estimation technique and describe the procedure for correcting the correlation coefficients for within cell sampling error. Since the industry differentials are estimated and since some of the industry-occupation cells are small, sampling error can lead to an upward bias in the standard deviations of industry wage effects within an occupation and a downward bias in the correlations of industry premiums across occupations. The raw correlations (uncorrected for sampling error) of the industry wage differentials across occupations lead to similar results, all quite positive. Dickens and Katz get results almost identical to those reported in table 3 when a full correction procedure for both within cell sampling error and the potential correlation in the estimation errors in the fixed effects across cells is utilized under the assumption of homoscedastic errors in the fixed effects regression.

influences of product market power, firm (or plant) size, and extent of unionization on wages. The industry characteristics that affect wage levels and the extent to which these variables matter appear to be quite sensitive to the specification (e.g., other control variables included) and to the particular sample analyzed (e.g., time period and use of only manufacturing vs. wider variety of industries). This suggests the effects are not uniform across industries and that multicollinearity is important for many industry variables. Nevertheless, some patterns emerge from these studies.

Industry wage levels are strongly positively correlated with industry concentration when no labor quality variables are utilized (L. Weiss 1966). The relationship is far more ambiguous when detailed labor quality controls are included. Pugel (1980) and Hodson and England (1985) find strong positive effects of industry profitability measures on average industry wages even with controls for average worker characteristics, extent of unionization, and other industry variables, including the rate of employment growth. Dickens and Katz (1986) find that profits as a percentage of sales are strongly positively related to industry wage premiums for nonunion workers. Kwoka (1983), Long and Link (1983), and Mellow (1982) find a positive and significant effect of industry concentration on wages, using individual-level data on earnings and worker characteristics combined with other industry level variables. This contrasts with L. Weiss's (1966) finding that concentration does not matter once individual worker controls are taken into account. Overall, industry wage differences appear to be related to product market power (ability to pay) although measurement problems in variables such as concentration and accounting profits mean these conclusions should be viewed as somewhat tentative.

The proportion of workers in an industry in plants of large or average size have typically been found to be positively related to industry wage levels even in the presence of detailed control variables (Kwoka 1983, Long and Link 1983, Pugel 1980, and others). Although establishment size and firm size appear to have quite important effects on wages within industries, they cannot explain much of interindustry wage differentials. The May 1979 CPS contains a special survey including questions on establishment and firm size. Krueger and Summers (1986) find in analyzing this data that the inclusion of plant size and firm size controls barely affects the estimates of industry wage differentials. They find the employment weighted standard deviation of two-digit industry log wage differentials falls only from 0.104 to 0.99 when plant and firm size controls are added to a log earnings equation with controls for occupation, region, union status, and individual characteristics. The raw correlation of the estimated industry differentials with and without employer size controls is .96. In regressions (not reported here but available upon request) using the 1979 CPS, I find that estimated industry differentials are only slightly affected by the inclusion of plant size and firm size dummies when nonunion workers are analyzed in isolation. These results correspond to the conclusion of Brown and Medoff (1985) that most of the employer size effect on wages occurs within detailed industries.

The percentage of workers covered by collective bargaining in an industry has a strong positive effect on average industry wages.[27] Dickens and Katz (1986) find that the extent of industry unionization has a strong positive effect on both union and nonunion wages. They also find that regional union density has a strong positive effect on nonunion wages and a much weaker impact on union wages. Dickens (1986) argues that this is the pattern of union density impacts that arises from an important role of a union threat in wage determination.

The impacts of industry variables on wages remain a bit of a puzzle. The findings of most studies are fairly consistent with some role for union threat effects since product market power and extent of unionization seem to explain a fair portion of interindustry wage differentials for nonunion workers. Sociological models of the Akerlof (1984) variety also seem to have some support. The findings of Hodson and England (1986) and Lawrence and Lawrence (1985) that capital intensity (capital to labor ratio) has a positive effect on industry wages provides some support for the shirking model since the cost of worker malfeasance is likely to be greater in capital-intensive industries. Capital–skilled labor complementarity suggests that the capital-labor ratio finding may simply proxy for unmeasured labor quality. The strong linkages of wages to product market variables even after controlling for a large number of individual and locational variables appear difficult to reconcile with a strict unobserved ability interpretation of industry wage differentials.

4.1.5. Direct Evidence on the Benefits to Firms of High Wages Efficiency wage models postulate that firms pay wages above the market clearing level because there are cost-reducing or productivity-enhancing reasons to do so. Some limited empirical evidence exists on the benefits to firms of higher wages. As noted previously, wage premiums are associated with lower quit rates. Thus, high wages help to economize on turnover costs. The direct cost savings from lower turnover do not appear to be large enough to justify the magnitude of observed wage differentials. For example, Freeman and Medoff (1984, p. 109) estimate that the cost

27. Lewis (1983) provides a comprehensive survey of estimates of the extent of unionization on wages in industry-level studies.

savings associated with lower quit rates from the presence of a union is 1 to 2 percent of labor costs. They also find that the impact of unionism on quit rates to be equivalent to the impact of a 40 percent wage differential. The indirect gains of enhanced teamwork from continuity in work relationships may be the more important element of the benefits of lower turnover.

Hammermesh (1977) finds that the deviation of a worker's wage from the wage predicted by the worker's personal and job characteristics is positively correlated with various measures of job satisfaction. High wages appear to raise morale, as suggested by the sociological models and many personnel professionals. A further unanswered question is whether job satisfaction measures have much to do with productivity. Freeman and Medoff (1984) conclude from surveying a larger number of studies on worker attitudes and unionization drives that worker dissatisfaction is strongly correlated with increased desire for unionization as expressed by greater union organizing activity and a higher likelihood of votes in favor of unionization in representation elections. High wages, by raising worker satisfaction, reduce the likelihood of union organization as predicted by the union threat model.

Krueger and Summers (1986) provide some further evidence linking wage premiums to worker behavior consistent with some of the supposed benefits to a firm of efficiency wage payments. Industry wage premiums are found to be negatively related to absenteeism (due to weather) and positively related to employee self-evaluations of work effort. The positive correlation of wage differentials and employee views of work effort may simply indicate that high wages are acting as a compensating differential for greater effort required on the job or a fast pace of work. Allen (1984) finds consistently in an analysis of several data sets that positive wage differentials are associated with reduced absenteeism. Although absenteeism is something that can easily be observed by a firm, the reasons for absenteeism are not easily monitored. High wages combined with the threat of job loss for too much absenteeism might be an effective personnel policy.

Bulow and Summers (1986) discuss the introduction of the five-dollar-a-day pay system at Ford in 1914. They note that historical observers found that the higher wages led to large increases in productivity and reductions in absenteeism and turnover. This case provides some support for the implications of the shirking and turnover model.

Industry wage differences not captured by observed worker characteristics, working conditions variables, and locational variables are large and persistent. These differentials are not well explained by compensating differentials or transitory rents arising from shifts in labor demand across sectors. More work using longitudinal data is required to determine the extent to which unmeasured ability may account for the estimated differentials. The union threat model appears quite consistent with industry differentials for nonunion production workers. The long-term stability of industry wage differences through periods with substantial differences in the extent of union organization indicate only a more limited role for union threats and direct union impacts. Large wage differentials across industries for occupations with little threat of collective action suggests that other factors must also be important. Industry differentials are strongly correlated across occupational groups. Sociological models in which industry wage contours or wage norms gain normative significance appear consistent with these similarities in the industry wage patterns across occupations. Economic efficiency wage rationales arising from monitoring, selection, or turnover problems can provide reasons why certain jobs in an industry require wage premiums. The concerns of firms with the perceived fairness of their internal wage structure may mean that these differentials come to permeate the entire wage structure in the industry. A combination of the economic efficiency wage models with the sociological (normative) efficiency wage models provides a fairly consistent, though far from elegant, account of the observed pattern of wage differentials. Much more empirical work is needed to uncover direct evidence of the gains to firms of high-wage policies. Better measures of the factors that economic efficiency wage models indicate should be important for wage differences (e.g., monitoring costs) are required to better determine the relevance of these models for understanding the apparent large impact of industry and firm affiliation on earnings.

4.2. LABOR MARKET DISCRIMINATION[28]

Efficiency wage models provide several reasons for persistent discrimination by race and sex in a competitive labor market. Group differences unrelated to productivity can potentially generate wage differences and occupational segregation. If two identifiable labor market groups differ in their rates of turnover or labor force withdrawal, the group with the higher turnover propensity will have a shorter horizon on a job and is likely to require greater inducement not to shirk. Bulow and Summers (1986) show that in the dual labor market version of the shirking model the higher turnover group must be overrepresented in the secondary sector since if the wage is the same for both groups in the primary sector,

28. This section is intended as a brief discussion of some of the implications of efficiency wage models for the analysis of labor market discrimination. I make no attempt to survey the vast empirical and theoretical literature on discrimination in the labor market.

the shorter horizon group is more likely to shirk unless the chances of being able to get a primary job in the future are lower than for the long horizon group. Since Poterba and Summers (1984) estimate a much higher rate of labor force withdrawal for women aged 25 to 59 than for men in the same age group, this yields a prediction of occupational and industrial segregation by sex with women tending to be found in lower-paying jobs that are easier to monitor. Bulow and Summers (1986) demonstrate that if labor market discrimination arises from a result of differences in separation probabilities by groups, then antidiscrimination policies such as affirmative action can increase welfare under a utilitarian welfare criterion.

Johnson and Solon (1984) estimate that the earnings of both males and females are negatively related to the proportion of females in the occupation even when a wide variety of individual control variables are included. Additionally, Johnson and Solon show that much of the difference in male and female earnings after controlling for differences in individual characteristics is related to differences in the industrial distribution of employment by sex. If industry wage differentials arise from efficiency wage considerations, then this is strong evidence that these factors play a major role in differences in earnings by sex.

Goldin (1986) presents evidence on widespread sex segregation across jobs within manufacturing requiring similar training and ability in 1890. She also finds that 50 percent of female operatives were paid piece rates as opposed to 13 percent of male operatives. Monitoring costs are found to be cheaper for piece rates than for time rates in female-dominated industries; the opposite is true for male-dominated industries. Goldin argues that deferred payment systems, such as discussed in Lazear (1979, 1981), conserved on monitoring costs and were feasible for males but not for females because of their shorter work horizons. Females were confined to jobs utilizing more expensive piece rates and thereby received lower wages than males. The same argument would apply to the use of efficiency wages rather than deferred payments for male-dominated jobs if full bonding were not feasible. Goldin also presents evidence showing that the feminization of the clerical occupations occurred only with standardization and division of tasks that made monitoring easier.

Occupational and industrial segregation arises in the shirking model because of the inability of high-turnover groups to post performance bonds. This suggests that groups facing capital market imperfections are more likely to be affected. Furthermore, even if groups do not differ in turnover propensities, if disadvantaged groups are liquidity constrained and unable to post bonds (accept deferred payment schemes), they will be less able to get primary sector jobs. Dickens and Lang (1985a, 1985b) find that nonwhites are overrepresented relative to their observed characteristics in secondary sector jobs.

4.3. CYCLICAL BEHAVIOR OF LABOR MARKETS

The behavior of labor markets in which efficiency wage payments are required in some sectors in response to demand or productivity shocks corresponds well with stylized facts concerning the cyclical behavior of actual labor markets.[29] Since in a downturn the pool of the unemployed increases and the duration of unemployment goes up, the cost of quitting increases in an efficiency wage model. This implies procyclical quit behavior. Additionally, dual market versions yield predictions of cyclical upgrading as the primary sector expands in response to a positive shock (Bulow and Summers 1986, Jones 1985). The quit rate increases in upturns as workers quit secondary jobs to take available primary sector jobs. In response to negative shocks, workers are displaced from primary sector jobs.

This cyclical upgrading and downgrading corresponds with empirical findings that most of the employment growth in an upturn is associated with jobs in high-wage sectors such as durable goods manufacturing, construction, transportation, and public utilities (Okun 1973, Abraham and Katz 1986). Furthermore, Bils (1985) finds in an analysis of panel data that the real wages of workers who switch employers in a given year are strongly procyclical. He finds that the real wages of workers remaining on the same job are only slightly procyclical. Vroman (1978) also finds that workers switching jobs over the cycle have lower wages on average than job stayers and far more procyclical real wages. Vroman's results indicate that industry switchers have the most procyclical wages of any group.

This process of worker upgrading also appears to be important in understanding movements in productivity over the business cycle. Calculations based on figures presented in Okun (1973, p. 215) suggest that about 40 to 50 percent of the increase in labor productivity associated with an expansion in business activity is attributable to shifts in employment from low- to high-productivity sectors. Bernanke and Powell (1984) find that productivity is most procyclical in durable goods manufacturing. Efficiency wage models in which worker effort is variable provide a plausible partial explanation. The simple shirking model predicts countercyclical productivity within a sector in response to aggregate-

29. Okun (1973) discusses in detail empirical regularities observed in the cyclical behavior of labor markets. Bernanke and Powell (1984) empirically analyze the differences in similarities in the cyclical behavior of industrial labor markets in the prewar and postwar United States.

demand-driven business cycles since the greater cost of job loss in recessions spurs greater work effort. Yet, efficiency wage considerations create incentives for long-term relationships in the labor market. In this case, effort should vary with the amount of work needed to be done. Labor hoarding and cyclical productivity shifts appear most important in sectors where efficiency wage considerations are likely to be most important (capital-intensive industries).

Most of the cyclical variation in labor input takes place in fluctuations in employment rather than in hours worked per employee. Bulow and Summers (1986) argue that in the shirking model the value of a job is greater to a full-time worker than to a part-time worker. Thus the use of work sharing in response to a downturn reduces the value of jobs to workers and means higher wages are required to prevent shirking. If layoffs are utilized, the remaining workers have stronger work incentives. This makes sense for permanent declines in demand, but may not be reasonable for temporary downturns. Firms should be interested in increasing long-term horizons by maintaining long-term relations with workers. Workers' shirking decisions should be based on the long-term value of the job. The adverse selection model of A. Weiss (1980) provides an alternative reason for the use of layoffs rather than wage cuts or work sharing in response to declines in demand. If workers differ in unobservables and more productive workers have better outside opportunities, wage cuts and work sharing reducing the value of the job mean that the better workers are the ones most likely to leave for alternative jobs or self-employment.

5. *Cyclical Fluctuations and Efficiency Wages*

Efficiency wage models provide several mechanisms through which cyclical fluctuations in output can be generated by aggregate-demand shocks. In the first place, a basic property of these models is that wages are set by firms to maximize profits as the interior solution to a maximization problem.[30] In this case, the failure of firms to adjust wages to small shocks leads to only second-order losses. This differs sharply from a competitive labor market model where firms face large losses from failing to pay the competitive wage. Akerlof and Yellen (1985b) demonstrate that if firms are efficiency-wage setters in the labor market and monopolistic competitors in the product market, then inertial wage and price behavior in response to small nominal shocks leads to only second-order

30. This follows directly from the structure of the model presented in section 2. Stiglitz (1984) and Akerlof and Yellen (1985a, 1985b) develop this point in detail.

losses to the firms that follow such behavior even though this behavior generates a macroeconomic response with first-order welfare consequences.[31] Imperfect competition in the product market combined with efficiency wages in the labor market can potentially yield a model of cyclical fluctuations in response to aggregate-demand disturbances.

Strong incentives for the creation of long-term firm-worker relationships arise from efficiency wage considerations. The emergence of long-term employment relationships means that wage payments may reflect installment payments on long-term obligations (Hall 1980). In this case, employment decisions are not completely guided by current wages. This may reduce the importance of sticky wages from near-rationality and menu costs as a potential rationale for real impacts of nominal shocks.

The importance of relative wage concerns in efficiency wage settings provides a further rationale for inertial wage policies in response to real and nominal shocks. This point has been illustrated for the turnover model by Stiglitz (1984, 1985). A drop in the money supply requiring a reduction in nominal wages to maintain the existing level of unemployment may lead to unchanged nominal wages with decentralized wage setting. Any individual firm reducing its wage will tend to experience a higher quit rate and lower profits. Frictions in wage setting, such as staggered contracts, can exacerbate the difficulties in adjusting to nominal shocks when relative wages matter to firms and workers (Taylor 1982). If wages at all firms could be adjusted to shocks in a coordinated manner, these difficulties would not arise.

Monetary policy can also affect real output and the unemployment rate in the shirking model if it can affect real interest rates (Bulow and Summers 1986). An increase in the real interest rate reduces the discounted value of keeping a primary sector job and thereby increases the incentive of workers to shirk. This can reduce employment by requiring higher wages to prevent shirking. The quantitative importance of this mechanism for monetary policy is likely to be quite circumscribed.

6. *Conclusions*

Efficiency wage theories suggest that firms may find it profitable to pay workers' wages above the market clearing level since such wage premiums can help reduce turnover, prevent worker malfeasance and collective action, attract higher-quality employees, and facilitate the elicitation of

31. Adjustment costs may be greater for output and employment than for prices and wages. The menu costs or "near-rationality" argument appears equally consistent with inertial output and employment policies with fluctuating wages and prices in response to small shocks.

effort by creating feelings of equitable treatment among employees. Simple versions of efficiency wage models can explain involuntary unemployment, segmented labor markets with queues for primary sector jobs, and large differences among firms in the wages paid for what appear to be similar workers. Suitably modified, these models can parsimoniously explain many of the major stylized facts concerning the behavior of labor markets over the business cycle.

The primary criticism of efficiency wage models is that bonding mechanisms can solve effort elicitation, turnover, and adverse selection problems in an efficient manner. Additionally, the primary rationales for the use of efficiency wages are all arguments for the emergence of long-term contracts and long-term employer-employee attachments. Such long-term relationships appear quite important in the primary sector of the labor market where efficiency wage considerations are typically viewed as most important. These long-term attachments help facilitate bonding through the use of deferred payment mechanisms. It is an open empirical question whether seniority wage systems and pensions provide full bonding or whether they are only partial solutions leaving room for efficiency wages. Future theoretical work is required to analyze efficiency wage problems in an explicitly contractual setting.[32] The reasons why the contract market fails to clear need to be more fully explicated. The presence of more than one efficiency wage consideration may mean that bonding mechanisms solving one efficiency wage problem exacerbate others. For example, Shapiro and Stiglitz (1985) argue that employment fees to clear the market in the presence of the shirking problem may exacerbate adverse selection problems. Complicated contracts required to perform implicit bonding functions may create misunderstandings and lead to feelings of inequity that harm morale and productivity.

Evidence on industry wage differences indicates that large differentials remain that are quite difficult to explain in terms of differences in labor quality or differences in important nonpecuniary aspects of work requiring compensating differentials. The persistence of industry wage premiums for long time periods implies that they are not just transitory differentials arising to facilitate the sectoral reallocation of labor in a dynamic market economy. Large, persistent wage differentials for similar workers and types of jobs provide strong evidence in favor of the importance of some type of efficiency wage behavior by many firms. The complex pattern of differentials is difficult to reconcile with individual variants of the efficiency wage argument. Further empirical research is required to iso-

32. Mookherjee (1984b) and Bester (1985) provide some interesting initial attempts to link efficiency wage and implicit contract theories. Stiglitz (1984) discusses future directions for research in this area.

late the primary benefits to firms of high wages, the determinants of the uses of alternative compensation systems (piece rate vs. time rate, etc.), and the industry characteristics associated with large wage premiums.

I am indebted to William Dickens for numerous discussions and for comments on previous drafts of this paper; a significant part of this paper grew out of our joint work. I thank George Akerlof, Joe Altonji, Charles O'Reilly, Kevin Lang, Lawrence Summers, and Janet Yellen for helpful discussions. I am grateful to Phil Bokovoy and Elizabeth Bishop for expert research assistance. The Institute of Industrial Relations at U.C. Berkeley provided research support. All remaining errors are my own.

REFERENCES

Abraham, K. G., and H. S. Farber. 1986. Job duration, seniority, and earnings. MIT Department of Economics Working Paper no. 407 (January).

Abraham, K. G., and L. F. Katz. 1986. Cyclical unemployment: Sectoral shifts or aggregate disturbances? *Journal of Political Economy*. 94 (June): 507–22.

Akerlof, G. A. 1982. Labor contracts as partial gift exchange. *Quarterly Journal of Economics* 87 (November): 543–69.

———. 1984. Gift exchange and efficiency wages: Four views. *American Economic Review* 74 (May): 79–83.

Akerlof, G. A., and L. F. Katz. 1986. Do Deferred Wages Dominate Involuntary Unemployment As A Worker Discipline Device? University of California at Berkeley. Mimeo.

Akerlof, G. A., and J. Yellen. 1984. Efficiency wage models of the labor market: Introduction. University of California at Berkeley. Mimeo.

———. 1985a. A near rational model of the business cycle, with wage and price inertia. *Quarterly Journal of Economics* 100 (August): 823–38.

———. 1985b. Can small deviations from rationality make a significant difference to economic equilibria? *American Economic Review* 75 (September): 708–20.

Allen, S. 1984. Trade unions, absenteeism and exit-voice. *Industrial and Labor Relations Review* 37 (April): 331–45.

Altonji, J., and J. Ham. 1985. The collective impact of sectoral shocks on aggregate employment fluctuations. Columbia University. Mimeo.

Altonji, J., and R. Shakotko. 1985. Do wages rise with job seniority? NBER Working Paper 1616 (May).

Antel, J. J. 1985. Costly labor contract negotiation and the labor mobility of young men. *American Economic Review* 75: 976–91.

Becker, G. S., and G. J. Stigler. 1974. Law enforcement, malfeasance, and the compensation of enforcers. *Journal of Legal Studies* 3 (January): 1–18.

Bell, L., and R. B. Freeman. 1985. Does a flexible industry wage structure increase employment? The U.S. experience. NBER Working Paper 1604 (April).

Bernanke, B., and J. Powell. 1984. The cyclical behavior of industrial labor markets: A comparison of pre-war and post-war eras. Stanford University. Mimeo.

Bester, H. 1985. Long-term wage contracts and dual labor markets. University of Bonn (February). Mimeo.

Bhattacharya, S. 1983. Tournaments and incentives: Heterogeneity and essentiality. University of California at Berkeley (March). Mimeo.

Bils, M. J. 1985. Real wages over the business cycle: Evidence from panel data. *Journal of Political Economy* 93 (August): 666–89.

Blanchard, O. J., and N. Kiyotaki. 1985. Monopolistic competition, aggregate demand externalities, and the real effects of nominal money. NBER Working Paper 1770 (December).
Bloch, F., and M. Kuskin. 1978. Wage determination in the union and nonunion sectors. *Industrial and Labor Relations Review* 31 (January): 183–92.
Bowles, S. 1985. The production process in a competitive economy: Walrasian, Neo-Hobbesian and Marxian models. *American Economic Review* 75 (March): 16–36.
Brown, C. 1985. Standard-rate wage setting, labor quality, and unions. NBER Working Paper 1717 (October).
Brown, C., and J. Medoff. 1985. The employer size wage effect. Harvard University. Mimeo.
Bulow, J. I., and Summers, L. H. 1986. A theory of dual labor markets with application to industrial policy, discrimination and Keynesian unemployment. *Journal of Labor Economics*. Forthcoming.
Calvo, G. 1979. Quasi-Walrasian theories of unemployment. *American Economic Review* 69 (May): 102–7.
———. 1985. The inefficiency of unemployment: The supervision perspective. *Quarterly Journal of Economics* 100 (May): 373–87.
Calvo, G., and S. Wellisz. 1978. Supervision, loss of control, and the optimum size of the firm. *Journal of Political Economy* 86 (October): 943–52.
Carmichael, L. 1983. Firm-specific human capital and promotion ladders. *Bell Journal of Economics* 14 (Spring): 251–58.
———. 1985. Can unemployment be involuntary?: Comment. *American Economic Review* 75 (December): 1213–14.
Cullen, D. 1956. The interindustry wage structure, 1899–1950. *American Economic Review* 46 (June): 353–69.
Dickens, W. T. 1986. Wages, employment and the threat of collective action by workers. University of California at Berkeley. Mimeo.
Dickens, W. T., and L. F. Katz. 1986. Industry wage patterns and theories of wage determination. University of California at Berkeley. Mimeo.
Dickens, W. T., L. F. Katz, and K. Lang. 1986. Are efficiency wages efficient? NBER Working Paper 1935.
Dickens, W. T., and K. Lang. 1985a. A test of dual labor market theory. *American Economic Review* 75 (September): 792–805.
———. 1985b. Testing dual labor market theory: A reconsideration of the evidence. NBER Working Paper 1670.
Doeringer, P. B., and M. J. Piore. 1971. *Internal labor markets and manpower analysis*. Lexington, Ma.: D. C. Heath.
Dunlop, J. 1985. Industrial relations and economics: The common frontier of wage determination. *IRRA Proceedings 1984*.
Eaton, C., and W. D. White. 1982. Agent compensation and the limits of bonding. *Economic Inquiry* 20 (July): 330–43.
———. 1983. The economy of high wages: An agency problem. *Economica* 50 (April): 175–81.
Foster, J., and H. Wan. 1984. Involuntary unemployment as a principal-agent equilibrium. *American Economic Review* 74 (June): 476–84.
Foulkes, F. 1980. *Personnel policies in large nonunion companies*. Englewood Cliffs, N.J.: Prentice-Hall.
Freeman, R. B. 1980. The exit-voice tradeoff in the labor market, unionism, job

tenure, quits, and separations. *Quarterly Journal of Economics* 94 (June): 643–73.
———. 1981. The effect of trade unionism on fringe benefits. *Industrial and Labor Relations Review* 34 (July): 489–509.
———. 1983. Unionism, price-cost margins and the return to capital. Harvard University (January). Mimeo.
Freeman, R. B., and J. Medoff. 1981. The impact of collective bargaining: Illusion or reality? in *U.S. industrial relations 1950–1980: A critical assessment,* ed. J. Stieber, R. B. McKersie, and D. Q. Mills. Madison: IRRA.
———. 1984. *What do unions do?* New York: Basic Books.
Gintis, H., and T. Ishikawa. 1983. Wages, work discipline and macroeconomic equilibrium. University of Massachusetts at Amherst. Mimeo.
Goldin, C. 1986. Monitoring costs and occupational segregation by sex: A historical analysis. *Journal of Labor Economics* 4 (January): 1–27.
Hall, R. E. 1975. The rigidity of wages and the persistence of unemployment. *Brookings Papers on Economic Activity* 2: 301–35.
———. 1980. Employment fluctuations and wage rigidity. *Brookings Papers on Economic Activity* 1: 91–132.
Hammermesh, D. 1977. Economic aspects of job satisfaction. In *Essays in Labor Market Analysis,* ed. O. Ashenfelter and W. Oates. New York: Halstead.
Hodson, R., and P. England. 1986. Industrial structure and sex differences in earnings. *Industrial Relations* 25 (Winter): 16–32.
Ippolito, R. A. 1985. The labor contract and true economic pension liabilities. *American Economic Review* 75 (December): 1031–1043.
Jacoby, S. 1983. Industrial mobility in historical perspective. *Industrial Relations* 22 (Spring): 261–82.
Johnson, G., and G. Solon. 1984. Pay differences between women's and men's jobs: The empirical foundations of comparable worth legislation. NBER Working Paper 1472 (September).
Jones, S. R. G. 1985. Dual labor markets, productivity and unemployment. University of British Columbia (April). Mimeo.
Katz, L. F. 1986. Inter-industry wage structure in historical perspective. University of California at Berkeley (January). Mimeo.
Kreps, D. 1984. Corporate culture and economic theory. Stanford Graduate School of Business (May). Mimeo.
Krueger, A., and L. H. Summers. 1986. Efficiency wages and the inter-industry wage structure. Harvard University (February). Mimeo.
Kwoka, J. 1983. Monopoly, plant, and union effects on worker wages. *Industrial and Labor Relations Review* 36 (January): 251–57.
Lawrence, C., and R. Lawrence. 1985. Relative wages in U.S. manufacturing: An endgame interpretation. *Brookings Papers on Economic Activity* 1: 47–106.
Lazear, E. 1979. Why is there mandatory retirement? *Journal of Political Economy* 87 (December): 261–84.
———. 1981. Agency, earnings profiles, productivity, and hours restrictions. *American Economic Review* 71 (September): 606–20.
———. 1983. Salaries and piece rates. NORC Working Paper No. 83–15, June.
Leibenstein, H. 1957. The theory of underdevelopment in densely populated backward areas. In *Economic Backwardness and Economic Growth,* ed. H. Leibenstein. New York: Wiley.
Lewis, H. G. 1982. Union relative wage effects: A survey. Duke University (April). Mimeo.

———. 1983. Union relative wage effects: A survey of macro estimates. *Journal of Labor Economics* 1 (January): 1–27.
Lilien, D. 1982. Sectoral shifts and cyclical unemployment. *Journal of Political Economy* 90 (August): 777–93.
Lindbeck, A., and D. J. Snower. 1984. Involuntary unemployment as an insider-outsider dilemma. Seminar Paper No. 282, Institute for International Economic Studies, Stockholm, Sweden.
Long, J. E., and Link, A. N. 1983. The impact of market structure on wages, fringe benefits, and turnover. *Industrial and Labor Relations Review* 36 (January): 239–50.
Malcolmson, J. 1984. Work incentives, hierarchy, and internal labor markets. *Journal of Political Economy* 92 (June): 486–507.
Mankiw, N. G. 1985. Small menu costs and large business cycles: A macroeconomic model of monopoly. *Quarterly Journal of Economics* 100 (May): 529–37.
Medoff, J., and K. G. Abraham. 1980. Experience, performance and earnings. *Quarterly Journal of Economics* 95 (December): 703–36.
Mellow, W. 1982. Employer size and wages. *Review of Economics and Statistics* 64 (August): 495–501.
Milkovich, G., and J. Newman. 1984. *Compensation*. Plano, Tx.: Business Publications Inc.
Montgomery, E., and D. Stockton. 1985. Evidence on causes of the rising dispersion of relative wages. (April). Carnegie-Mellon University. Mimeo.
Mookherjee, D. 1984a. Involuntary unemployment and worker self-selection. Research Paper 741, Graduate School of Business, Stanford University (April).
———. 1984b. Involuntary unemployment and worker moral hazard. Research Paper 745, Graduate School of Business, Stanford University (June).
Murphy, K. M., and R. Topel. 1986. Unemployment, risk, and earnings: Testing for equalizing wage differences in the labor market. UCLA (March). Mimeo.
Oi, W. 1983. Heterogeneous firms and the organization of production. *Economic Inquiry* 21 (April): 147–71.
Okun, A. 1973. Upward mobility in a high-pressure economy. *Brookings Papers on Economic Activity* 1: 207–52.
Pencavel, J. 1970. *An analysis of the quit rate in American manufacturing industry*. Princeton, N.J.: Industrial Relations Section, Princeton.
———. 1977a. Work effort, on-the-job screening and alternative methods of remuneration. In *Research in Labor Economics*, ed. R. Ehrenberg. Greenwich, Ct.: JAI Press.
———. 1977b. Industrial morale. In *Essays in Labor Market Analysis*, ed. O. Ashenfelter and W. Oates. New York: Halstead.
Poterba, J., and L. H. Summers. 1984. Adjusting the gross changes data: Implications for labor market dynamics. NBER Working Paper 1436 (August).
Pugel, T. 1980. Profitability, concentration and the interindustry variation in wages. *Review of Economics and Statistics* 62 (May): 248–53.
Reder, M. 1962. Wage differentials: Theory and measurement. In *Aspects of Labor Economics*. Princeton, N.J.: Universities-NBER, Princeton U. Press.
Reynolds, L. 1978. *Labor economics and labor relations*, 7th ed. Englewood Cliffs, N.J.: Prentice-Hall.
Rosen, S. 1985. The theory of equalizing differences. NORC Discussion Paper No. 85–3 (January).

Ruback, R., and M. Zimmerman. 1984. Unionization and profitability: Evidence from the capital market. *Journal of Political Economy* 92 (December): 1134–57.
Salop, S. 1979. A model of the natural rate of unemployment. *American Economic Review* 69 (March): 117–25.
Shapiro, C., and J. E. Stiglitz. 1984. Equilibrium unemployment as a worker discipline device. *American Economic Review* 74 (June): 433–44.
———. 1985. Can unemployment be involuntary?: Reply. *American Economic Review* 75 (December): 1215–17.
Slichter, S. 1950. Notes on the structure of wages. *Review of Economics and Statistics* 32 (February): 80–91.
Solow, R. 1979. Another possible source of wage stickiness. *Journal of Macroeconomics* 1: 79–82.
———. 1985. Insiders and outsiders in wage determination. *Scandinavian Journal of Economics* 87 (2): 411–28.
Stiglitz, J. E. 1974. Wage determination and unemployment in L.D.C.'s: The labor turnover model. *Quarterly Journal of Economics* 88 (May): 194–227.
———. 1976. Prices and queues as screening devices in competitive markets. IMSS Technical Report No. 212, Stanford University (August).
———. 1984. Theories of wage rigidity. NBER Working Paper 1442 (September).
———. 1985. Equilibrium wage distributions. *Economic Journal* 95 (September): 595–618.
Stoft, S. 1982. Cheat threat theory: An explanation of involuntary unemployment. Boston University (May). Mimeo.
Taylor, J. 1982. The role of expectations in the choice of monetary policy. NBER Working Paper 1044 (December).
Topel, R., and L. Weiss. 1985. Sectoral uncertainty and unemployment. UCLA Department of Economics Working Paper 384 (September).
Vroman, W. 1978. Cyclical earnings changes of low wage workers. In *Research in Labor Economics,* vol. 2, ed. R. Ehrenberg. Greenwich, Ct.: JAI Press.
Weiss, A. 1980. Job queues and layoffs in labor markets with flexible wages. *Journal of Political Economy* 88 (June): 526–38.
Weiss, L. 1966. Concentration and labor earnings. *American Economic Review* 56 (March): 96–117.
Wing, R. 1984. Achieving internal equity through job measurement. In *Handbook of Wage and Salary Administration,* ed. M. Rock. New York: McGraw-Hill.
Yellen, J. 1984. Efficiency wage models of unemployment. *American Economic Review Proceedings* 74 (May): 200–205.

Comment

JOSEPH G. ALTONJI
Columbia University and NBER

Larry Katz has made a valiant attempt to evaluate recent theoretical and empirical work on efficiency wage models—models in which wages have a direct influence on labor productivity and turnover costs. It would take a monograph to provide a complete survey of the many variations on the efficiency wage theme. Furthermore, a large empirical and theoretical literature in labor economics on the structure of wages, turnover behavior, firm and worker search behavior, and the composition of unemployment is potentially relevant for an assessment of efficiency wage models.

My comments fall into four areas. First, a few remarks about efficiency wage theory. Second, I discuss some general issues concerning the empirical assessment of efficiency wage models. Third, I consider the evidence reviewed in the article. In closing, I briefly comment on the relevance of efficiency wage models for business cycle fluctuations.

1. *Comments on the Theoretical Discussion*

Katz provides a brief summary of the links from wages to labor productivity that have received the most attention in the theoretical literature. The first mechanism is the shirking model, in which high wages induce high effort levels. The second is the labor turnover model, in which high wages reduce quits and thus lower turnover costs. The third is the adverse selection model in which firms use high wages to sort out high-quality workers from lower-quality workers when quality is difficult to observe directly. The fourth are sociological models in which worker perceptions of the fairness of the wages offered by the firm affects their effort level and perhaps their turnover behavior. In addition, Katz devotes considerable attention to the union threat model. In this model profit-maximizing nonunion firms choose to pay wages above competitive levels to avoid unionization. The union threat effect model has received considerable attention in discussions of the link between unionism and the structure of wages, although the model is not usually included in lists of efficiency wage mechanisms.

The exposition of the theories is generally evenhanded and clear. A few points deserve special emphasis. The first is that the importance of the shirking and adverse selection models depends critically upon the extent to which workers acquire reputations. Most men spend more than thirty-five years as full-time workers, and many women also spend long periods of time in the labor force. Although it may be difficult for employers accurately to evaluate performance in a given period, the cumulative effect of such evaluations may have a key influence on a worker's prospects in and outside the firm. Evidence from panel data suggests that wages evolve over time for a given individual. (See, for example, MaCurdy (1982)). A large proportion of wage changes have permanent effects on future wages. In an expected value sense, the rewards to good performance may be substantial.

A note on the sociological theories. There is a long tradition in industrial relations and personnel literature stressing the importance of interpersonal comparisons and notions of fairness in the determination of wage rates. I have no doubt that these factors play a role. However, the sociological theories are vague about how such standards are determined or what the appropriate reference group is. Do workers compare themselves to other workers in the same industry, in the same firm, in the same occupation, or in the same position within a firm? Are these standards of comparison constant over time?

Evidence from panel data sets suggests that wages of individuals are subject to substantial variation from year to year, even after the substantial measurement error in such data is accounted for. It would be very interesting to perform similar calculations using data from workers in the same firm. This could be done with information from firm personnel files. If the results were to show little dispersion in wage growth for employees within a given firm, they would be consistent with the notion that interpersonal comparisons have an important influence on the wage structure, and that the wage structure within firms is fairly rigid. My guess is that there is in fact a substantial amount of dispersion in wage growth within a given firm over an interval of two or three years. The importance of interpersonal comparisons and notions of fairness may slow down relative wage adjustments. However, I doubt if these factors can explain differentials across firms, occupations, or industries that persist for many years.

I wish to highlight a point made in the article concerning the possibility that firms may use entrance fees, deferred wage payments, and fringe benefits tied to seniority as a way to induce workers not to shirk, quit, etc. I think that it would be possible to devise a market clearing optimal compensation package that deals with the shirking problem, or that generates optimal turnover decisions, given training costs. However, it may be very costly to provide such a package if several efficiency wage mechanisms operate simultaneously, and if wages are also influenced by the risk-sharing considerations emphasized in the implicit contracts literature. It may be even more difficult to do so in a stochastic environment in which wages must be renegotiated, for many of the same reasons discussed in the literature on the feasibility of efficient contracts (see Hall and Lazear (1984) and Hart (1983)). Consequently, I find the view that in many situations firms will resort to raising the wage profile above market clearing levels to be fairly persuasive on a priori grounds.

In discussing the role of bonding mechanisms in efficiency wages, a number of economists have argued that demographic and skill groups who suffer from liquidity constraints and thus cannot post performance bonds are most likely to be affected by unemployment. However, this argument ignores the fact that a spell of unemployment is likely to be most costly for those who are liquidity constrained. Consequently, it is not clear that limits on the feasibility of bonding arrangements arising from imperfect capital markets can provide an explanation for age and skill differentials in unemployment.

2. *General Issues in Testing Efficiency Wage Models*

The term "efficiency wage model" is given a very broad interpretation in Katz's article. The following simple framework may help to sharpen the distinction between these models and neoclassical alternatives and to show the main issues involved in testing the efficiency wage models. The null hypothesis against which efficiency wage models are evaluated is a Reder or Rosen type hedonic model. In this competitive model, wages and employment levels adjust over time to equate the demand and supply for labor and jobs of various types. More formally, let the demand and supply equations be

$$D_{ij} = D(w_{ij} \; ; \mathbf{Z}_i, \mathbf{Z}_j, \mathbf{Z}_{ij}, \mathbf{w}) \quad (1)$$

$$S_{ij} = S(w_{ij} \; ; \mathbf{Z}_i, \mathbf{Z}_j, \mathbf{Z}_{ij}, \mathbf{w}, \mathbf{U}), \quad (2)$$

where S_{ij} is the supply of workers of type i to jobs of type j, D_{ij} is the demand for workers of type i in jobs of type j, w_{ij} is the current wage for workers of type i in job j, $\mathbf{Z}_i$ is a vector of personal characteristics variables which affect the supply or the demand for workers in all types of jobs, $\mathbf{Z}_j$ is a vector of job characteristics which affect the supply or the demand for workers of all types for job j, $\mathbf{Z}_{ij}$ is a vector of interaction variables which reflect variation across jobs in the productivity of workers of type i or variation in their evaluation of the characteristics of the job, $\mathbf{w}$ is a vector of wages for all other worker/job combinations, and $\mathbf{U}$ is a vector of the balance between the supply of workers and the number of jobs for each of the various worker/job combinations. It should be noted that $\mathbf{Z}_j$ and $\mathbf{Z}_{ij}$ include variables describing the wages and fringe benefits which worker i may expect to receive in future periods. (The human capital model implies differences across firms in wage profiles which arise from differences in the levels of specific and general training that are provided.) The form of the demand and supply functions depends on the distribution of $\mathbf{Z}_i$, $\mathbf{Z}_j$, and $\mathbf{Z}_{ij}$ over the economy. Conventional labor supply/search models imply that employment prospects affect the supply of labor to a particular type of job. For this reason, the vector $\mathbf{U}$ of excess demands for matches of various types is included in the equation.

The key assumption of the hedonic model is that the market clears in a stochastic sense for all types of workers and all types of jobs, with

$$D(w_{ij}\ ;\ \mathbf{Z}_i, \mathbf{Z}_j, \mathbf{Z}_{ij}, \mathbf{w}\,) = S(w_{ij}\ ;\ \mathbf{Z}_i, \mathbf{Z}_j, \mathbf{Z}_{ij}, \mathbf{w}, \mathbf{U}). \quad (3)$$

Thus, the excess demand vector $\mathbf{U}$ is 0 in equilibrium. The solution implies an equilibrium relationship between the wage and employment level for a given ij combination. These functions are

$$w_{ij} = w(\mathbf{Z}_i, \mathbf{Z}_j, \mathbf{Z}_{ij}) \quad (4)$$

$$E_{ij} = E(\mathbf{Z}_i, \mathbf{Z}_j, \mathbf{Z}_{ij}), \quad (5)$$

where E_{ij} is the employment of workers of type i in jobs of type j. Although the excess demand vector is 0, a stochastic version of the hedonic market story would add that product demand variations across firms, changes in labor supply preference, and other factors generate labor turnover and movements in and out of the labor market. The associated frictional unemployment rates may vary with the type of job and the individual.

Efficiency wage models replace the hedonic market equilibrium condition, equation (3), with a wage setting equation that is based upon a model of how wages affect labor productivity and nonwage labor costs.

$$w^e_{ij} = f(\mathbf{Z}_i, \mathbf{Z}_j, \mathbf{Z}_{ij}\ ;\ \mathbf{w}, \mathbf{U}) \quad (6)$$

In equation (6) w^e_{ij} is the optimal wage chosen by the firm. The equation makes explicit the fact that the efficiency wage may depend upon a vector $\mathbf{w}$ of wages in all other ij matches as well as the vector $\mathbf{U}$ summarizing the differences $(S_{i'j'} - D_{i'j'})$ between supply and demand for matches of various other $i'j'$ types. This dependence arises because efficiency wage theories emphasize that alternative wages and unemployment rates serve as a discipline on worker behavior.

Associated with equation (6) is a labor demand function, equation (7). This function also accounts for the fact that in the efficiency wage models alternative wages and the tightness of the labor market affect worker productivity and thus labor demand.

$$D_{ij} = D^e(w_{ij}\ ;\ \mathbf{Z}_i, \mathbf{Z}_j, \mathbf{Z}_{ij}, \mathbf{w}, \mathbf{U}) \quad (7)$$

Equations (6) and (7) determine employment. Subtraction of equation (7) from equation (2) yields the excess demand U_{ij} for job matches of type *ij*.

$$U_{ij} = S_{ij} - E_{ij} \quad (8)$$

Simultaneous solution across *ij* combinations in conjunction with the supply equation (2) yields the wage vector **w** and the excess demand vector **U**. In equilibrium, there may be excess demand for some types of matches and excess supply for other types. The solution to the model implies an equilibrium relationship of w_{ij}, E_{ij}, and U_{ij} to characteristics of *i*, *j*, and the match *ij*:

$$w_{ij} = w^e(Z_i, Z_j, Z_{ij}) \quad (9)$$

$$E_{ij} = E^e(Z_i, Z_j, Z_{ij}) \quad (10)$$

$$U_{ij} = U^e(Z_i, Z_j, Z_{ij}). \quad (11)$$

How can one distinguish empirically between the hedonic model and the efficiency wage model? There are likely to be few exclusion restrictions from the wage and employment loci for the two models. One approach is to estimate the wage locus and consider whether the relationship is more consistent with the hedonic model or with the various efficiency wage models. Most of the empirical evidence discussed in the article involves this approach. This may be done in two levels. The first is to see whether wages vary across types of firms or across personal characteristics in ways that, given what we know about labor supply and labor demand, are hard to square with the hedonic model. If the results seem unfavorable to the hedonic model, then the second level of the analysis is to see if the results may be explained with other models, such as the various efficiency wage models. The problem, however, is that given available data it is very difficult to control for the many variables that may be correlated with supply and demand for particular job matches.

A second strategy is to examine the distribution of employment. This approach receives less attention in Katz's paper. To give an example, the discussion of dual labor markets in Bulow and Summers (1986) focuses on the distribution of various types of workers across job types. Again, there are often several alternative explanations for such distributions. For example, some economists argue that differences between men and women in an industry and the occupational distribution of employment arise from sex differences in schooling choice, labor force attachment, and preferences for various job attributes. Others interpret the differences as evidence of discrimination in the labor market. (See Cain's (1984) survey for many references.)

The third strategy is to look for evidence of imbalance in the supply and demand for various worker/job combinations. In my view, a key implication of the efficiency wage models is that such imbalances will persist over time. One can only get rough indicators of such imbalances by examining industry/occupation unemployment rates, patterns of job mobility broken down by quit/layoff, and vacancy data. Nevertheless, I think a careful survey of the literature on the structure of unemployment and on mobility patterns would be helpful, particularly since "stylized facts" on this issue seem to have motivated much of the work on efficiency wages.

3. *Comments on the Empirical Work*

Most of the empirical evidence discussed in the article concerns the wage structure. First, Katz notes that area wage surveys find large differences across firms in wages for a given job classification within a geographical area.

Second, he cites evidence from several studies on industry wage differentials, including some of his own work. These differentials are substantial, stable over time, and remain after one controls for a set of observed individual and job characteristics. I am impressed by Krueger and Summers's (1986) and Vroman's (1978) finding that large industry effects are found even if one uses a first-difference estimator. Such a procedure is less sensitive to the criticism that the wages premiums reflect unmeasured differences in the quality of workers employed in the various industries.[1]

Many labor economists have argued that industries provide different levels of specific and general training, and that these underlie the indus-

1. If anything, measurement error in industry classifications and selection bias are likely to result in a downward bias in the first difference estimates. Krueger and Summers's first-difference estimates contain a rough correction for the effects of measurement error. Without this correction their first-difference estimates of industry wage differentials are considerably smaller than the estimates based on level equations. More research on this will be needed, especially in light of the recent study by Kevin Murphy and Robert Topel (1986). As Katz notes, Murphy and Topel have obtained estimates of industry differentials that are well below those of Krueger and Summers, despite the fact that Murphy and Topel use similar data and work with first differences. They use an instrumental variables procedure to deal with the measurement error problems.

try differentials. I found Katz's evidence suggesting that industry differentials have a fairly high correlation across experience levels to be an interesting challenge to this view. On the other hand, I am not sure if Katz's finding of .74 correlation among the industry differentials for workers with less than a year of tenure should be considered large or small. A much more detailed analysis of these issues seems warranted.

The article discusses the possibility that compensating differentials for other job attributes, such as work hours, work pace, safety, and unemployment risk can reconcile the industry differentials with a hedonic model of the labor market. I think this is very much an open question. Abowd and Ashenfelter, Topel, and others suggest that unemployment risk does play a role in industry wage differentials, as does safety. Furthermore, the fact that industry differentials survive an attempt to control for a set of job characteristics is not decisive evidence against the compensating differentials view, since micro data on job characteristics are not only incomplete but noisy. If the wage premiums do not reflect compensation for training opportunities and other job characteristics, we need to know why workers move from high-wage industries to low-wage industries. Some tabulations on the relationship between the industry wage differentials and interindustry job changes broken down by quit and layoff, with and without intervening spells of unemployment, would be very interesting. If the movements from high-wage to low-wage industries are dominated by layoffs, this would be further evidence that the industry differentials are not compensating. This type of evidence relates to the central issue of whether markets clear for various worker/job combinations.

The article also discusses recent work by the author (in collaboration with William Dickens) indicating that workers in all occupations within an industry are affected more or less equally by the industry wage differentials, although they also find that the dispersion of the industry effects is larger for managerial, professional, and supervisory workers than for other groups. As Katz points out, these findings do not support the hedonic model, since the job characteristics are presumably highly occupation-specific. But as he also recognizes, they are not very favorable to the different variants of the efficiency wage hypothesis either, with the possible exception of the sociologically based models.

There does not seem to be much evidence for the hypothesis that employers derive benefits from paying higher wages. The finding that quits are a negative function of the wage is predicted by virtually any model of the labor market. Unfortunately, there is little information on the costs to firms of turnover. Since absenteeism can easily be monitored and penalized, the fact that higher wages reduce absenteeism would seem to be more consistent with the hedonic model in which workers trade off the right to be absent for higher wages. Indeed, Katz mentions a number of facts that do not sit well with the various efficiency wage models.

4. *Efficiency Wages and Business Cycle Behavior*

My final comments concern the efficiency wage models and business cycle behavior. Katz does not devote much space to these issues. He cites evidence from several studies that low-skill workers are more likely to be employed in high-wage sectors such as durable goods manufacturing, construction, transportation, and public utilities during booms than during recessions. This in itself is not surprising, since labor demand in these sectors is the most sensitive to the business cycle. However, competitive theories of the labor market do not provide an adequate explanation for why low-skill workers who switch industries during expansions experience wage gains that exceed the cyclical wage adjustment for workers who were already employed in the high-wage sectors.[2] More work on the effects of labor demand shifts on wage adjustments, promotion patterns within firms, and mobility patterns of workers of various skill levels would be useful.

Finally, the article only briefly discusses the macroeconomic implications of efficiency wage models. I think that efficiency wage theories will ultimately prove useful in explaining the wage and employment decisions of firms over the cycle. The papers of Phelps (1970) and Mortensen (1970), which stress labor turnover and recruiting costs and the short-run monopsony power of firms, are early prototypes of such models. I think that we must explicitly account for the wage decisions of firms if we are to understand wage and employment dynamics, rather than simply treat wages as determined in a passive way by the balance of supply and demand. However, a well-worked-out theory with supporting empirical evidence is still not available despite much interesting research.

REFERENCES

Altonji, J. G., J. Mincer, and R. Shakotko. 1984. *Employer/employee attachments,* Final report to the Office of the Assistant Secretary for Policy and Evaluation, U.S. Department of Labor, Washington, D.C.

Bulow, J. I., and L. H. Summers. 1986. A theory of dual labor markets with appli-

2. Although Katz cites two studies that find large cyclical wage changes for job changers, my own work with the Panel Study of Income Dynamics indicates that the response of wages to changes in aggregate unemployment, state employment growth rates, and county unemployment rates is about the same for workers who have been on the job for less than a year as for workers with higher levels of job seniority. See Altonji, Mincer, and Shakotko (1984, chapter 4).

cations to industrial policy, discrimination and Keynesian unemployment. *Journal of Labor Economics*. Forthcoming.
Cain, G. G. 1984. The economic analysis of labor market discrimination: A survey. Institute for Research on Poverty Special Report 37 (August) forthcoming in *Handbook of Labor Economics*, ed. O. Ashenfelter and R. Layard.
Hall, R. E., and E. Lazear. 1984. The excess sensitivity of layoffs and quits to demand. *Journal of Labor Economics* 2 (2): 243–58.
Hart, O. D. 1983. Optimal labour contracts under asymmetric information: An introduction. *Review of Economic Studies* 50 (1) (January): 3–35.
Krueger, A., and L. H. Summers. 1985. Efficiency wages and the inter-industry wage structure. Harvard University, Department of Economics (October). Mimeo.
MaCurdy, T. E. 1982. The use of time series processes to model the error structure of earnings in a longitudinal data analysis. *Journal of Econometrics* 18: 83–114.
Mortensen, D. T. 1970. A theory of wage and employment dynamics. In *Microeconomic foundations of employment and inflation theory,* ed. E. S. Phelps et al. New York: Norton.
Murphy, K. M., and R. H. Topel. 1986. Unemployment, risk, and earnings: Testing for equalizing wage differences in the labor market. (March). Mimeo.
Phelps, E. S. 1970. Money wage dynamics and labor market equilibrium. In *Microeconomic foundations of employment and inflation theory,* ed. E. S. Phelps et al. New York: Norton.
Vroman, W. 1978. Cyclical earnings changes of low wage workers. In *Research in Labor Economics,* vol. 2. ed. R. Ehrenberg. Greenwich, Ct.: JAI Press.

Comment

LAURENCE WEISS
Goldman Sachs & Co.

Any paper entitled "Efficiency Wages—A Partial Evaluation" is not likely to be too far wrong. Larry Katz's tone is somewhat agnostic and steadfastly fair and impartial. He plays his cards pretty close to his vest and I can't really tell if he's rooting for these theories or thinks they miss the mark.

The title of this paper could have been "Is Life Fair?" The theories examined here have the common theme that identical individuals wind up with very different levels of utility in economic equilibrium. These theories purport to "explain" why there are wide wage differentials across various industries not explained by observable worker characteristics. In a business cycle context, the theories seek to find an explanation for that incubus of economic thought termed "involuntary unemployment," which has been interpreted here to be a situation in which one jobless person envies an employed person, even though they are considered by everyone else to be identical. After reading Katz's paper and the paper by Krueger and Summers referenced in it, I am skeptical about both the prevalence of these sorts of phenomena and the usefulness of these theories for explaining them.

I have asked some of my colleagues what they thought about the proposition that employees work harder when they're paid more, a key observation of the "shirking" model of efficiency wages. Two of them told me (independently) that they pay their baby-sitters more than is really necessary. Their reasoning is broadly consistent with the underlying logic of the model; higher wages would induce more responsible behavior. What features of baby-sitting make it particularly relevant for the shirking model? The answer is obvious: baby-sitting is a dead-end job without much hope for advancement. This I take to be an important (and unstated) assumption of the model; not only must there be a lack of punitive measures against employees for dereliction of duties, but there cannot be any rewards for superlative performance. The relevance of this sort of model would appear to be confined to the rather small minority of people with menial jobs. Casual empiricism suggests that there is no shortage of carrots out there and the fear of getting fired is low on the list of people's motivation for working hard.

I then asked my wife if people work harder when they're paid more. "Ridiculous," was her unabashed answer. "People work as hard as the people around them. There's a lot of peer pressure." This latter effect is, upon reflection, very important and noticeably missing from the formal development of shirking models. Employees tend to be able to monitor the performance of similar workers fairly accurately. In situations where the group's output as a whole is observable, it is the job of management to elicit and use peer review to compensate and promote employees. In this context, an employee's perception of management's "fairness" is not merely a nonpecuniary aspect of the employee's compensation (as some of these theories suggest), it is a vital managerial attribute necessary for the hiring and retention of employees.

The evidence concerning the industry effects on individual wages is impressive, but I do not think it suggests a radical departure from the neoclassical paradigm. What this evidence tells me is that there are enormous unobserved quality differences among individuals and enormous unobserved job-attribute differences across industries. I do not find the fact that these industry effects hold across different occupations within an industry especially hard to explain—I would expect to find the most productive secretary working with the most productive executive.

The "sociological" theories in this article appear vacuous. I have no doubt that any successful enterprise must have shared goals, ideals, and tastes that transcend mere money-making. I also have no doubt that the best way to make profits is to convince employees to share management's fidelity to these higher concerns. Thus I see no power of these alternative theories to refute the conventional view.

As for the ability of these theories to enhance our understanding of cyclical unemployment, I think they are worse than useless. I can think of no substantive issue for which they are even slightly helpful. Examples of what I take to be substantive questions are: Why was unemployment higher in 1982 than in 1965? Why has black teen-age unemployment doubled? Why has the return to going to college in terms of decreased unemployment gone up since 1973? Why has the traditional male-female pattern of unemployment changed recently?

These models may have something to say about why reductions in aggregate labor input fall disproportionately on that small fraction of the labor force that reports itself as unemployed. However, this is hardly the biggest puzzle in macroeonomics and there are other alternative explanations for the relative lack of work sharing. The big question continues to be the sources of fluctuations in aggregate demand for labor. These efficiency wage theories do not suggest any new candidates for aggregate disturbances. Their relevance in macroeconomic dynamics appears confined to perhaps explaining some propagation mechanism of cycles and possibly explaining their persistence, but the model that formally develops this intuition has yet to be written.

Discussion

In responding to the discussants, Lawrence Katz pointed out that Weiss's emphasis on group pressure rather than the efficiency wage has been developed by Akerlof in his gift exchange model. He argued that it is difficult to find a competitive model that explains wage differentials across industries, and that efficiency wage explanations are very likely to account for much of the difference.

Maurice Obstfeld commented that peer pressure may work well in eliciting effort in small groups, but that the efficiency wage argument may be more important in large groups where individual effort is more difficult to identify.

The ability of efficiency wage theory to explain fluctuations of the aggregate level of employment was questioned by Robert Barro. The main problem in business cycle theory is to identify possible sources of large and frequent disturbances, whereas efficiency wage theory appears to explain the average level of output and unemployment rather than fluctuations.

Martin Weitzman doubted the empirical significance of efficiency wages as a mechanism for producing output fluctuations, despite the theoretical appeal of models with small menu costs of changing wages and prices in which prices become relatively rigid and output flexible. The difficulty with this argument is that it is entirely symmetric. We could as well argue that the costs of changing output are high and the costs of changing price low—then the result would be price flexibility with relatively stable output. There is a serious need for research on adjustment costs to establish which approach is more accurate.

Robert Hall argued that the primary issue in the efficiency wage literature is whether potential workers line up for higher-wage jobs. There is some evidence that at the lower end of the job market, people do stand in line for jobs. On the other hand, a variety of sophisticated effort-eliciting mechanisms—such as tournaments and rising wage profiles—exists at the higher end of the job market. Consideration of these alternative mechanisms is missing from the Katz article. Hall also argued that evidence that wages change when workers change jobs is not convincing support for efficiency wage theory. The wage changes may simply reflect successful selection by firms. Hall also doubted that there was a connection between efficiency wage theory and cyclical fluctuations. Efficiency wages suggest long-term employment relationships, which would surely mitigate employment fluctuations.

On the question of the relation between efficiency wages and economic fluctuations, Lawrence Summers noted that many theories show that wage rigidity is related to fluctuations: efficiency wage theory, which states it is profitable for firms to fix the real wage, is a promising explanation of real wage rigidity. The evidence that firms with different wages can survive in the product market suggests that cost of production is not proportional to the wage, providing support for the theory.

John Taylor stressed the role of relative wages in wage and price dynamics. Theories in which the efficiency of labor is a function of a firm's wage relative to other wages may therefore provide an important element in explaining business cycles.

Olivier Blanchard was worried about the relation between efficiency wage theory and real wage rigidity. One way to put the problem is to consider two models with competitive product markets, one of which has an efficiency wage labor market and the other a competitive classical labor market. Comparison of the degree of wage rigidity demonstrated in the responses of these two economies to a technological shock is completely ambiguous. The only efficiency wage model that gives unambiguously more rigidity is the social norm model of real wages, but that model leaves the norm itself unexplained.

Katz concluded the discussion, maintaining that efficiency wage theories are indeed promising for explaining real wage differentials. He accepted the existence of other mechanisms for eliciting effort, particularly in the high-quality job market, but believed there was still room for efficiency wages. He also stressed the importance of wage rigidity in business cycle theories through possibly temporary wage rigidity, although it is true, as Blanchard commented, that efficiency wage theory does not generate wage rigidity in a general equilibrium model.

Martin L. Weitzman
MASSACHUSETTS INSTITUTE OF TECHNOLOGY

Macroeconomic Implications of Profit Sharing

Introduction

My point of departure is the idea that standard macroeconomic policy may not always be enough to create full employment with price stability. In a capitalist economy, most decisions about employment, output, and prices are made by private firms. Of course such decisions are profoundly influenced by government macroeconomic policies, yet the purposeful manipulation of financial aggregates may be a clumsy way of attaining desirable macroeconomic goals. Under certain circumstances the best place to attack macroeconomic problems may be directly at their source. Make it in the strong self-interest of firms to maintain full employment with low prices, and macroeconomic problems might, to a greater extent than now, largely take care of themselves. To be sure, control of government spending, the "money supply," tax receipts, and the like will always have an important role in influencing how the economy behaves. But perhaps the time has come to think seriously about basic reform of microeconomic incentives as a kind of alternative, or at least complementary, approach.

While macroeconomic theory is currently in a state of great controversy, most economists still agree that mainstream IS-LM policies can be used as a crude rudder for aiming the economy in one direction or the other. Illusions of being able to fine-tune aside, we know how to get unemployment down and output up by the usual expansionary monetary and fiscal measures. We also know how to break inflation by policy-induced recessions. What we do *not* know—and this is the central economic dilemma of our time—is how *simultaneously* to reconcile reasonably full employment with reasonable price stability.

At this point the honest Keynesian puts in the awkward if obligatory footnote about the need for some form of incomes policy. But this phrase is usually added rather mechanically, as an afterthought, with little enthusiasm or follow-up. I think it may be time to reverse the emphasis. In countries like Britain and France (or, for that matter, Argentina and Israel) today, the main operational issue is how to introduce greater wage restraint and "flexibility" into the labor market, especially as it starts to become tight. Compared with this issue the nuances of how best to reflate the economy are relatively straightforward. Although the dilemma being described is currently seen most starkly in some European economies, the same basic issues are involved almost everywhere. Things have reached a point where a surprising number of macroeconomists of Keynesian or classical persuasion have essentially abandoned the hope that traditional macroeconomic policies can do a great deal to promote prosperity. I would argue, as a general proposition, that structural changes should be a relatively more pressing concern than the demand management policies currently occupying the attention of most macroeconomists.

The plan of the article is as follows. First, I attempt to place the problem of labor payment mechanisms in historical perspective. Then I provide an analytic framework for comparing wage and profit-sharing systems, including a detailed description of the relevant theoretical and empirical aspects of profit sharing. Major criticisms of profit sharing are discussed in a question-and-answer format. Next, I try to assess critically what I see as three major alternative prototypes for structural reform of the labor market: incomes policy, two-tiered pay, and employee control. I argue that, although each may reduce unemployment, profit sharing is overall the most likely to succeed. I then examine the Japanese experience with an eye to evaluating the possible macroeconomic impact of the bonus system and implications for profit or revenue sharing. The article concludes by again stressing that basic reforms in the way labor is paid could be a precondition to improved macroeconomic performance.

The Historical Context

Before discussing possible labor market reforms, I think it useful to place my main subject in a somewhat broader context by reviewing the intellectual history of the problem. Such a review is necessarily prone to being interpretive and subjective.

The modern mainstream approach to macroeconomics began with Keynes. Previous economists by no means disregarded business cycles—the subject has a long history. But the prevailing attitude before Keynes was that economic fluctuations represent a normal, and sometimes even desirable, condition. Classical macroeconomics held (and still holds) that all markets are practically competitive and practically always in equilibrium. The old-fashioned classical macroeconomics admitted that the economy might not always be in equilibrium due to "temporary derangement of markets" (Mill) or "crises of confidence" (Marshall). Old classical macroeconomists also felt some obligation to explain how an economy out of equilibrium gets back into equilibrium (as opposed to tautologically postulating that an economy must always be in some kind of market-clearing equilibrium). But such states of disequilibrium were not viewed as terribly important in the overall scheme of things.

The Great Depression dealt a death blow to classical macroeconomics of the old school. There was no lack of contemporary explanations for the depression, but none of them sounded convincing. Most damning of all in the eyes of the public, few economists had any constructive suggestions about what to do to correct the worst economic catastrophe in history. Hayek and Haberler talked of abstract Austrian-capital building cycles. Schumpeter found depression a necessary, if distasteful, medicine for sweating out inefficiencies. Perhaps the most common interpretation among economists—certainly the one most aggressively targeted for attack by Keynes—was that of A. C. Pigou.

Pigou, along with a possible majority of economists at the time, held that the wage issue was central. If labor was unemployed, what else could it mean except that wages were too high? As Pigou, the distinguished economist of world stature, Keynes's teacher, and the foremost representative of the prevailing orthodoxy put it in 1933, at the very bottom of the worst depression in history: "Such unemployment as exists at any time is due wholly to the fact that changes in demand conditions are continually taking place and that frictional resistances prevent the appropriate wage adjustments from being made instantaneously"[1]. If workers were unemployed, it meant that labor costs were too high and there was nothing the government could, or should, do, aside from possibly urging that wages be cut more vigorously.

Keynes was quick to seize on two serious problems with the Pigouvian position. For one thing, it was not exactly clear what it meant for wages to be "too high" in a depression. "Too high" relative to what? Presumably wages were "too high" relative to the state of aggregate demand, properly defined. But that must mean the same thing as aggregate demand being "too low" relative to wages. Furthermore, it was far from clear how the "too high" wages could be lowered. Even if labor wanted to cooperate by reducing money wages to restore full employment, would not universal wage cutting lead primarily to further price cut-

1. See Pigou (1933), p. 252.

ting—which would leave the real economic situation nearly unchanged? The practical moral of this dilemma was clear enough to Keynes, who was not the type to ponder long over theoretical paradoxes when actual solutions were close at hand. As a purely practical matter, discretionary fiscal and monetary policy represented a far more pragmatic approach to attacking unemployment than any conceivable series of wage reductions. And this remained true with or without the afterthought of Pigou's real balance effect to rescue the concept of a full-employment equilibrium attainable by flexible wages. Thus was born one of the greatest disappearing acts in history. Like a fantastic magician, Keynes removed the malfunctioning labor market and the wage issue from right before the public's eyes and replaced it by discretionary government policy to manage aggregate demand via the skillful manipulation of financial aggregates.

The rest is history. The Keynesian approach of actively manipulating financial aggregates to improve macroeconomic performance became virtually synonymous with macroeconomics and, rightly or wrongly, was credited with the quarter-century of strong stable economic growth that followed World War II. When, after an initial period of success, activist Keynesian policies for spending ourselves into full employment were blamed, rightly or wrongly, for the double-digit inflation of the 1970s, the stage was set for the monetarist version of which particular financial aggregates should be manipulated—how, when, and by whom. The basic message of monetarism is that if the economy concentrates on achieving price stability by rigidly controlling the "supply of money," at worst there may be a few awkward transition years when slightly less ambitious targets for full employment will have to be accepted. But when the system finally settles down at a stable low rate of inflation, steady slow growth of the "money supply" will yield no more unemployment over the long run than discretionary Keynesian interventionism. Unfortunately, as many central banks have had to learn the hard way, in a monetary technology that includes plastic and electronic money tied to deregulated banks and financial institutions, the "quantity of money" is not a terribly operational concept. More to the point, the deep policy-induced recession of 1981–83, which yielded the highest unemployment rates since the Great Depression, is widely viewed, rightly or wrongly, as discrediting simple-minded monetarism. Monetarism, it appears, does not eliminate the stagflation dilemma.

Where do we go from here? Most of the advanced capitalist economies (except Japan), after experimenting with Keynesianism and monetarism, are obviously in trouble on stagflation. Since the problem originates in wage behavior, that is the logical place to look for a solution.

From this perspective, the major macroeconomic problems of our day go back, ultimately, to the wage system of paying labor. We try to award every employed worker a nominally predetermined piece of the income pie before it is out of the oven, before the size of the pie is even known. Our "social contract" promises workers a fixed nominal wage independent of the health of their company, while the company chooses the employment level. This stabilizes the money income of whoever is hired, but only at the considerable cost of loading unemployment on low-seniority workers and inflation on everybody—a socially inferior risk-sharing arrangement that both diminishes and makes more variable the real income of workers as a whole. The individual worker who is promised a fixed number of pieces of green paper may feel secure, but it is an illusion from a social standpoint because, when all workers are so promised, a difficult burden of adjustment has been placed on simultaneously maintaining full employment while preserving what the pieces of green paper can buy.

In my opinion it is time to focus more directly on the labor market itself, to build in automatic flexibility and to reform out structural rigidities so that we do not have to rely quite so exclusively on macroeconomic sledgehammer "cures" to maintain noninflationary full employment. What is required is institutional change in incentive structures on the micro level to make it in employers' strong self-interest automatically to react to unfavorable shocks by maintaining high levels of employment while lowering prices rather than the other way around.

Profit Sharing

The reason profit sharing has more favorable macroeconomic consequences than a wage system is quite simple. Suppose the firm controls the employment decision. Then, other things being equal, under a profit-sharing system the firm is more inclined to expand employment and output in the face of shocks than under the corresponding wage system.

The following example illustrates the basic point. Suppose the typical firm can produce output Y out of labor L by the production function $F(L)$. Let the firm's revenue function be $R(Y)$. If the firm pays a fixed wage w it will hire labor and produce output at the level where profits $R(F(L)) - wL$ are being maximized, or where the marginal revenue product of labor $R'F'$ equals the wage w.

Now imagine, as a kind of thought experiment, that a profit-sharing system is put in place promising to pay each worker a base wage ω and a share λ of gross profits per capita. Each worker is now paid $W = \omega +$

$\lambda\Pi/L$, where $\Pi = R(L) - \omega L$ represents the gross profits of the firm, before profit-sharing bonuses are paid. The firm's net profits are now $\pi = (1 - \lambda)(R(F(L)) - \omega L)$, and the net marginal value of an extra worker is $(1 - \lambda)(R'F' - \omega)$. Provided only that $\omega < w$, the firm will wish to expand output and employment from its previous position. No matter how one interprets the "other things being equal" in this comparative statics thought experiment, a profit-sharing system is more expansionary than a wage system. If pay parameters are set so that workers are initially paid the same amount immediately after conversion from a wage into a profit-sharing system, the firm will wish to expand employment and output, thereby contracting its price (and pay) compared with the previous situation. If pay parameters are set so that, after the firm's reaction to the introduction of a profit-sharing contract, each worker ends up being paid the same as under the previous wage contract, then output and employment must be higher, with prices lower. The expansionary effects are stronger the smaller is the base wage ω, irrespective of the profit-sharing coefficient λ.

There is a simple explanation of all this. When factor costs are lowered, a profit-maximizing monopolist will want to hire more input, produce more output, and charge a lower price. When faced with a pure profits tax, on the other hand, the monopolist will choose to hire the same amount of input, produce the same output, and charge the same price. So far as the monopolist is concerned, conversion from a wage system to a profit-sharing system (with a smaller base wage) is equivalent to lower factor costs coupled with a pure profits tax. Hence the expansionary bias of a profit-sharing system over a wage system.

At some risk of oversimplification, let me give a concrete if highly idealized (and extreme) example of what I have in mind. Suppose that wages plus fringe benefits of the average General Motors automobile worker come to \$24 per hour. This means that the cost to GM of hiring one additional hour of labor is \$24. The extra hour of labor is used to produce more automobiles, which are then sold to yield increased revenue. If the increased revenue exceeds the increased cost, more workers will be hired; in the opposite case, workers will be laid off. Since GM is trying to maximize profits, it will take on (or lay off) workers to the point where the additional revenue created by the extra hour of labor is neither more nor less than the additional cost, in this case \$24. The average revenue per hour of labor will naturally be higher, say \$36, to cover overhead, capital, profits, and the like.

Now imagine that the auto workers agree to a different type of contract with GM. Instead of a fixed wage of \$24 an hour, they go for a fixed two-thirds share of GM's average revenue of \$36. At first glance there seems to be no difference between the two systems, since in both cases the workers get $24 an hour. However, GM's incentive to hire or fire is subtly but dramatically changed.

If GM now hires an extra worker, its revenue goes up by $24 as before, but its total labor cost in fact only increases by two-thirds of $24, or $16. It clears a profit of $8 on the extra worker, and understandably wants to go on hiring and expanding output more or less indefinitely. There is a secondary effect: in order to sell the extra output, GM has to reduce the price of its cars relative to other auto makers.

The benefits for the whole economy are thus clear: the new labor contract means more output and jobs—and lower prices. Firms want to hire more workers for the same reason they would be keen to acquire more salesmen on commission—nothing to lose, and something to gain.

So what is the rub? Clearly the revenue per worker—and therefore pay—has declined because the marginal revenue brought in by the extra worker is less than the average revenue. Senior workers who are not unduly at risk of being laid off might resist the plan.

However, this conclusion does not necessarily follow if a large number of important firms introduce profit (or revenue) sharing, because as each firm expands and hires more workers, total workers' purchasing power rises, and so does the demand for GM's products. Not for the first time, the sum of the economic parts adds up to more than the parts themselves. The conclusions reached from this example readily generalize to formulas encompassing more realistic "mixed" systems of base money wages plus shares of per capita profit (or revenue).

Somewhat more abstractly, consider a typical monopolistically competitive firm in a partial equilibrium setting. Suppose the wage is treated as a quasi-fixed parameter in the short run. If the firm can hire as much labor as it wants, it will employ workers to the point where the marginal revenue product of labor equals the wage rate. This is familiar enough. Consider, though, what happens with a profit-sharing contract that names a base wage and a certain fraction of profits per worker to be paid to each worker. Suppose these two pay parameters are treated as quasi-fixed in the short run. A little reflection will reveal that if the profit-sharing firm can hire as much labor as it wants, it will employ workers to the point where the marginal revenue product of labor equals the base wage, independent of the value of the profit-sharing parameter. (Note, though, that what the worker is actually paid depends very much on the value of the profit-sharing coefficient.) When a standard IS-LM type macro-model is constructed around such a model of the firm, the following isomorphism emerges. A profit-sharing macroeconomy will find itself with the same output, employment, and price level as the corresponding wage economy whose wage is set at the profit-sharing economy's base wage level. In other words, the aggregate macroeconomic characteristics of a profit-sharing economy, excepting the distribution of income, are determined (on the cost side) by its base wage alone. The profit-sharing parameter does not influence output, employment, or prices, although it does influence the distribution of income. If the employed workers can be persuaded to take more of their income in the form of profit shares and less in the form of base wages, that can result in a Pareto improvement—with increased aggregate output and employment, lower prices, and higher real pay.

For concreteness, let the aggregate demand specification be

$$Y = \alpha A + \beta M/P,$$

where Y is real national product, A is aggregate autonomous real spending, M is the money supply, and P is the price level. Coefficients α and β represent the relevant fiscal and monetary multipliers.

The aggregate demand equation is an underdetermined system. Given A and M (and the parameters α and β), there is an extra degree of freedom between the two major macroeconomic variables Y and P. The Keynesian tradition essentially fixes the price level P in the short run, implicitly relying on a more or less constant markup over sticky wages. Suppose, again for concreteness, that the economy consists of a large number n of symmetric monopolistically competitive firms, each of which produces output y from labor l according to the identical (linear) production function

$$y = \gamma(l - f),$$

where γ is the marginal productivity of an extra worker and f represents a fixed amount of overhead labor that must be employed to produce any output at all[2]. Each firm faces the (isoelastic) demand curve

$$y = (p/P)^{-E}(Y/n)$$

as a function of the price p it charges and the relevant aggregate demand variables. Then

$$\mu = E/(E - 1)$$

2. This production function can be viewed as a first-order approximation in the relevant operating range. That unit variable costs are roughly constant over some range is, I think, a decent enough stylized fact to be used as a point of departure for the purposes of this article.

is the markup coefficient for each firm, representing the ratio of its average revenue (price) to marginal revenue.

In the short run, suppose each firm pays its l workers by the profit-sharing formula

$$W(l) = \omega + \lambda(R(l) - \omega l)/l,$$

where $R(l)$ stands for total revenue as a function of labor, given the relevant demand and production functions. The pay parameters ω, representing the base wage, and λ, representing the profit-sharing coefficient, are both treated in the short run as exogenously fixed. A wage system here is just a special case of a profit-sharing system with the share coefficient $\lambda = 0$.

When l workers are hired by the firm, total net profits are

$$\pi(l) = (1 - \lambda)(R(l) - \omega l).$$

If unlimited amounts of labor are available to be hired on the given share contract, the firm will choose to hire workers to the point where

$$R'(l) = \omega.$$

But the marginal revenue product of labor with isoelastic demand curve and linear production function is related to price charged, p, by the formula

$$R'(l) = \gamma p/\mu.$$

Combining the above two expressions, with unlimited supplies of labor available on the quasi-fixed pay contract, each firm would choose to set its price at the level

$$P' = \mu\omega/\gamma.$$

The corresponding desired or target aggregate output level of the profit-sharing system with fixed pay parameters (ω,λ), denoted Y', would then be, from the aggregate demand specification,

$$Y' = \alpha A + \beta M\gamma/\mu\omega.$$

The strictly hypothetical variable Y' measures what firms would like to produce in the aggregate on the given pay contract if there were no overall labor constraint. Let the actual full employment output level of the economy be Y^*. Real aggregate production Y must then be the smaller of the demand-determined target Y' and the supply-determined capacity Y^*, i.e.,

$$Y = \min \{Y', Y^*\}.$$

The price corresponding to the full employment case $Y = Y^*$ is, from the aggregate demand specification,

$$P^* = \beta M/(Y^* - \alpha A).$$

We have thus derived a complete theoretical description of the short-run behavior of the macroeconomic variables (Y,P) as a function of the quasi-fixed parameters α, β, A, M, ω, λ. To recapitulate the methodology, each firm makes its short-run pricing, output, and employment decisions to maximize profits given the rigid labor payment parameters, the state of aggregate demand, and the prices that all the other firms are charging. The economy's short-run behavior is modeled as the Nash equilibrium outcome of this individualistic profit-maximizing process, which simultaneously satisfies the basic macroeconomic aggregate demand condition.

The economy in the regime $Y' < Y^*$ exhibits textbook Keynesian behavior in the short run when pay parameters can be treated as quasi-fixed. The price level P' cannot be directly affected by government policy. But output Y' responds via the standard Keynesian multipliers to changes in autonomous real spending A or money supply M.

By contrast, when $Y' > Y^*$ the economy displays classical or monetarist characteristics in a short run where pay parameters are quasi-fixed. Government aggregate demand management has no influence on real output, already at full employment, but directly influences the price level. Monetary policy is strictly neutral, with prices directly proportional to M. Expansionary fiscal policy has only an inflationary impact, since it crowds out private spending.

An immediately striking result is that the share parameter λ does not affect real national product or the price level (although it does affect real pay and the distribution of income). Only the value of ω, representing to a firm the "hard" money cost of taking on an extra worker (as opposed to the "soft" cost of a share of incremental gross profits), influences the overall level of national income. If workers in a wage economy agree to receive 80 percent of their pay in the form of base wages and 20 percent in the form of a profit-sharing bonus, the effect on national product, employment, and prices is "as if" wages had been cut by 20 percent while aggregate demand (real autonomous spending and the money supply) was being maintained at the same level.[3]

When a wage economy ($\lambda = 0$) suffering from unemployment converts to a profit-sharing formula whose parameters are initially set so that each employed worker is at first paid the same amount, the change will make all workers better off after the economy adjusts. Real pay in a profit-sharing system is

$$W/P = (1 - \lambda)\omega/P + \lambda y/L.$$

After conversion from a wage system to an "equivalent" profit-sharing system initially yielding the same pay, the share economy firms are induced to expand output and employment while lowering price. If labor productivity Y/L is not countercyclical, real pay must increase. In addition, new jobs have been created, so there are more employed workers, each of whom is receiving higher real pay. In this sense a seemingly neutral move toward profit sharing represents an unambiguous improvement for the working class.

Note that the argument applies only when a sufficiently large number of firms of a wage economy simultaneously convert to profit-sharing plans. If one firm alone converts, and if it attempts to hire new workers, it will only be at the expense of driving down the pay of its original workers. So coordination may be required to induce people to convert to a share system: one possibility is to have the government reward profit-sharing workers, by preferential tax treatment of share income, for their part in creating the positive externality of a tight labor market.

Consider next a longer-run situation where the set-up is the same as before except that pay parameters are now endogenously determined. For simplicity I will treat the base case of perfect competition in the labor market. The interested reader can consult a more complicated formulation of an imperfectly competitive labor market where it is shown that the same conclusions hold a fortiori.[4] I should point out that I view the hypothesis of competitive equilibrium in the labor market not as a literal description but more as a long-term approximation or norm that is never actually attained, yet forms a useful basis for talking about possible departures from normalcy.

In a wage economy ($\lambda = 0$), under thorough-going competition where each firm is free to set its own wage rate and does so to maximize

3. The reader will note that this conclusion holds under much more general conditions than the specific model being treated here.
4. See Weitzman (1986), forthcoming.

profits taking as given the prevailing level of pay throughout the economy, the limiting Nash equilibrium behavior as each firm becomes a negligible buyer of labor yields the full employment wage

$$w^* = \beta M\gamma/\mu(Y^* - \alpha A).$$

The next question is what happens when $\lambda > 0$. The basic concept of competitive equilibrium in the labor market is essentially the same for a share system as for a wage system. Given the pay parameters every other firm is selecting, each firm is free to choose its own pay parameters but must live with the consequences of labor shortage if it selects values that are too low. The underlying solution concept is a symmetric Nash equilibrium in pay parameters, which means that if all firms are selecting (ω,λ) as parameter values, it is not profitable for any one firm to deviate from that pattern.

A basic theoretical result is that any pair (ω,λ) constitutes a long-run competitive equilibrium in pay parameters if and only if it delivers to each worker the same pay as the equilibrium wage system $(w^*, 0)$ operating under otherwise identical circumstances. There is thus an inverse relationship between long-run equilibrium values of λ and ω and, hence, one extra degree of freedom in determining the pay parameters of a profit-sharing system. The intuitive explanation is roughly as follows. In long-run competitive equilibrium, because of migration pressure, each worker must end up with the same pay no matter what the ostensible form of the payment (how it is split between straight money wages and shares of profit). Given the fact that every firm must end up paying the prevailing wage whatever parameter values it selects, the profit-sharing firm can do no better in the long run than to hire labor to the point where the marginal revenue product of an extra worker is equal to the prevailing wage, then setting its pay parameters accommodatingly during contract time to yield that going compensation for its workers.

There are two major implications of this result. The first is that wage and profit-sharing systems are essentially isomorphic in a long-run stationary equilibrium with competitive labor markets. But, and this is the more important implication, the short-run properties of the two systems (when pay parameters are quasi-fixed) are quite strikingly different in the neighborhood of a long-run equilibrium position. As λ goes up, the corresponding competitive value of ω goes down. A genuine profit-sharing system in equilibrium will then be operating well inside the full employment region, with plenty to spare, while a wage economy is borderline full employment at best. A formal way of stating this idea is as follows.

When identical-twin wage and profit-sharing economies are placed in the same stationary environment, with competitive labor markets, both economies will gravitate toward the same long-run full-employment equilibrium. But then perform the following thought experiment. Disturb each economy and observe the short-run reaction when pay parameters are quasi-fixed but everything else is allowed to vary. The profit-sharing economy will remain at full employment after a disturbance, because the base wage determines desired aggregate output Y', while a contractionary shock will cause a wage economy to disemploy labor. And, after the identical adverse shocks to both systems, the wage economy will essentially display Keynesian characteristics, while the profit-sharing economy will continue to have essentially monetarist properties. It should not be hard to imagine why a profit-sharing system is then more resistant to stagflation than a wage system.

Let me note in passing that a profit-sharing system does not eliminate unemployment by, "in effect," lowering wages to the point where equilibrium is automatically maintained. The driving force behind full employment in a profit-sharing system is not a disguised form of wage flexibility in the usual, classic sense of that term. A profit-sharing system will remain at full employment even when worker pay is above the marginal revenue product of labor. The point is not that one system operates closer to equilibrium than another, but rather that the *form* of disequilibrium response to unexpected disturbances is different. Roughly speaking, the short-term response of a share economy holds the quantity of hired labor (and output) at its full-employment level, with the disequilibrium showing itself on the price (or value) side (workers are temporarily not paid their marginal value). Wage economies, on the other hand, tend to respond to contractionary shocks by holding equilibrium prices (or values) in line (workers are always compensated their marginal value) while the quantities of employment (and output) decline. In the long run both systems tend to the same equilibrium, but their short-run behavior out of equilibrium is quite different. And, of course, it is far more important for overall economic welfare that the system as a whole maintains a full-employment flow of goods and services throughout a contractionary shock than that some secondary marginal-value efficiency conditions on the level of the firm are being satisfied.

SOME BASIC QUESTIONS AND ANSWERS ABOUT PROFIT SHARING

So far I have outlined, in general form, the basic argument why, for a given level of autonomous spending and money supply, profit sharing tends to result in higher levels of employment and output with lower prices. The technical aspects of modeling a profit-sharing economy have been treated in the literature.[5] Here I would like to deal with some of the major objections that have been raised. The most effective way to do this, I believe, is to answer questions the way they are typically posed by astute critics.

A system that shares profits is analogous to the notorious sharecropping system in agriculture. As everyone knows, and many of the classical economists pointed out, such a system reduces the incentives to invest because the capitalist must share some part of increased profits with the workers. Wouldn't profit sharing cause underinvestment, too little capital, and too low labor productivity?

The classical economists were wrong on this point, or at least incomplete. They had in mind a situation where pay parameters were more or less permanently frozen. In that case profit sharing would, indeed, cause underinvestment for the well-publicized reason that any incremental profits would have to be shared with labor. But over the longer time horizon relevant to decisions about durable capital investments, where either base wages or profit-sharing coefficients (or both) are relatively plastic and respond to quasi-competitive long-run labor market forces, both wage and profit-sharing systems stimulate equal efforts toward output-increasing improvements—to the point where the marginal revenue product of capital equals the interest rate. Even if this theoretical isomorphism between investment in wage and profit-sharing systems did not exist, the cost of capital is only one side of the picture, and probably the less important side. The other consideration is the demand side. If profit sharing results in a macroeconomic environment where output is being stabilized at or near the full-employment, full-capacity level, while a wage economy results in erratic, fluctuation-prone output and capacity utilization levels, there is bound to be more investment in a profit-sharing economy. And, as if these two arguments were not enough, interest rates, investment tax credits, and the like could be used to influence investment decisions in any system. The really important distinction concerns the average level of unemployed resources.

A key part of the mechanism causing a profit-sharing firm to want to expand employment is that the marginal revenue product of labor under such a system exceeds the marginal cost of labor. But this occurs because, in effect, the additional hired worker dilutes the profits per worker which the previously hired workers receive. Wouldn't this cause resentment by the already existing labor

5. See Weitzman (1983), (1984), (1985), (1986).

force against newly hired workers and, in extreme cases, lead to restrictions against new hires?

First of all, it is important to keep things in perspective by realizing that even a worse-case scenario where profit sharing "merely" dampens economic downturns by encouraging employers to lay off fewer workers during recessions still represents an economic benefit of potentially enormous magnitude. If profit sharing did nothing more than reduce downside risks to an economy, it would still be tremendously important. And when it comes to internal labor relations, let us not forget that the wage system is hardly a bed of roses. Younger, untenured workers are pitted against older, high-seniority workers in the jobs vs. wages decision. Featherbedding is widespread. Workers resist the introduction of new labor-saving technology and, more generally, take relatively little interest in the fortunes of the firm because they do not have any direct stake in its profitability. Worker alienation is widespread in an environment where the employer is essentially indifferent on the margin to whether the worker stays or goes.

Any system where a substantial number of the major firms are operating with the marginal cost of labor lower than the marginal value of labor will have an inherent predilection toward providing more employment and expanding output. This tendency may take a long time to be fully realized, it may be frustrated by aggressive unions (where they exist) or voluntarily slowed by the employers themselves. But if the incremental, hardly noticed decision at the margin has more of a bias than before to lean toward letting go of fewer workers during bad times and taking on more of them during good times, then gradually, perhaps imperceptibly, the system will ratchet itself toward an ever-tighter labor market. The point is not that widespread conversion to profit sharing would instantly result in full employment. To eventually create a tight labor market it suffices that during downswings a few less workers than under a wage system are laid off and during upswings a few more workers than under a wage system are hired. Why is the employers' incentive to maintain or even slowly increase employment in a system of widespread profit sharing likely to prevail over the insider workers' possible incentive to resist?

When an entire economy of profit-sharing firms is geared up and functioning smoothly, there is a significant excess demand for labor as a whole and there are no long-term jobless people to be picked up easily. New labor must come primarily from other share firms, presumably yielded up in grudging amounts. In a tight labor market the tenuous aftermath of hiring a few more workers in one profit-sharing firm will scarcely be noticed, disguised as it must be behind a myriad of more important economic changes that much more directly influence short-term profitability. In a profit-sharing system, effort spent to enhance productivity and profits has a much higher payoff for the already-employed workers of a profit-sharing firm than effort spent on restricting new hires. It is worth noting that restriction of new hires becomes an issue only in those exceptional firms or industries where senior workers are trying to protect a noncompetitive pay level held artifically above the going market rate for that job category—new workers will have no incentive to join a firm in the first place unless they can receive a higher pay there than elsewhere.

So, as I see it, there will most likely be little trouble persuading unions to retain their working members once a profit-sharing system is geared up and running smoothly. (Can anyone imagine a situation where a union is pressuring the employer to lay off some of its members?) The more relevant issue concerns getting from here to there in an environment of less than full employment. For this purpose I advocate strong tax incentives making it in workers' strong self-interest to want to take some significant fraction of their pay in the form of profit sharing no matter what other workers in other firms are doing. In the U.S. context such tax incentives might take the form of a "working person's capital gains tax" which would tax profit-sharing income at the same reduced rates as long-term capital gains, up to some reasonable limit. I have calculated[6] that even under very extreme assumptions a substantial tax reduction for profit-sharing income would break even and pay for itself as a tax reform if it reduced the unemployment rate by just one percentage point. Any further reduction of unemployment from widespread profit sharing would translate into a federal budget surplus of some $30 billion per percentage point of reduced unemployment. The tax benefits would only be granted in situations where the union and employer explicitly agree to forswear any restrictive hiring practices. No union is compelled to petition for the special tax status of a share plan. But when it chooses to participate, a union cannot enjoy the considerable tax benefits without reaffirming an already existing legal commitment to open its ranks to as many qualified members and apprentices as the company wishes to hire under the agreed-upon share contract. This is a logical requirement for the government to insist on, since the entire raison d'être of the differential tax treatment is to encourage increased employment. In the U.S. today, approximately 17 percent of the work force is unionized and that percentage is currently declining at a rate of about one point per

6. See Weitzman (1984).

year. I cannot think of any compelling reason why the U.S. economy could not be purposely put on more of a profit-sharing basis. The European economies have a more solidaristic labor movement, are much more highly unionized, and in general display less flexible attitudes toward social and economic change. There is no question but that the introduction of widespread profit sharing would require a cultural revolution of sorts for European-style economies. On the other hand, these economies are suffering from extremely high unemployment rates, there is a pervasive sense that the old ways of doing things are inadequate, and there is some feeling that perhaps radical structural reforms are required.

It is best to be under no illusions about the political realities involved in making an economywide transition to a system based on profit-sharing principles. Some people are hurt by change, any change, and they will shout loudest to preserve the status quo even though, as with free trade, a share system is highly beneficial to the population as a whole. I believe that pure self-interest based on strong tax incentives in favor of profit-sharing income will go a long way toward convincing unions and others to look favorably upon a system that guarantees that aggregate output will be produced, and consumed, at the full-employment level even if it erodes the monopoly rent above the competitive pay which they currently enjoy. If the tax incentives are strong enough, a unionized firm will not only be enticed to join the share economy, but in a sense will be driven to enroll. It will be compelled because, if many other firms adopt share plans and if the pecuniary advantages in the form of tax savings are significant enough (larger than the union premium), a union will be unable to compete for members without following course. And the potential tax benefits could be made extremely attractive without doing fiscal harm to the federal budget since the increases in government revenues and decreases in outlays obtained from maintaining permanent full employment are so enormous. No union would be compelled to petition for the special tax status of a share plan. But when it chooses to participate, a union cannot enjoy the tax benefits without forswearing restrictive hiring practices. No matter how well-designed the incentives, such change will require genuine consensus, a general agreement cutting across left-right political lines, that the broad social gains of permanent full employment without inflation are worth more than the narrow private losses that will inevitably be incurred here and there.

In summary, then, it must be admitted that widespread profit sharing will probably alter the nature of industrial relations. There is no question but that workers sharing profits with management represents a different way from the wage system of doing business in the labor market. In an imaginative paper, Daniel Mitchell has argued that share bargaining is likely to prove healthy and invigorating for American labor unions—calling for new expertise and an expanded role—even though most of the old guard will initially oppose it.[7] The relevant theory shows that if the firm retains control of the employment decision, other things being equal a profit-sharing system results in greater output, higher employment, and lower prices. The trick is to make the transition to profit sharing while preserving the employer's traditional right to decide, ultimately, the employment level, at the same time allowing workers to bargain over base wages and profit-sharing coefficients. I do not think this trick is all that difficult to accomplish because, in contrast to other "incomes policies," it builds on already existing natural tendencies. (Profit sharing is not an exotic innovation or a completely externally imposed artifice, but an already existing reality for many tens of millions of workers.) Besides, widespread conversion to profit sharing will probably require government incentives anyway (this point will be expanded later) and the issue then reduces to building into such incentives management's traditional right to expand employment.

Under a wage system the firm bears all the risk, while under a profit-sharing system the worker bears some risk. Doesn't profit sharing therefore represent a socially inefficient form of risk bearing, since the stockholder can naturally diversify risks more easily than the worker?

The reasoning traditionally put forward to support this "insurance" argument is fallacious, being based on a partial equilibrium view that does not take into account the radically different macroeconomic consequences of the two systems for overall employment and aggregate output. The fixed wage does not stabilize labor income. What is true for the individual tenured worker is not true for labor as a whole. When a more complete analysis is performed, which considers the situation not as seen by a tenured, high-seniority worker who already has job security, but as seen by a neutral observer with a reasonably specified social welfare function defined over the entire population, it becomes abundantly clear that the welfare advantages of a profit-sharing system (which delivers permanent full employment) are enormously greater than a wage system (which permits unemployment). The basic reason is not difficult to understand. A wage system allows huge first-order Okun-gap losses of output and welfare to open up when a significant slice of the national-

7. See Mitchell (1985).

income pie evaporates with unemployment. A profit-sharing system stabilizes aggregate output at the full-employment level, creating the biggest possible national-income pie, while permitting only small second-order Harburger-triangle losses to arise because some crumbs have been randomly redistributed from a worker in one firm to a worker in another. It is extremely difficult to cook up an empirical real-world scenario, with reasonable numbers and specifications, where a profit-sharing system with a moderate amount of profit sharing (say 20 percent of a worker's total pay) does not deliver significantly greater social welfare than a wage system. As if this argument alone were not enough, it would be a mistake to extrapolate the demand variability now observed in the firms of a wage economy to a share economy. Cyclical industries such as machine tools, metals, building materials, construction, and the like would not fluctuate nearly so much, since the share economy is permanently operating at or near full capacity. Every firm of a profit-sharing system would exhibit significantly greater demand stability than we are now accustomed to because a budding recession cannot feed upon itself in a fully employed economy. In addition, enterprising insurance companies are sure to offer to reduce risk further for the employees of big profit-sharing corporations by offering neatly packaged policies that will insure share fluctuations for a premium. (The insurance companies can cover themselves to some degree by selling the company stock short.)

If profit sharing represents such a great idea for operating a market economy, why don't we see more examples of it arising spontaneously?

There *are* some significant examples of profit sharing. In Japan, Korea, and Taiwan, it can be argued, modest (although significant) steps have been taken in this direction. The performance of these economies hardly supports the view that widespread profit sharing is likely to prove deleterious. In the U.S. economy, about 15 percent of firms have what they call profit-sharing plans. (It is questionable how many of these plans would satisfy reasonably objective economic criteria.) Although the issue has not been studied in a rigorous way, it is clear that many of these profit-sharing firms are among the most progressive, advanced companies in the economy. As just one informal indication, in a well-known book called *The 100 Best Companies to Work for in America*, over half of the cited companies identify themselves as having profit-sharing plans of some kind.

The reason profit sharing is not more widespread involves an externality or market failure of enormous magnitude. In choosing a particular contract form, the firm and its workers only calculate the effects on themselves. They take no account whatsoever of the possible effects on the rest of the economy. When a firm and its workers select a labor contract with a strong profit-sharing component they are contributing to an atmosphere of full employment and brisk aggregate demand without inflation because the firm is then more willing to hire new "outsider" workers and to expand output by riding down its demand curve, lowering its price. But these macroeconomic advantages to the outsiders do not properly accrue to those insiders who make the decision. Like clean air, the benefits are spread throughout the community. The wage firm and its workers do not have the proper incentives to cease polluting the macroeconomic environment by converting to a share contract. The essence of the public-good aspect of the problem is that, in choosing between contract forms, the firm and its workers do not take into account the employment effects on the labor market as a whole and the consequent spending implications for aggregate demand. The macroeconomic externality of a tight labor market is helped by a share contract and hurt by a wage contract, but the difference is uncompensated. In such situations there can be no presumption that the economy is optimally organized and societywide reform may be needed to nudge firms and workers toward increased profit sharing.

Alternative Structural Approaches

Profit sharing is not the only proposal for structural reform of the labor market that might help with the stagflation policy dilemma. In the next three sections I will try to assess critically what I see as three other major prototypes for structural reform of the labor market: incomes policy, two-tiered pay, and employee control. In effect I will be arguing that, although each may have a positive, constructive role to play, profit sharing is overall the most promising of the alternatives. But it is important, in my opinion, to have an open mind and to maintain a constructive attitude toward almost any structural plan that might have a reasonable chance of lowering unemployment. This is especially true for a world where, in the final analysis, political feasibility may well be the dominant constraint.

INCOMES POLICY

Understanding the term liberally, "incomes policy" is a tremendously broad subject with an enormous literature.[8] All I can hope to do here is

8. Two recent books contain good bibliographies. For the United States see Rockoff (1985). For Europe see Flanagan et al. (1983).

place the subject in some comparative perspective as a labor-market policy.

The common strand of incomes policy is a desire to bring the economy back closer to the old-fashioned textbook Keynesian model by exerting some control over the upward pressure of wages and prices. The point of departure is the empirical observation that cost-push or sellers' inflation typically sets in well before the economy reaches full employment. If only prices and wages could be held down, Keynesian expansionary policies might be carried further toward full employment without triggering inflation.

Initially, incomes policy was primarily conceived as wage and price controls of the typical wartime variety. A major problem is that it is an enormous administrative task to control all, or even just the most important, prices in a market economy without introducing allocative distortions all over the economic landscape. During wartime, when the priorities are few and simple and the population is motivated to cooperate, this problem is perhaps not insurmountable. But it can become overwhelming during more normal times. Critics of incomes policy are typically quick to seize upon the microeconomic distortions as fatally damaging. Actually, the relevant consideration is whether the microeconomic distortions are more costly than the macroeconomic losses of income and output from conducting anti-inflationary campaigns without incomes policy. Here the answer is not so clear-cut, but old-fashioned wage-price controls still probably get the lowest grades out of the class of all incomes policies.

Wages are somewhat easier to control than prices, and, economic theory teaches us, it probably suffices to control them since prices are largely determined by wage costs. But wage control, while easier than price control, is still a difficult, messy business to administer. And, perhaps more to the point, controlling wages alone is widely viewed in a political context as being inequitable. There are schemes to get back some symmetry by also controlling "excess profits," but I doubt that this abstraction would much appease labor.

Another problem with traditional wage-price controls is what happens when they are removed. If in the meantime macroeconomic policy has not been appropriately adjusted, and it is frequently difficult to make the appropriate adjustments (both for informational reasons and lack of willpower), the economy may roar back to its previous position and much of the intended benefit will have been undone. The removal of wartime controls after the war is almost always a ticklish issue because of this problem.

While there is some debate about their empirical efficacy, the postwar experience of several mixed economies that experimented with wage-price controls has not, on the whole, been very encouraging. There may be a legitimate short-period function for controls as part of a coordinated inflation-fighting strategy, but they are probably not viable in peacetime as a long-term device. This is especially true in a political climate where government intervention into individual markets is already viewed with no small degree of suspicion.

The United States experimented on a sporadic basis with voluntary wage-price restraints during the Kennedy-Johnson and Carter administrations. While a few studies have attempted to assess the impact,[9] no consensus has emerged concerning whether or not—or how much—good was done in halting inflation.

A more market-oriented class of incomes policy has emerged in the last fifteen years. Called TIPs (tax-based incentive policies),[10] this approach attempts to defeat cost-push inflation by making it expensive. A number of variants have been proposed. Most would tax wage and price increases above a certain prescribed norm. The advantage over straight wage-price controls is that the firm is allowed a certain degree of flexibility since it makes the choices, thus mitigating somewhat the degree of inefficiency in resource allocation that inevitably accompanies any form of incomes policy.

Like traditional wage-price controls, TIPs come in several variants—wages alone, wages and prices, wages and profits, etc. Any TIP plan shares with its wage-price control analogue the problem of administration because TIP is essentially a form of wage-price control where the penalty system is more flexible. Basically the same norm-setting dilemmas and bureaucratic problems are involved—if anything, it may be more complicated to administer TIP than wage-price controls because the exact *degree* of compliance must now be monitored.

Some proponents of TIP-like plans would maintain the plans permanently while others would use them only temporarily. One imaginative plan calls for a permanent wage tax offset by an employment subsidy.[11] The argument is that such a plan would help to lower the NAIRU[12] to the extent that it has been caused by monopolistic wage-setting practices. This approach seems more appropriate to the European context, and, indeed, most such ideas have originated in Britain.

There has been very little actual experience with TIP-like plans. The

9. See for examples the references cited in Colander (1986), especially in chapters 11 and 12.
10. Colander (1986) contains an extensive bibliography.
11. Jackman and Layard (1985).
12. Non Accelerating Inflation Rate of Unemployment.

closest we have come in the United States is the Carter administration's "real wage insurance plan," which was proposed by the administration but was never passed by Congress. The history of the real wage insurance plan, with its ever-increasing complexity attending each new rewriting, makes instructive reading for TIP enthusiasts looking for clues as to how such plans might have to look in practice to gain political acquiescence.

Despite the administrative drawbacks, and despite the inevitable loss of some allocative efficiency, the only fair economic comparison has to be made with the alternative of fighting inflation by purely macroeconomic strategies like policy-induced recessions. TIP-like policies might well form part of a policy package assault on bringing unemployment rates down without triggering inflation—in the United States and even more so in Europe—but the economics profession has been lukewarm or cynical and the public is no better than indifferent. I believe the essential problem is that such plans are viewed as inherently involving widespread government interference at a detailed microeconomic level, which goes against the political currents now flowing.

An even more ambitious type of incomes policy is MAP (market-based anti-inflation plan), which essentially makes a tradeable market in rights to inflate, the total number of certificates to be issued by the government. On a purely intellectual level it is quite a clever proposal. But, in a way, its cleverness is its own undoing in a world that can barely understand the logic of considerably simpler TIP-like plans. It seems hardly worth fighting for a plan that might involve somewhat superior theoretical properties than the better-known TIP but would probably face even greater difficulty in public acceptance.

My conclusion about incomes policies is this. They are capable of being a good short-term measure under certain circumstances as part of an overall strategy. Their principal drawback is political and social. Incomes policies are perceived as nonindigenous species. They have no counterpart or analogue in the private market, which the public can view as a natural antecedent. Instead, incomes policies are widely seen as representing a pure form of government interference directly at the microeconomic level where it is most threatening and least well tolerated.

TWO-TIERED PAY

While most pay systems are based, at least in theory, on the egalitarian principle of "equal pay for equal work," recently in the United States there have sprung up examples of inequalitarian two-tiered pay systems that explicitly pay new hires at a lower rate than previously hired workers were at first paid. Thus, a newly hired worker this year might be paid significantly less than last year's new hire and be tracked onto a significantly lower pay ladder. Sometimes it is intended that such discrimination be "temporary"—say, for five years, or until the company regains greater profitability, or whatever—while in other instances the intended duration of the two different pay profiles is vague. The motivation behind two-tiered systems is fairly clear. In the present internationally competitive and deregulated environment, many firms have found themselves under great pressure to lower labor costs. But frequently there is resistance to so doing by noncompetitive forces—usually in the form of a militant labor union. To an extent that is astonishing by pre-1980s standards, there have been a fair number of union givebacks in cases where the company has forcefully threatened to otherwise shut down operations and produce mass layoffs. Two-tiered systems represent a kind of compromise position where the union retains higher pay than would otherwise be the case for its current members, but accepts reduced pay for new employees. It is not difficult to understand why unions basically dislike two-tiered pay systems and occasionally accept them, but with great reluctance, only as a lesser evil than lowering their own current members' wages. In industries with large turnover, two-tiered wage systems amount to a phased-in wage cut. But even without the turnover issue, acceptance of two-tiered pay poses a very unpleasant dilemma for a union. If "old" union members allow discriminatory pay, lower than they were themselves initially offered at a corresponding level of experience, for entering "new" members, why should the "new" union members, whose proportion is naturally increasing over time, defend the right of the "old" members to keep their arbitrary differential if and when the company seeks to lower or even eliminate pay differences the next time around? For this cogent reason, as well as the fact that union membership is diminishing (17 percent of the current work force and declining at a rate of about 1 percent per year), two-tiered pay systems are unlikely to become a significant phenomenon in the United States.[13]

As a theoretical matter, could the two-tiered wage system we now see occasionally springing up in the United States serve as a kind of model

13. Two-tiered wage systems are probably even more unlikely to become a significant factor in the solidaristic labor markets of Europe. The Japanese *nenko* system, as we shall see, has a relatively steep age-earnings profile, so that it is, de facto, a multi-tiered pay system. But the profile of length-of-service wage ratios is traditionally quite rigid, and therefore nondiscriminatory, so that the unions do not fear the playing off of one segment against the other or the lowering of "new" compared with "old" workers' pay. The type of two-tiered, or even multi-tiered, systems being discussed here are conceptually quite different, therefore, from the Japanese *nenko* system, wherein the firm, making a lifetime commitment to employment, presumably decides about new hires on the basis of something like a present discounted cost and benefit calculation.

approach to eliminating or greatly reducing unemployment on the macroeconomic level? This is not an easy question to answer. Probably a more widespread use of two-tiered systems might reduce unemployment somewhat. (It would certainly be difficult to argue otherwise—how could it possibly *increase* unemployment?)

One strike against such approaches is their explicitly inequalitarian nature, which, with or without labor unions, could be viewed as unfair, repugnant, or inherently conflictual. As opposed to this view one must ask, as always, whether the alternative of greater unemployment is less unfair, less repugnant, or less inherently conflictual. Still, I think there is a very fundamental difficulty with inequalitarian pay scales and with blatant violations of "equal pay for equal work," at the same level of experience and job tenure, in the American workplace at least, that are not so easy to wave away. I am not sure that creating a second-class citizenry within the same work organization will not lead to strong internal tensions, as it typically does in a wide variety of other contexts. The concept that all hired workers should be treated symmetrically (if not equally) by their company is, to my mind, a very deeply rooted culture myth.

Suppose it were conceded that two-tiered wage systems are likely to reduce unemployment somewhat. We might legitimately still wonder how far this effect is likely to go. The mainstream explanation of cyclical unemployment involves wage stickiness as a central ingredient. Why would not the second-tier wage also become sticky, even if not so sticky as the first-tier wage? The answer must depend greatly upon what one believes is behind the original first-tier wage stickiness. Whatever the ultimate explanation—and we have, of course, seen a great many theoretical attempts—it is difficult to envision circumstances that would make the second tier of wages singularly free of stickiness. While I am prepared to believe that more widespread adoption of two-tiered wage systems might help somewhat to reduce unemployment, it is difficult for me to think of this as a breakthrough solution concept worthy of any great proselytizing effort. The problem is that whatever forces are causing first-tier wage stickiness are likely, although perhaps in somewhat attenuated strength, to cause second-tier wage stickiness. Of course one could go to three-tier wage systems, and so on, but the endeavor seems remarkably like trying to sneak through the back door a wage flexibility that simply will not be allowed to pass through the front door. Far more desirable than the inequalitarian principle of unequal pay for equal work in the same workplace, I believe, would be a system that automatically preserves full employment even when sluggish pay parameters are frozen at the "wrong" levels.

EMPLOYEE CONTROL

"Employee control" is a term encompassing a broad spectrum of proposals for labor market reform. For some, the term connotes a quite radical reorganization of work relations—really some form of socialism or anarcho-syndicalism following loosely in the utopian tradition of, say, Robert Owen. Others see employee control as a minor but important variation on the prevailing capitalist theme, where workers merely own more of their company's stock, and thereby exert more control over its decisions. As might be expected, the kinds of suggestions for improving capitalism being considered here are often heavily tainted with ideological overtones. Indeed, ideology, rather than strictly economic considerations, usually determines a typical proponent's attitude. At the one extreme, worker management represents to some a kind of idealized democratic socialism. At the other, those who strongly advocate employee stock ownership plans are frequently attached to some vision of peoples' capitalism. In between are often-fuzzy images of workers' councils helping to create a more humane and more productive world. In this kind of potentially charged environment, I should make my own position clear. I am primarily interested in whether or not a proposed reorganization increases employment without accelerating inflation. The key operational question is whether or not, after a particular form of "employee control" is put into place, forces are set in motion that tend to increase, or at least to facilitate, the hiring of currently unemployed workers.

A common, typically implicit, article of faith among those advocating increased employee control is that by eliminating the sharp distinction between "us" who work for the company and "them" who own or direct the company, economic performance will be bettered. After all, if the workers own or control the firm, the distinction between wages and profits largely vanishes, or at least becomes blurred. Isn't it then reasonable to suppose that macroeconomic polices aimed at full employment in such an environment would be more effective because the push on wages, which bedevils current efforts to reconcile low unemployment with low inflation, would be greatly diminished? It is hard to have a problem of wage explosion, after all, when, at least in the extreme case, there are no wages.

A major problem with this line of reasoning is that it is not supported by the relevant theory.[14] Actually, the standard model of a labor coopera-

14. A good summary discussion with references to the literature is contained in Meade (1982).

tive whose members share an "earned surplus" dividend (instead of a wage) has rather perverse employment properties. When the objective of the cooperative is to maximize the dividend per member, what one normally thinks of as expansionary shocks actually cause the organization to contract membership, while what one normally thinks of as contractionary shocks induce expansion. Even granted that the model specification may not be entirely appropriate, one is left with the uneasy feeling that labor-managed firms are likely to have a contractionary bias compared with their capitalist cousins. The reason is that the existing members of the cooperative will desire to maximize not the total earned surplus, but the earned surplus *per member*. If existing members control the employment decision, they will be willing to expand output by taking on new members only so long as profits are increased at least in proportion to the increase in membership size. But this is a more restrictive criterion for expansion than the ordinary monopolist (who is interested primarily in increasing total surplus) typically applies. Hence, turning firms into worker co-ops whose members control the employment decision is likely to result in fewer, not more, new hires. Consequently, I would say, there is little basis for believing that labor cooperatives will aggressively attempt to integrate unemployed workers into their system. The absorption of unemployed outsiders would come about presumably through the creation of new cooperatives, which is, in my opinion, likely to prove at least as unreliable a stimulus to new hires as wage cuts in the more conventional setting.

There exists, additionally, a problem of risk sharing. As the point is usually made, there is a good reason why capital should bear more risk than labor—capital can be diversified in any portfolio, whereas labor tends to have but one job at a time. Therefore, it is better if the variable component of business income would accrue largely to capital, while the worker is paid a fixed wage. This argument, so widely parroted by economists and seemingly so plausible, is in fact deeply fallacious. An elementary fallacy of composition is involved. What is a correct statement for the individual high-seniority worker who already has job tenure is not necessarily true for the working class as a whole. The problem of unemployment is in fact the largest income risk that labor as a whole (as opposed to the median worker) faces. If more variable pay for the individual helps to preserve full employment for the group, while fixed pay tends to cause unemployment, it is not the least bit clear why overall welfare is improved by having the median worker paid a fixed wage. Actually, the correct presumption runs the other way around. For present purposes it suffices to concentrate on the fundamental issue of whether or not the particular variable-income proposal under consideration tends to decrease unemployment. As I have indicated, the egalitarian cooperative does not appear to score high in this dimension.

James Meade proposes an imaginative variant of a labor-managed cooperative based on the "inequalitarian principle" that new hires are offered a different (presumably lower) number of shares than old hands. The proposal is somewhat of a hybrid between the two-tiered (or multitiered) payment system and the worker coop.[15] The major problem I have with all multitiered payment systems (whether based on inequalitarian wages or inequalitarian dividends) is in wondering why the *n*th tier of an *n*-tiered system should be assumed to be a perfectly flexible subject of rational discourse when the heart of the macroeconomic problem, or so it seems to me, is the disequilibrium created when pay parameters (of whatever sort) are inflexible in the face of changed demand conditions. Virtually any system assuming perfect flexibility of pay parameters for the marginal worker will yield full employment. But is this a reasonable assumption? Perhaps it is. Perhaps society can be turned in this direction. But I think that a more promising line is not to abandon the egalitarian principle, and not to abandon the idea that the capitalist determines the employment level, but rather to motivate that capitalist to hire more workers, expand output, and charge lower prices.

If, as most observers have believed, the very essence of a cooperative organization involves each member being treated equally with every other, so that no member has the feeling of being a second-class hired hand, then a legitimate question arises concerning why we do not see more examples of this organizational form. It is not for lack of trying. History is littered with examples of transient cooperative movements. Most failed to keep or attract members. A handful succeeded so well that they became bona fide corporations in their own right. Either way, there are remarkably few producer cooperatives in the modern industrial landscape.

Why this should be so was first addressed and, to my mind, brilliantly analyzed by the Russian Marxist economist Tugan-Baronovsky.[16] Tugan-Baronovsky wondered whether producer cooperatives might be an inherently unstable form of economic organization. His answer was yes. The reasoning is as follows. There are essentially two cases. If the cooperative fails to keep its dividend per worker up to the competitive wage level, its members, no matter how highly ideologically motivated, will begin to drop out in favor of jobs elsewhere (or if the current mem-

15. See Meade (1986).
16. See Tugan-Baronovsky (1921). Ben-Ner (1984) contains an excellent discussion of these issues.

bers don't, their children will). If, and this is the more subtle case, the cooperative succeeds so well that its members are earning dividends above the competitive wage, there will be strong economic pressures to expand. But why should the current members dilute their above-market earnings by admitting new members? If the present members would instead incorporate themselves and hire outsiders at the going rate, they would make more money. In the case of a successful co-op there is then a conflict between the economic motive of making money and the egalitarian motive, which constitutes the essence of the cooperative philosophy, of treating all members equally. As we know from many actual historical examples, the economic motive tends to win out and the original members of a successful co-op tend to evolve into capitalists of some sort while the new members become more like hired workers. In either of the two cases, then, the egalitarian producer cooperative is a transient, essentially unstable economic organization.

What about the more openly capitalistic variants of "employee control," such as employee stock ownership plans (ESOPs)? Proponents of this approach typically adhere to the following philosophy. Capitalism, they believe, is basically a very fine system. But it is marred by a too-concentrated ownership of the means of production in too few hands. Corrective measures should be taken to spread capital around, so that the community is more of a nation of capitalist-workers or worker-capitalists. Especially desirable would be a situation where the worker-capitalists essentially own the company they work for. Hence the motivation for a spate of tax gimmicks encouraging employers to pay workers stock in lieu of wages.

Whatever the possible political and social merits or drawbacks of a world of worker-capitalists, it is difficult to find a hard economic rationale in favor of worker capitalism as opposed to ordinary capitalism. When workers are paid stock in lieu of wages, why does that encourage the company to hire the unemployed or to keep down prices? It is true that certain delicately designed stock plans are actually much like profit sharing and do encourage additional employment on the margin. But the typical ESOP is not like this at all. (Perhaps it could be made more like this, for example by making the value of stock distributions proportional to profits per worker—and maybe the tax benefits should be only granted in these cases.) In any event such considerations are not usually what the typical ESOP supporter has in mind. Perhaps the fact that workers "own" a part of the company helps to moderate wage demands or motivates harder work. These might conceivably have macroeconomic consequences, although it is hard to believe they would be substantial. The idea that part of a worker's pay is linked to the well-being of the company (through the price of the stock) seems like a good idea that presumably helps to stabilize employment. What is typically lacking in such discussions is any kind of hard economic theory that clearly identifies motives and behaviors under employee stock ownership that would result in improved macroeconomic performance. Perhaps such a connection can be made, but it is presently elusive, at least for me. In this sense there is a strong contrast with profit sharing, where a relatively much more tight economic theory can be used to argue that there might be favorable employment consequences.

The one argument for worker capitalism I have found convincing concerns situations where particular industries or regions are under duress due to structural changes in the economy.[17] Plant closings can cripple a community. Sometimes unions that vehemently oppose concession bargaining or worker givebacks as an alternative to a plant closing will look less unfavorably upon employee ownership. The union's attitude in such situations is paradoxical because the very first thing the new worker-owners typically find themselves doing is taking a "temporary" pay cut. The same forces that made the plant uneconomical for the capitalist owners will invariably make it unviable also for the new worker-owners if the old wages must be paid. But since the mass layoffs attending plant shutdowns can be such a traumatic event for a community of workers and their dependents, we should not look lightly upon any measures, however much they might involve face-saving gimmicks, that can keep people employed a little longer. If the worker-owned plant is economically unviable, eventually the workers, or their children, will relocate to other industries or other regions. But in the meantime the forces necessitating such relocation will have been blunted somewhat, and the migration itself will take on more of a voluntary, gradual character, spurred on by the de facto pay cuts that invariably accompany worker ownership of a declining plant. In my opinion, temporary tax relief is warranted for workers wishing to own and manage a plant that would otherwise be shut down. However, I do not see in this particular argument, intended to give short-term relief under special circumstances, the germ of a valid general case for tilting an economy toward worker ownership.

Actually, my general instinct is that worker ownership, or even worker control, is basically not a good idea under most circumstances. It is hard to believe that the modern corporation (especially in an internationally competitive environment) can be effectively run by a committee of workers. The transience of worker cooperatives seems to me indirect evidence of this thesis. While there are bound to be specific exceptions, I fear that

17. This theme is developed more fully in Bradley and Gelb (1984).

a worker-managed firm would generally have difficulty making the hard choices that need to be made quickly in a fast-moving environment where specific circumstances of time and place are important. Managers representing workers would also, I believe, have some difficulty keeping up the torrid pace of technological innovation upon which all economic growth and welfare is ultimately based. I think it is ultimately in the workers' own self-interest (just as it is ultimately in the consumers' self-interest) not to sit on committees that democratically vote for what is to be produced and how it is to be produced, but rather to be presented with so many viable alternative job opportunities in a tight labor market that the capitalist overseers simply have no choice but to provide high pay and good working conditions.

Is Japan a "Share Economy"?

The task of comparing a particular theoretical model with the historical experience of an actual functioning economy and drawing from such an association the correct implications is one of the most challenging issues in economics. Again and again we are required to make such judgments because of the nature of economics. We cannot perform meaningful controlled experiments on the level of a national economy. Nor are the time series we confront sufficiently stationary, long enough, or possessed of enough variation to settle many vital questions. So, like it or not, we are forced back on the eclectic methodology of the historian to try to resolve many important issues. As is often the case in historical analysis, however, there is room for many coexisting interpretations. It is in this spirit that I want to report some empirical investigations of the Japanese bonus system.

It has long been noted that the Japanese labor market is "different." Perhaps the best operational statement of this observation is something like the following. If one makes pairwise comparisons of labor markets in OECD countries, they are more similar to each other than any one is to the labor market of, say, the Soviet Union. But the OECD country that looks least like the other OECD countries in pairwise comparisons is Japan. There are several ways in which Japanese labor markets look different.[18] The following stylized facts might be taken as roughly descriptive of how the "Japanese model" of the labor market differs somewhat from others.[19]

18. The remainder of this section contains some descriptive and summary material from Freeman and Weitzman (1986), q.v. for a more complete analysis of the Japanese bonus system.
19. Shimada (1983) contains an excellent survey of the English-language literature.

1. Firms hire workers for "lifetime employment" (the *shushin koyo* system). In fact this is done primarily by the large firms, and only for their so-called "permanent" or "regular" employees (who constitute, typically, over three-fourths of the total). Nevertheless, the "lifetime commitment mentality" seems to be a fair characterization of the Japanese system as a whole, which, if anything, is probably becoming more valid over time as the distinction between permanent and temporary employees seems to be breaking down.[20]

2. There is a steep age-earnings profile for permanent workers up to the retirement age of 55 or 60. Pay is determined primarily, but not exclusively, by seniority. (This *nenko* system is beginning to erode in many places as it increasingly comes to be viewed as anachronistic.)[21]

3. The Japanese workplace is a relatively cooperative and equalitarian environment. There are few work rules, job reassignments are common, and a high degree of company loyalty motivates productivity-enhancing behavior. Unions are organized along enterprise or company lines. Blue- and white-collar workers in the same firm are comparatively less differentiated than elsewhere in terms of perquisites, treatment, union coverage, method of payment (monthly salaries rather than hourly wages, with meaningful bonus payments), and how much they are paid.[22]

4. Japanese society as a whole displays a relatively intense commitment at a grass-roots level to maintaining full employment. Companies and unions seem almost ashamed to lay off workers outright. Layoffs are *not* by seniority. There appears to be a somewhat higher degree of social responsibility in wage setting, as was dramatically shown by labor heeding the 1975 call for wage restraint in the face of strong inflation caused by the first oil shock. Work sharing is common, as Japanese firms tend to adjust hours (±4 percent compared with ±2 percent in other OECD countries) rather than employment.[23]

5. A significant fraction of the average worker's pay is in the form of a semiannual bonus.

I will now describe the Japanese bonus system in some detail. But it should always be kept in mind that the bonus system is just one part

20. Koike (1983a), (1983b), and references therein, sometimes argues the contrarian view that Japanese industrial relations, and particularly the lifetime employment system, are not nearly so unique as is sometimes supposed. He has a point when he does not push this view too hard. Perhaps a more balanced view is contained in Hashimoto and Raisian (1985).

21. For discussion of the *nenko* system, see, e.g., Shimada (1983) or Shirai (1983b).

22. For descriptions of the Japanese workplace, see Koshiro (1983a).

23. On many of these points see Shirai (1983b). Hours adjustments are discussed in Hamada and Kurosaka (1984).

of the complicated, interrelated web of institutions and attitudes that constitutes Japanese labor relations. It is difficult to sort out the pure economic role of the bonus from the roles of lifetime employment commitment, layoffs not by seniority, the *nenko* system, and so forth.

The typical Japanese worker's pay is divided into two categories. The first component is officially called *kimatte shikyusuru kyuyo,* "the wage that is surely paid," which we will refer to simply as base wages, or wages—although they are not really hourly wages at all, but rather a monthly salary. (Actually the whole concept of "overtime" payments and work is not sharply differentiated in Japan, suggesting that employment rather than person-hours is the fundamental unit of labor usage for regular workers.) The second component is called "special cash payments" in the official statistics and the defining characteristic is held to be that it is a payment made "temporarily, unexpectedly, or erratically at the discretion of the employer." This category consists overwhelmingly of bonus payments, even when their terms and amounts are established by collective agreements.

The bonus payments are a significant economic entity. In recent years they have constituted about one-fourth of a worker's pay. Economy-wide, aggregate bonus payments typically exceed before-tax profits.

Bonuses are usually paid twice a year—in summer (most frequently in June and July), and at year end (December). Insignificant amounts are sometimes paid in August, March, and January. The bonus probably traces back in history to the time when merchants gave small gifts to employees at Buddhist festival times. Although blue-collar and low-status white-collar workers before the war often received a lump sum of money twice a year in addition to their regular pay, the amount of money involved was tiny and in no way compared with the significant semiannual profit-sharing bonuses received as a mark of honor by high-status white-collar employees with advanced educational backgrounds.

Only after World War II did the payment system emerge in its present form, as part of a broader trend. The main feature of this trend was a deemphasis, to the point of near-elimination, of the invidious status categories of prewar Japan with their implicit legacies of a feudal past. As one byproduct of the immediate postwar process of democratizing the workplace, which the unions fully supported, all regular employees—blue-collar and white- —were henceforth to be paid a monthly salary instead of an hourly wage, supplemented by meaningful semiannual bonuses for every regular employee irrespective of category.[24] While

24. This interpretation is emphasized by, among others, Shirai (1983b), p. 131.

large relative to prewar and in comparison with other countries, at first the bonus payments constituted less than two months' worth of supplement rising gradually to over four months' by 1973 and falling back to slightly more than three-and-one-half months' currently. Economywide average bonus payments for regular private employees from 1958 through 1983 are shown in table 1 (expressed in months of base wages, which is how most Japanese think of it).

The bonus system is widely viewed as serving three purposes. One purpose is to compensate individual effort. Since the bonus is largely discretionary, as opposed to the base wage of the *nenko* system (which is primarily related to length of service), management typically makes some part of a particular employee's bonus depend on the merit ap-

Table 1 JAPANESE BONUS PAYMENTS
(in months of base wages)

Year	*Bonus*
1958	2.21
1959	2.38
1960	2.65
1961	2.90
1962	2.87
1963	2.99
1964	2.97
1965	2.97
1966	3.07
1967	3.17
1968	3.29
1969	3.54
1970	3.64
1971	3.79
1972	3.86
1973	4.26
1974	4.43
1975	3.96
1976	3.91
1977	3.83
1978	3.70
1979	3.76
1980	3.78
1981	3.77
1982	3.70
1983	3.60

Source. Bonus divided by wages; data from appendix.

praisal of the individual worker's job performance.[25] A second purpose of the bonus is to emphasize, symbolically and practically, the common bond linking the company's well-being with the well-being of its regular workers. Finally, the bonus system provides some pay flexibility to help firms maintain the lifetime employment commitment over bad times and good.

The timing of wage and bonus decisions frequently differs. Across typical unionized companies the general features of base wage determination are quite similar, being the primary concern of the economy-wide pattern-bargaining spring wage offensive (*shunto*) which typically starts in February and peaks in April. Bonus determination is by comparison a much more idiosyncratic process, with several different possible time patterns of negotiation, depending upon the particular firm or industry.

Bonus payments are also much more variable in amount than base wages, on an aggregate level having almost three times the standard error and displaying even more variability relative to wages on an industry level.[26] This reflects a prevailing philosophy that base wages are essentially related to the economy's national performance, while the bonus is more sensitive to a company or industry's specific circumstances. Firms typically try to pay a fairly steady number of months' wages as a bonus, and can often succeed in an expanding market, but will seek to impose a substandard bonus if the company suffers economic reverses.[27] Toyota, as an example of the first type, has paid about the same months' worth of bonus in each year since 1968. But for every Toyota Motor Company there are companies in, say, machine tools or shipbuilding where it is reluctantly accepted that bonuses may vary from zero to ten months' pay in extreme economic conditions. (At Okuma Machine Works, the standard deviation of the percentage change of wages is 7, compared with a standard deviation of the percentage change of bonuses of 29.) The majority of firms hold a position in between Toyota and Okuma. Surveys conducted by *Nikkeiren,* the employers' federation, show that most firms think of bonuses as being influenced by profitability. Among corporations that make an *explicit* agreement with employees about bonus payments, some 15 percent of such contracts contain profit-sharing clauses.[28]

25. See, e.g., Okuno (1984).
26. See Ishikawa and Ueda (1984), p. 141 and tables v-2 and v-3.
27. Koshiro (1983b), pp. 241–242, contains a good discussion of bonus responsiveness to profits.
28. See (Japanese Ministry of Labor, *General Survey on Wage and Working Hours System.*) It is useful to bear in mind that the aggregated data are masking a fair degree of diversity by

All this notwithstanding, I have also heard it said more than once by some specialists on the Japanese economy that bonus payments are so regular as to constitute a form of disguised wage. When pressed, such experts will cite examples like Toyota, where companies they know change only slowly, if at all, the number of months paid as bonus. A more sophisticated response observes in the data of table 1 some clear secular trends but no discernible yearly pattern of reacting to current business conditions. Clearly, bonuses have increased more or less stead-

Table 2 REAL JAPANESE PROFITS
(Fiscal year: in trillions of 1980 Yen)

Year	*Profits*
1959	1.74
1960	2.94
1961	3.29
1962	3.21
1963	3.82
1964	3.97
1965	3.93
1966	5.30
1967	7.08
1968	8.80
1969	11.82
1970	12.38
1971	10.32
1972	13.73
1973	22.55
1974	16.14
1975	7.11
1976	11.13
1977	11.25
1978	14.32
1979	19.51
1980	19.70
1981	15.18
1982	14.05
1983	14.62

Source. Nominal fiscal-year profits divided by appropriate price index; data from appendix.

---

firm size and industry. For example, small companies pay less wages *and* bonuses than large companies, have a lower bonus to wage ratio (by about 40 percent on average), and also display greater bonus variability. In finance, insurance, and chemicals, bonuses constituted about half of wages in 1974, while in construction or textile products they amounted to about one fourth.

ily from 1958 to 1974 and afterward have slowly declined. But there is no evidence in the regular time series of table 1 that a meaningful response is occurring to a volatile business cycle indicator like annual profits. Or is there?

In table 2 are listed real profits for Japanese companies.[29] The data are on a fiscal year basis, ending March 31. Coverage is roughly similar to table 1.

A first glance at tables 1 and 2 might appear to confirm the stereotype that bonus payments are independent of profitability. After all, real profits are fluctuating rather violently, while months of bonus paid, despite an undeniable trend, looks to be about as steady a sequence as one is likely to encounter in economic data.

But a second reading discloses some interesting possibilities. Look at deviations of real profits from their trend values. When profits deviate substantially from trend, there frequently seems to be a corresponding change of bonus payments in the same direction. A way of capturing this relationship is a standard lagged adjustment model of the form

$$B(t)/B(t-1) = [\pi(t)/\pi^*(t)]^a f(t).$$

In the above expression $B(t)$ represents bonus payments in calendar year t (expressed as months of base wages in the same year), $\pi(t)$ is real profits in fiscal year t (April 1 of year $t - 1$ to March 31 of year t, which builds in a natural lag consistent with most stories of bonus formation), $\pi^*(t)$ represents target or normal profits for fiscal year t, and $f(t)$ is a time term capturing trends in bonus growth that would occur even if profits were normal. The story being told by this equation is that bonus growth is possibly influenced by abnormally high or low profitability.

Taking logarithms of both sides, equation (1) might be estimated by the linear regression:

$$\log B(t) - \log B(t-1) = a \log \pi(t) + G(t), \quad (1)$$

where

$$G(t) = \log f(t) - a \log \pi^*(t)$$

29. Real profits are just nominal profits, from the data appendix, divided by an appropriate price index. Because profit data is on a fiscal year basis from March 31 to April 1, the deflator I have used is one-fourth of the current year's wholesale price index plus three-fourths of the previous year's wholesale price index. There are no dramatic changes in my story if I use other reasonable deflators. Note that because the bonus is subtracted out to obtain profits, if anything the regressions are biased against finding a positive relation.

is, for convenience, taken to be a polynomial in time. (In practice, additional polynomial terms of higher order are added until the coefficients start to become insignificant.)

Equation (1) is the prototype regression for this article. I hasten to add that I have tried a wide variety of alternative specifications, different data sets, etc.—all of which are consistent with the results I will report for equation (1) and tend to verify that the conclusions are quite robust. Regression results are summarized in table 3. They indicate that, in the aggregate, every 10 percent of profits below trend translates into a bonus payment about 1.4 percent lower than it otherwise would be. At 0.14, the elasticity of bonus response to profitability is not large, but at eight standard deviations from zero the coefficient is highly significant. Similar results are obtained when aggregate bonus changes are regressed on aggregate value added or revenues. In this case the elasticity of response is about 0.4. Overall, there is little question that the Japanese bonus contains a statistically significant profit- or revenue-sharing component.

We come now to an interesting and perhaps important question. Does the Japanese bonus system influence macroeconomic performance? Japan has had the lowest average unemployment rate among the major industrialized capitalist economies over the last quarter-century. This comparatively outstanding employment record survives corrections for discouraged workers, relatively flexible hours, definitional differences, and the like.[30] Does the existence of a revenue- or profit-sharing bonus

Table 3 THE BASIC REGRESSION: DEPENDENT VARIABLE: $\log B_t - \log B_{t-1}$

Independent variable	*Estimated coefficient*	*Standard error*	*T-statistic*
$\log \pi_t$	.14	1.76E-02	7.9
constant	3.2	.59	5.5
t	−.12	1.9E-02	−6.2
t^2	7.4E-04	1.3E-04	5.7

$R^2 = .82$
D-W = 2.39
Sample period: 1958–1983

30. It should be noted that Japan's number one status in having the lowest unemployment rate among major industrialized economies did not emerge until the 1970s. In the 1960s, some other countries like Germany had equally good employment records. There has been some discussion in the literature about the extent to which Japanese statistics may underestimate the unemployment rate by international standards. Taira (1983) and a few others have tried to argue this case. But it is not very convincing (see, e.g., Sorrentino (1984), Hamada and Kurosaka (1985)). The basic point is that when

component of pay help in any way to account for the comparatively low, stable unemployment rate in Japan?

This is a very difficult question to answer.[31] It is not even clear how to pose the appropriate hypothesis formally so that the existing data might, at least in principle, allow us to extricate an answer reasonably free from controversy. Yet the question is so tantalizing that one strains to get some sense of an answer, however tentative. Rather than trying to confront the issue head on with a formal model, I propose to limit myself here to some crude calculations based on a more pedestrian approach.

The first issue is to distinguish between the familiar pay flexibility that comes from responsiveness of pay parameters (such as base wages) to economic conditions, and the automatic pay flexibility that arises under revenue or profit sharing. From a wide variety of regression experiments run with the data presented here, I cannot find any formal statistical evidence that base wages alone respond to profitability. Some of the Phillips-curve-like pay-formation regressions in the literature have picked up, in some instances, a dependence upon profits.[32] But in many of these exercises the authors are attempting to explain the formation of total pay, defined as wages plus bonuses (and profits may be primarily affecting the bonus component), or else it is not clear what is included as "wages." The entire subject of empirical Phillips curve measurements for Japan is worthy of reexamination, with more careful attention focused on separating out base wages from bonuses in the pay-formation process. Meanwhile it seems safe to conclude, from results like those reported in table 3, that bonuses respond more than base wages to profitability, even if the issue of just how responsive to profits base wages are remains unsettled.[33]

It stands to reason that the existence of a bonus component of pay

---

reasonable adjustment measures are applied uniformly to all countries in an attempt to make international standards more uniform, then all countries' unemployment rates increase slightly, but without much altering their relative standing. Japan's unemployment record remains outstanding even after reasonable readjustments.

31. Issues of causality are immediately involved in a heavily interdependent social design like Japanese labor relations. Is the bonus system causing lifetime employment, or is lifetime employment causing the bonus system?

32. See, e.g., Grubb, Jackman, and Layard (1983), Koshiro (1983b), or the results reported in Hamada and Kurosaka (1985).

33. The lack of formal analysis convincingly identifying the degree of Japanese wage flexibility should not blind us to the probable fact that wages are, indeed, likely to be quite flexible, and this is almost undoubtedly playing some role in maintaining relatively high employment. The history of response to the first oil shock, recounted later in this article, while not easy to fit mechanically into a wage equation, bears ample testimony to this thesis. On this interpretation see Hamada and Kurosaka (1985).

with a more automatic procyclical link than base wages should help an economy to maintain a higher level of employment, other things being equal, than if wages alone were paid.[34] But how important a factor, quantitatively, is this likely to be in the Japanese case? Some very rough calculations can be used to indicate the orders of magnitude possibly involved.

The bonus itself is about one-fourth of an average worker's total pay. By running regressions in logarithms the elasticity of aggregate bonus response to changed aggregate profits was estimated at about 0.14. Converting this interpretation to a linear formula, the same elasticity of 0.14 is obtained if 14 percent of the bonus payment is strictly proportional to profits, while the other 86 percent is like a fixed constant. The following crude imputation can then be made. About 3.5 percent (14 percent × 25 percent) of a Japanese worker's total pay can be treated as genuine profit-sharing income, compared with the other 96.5 percent, which for economic purposes is better described as being like an imputed base wage.

A rough check on this calculation is possible. The elasticity of aggregate bonus payments with respect to aggregate value added, or revenue, was estimated to be about 0.4. Converting to an equivalent-elasticity linear revenue-sharing formula makes 40 percent of the bonus payment strictly proportional to revenues, while the other 60 percent is like a fixed constant. If aggregate imputed base wages are roughly three-fourths of aggregate revenues, that leaves one-fourth for gross profits. By this calculation, roughly 10 percent (¼ × 40 percent) of the bonus payment is strictly proportional to profits, while the other 90 percent is like a fixed constant. Following this line of reasoning, about 2.5 percent (10 percent × 25 percent) of a typical Japanese worker's total pay can be treated as genuinely proportional to profits, while the remaining 97.5 percent is like an imputed base wage.

Splitting the difference between these two calculations, we can make the following very rough statement. In any year about 97 percent of an average Japanese worker's total pay is like a fixed imputed base wage, while 3 percent automatically responds directly to profits. If pay contracts are annually renegotiated, the marginal cost to the employer of hiring an extra unit of labor in any given year is just the (imputed) base

34. This is akin to the proposition that a profits tax causes less unemployment than an equivalent tax on labor. A cynic might argue that the bonus is merely a label for the (more) flexible component of pay, there otherwise being not much essential difference between overall pay response to profitability between Japan and other countries. While this is a logically consistent position, I think the fact that the Japanese have a category called "bonus" that is significantly more dependent on profitability than "wages" is a relevant piece of information suggestive of a direct profit-sharing link.

wage, as opposed to total pay.[35] The relevant theory[36] then predicts that the Japanese economy should behave like an otherwise absolutely identical (but strictly hypothetical) wage economy whose wages are 3 percent lower than actual Japanese pay (base wages plus bonus) but whose maintained levels of aggregate demand (autonomous spending, the money supply, and world demand for Japanese exports) are the same. In other words, if someone who thought that Japan was a wage economy and has just now been informed that it is in fact (partially) a revenue- or profit-sharing economy wants to know what difference that makes, the answer is: the same difference *as if* money wages were perpetually devalued 3 percent below what you had previously believed them to be. While the exact ramifications of a 3 percent wage cut depend on a lot of assumptions about the magnitudes of various elasticities, my intuitive reaction is neither to dismiss this as being an altogether negligible effect nor to be impressed that it is likely to represent a major economic force.

This kind of counterfactual historical exercise should be understood in proper perspective. First, the calculations are extremely crude. Second, they are based on a particular interpretation of a particular theory. Third, the "thought experiment" is necessarily artificial. (If there were lower bonuses but higher base wages, it could be argued, wages might become more flexible, timing in the economy might be altered, or fiscal or monetary policy might be changed, perhaps thereby neutralizing some of the effects calculated here.)

These limitations notwithstanding, I think the exercise is useful for gaining some rough insight into the likely size of what might be called the "pure bonus effect." The numbers seem to point out a middle ground between two extremes. I would interpret the orders of magnitude involved as suggesting that the Japanese bonus system may have exerted a non-negligible macroeconomic influence by helping automatically to boost employment without inflationary pressure. But the significance of an "as if" 3 percent money wage cut is not nearly so great as to account for the entire unemployment story, nor to eliminate output fluctuations,[37] nor to repeal the laws of macroeconomics, nor to do away with

35. If the relevant contract adjustment period is more than a year because of pay parameter stickiness, the profit-sharing component grows in importance relative to the base wage component because of the distributed-lag difference equation buildup. In that case the effect of profit-sharing is somewhat more pronounced. It is hard to imagine how imputed base wages as seen by the employer could decline much more than about 5 percent below total pay.

36. See Weitzman (1985). The basic idea is that the effect on the firm of converting 3 percent of pay from base wages to profit shares is to lower wages by 3 percent while simultaneously being subjected to a compensating tax on profits.

37. Depending on how output is detrended from its high growth rates, Japanese output

the need for discretionary policy to maintain full employment, especially in the face of severe economic shocks.

That the bonus system alone cannot possibly be explaining the entire macroeconomic adjustment story is made abundantly clear by the rather non-neoclassical history of Japan's response to the energy crisis. After the first oil shock, in 1974, consumer prices increased by about 25 percent and wholesale prices by over 30 percent. At first the unions had no better premonition than anyone else that a permanent terms-of-trade deterioration was under way, and were concerned to recoup lost purchasing power as well as to obtain their customary pay increase. In the spring offensive of that year, base wages jumped by 33 percent. At this point, when the mechanics of a potentially vicious wage-price spiral started to become evident, the famous Japanese consensus took over. Government officials, labor experts, businessmen, and labor union leaders began preaching wage and price restraint. The 1975 *shunto* saw base wages increase by only 13 percent, and they have been held to the single-digit range since then. However much the Japanese bonus system may be helping as an automatic employment stabilizer (months of bonus pay declined sharply after 1974—see data appendix), it is but a drop in the ocean when a major macroeconomic shock impacts.

Conclusion

In this article I have argued that substantial progress in the struggle for full employment without inflation will have to come largely from basic changes in pay-setting arrangements rather than from better manipulation of financial aggregates. I think the analysis presented here suggests that widespread profit sharing, along the lines of what is practiced in Japan, represents a structural reform of the labor market likely to improve the unemployment-inflation tradeoff.

REFERENCES

Aoki, M. ed. 1984. *The economic analysis of the Japanese firm.* Amsterdam: North-Holland.

stability might be judged outstanding or mediocre. Actually, Japan has the steadiest growth rate among all OECD countries over the past quarter-century if it is measured by *relative* deviations from a standardized mean of one. In terms of *absolute* deviations (from a nonstandardized mean), Japanese growth shows much more cyclical variability. Note that, with a sprinkling of temporary price stickiness, the relevant model of a profit-sharing economy would predict relatively full employment but some building up of inventories, make-work, or labor hoarding during slack periods. Thus, the large Okun coefficient for Japan (see Hamada and Kurosaka (1984)) is not in itself a theoretical contradiction with share-economy-like interpretations.

Ben-Ner, A. 1984. On the stability of the cooperative type of organization. *Journal of Comparative Economics* 8 (3) (September): 247–60.
Bradley, K. and D. Gelb. 1983. *Worker capitalism: The new industrial relations*. London: Heinemann.
Colander, D. C., ed. 1986. *Incentive-based incomes policies*. Cambridge: Ballinger.
Flanagan, R., D. Soskice, and L. Ulman. 1983. *Unionism, economic stabilization, and incomes policy*. Washington, D.C.: Brookings Institution.
Freeman, R. B., and M. L. Weitzman. 1986. Bonuses and employment in Japan. NBER Working Paper 1878 (April).
Grubb, D., R. Jackman, and R. Layard. 1983. Wage rigidity and unemployment in OECD countries. *European Economic Review* 21 : 11–39.
Hamada, K., and Y. Kurosaka. 1984. The relationship between production and unemployment in Japan: Okun's law in comparative perspective. *European Economic Review* 25 (1) (June): 71–94.
———. 1985. Trends in unemployment, wages, and productivity: The case of Japan. Paper prepared for the Conference on the Rise in Unemployment (May).
Hashimoto, M., and J. Raisian. 1985. Employment tenure and earnings profiles in Japan and the United States. *American Economic Review* 75 (4) (September): 721–35.
Ishikawa, T., and K. Ueda. 1984. The bonus payment system and Japanese personal savings. In *The economic analysis of the Japanese firm*, ed. M. Aoki.
Jackman, R., and R. Layard. 1985. A wage-tax, worker subsidy policy for reducing the "natural" rate of unemployment. L.S.E. Centre for Labour Economics Working Paper 752.
Koike, K. 1983a. Internal labor markets: Workers in large firms. In *Contemporary Industrial Relations in Japan*, ed. T. Shirai.
———. 1983b. Workers in small firms and women in industry. In *Contemporary industrial relations in Japan*, ed. T. Shirai.
Koshiro, K. 1983a. The quality of working life in Japanese factories. In *Contemporary industrial relations in Japan*, ed. T. Shirai.
———. 1983b. Development of collective bargaining in postwar Japan. In *Contemporary Industrial Relations in Japan*, ed. T. Shirai.
Lerner, A., and D. C. Colander. 1980. *Map: A market anti-inflation plan*. New York: Harcourt, Brace, Jovanovich.
Meade, J. E. 1982. *Wage-fixing*. London: George Allen & Unwin.
———. 1986. *Alternative systems of business organization*. London: George Allen & Unwin.
Mitchell, D. J. B. 1985. The share economy and industrial relations. UCLA Institute of Industrial Relations Working Paper 99 (November).
Okuno, M. 1984. Corporate loyalty and bonus payments. In *The economic analysis of the Japanese firm*, ed. M. Aoki.
Pigou, A. C. 1933. *Theory of unemployment*. London: Macmillan.
Rockoff, H. 1984. *Drastic measures: A history of wage and price controls in the United States*. Cambridge: Cambridge University Press.
Shimada, H. 1983. Japanese industrial relations—A new general model? A survey of the English-language literature. In *Contemporary Industrial Relations in Japan*, ed. T. Shirai.
Shirai, T., ed. 1983a. *Contemporary industrial relations in Japan*. Madison: University of Wisconsin Press.

———. 1983b. A theory of enterprise unionism. In *Contemporary Industrial Relations in Japan*, ed. T. Shirai.
Sorrentino, C. 1984. Japan's low unemployment: An in-depth analysis. *Monthly Labor Review* 107 (3) (March): 18–27.
Taira, K. 1983. Japan's low unemployment: Economic miracle or statistical artifact? *Monthly Labor Review* 106 (7) (July): 3–10.
Tugan-Baronovsky, M. I. 1921. *Sosialnyia osnovy kooperatsii.* Berlin.
Wadhwani, S. 1985. The macroeconomic implications of profit sharing: Some empirical evidence. LSE Working Paper.
Weitzman, M. L. 1983. Some macroeconomic implications of alternative compensation systems. *Economic Journal.*
———. 1984. *The share economy.* Cambridge: Harvard University Press.
———. 1985. The simple macroeconomics of profit sharing. *American Economic Review* (December).
———. 1986. Steady state unemployment under profit sharing. *Economic Journal.* Forthcoming.

Table 4 THE BASIC DATA SERIES

Year	*Wage*	*Bonus*	*Profits*	*WPI*
1958	15.733	2.895	NA	41.7
1959	16.676	3.301	.821	42.1
1960	17.818	3.929	1.401	42.6
1961	19.487	4.712	1.585	43.0
1962	21.896	5.235	1.550	42.3
1963	24.231	6.030	1.832	43.1
1964	26.801	6.624	1.931	43.2
1965	29.485	7.294	1.916	43.5
1966	32.424	8.288	2.617	44.5
1967	35.778	9.465	3.570	45.4
1968	40.439	11.090	4.512	45.7
1969	46.078	13.586	6.128	46.7
1970	53.228	16.150	6.578	48.4
1971	61.165	19.353	5.619	48.0
1972	70.456	22.644	7.449	48.4
1973	83.674	29.701	12.799	56.1
1974	104.311	38.478	11.015	73.7
1975	122.766	40.463	5.956	75.9
1976	137.180	44.666	9.648	79.7
1977	150.921	48.197	10.163	81.2
1978	162.078	50.041	13.030	79.1
1979	170.416	53.341	17.722	84.9
1980	181.102	57.073	19.704	100.0
1981	190.832	60.015	17.174	101.4
1982	198.736	61.231	16.132	103.2
1983	205.610	61.702	16.924	100.9

DATA APPENDIX

Table 4 contains the basic data behind the regression results. Data are from the following sources.

Wages and bonuses are from the Japanese Ministry of Labor, *Yearbook of Labor Statistics.* Wages are average monthly contractual cash earnings and bonus is average monthly special earnings. Both are for regular employees, expressed in thousands of yen, covering establishments employing five or more people in all industries.

The profits data are from the *Japan Statistical Yearbook* and refer to net recurring profits valued in trillions of yen. Data are on a fiscal year basis (March 31 to April 1), covering all for-profit corporations except financial and insurance corporations.

The wholesale price index is from the *Japan Statistical Yearbook.* The price index used to deflate fiscal year profits is one-fourth of the current WPI plus three-fourths of the previous year's WPI.

Comment

ALAN S. BLINDER
Princeton University, The Brookings Institution, and NBER

Since my assignment is to discuss a document of persuasion, I feel compelled to begin with a truth-in-packaging warning: when Weitzman preaches to me, he is preaching to the converted. I still remember the excitement with which I read his first paper on the subject in 1982. Shortly thereafter, I invited him to start spreading the gospel to macroeconomists at an NBER meeting at Princeton. It was my *Boston Globe* and *Washington Post* columns in February 1985 that helped launch the media blitz for his book that led up to the *New York Times* branding the share economy "the best idea since Keynes."[1] And I was the organizer of the AEA session on the share economy in December 1985 in New York, and the only speaker who came there to praise Weitzman rather than to bury him.[2] So what you are about to read may smack of Aaron criticizing the Ten Commandments.

1. See my "Work-for-all Scenario," *Boston Globe,* February 5, 1985 and "Share the Wealth," *Washington Post,* February 10, 1985. The quotation from *The New York Times* is the title of a March 28, 1985 editorial.
2. The other speakers were R. E. Hall, W. D. Nordhaus, and L. H. Summers. The proceedings of the session will be published in a forthcoming issue of *Challenge.*

However, not even Moses was flawless. (As we know, he led the Jews to the only spot in the Middle East that is devoid of oil.) So let me start by criticizing something in Weitzman's explanation of the share economy—something that I and others have often found confusing. After reading his latest offering twice, I am convinced that Moses here is largely to blame for the confusion.

Despite Weitzman's many disclaimers, I have heard it said many times that he claims to have found a way to lower the natural rate of unemployment. My understanding is otherwise. A share economy does not have a lower natural rate of unemployment than a wage economy because the two have exactly the same long-run equilibrium. But a share economy should have a lower average rate of unemployment over any particular historical period because disequilibrium in a share economy does not manifest itself as unemployment.

I believe this is Weitzman's position, but the reader can perhaps be forgiven for drawing the wrong conclusion from statements like these (there are others):

"No matter how one interprets the 'other things being equal,' a profit-sharing system is more expansionary than a wage system."

"Conversion from a wage system to a profit-sharing system (with a smaller base wage) is equivalent to lower factor costs coupled with a pure profits tax."

"The relevant theory then predicts that the Japanese economy should behave like an otherwise identical wage economy whose wages are 3 percent lower than actual Japanese pay."

The difficulty comes in reconciling short-run and long-run behavior. Suppose labor is paid a base wage, w, plus a share, s, of the profits per worker after base wages are deducted:

$$W = w + s((R - wL)/L) = (1 - s)w + s(R/L). \quad (1)$$

Since the firm wants to maximize

$$R - WL = (1 - s)R - (1 - s)wL, \quad (2)$$

its short-run equilibrium condition, Weitzman seems to suggest, is:

$$R'(L) = w. \quad (3)$$

Since $w < W$, this implies higher employment than under a wage system that pays wage W.

In the long run, however, Weitzman stresses again and again that the pay parameters w and s will adjust so that the total compensation implied by equation (1) is precisely equal to W^*, the neoclassical real wage, when L is at its neoclassical equilibrium value, L^*. Now, we know that L^* and W^* are related by

$$R'(L^*) = W^*. \quad (4)$$

How can equations (3) and (4) hold at the same time when the full-employment version of equation (1),

$$W^* = w + s((R(L^*) - wL^*)/L^*), \quad (1')$$

implies that $w < W^*$ if $s > 0$? The answer is that they cannot. A firm in a share economy typically cannot acquire enough labor to satisfy equation (3); it is left in a position with excess demand for labor since $R'(L) - w > 0$.

Figure 1[3] may help explain what is going on, and suggest what Weitzman still needs to clear up. In this diagram, $AC = (1 - s)w + s(R/L)$ is the average cost of labor given by equation (1), $MC = (1 - s)w + s R'(L)$ is the corresponding marginal cost, and $R'(L)$ is the marginal revenue product. Point A, where $MC = R'$, satisfies equation (3), and seems to be—but probably is not—the short-run equilibrium of the firm. Point B is the neoclassical long-run equilibrium defined by equation (4). Long-run equilibrium is generated, Weitzman explains quite clearly, by the adjustment of the pay parameters s and w until the AC curve rises or falls to pass through point B.

The figure illustrates the two key features of a share system. First, the firm has an excess demand for labor at its long-run equilibrium in the sense that, given the pay parameters, it wants to hire more labor because $R' > MC$. Second, if long-run equilibrium is perturbed by a contractionary shock that lowers R', the firm will not reduce its employment. Both $\hat{L}$ and L^* will fall; but so long as the *new* $\hat{L}$ remains above the *old* L^*, employment will not be reduced.

The question that Weitzman needs to clear up is precisely what happens in the short run. Sometimes he seems to suggest that the firm actually atttains point A. But that is possible only if workers are willing to work at a total compensation below the competitive wage. The essence of Nordhaus's criticism is that workers ought not to behave this way.[4]

One possible answer is that workers in a share system are tied contrac-

3. From William D. Nordhaus, "Can the Share Economy Conquer Stagflation?", mimeo, Yale University, May 1985.
4. Ibid.

Figure 1

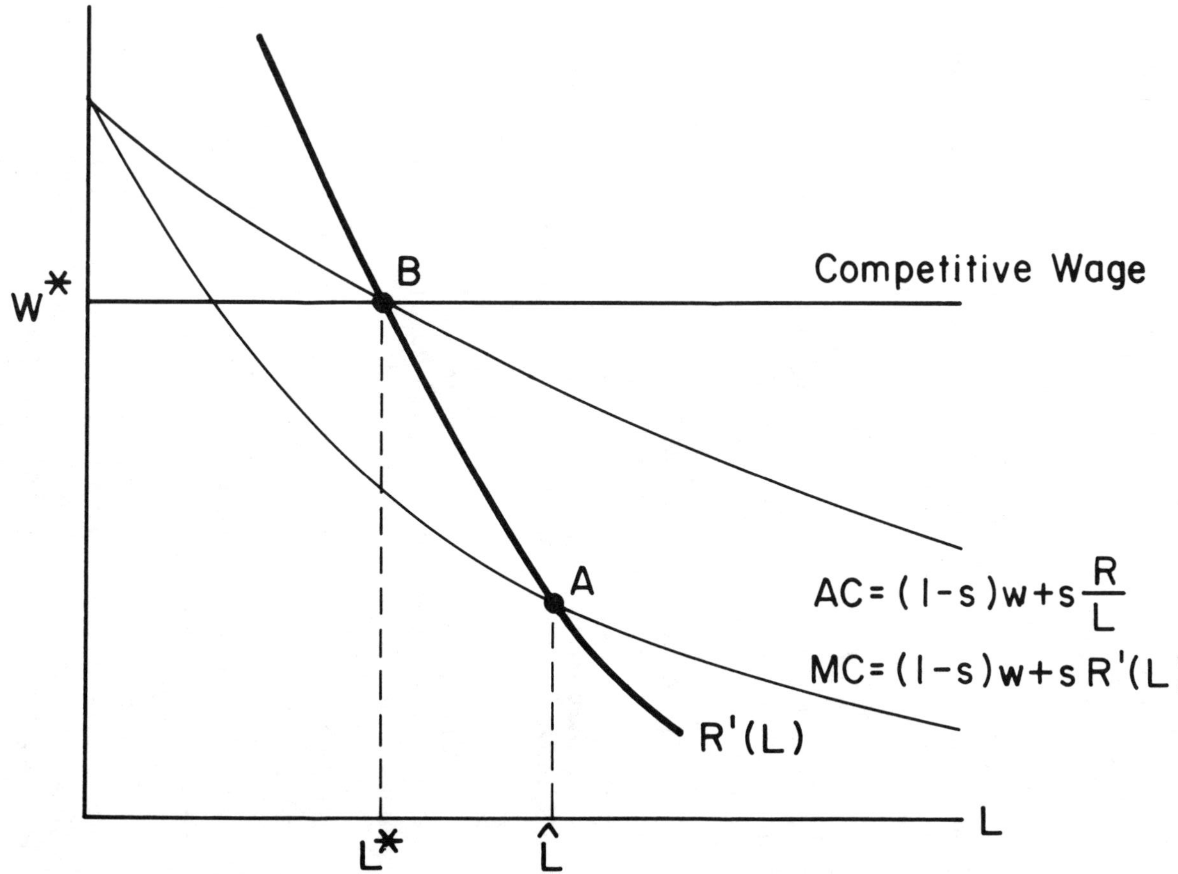

tually to a firm for a period of time. Their implicit or explicit contract includes an understanding that the profit-sharing component of compensation may sometimes decline enough to bring W below W^*. In return for accepting this risk of lower compensation, workers are guaranteed that they will not be laid off. If this share contract is preferred to a standard wage contract with wage W^*, the worker takes the job. If not, he refuses it in favor of the standard wage contract. Long-run equilibrium would then require that the contract terms, w and s, be set to make workers indifferent between the two contracts. To Weitzman, who assumes risk neutrality, this means that (1′) holds. But the equilibrium condition in the contract model I have just sketched is different. It says that *risk-averse* workers must get the same *expected utility* from a wage contract that offers W^* when employed and zero when unemployed as they do from a share contract that offers equation (1), which is random because L is random.

In one section of his article, Weitzman poses and answers four questions. My next point pertains to the second and third of these. The main reason, as I see it, why share systems are not generated spontaneously by the free market is that they are against the interests of senior workers. In forgoing a fixed wage contract for a share contract, a junior worker accepts some wage-rate risk in return for eliminating the presumably much greater risk of unemployment. That sounds like a potentially attractive bargain. But senior workers bear none of the unemployment risk, and so have no incentive to change from a wage system to a share system. In fact, they have an incentive to switch in the opposite direction should a share system be adopted.

That is why Weitzman proposes a tax subsidy plan to encourage the adoption of share contracts. Note that this plan is not a *temporary* measure designed to shove the economy from a bad equilibrium to a good one, but a *permanent* feature of the economic landscape that would change the free-market allocation. I would like to propose an alternative plan—or rather, half a plan because it creates a problem of its own—for achieving the same end without tax distortions.

Instead of Weitzman's prototypical profit-sharing plan, suppose firm i pays a nominal wage rate that is indexed to its own price:

$$w_i = b\, p_i.$$

If the firm has a downward-sloping demand curve, this compensation system has the critical property that drives Weitzman's analysis: $dw_i/dL_i < 0$, so that marginal labor cost is below average labor cost. So far this is no better than profit sharing. Instead of bearing the risk of profit fluctuations, workers now bear the risk of relative price fluctuations because the real wage paid by firm i is

$$w_i/p = bp_i/p,$$

where p is the aggregate price index. That is not an obvious improvement; indeed, the two risks are quite similar.

The difference is that relative price risk can be diversified away because an appropriately weighted average of all relative prices must always be 1. Let a mutual fund be established into which each firm pays bp_i per worker. If the fund gets the weights right, each worker, regardless of which firm he works for, can then draw out bp, where p is the weighted average. So the firms get the hiring incentive that Weitzman seeks, the workers get an indexed wage contract with little if any risk of unemployment, and the fund is perfectly self-insured.

There is, however, a difficulty with this scheme. I first worked it out about ten years ago as a way to create indexed wages for workers without requiring risk-averse firms to pay indexed wages.[5] At that time, I suggested that each firm should pay wages tied to an industrywide price index (say, a piece of the PPI), or to a weighted average of such indexes, to prevent it from manipulating its price index to reduce its wage rate, e.g., by running a sale or by outright cheating and misrepresentation.

Of course, reducing the wage rate by running a sale is exactly what we want firms to do under Weitzman's plan. So we really do need firm-specific, not industry-specific, price indexes to create the proper employment incentives. That leaves the cheating problem.

It is a genuine problem but not, I believe, an insuperable one. If both a firm and its union wish to avail themselves of Weitzman's plan, the mutual fund should be able to create firm-specific price indexes that are agreeable to both parties. The critical features are:

(a) that the weights be known and fixed for the duration of the contract (so the firm cannot manipulate the index by changing its product mix);

(b) that the specific prices that comprise the index be well defined and readily observable (so both firm and union can monitor the index).

I know there would be many little practical problems in creating such

5. Alan S. Blinder, "Indexing the Economy through Financial Intermediation," in K. Brunner and A. H. Meltzer, eds., *Stabilization of the Domestic and International Economy*, Carnegie-Rochester conference series, vol. 5, 1977, pp. 69–105.

price indexes. But the BLS copes with such problems every day. And the private sector would quickly learn to use the BLS as a training ground. Besides, like Weitzman, I am disinclined to let a few little Harberger triangles stand in the way of destruction of a big Okun gap.

The Japanese evidence is important to Weitzman's proselytizing campaign since Japan, among all the major countries on earth, seems closest to the share economy ideal. I have a few comments on Weitzman's empirical work.

First, the regression does not represent the profit-sharing formula. Multiply equation (1) by employment and take L to the other side to get

$$WL - wL = s(R - wL). \quad (5)$$

It is s that Weitzman should be trying to estimate, though his regression estimates an elasticity instead. The lefthand side of equation (5) is the bonus: total compensation minus base wages; call that B. The righthand side, however, is not profits but revenues minus base wages, that is, the sum of bonuses plus profits; call that Z. If profits are replaced by Z in Weitzman's regression, the estimated elasticity rises from 0.15 (in my replication of his regression) to 0.25.[6] The implied slope coefficient, s, however, is essentially the same as Weitzman's since Z is so much larger than profits.[7]

Second, the nine-month lag between profits and bonuses that Weitzman builds into the equation seems contrary to the spirit of the share economy. If marginal labor costs are to be below average labor costs, then labor must get a share of *this period's* revenue. If it gets, instead, a share of *last period's* revenue, then the bonus is actually a fixed cost relative to this period's employment decision.

Third, Weitzman's equation does not look to me like a standard lagged adjustment equation. I would have thought the partial adjustment model is something like

$$B(t) - B(t-1) = a(B^*(t) - B(t-1)),$$
$$B^*(t) = sZ(t);$$

6. All my regressions use a cubic time trend. The 0.25 estimate has a standard error of .035. When the right-hand variable is changed in this way, the fit of the equation hardly changes.

7. If e denotes the estimated elasticity, then the desired slope is $dB/dZ = eB/Z$, which is 0.11 evaluated at the means. In Weitzman's regression, which uses profits in place of Z, the corresponding slope is 0.12.

in levels or

$$b(t) - b(t-1) = a(b^*(t) - b(t-1)),$$
$$b^*(t) = \log(s) + z(t),$$

in logs (where lowercase symbols are logs of corresponding uppercase symbols). These lead to the following two empirical models:

$$B(t) = (1 - a)B(t-1) + asZ(t) \quad (6a)$$

$$b(t) = (1 - a)b(t-1) + az(t) + a\log(s) \quad (6b)$$

Equation (6b) comes close to what Weitzman estimates, except that he uses $b - \log(wL)$ rather than b and constrains the coefficient of the lagged dependent variable to be 1. Note, however, that the coefficient of z in (6b) is an estimate of the *adjustment speed*, not of the *share parameter.* Extracting an estimate of s from the log specification is more than a little tricky since it comes strictly from the constant—which can pick up anything. In any case, if we drop Weitzman's constraint that the coefficient of the lagged dependent variable is 1.0, the estimate of a rises from 0.15 to 0.87. By comparison, if we run equation (6b) without constraining the coefficients of $b(t-1)$ and $z(t)$ to sum to unity,[8] the estimated adjustment speed is 0.88. So substitution of z for profits seems unimportant. Remember, however, that these very rapid estimated adjustment speeds are layered on top of a built-in nine-month data lag.

To estimate s, which is the parameter of interest, directly, I ran three versions of equation (6a). The first was equation (6a) precisely; it yielded an implied estimate of s of 0.09. With no partial adjustment (a constrained to 1.0), the corresponding estimate was 0.07. Generalizing slightly beyond the Procrustean bed of geometric distributed lags by adding $Z(t-1)$ to the regression reduced the estimate of s to essentially zero, however. In this richer specification, $Z(t)$ and $Z(t-1)$ receive coefficients that are roughly equal in magnitude and opposite in sign, suggesting perhaps that changes in Z, not levels, influence bonus payments.

Suppose that s is between zero and 0.1. What do we do with this estimate? Based on mean values of all the variables in equation (1), s in this range implies that, on average, between 0 and 6.3 percent of Japanese labor compensation has taken the form of true bonus payments.[9]

8. Unconstrained, the two coefficients add up to 0.97. That seems more than close enough to me.

9. For comparison, putative bonus payments averaged 30.7 percent of base wages in the sample.

Weitzman's estimate is squarely in the middle of this range so, having wondered about the method he used to arrive at his estimate, I wind up having no quarrel with the number.

Finally, I would like to close with an intriguing question that Lawrence Summers posed at the 1985 meetings and that I would like to hear Weitzman answer. Capital gets 100 percent profit sharing in our economy now. Yet it is unemployed as frequently as labor. Why? I suspect the answer has to do with ex post fixed proportions; firms lay off labor when the price it must pay for the marginal unit of labor-cum-capital is too high. But Weitzman, not Blinder, should be answering these questions.

My thanks to Lori Grunin for research assistance, The Brookings Institution for hospitality, and Martin Weitzman for dreaming up the share economy.

Comment

RUSSELL COOPER
University of Iowa and NBER

Weitzman's article is part of his continuing research on the macroeconomic implications of alternative compensation schemes. The key issue addressed is whether or not privately determined labor arrangements are socially optimal. In particular, can the employment and compensation rules negotiated by workers and firms produce inefficiencies that are of macroeconomic significance? Weitzman answers with a loud and resounding "Yes" and advocates the adoption of a share system to correct these problems.

I think Weitzman deserves an enormous amount of credit for directing attention to this line of inquiry. This area of research is important from the viewpoint of both standard macroeconomic analysis and the theory of labor contracts. From the perspective of macroeconomic policy making, it forces one to think more deeply about the source of the inefficiency that aggregate policies are supposed to correct and augments the set of policy tools one may consider. As Weitzman suggests, it is important to think beyond the conventional set of aggregate stabilization policies. From the perspective of labor contracting theories, it forces one to consider the design of labor contracts between private agents from a general equilibrium perspective. Perhaps labor contracts can be optimal from the viewpoint of the contractants and yet, in the presence of externalities, produce inefficiencies at the macroeconomic level. Given all of the difficulties in finding a convincing model of employment inefficiencies at the worker-firm level, this alternative view should be welcomed.

The problem of evaluating alternative compensation schemes is amenable to standard welfare analysis. First, we need to carefully specify preferences, endowments, technology, and the like for the economy in question and then proceed to characterize the decentralized allocations. Second, holding the environment fixed, we solve for the set of constrained Pareto optimal allocations—where the constraints on the planner reflect those faced by private agents. Finally we ask whether the decentralized solution is in the set of Pareto optimal allocations. If not, interventions can be designed to correct these inefficiencies.

This methodology forms the heart of traditional economic analysis. The key to doing it properly is to carefully keep track of the economic environment, in particular, the informational and trading constraints that agents face. Both the welfare evaluation of the decentralized solution and the prescription of policy must be consistent with the environment of the decentralized solution.

Given this ideal methodology, how does Weitzman perform his analysis and arrive at his conclusion? To answer this, I turn to an evaluation of the type of model he has used.

The model is outlined in the "Profit Sharing" section of the article and corresponds closely to that used in Weitzman (1985). The emphasis is on the behavior of a monopolistically competitive firm and, in particular, how alternative compensation schemes influence the firm's decisions on output and employment. The basic intuition comes from observing that a monopolist facing a fixed wage might have a tendency to underproduce relative to the social optimum. A profit-sharing scheme lowers the marginal cost of labor and induces the monopolist to move along the demand curve so that output increases and price falls. Introducing a compensation scheme of this type is equivalent to subsidizing the monopolist and then taxing away profits.

This argument is then extended to a model with many monopolistically competitive firms in which each firm faces a downward-sloping demand curve parameterized by the level of autonomous spending, the real money supply and the average of prices charged by the other firms. This latter effect captures the strategic interaction between the firms.

Weitzman characterizes the output and pricing decisions of an individual firm and then looks at a symmetric Nash equilibrium in an economy composed of many such firms. The equilibrium is computed for a given share contract—i.e., a given base wage and a given share parameter. This is called a short-run equilibrium since the parameters of the compensation scheme are taken as independent of the values of the exogenous variables describing the state of the economy. The equilibrium is then compared to one in which workers are paid a constant wage (i.e., the share parameter is set at zero).

As I think is now well understood, an appropriately chosen share contract can generate incentives for the economy to operate at or near full employment even in the short run. If the base wage level is set sufficiently low, firms will always have an incentive to expand their production and are only inhibited from doing so by the presence of economywide employment constraints. Hence for small fluctuations in the exogenous components of demand, employment and output will not fluctuate. One interesting property of this short-run equilibrium is that the share parameter does not influence the level of prices or activity in the economy. Instead, it is the level of the base wage alone that determines the equilibrium. As an aside, it should be noted that if profit sharing is replaced with revenue sharing, the share parameter does enter into the equilibrium since the share contract is now similar to a tax on revenues rather than a profits tax.

This short-run equilibrium is contrasted with a long-run equilibrium in which the parameters of the share contract are determined in a competitive labor market. As argued in Weitzman (1983, 1985), the equilibrium of the model is independent of the way in which labor services are traded. That is, the total payment made to workers is independent of how offers to workers are quoted and the labor market clears at the same level of compensation and employment regardless of the system. Hence the wage and share system have identical long-run equilibria.

I must admit that I have never fully understood this equivalence in a world of uncertainty since the contracts do have radically different implications for the sharing of risk. As best as I can tell, Weitzman chooses to ignore uncertainty in describing the long-run equilibrium and then views short-run deviations as unanticipated shocks in a certain world.

Suppose, though, that we accept the long-run equivalence of these two compensation systems. Weitzman's main point is that the short-run response of the economy to unanticipated shocks is influenced by the choice of compensation scheme in an important way. Since the introduction of the share contract permits firms to pay low base wages, the economy remains close to full employment even in the presence of adverse demand shocks. Hence, Weitzman argues, it is socially desirable for agents to trade labor services in this fashion.

With this structure in mind, we can contrast the argument for the share economy with the methodology outlined earlier. I think this is important not because all theoretical exercises must be performed in a particular way but because of the fear that inconsistencies may be introduced by not following the procedure outlined earlier.

First, with regard to the statement of the decentralized solutions, the model Weitzman develops provides considerable insight into the product-market behavior of monopolistically competitive firms.[1] However, the development of labor-market behavior is relatively incomplete. This is an important issue since we know from other work in this area that labor-market behavior tends to drive product-market behavior.

Weitzman takes as a benchmark a wage system in which the wage is predetermined and firms are given the latitude of selecting employment levels. This generates some undesirable behavior of the economy (such as inefficiently low levels of output and employment) in the short run. However, the real source of this inefficiency is never made clear. The model contains three deviations from the Arrow-Debreu model. First, there is the absence of perfect competition in product markets. Second, there is the inflexibility of wages. Third, there is a nonconvexity in the production function. Which of these changes is the source of the problem here? Simply put, what is wrong with this economy?

The article focuses mainly on the stickiness of wages as the source of the problem. The structure of technology and preferences coupled with the monopolistically competitive product markets then creates price inflexibilities. Hence the model without share contracts operates as a traditional Keynesian fix-price model with its well-known inefficiencies, multipliers, etc. One is led to wonder whether share contracts simply reintroduce the wage flexibility arbitrarily assumed away at the start of the analysis.

To answer this point directly requires the formulation of a model predicting these wage inflexibilities or strong empirical evidence of their existence. Weitzman does not supply either of these pieces of the argument. Instead he appeals to a general consensus that the wage system is a good representation of the common form of labor exchange. I think this is unfortunate for a couple of reasons.

First, I am not certain there really is a general consensus that the wage system typifies labor arrangements. Models of this type have the strong empirical prediction that real wages should be countercyclical. My understanding of the empirical evidence is that this prediction is not obviously consistent with the data.[2] Furthermore, as I will discuss in a moment, there is a lack of theoretical support for the wage system as an optimal labor contract. Simply put, the wage system is a suboptimal private contract. Hence, why should we be interested in the social inefficiencies that such a compensation system produces?

Second, the theoretical argument for the wage system is needed to be

1. Akerlof and Yellen (1985), Cooper (1985), Hart (1982), Heller (1984), Roberts (1984) and Weitzman (1982) all stress the macroeconomic consequences of strategic product market behavior.
2. See, for example, Geary and Kennan (1982) and Bils (1985).

sure that the environment in which agents interact is modeled properly in the welfare analysis. Let me illustrate this point in two ways. Suppose that the argument for the wage rigidity stems from an insurance story along the line told by Azariadis (1975), Baily (1974) and others. If so, then we need to keep in mind the fact that risk sharing is important in calculating the costs and benefits of the share system. The share system is not privately optimal because it forces workers to bear too much risk. To show that the share system may be socially desirable requires proof that in equilibrium workers can be compensated for the extra risk they bear.

The insurance argument alone does not deliver the full features of Weitzman's wage system. As is well known, the contracting model does not predict that employment will lie along the firm's demand curve. Instead, terms of compensation and employment should be negotiated separately. Hence, the problem that Weitzman sees in the wage system stems jointly from the rigidity of wages and the fact that firms choose employment levels.

There is a class of contracting models in which the firm is given the latitude to select employment levels. This arises in a setting in which the firm is better informed than workers about current demand or technological conditions. Unfortunately, this class of models will not generally predict fixed wages. More important, though, the presence of this asymmetric information may itself lead to problems with implementation of a share system in which compensation depends on profits.

My point is that it is important to specify the environment (such as attitudes toward risk and the information structure) which generates a problem as we attempt to find solutions to that problem. Otherwise, we face the danger that we may miss some costs of the solution or, worse, it may not be feasible.

The article also does not provide a full analysis of the planner's problem. That is, the welfare criterion is never made explicit and there is no consideration of alternatives to share contracts within a common environment. I found the discussion of alternatives such as TIPs, worker-managed firms, and so on, helpful but not convincing.

So my overall view of this line of research is that its main theme is very important and very interesting. Nonetheless, the models used thus far appear to be less than convincing relative to the enticing stories that accompany Weitzman's work. I think that a more specific statement about the source of the inefficiencies in the private labor markets needs to be provided as well as a more precise statement of the costs and benefits of introducing the share system.

Since it is easy to be critical and harder to be constructive, I will offer some specific suggestions. The most pressing issue is to carefully incorporate labor-market behavior into the monopolistically competitive economy outlined in the article. We know from the work of Hart (1982) that the structure of labor markets can both create and cure many ills in this class of models. The point is to determine whether optimal labor arrangements (as opposed to the wage system) can lead to interesting social inefficiencies.

This model of the labor market would then provide the basis for the welfare analysis to follow. That is, the union's objective function would be carefully specified so that trade-offs between types of workers (such as issues of seniority) could be addressed. This analysis of the labor market would also be a vehicle for making the source of the externalities very explicit.

In light of recent attempts to understand macroeconomic inefficiencies from the perspective of labor contracting theories, developing such a model will not be an easy task. Further, we should remember that the type of model that Weitzman outlines has a very different form of product-market behavior than that found in the partial equilibrium contracting models. This interaction between labor contracts and strategic product-market behavior is an important research area. Depending on the level of union representation, I believe it is possible to develop a model in which privately optimal labor arrangements are socially inefficient. Weitzman's arguments may then apply to this setting.

I also think that some interesting questions about the level of union representation and negotiation would emerge from such an exercise as a by-product. That is, one could investigate the implications of negotiations at the firm level, the industry level, or the aggregate level for the types of externalities that Weitzman alludes to in his discussion.

Besides these general thoughts on the model Weitzman uses in this and related research, I want to offer other comments on some specific points raised in the text. First, in the question and answer section, Weitzman addresses the allocation of risks by asking whether or not the share system provides socially inefficient risk sharing. In a related comment, he argues that the fixed-wage system provides good insurance only for senior workers who face no employment risk. Leaving the important question of severance pay aside, it is still the case that risk-averse junior workers facing employment risk will prefer that their wages be stabilized. As I stated earlier, the problem with this wage system is not its incomplete insurance over employment risk alone but that firms have discretion over terms of employment as well. This implies that wage-setting practices have an influence over both insurance and employment incentives.

One way to view Weitzman's argument is that private contracts lean too far in the direction of insurance and neglect the external effects of employment practices. Share contracts provide better social incentives at the cost of less insurance. So what is the best balance between insurance and incentives? This depends on the attitudes toward risk of the agents in the economy and the nature of this externality in the system.

Also, we see that individual worker-firm pairs will have an incentive to deviate from the share system to avoid the privately inefficient allocation of risks imposed by the government. Hence, the tax and subsidy system used to induce the adoption of share contracts needs to reflect these private gains from deviating from the government's plan. I am not convinced that all of these costs have been appropriately included in the arguments for adopting a share system.

My second comment stems from work on moral hazard problems within the firm—a topic addressed in Lawrence Katz's article. In the presence of internal incentive problems, firms have a private incentive to adopt compensation schemes that will induce their workers not to shirk. These include elaborate systems of bonuses, tournaments, and the like. In some settings, these schemes may produce something that looks quite close to a profit-sharing system. In fact, Weitzman observes that a significant number of firms in the United States have adopted such schemes.

If so, is this evidence that we are moving closer to a share system? I think not. The adoption of these schemes by private agents reflects their own private costs and benefits from trading off insurance for incentives. The crux of Weitzman's view, at least as I understand it, is that there is an externality that is not internalized by individual agents establishing terms of employment.[3] Hence the movement toward share contracts by these agents is presumably still insufficient.

Third, I want to comment on the point I raised earlier about whether a share system is simply a way to reintroduce wage flexibility into a model in which wages were arbitrarily fixed at the start. Weitzman argues that the share system is not a disguised form of wage flexibility since workers' pay exceeds the marginal revenue product of workers' labor. Furthermore, he points out that the share system also has some built-in rigidities in that the base wage and the share coefficient are not state dependent. With profit sharing, the marginal decisions are based on the level of the base wage and are independent of the share parameter. The point is then to create incentives by selecting the correct base wage and then using the share parameter to redistribute income. As far as I can see, the equilibrium is equivalent to one with flexible wages coupled with nondistortionary redistributions of firm profits.

3. Cooper (1985) attempts to model this externality explicitly.

Finally, I would like to say a few words on the case of Japan. There are really two important points in this section. First, is Japan an example of a share economy at work? Second, has the Japanese compensation system with its bonus payments contributed to Japan's macroeconomic performance?

To determine whether or not Japan operates as a share system, Weitzman uses aggregate data on wages, bonuses and profits. Regression results of bonuses relative to wages on deviations of profits from trend are reported. Weitzman finds a significant positive correlation between these variables.

The specification of this equation is somewhat difficult to reconcile with the theoretical model outlined in the article. In particular, the specification includes costs of adjustment and the regression of changes in the bonus/wage ratio on the level of profits.

Even if we determine that bonuses do respond to profits, is this evidence of a share system at work? One can imagine a bargaining setting in which total compensation reflects anticipated profits for the near future. This payment may be reflected in increased bonuses over the next year which, on average, will be correlated with the higher profits of firms. However, this correlation is not really evidence that bonuses respond to unforeseen economic circumstances as is required of a share system. It would be interesting to see whether or not bonuses respond to unanticipated profits.

Weitzman also argues that base wages are independent of economic conditions. I presume that these results would imply that compensation is also sensitive to profits. Is this peculiar to Japan? It would be interesting to investigate whether the U.S. data exhibit similar correlations.[4] This would help us know whether these correlations are a distinguishing feature of a share system.

More important, though, is the question of whether the bonus system has significant macroeconomic implications. Comparing Japan to other OECD countries may indicate that Japan is different but does not tell us why. Are the time series for Japan comparable to those that would be generated by a share economy? It might be useful to carefully write down a share economy and perform some of these comparative dynamic exercises.

One way to investigate the influence of bonuses on employment and

4. I have attempted this exercise by looking at U.S. data on real profits and real average weekly earnings in the manufacturing sector for the years 1963–1984. Using first differences of these variables, there appears to be a strong correlation between changes in profits and changes in wages. Nonetheless, one would not argue that the United States is a share system.

output would be to look at disaggregated data. If there are significant differences across industries in their use of bonuses, then perhaps we can gain some insights into the importance of the bonus system in regard to fluctuations.

I find this paper, like others Weitzman has written on this topic, very stimulating. As I have tried to argue, I am not convinced that we have yet answered the basic question of whether or not privately optimal labor contracts are responsible for our macroeconomic problems. Without an answer to this question, I don't see that we are in a position to advocate the adoption of alternative compensation schemes on a national basis. Nonetheless, these issues are yet to be fully addressed and I hope others will be persuaded to join in the search for answers.

REFERENCES

Akerlof, G., and J. Yellen. 1985. A near-rational model of the business cycle, with wage and price inertia. *Quarterly Journal of Economics* 100:823–38.

Azariadis, C. 1975. Implicit contracts and underemployment equilibria. *Journal of Political Economy* 83:1183–1202.

Baily, M. 1974. Wages and employment under uncertain demand. *Review of Economic Studies* 41:37–50.

Bils, M. 1985. Real wages over the business cycle: Evidence from panel data. *Journal of Political Economy* 93:666–89.

Cooper, R. 1985. Sharing some thoughts on Weitzman's *The Share Economy.* NBER Working Paper 1734.

Geary, P., and J. Kennan. 1982. The employment-real wage relationship: An international study. *Journal of Political Economy* 90:854–71.

Hart, O. 1982. A model of imperfect competition with Keynesian features. *Quarterly Journal of Economics* 97:109–38.

Heller, W. 1984. Coordination failure with complete markets in a simple model of effective demand. Department of Economics, University of California.

Roberts, J. 1984. General equilibrium analysis of imperfect competition: An illustrative example. Stanford University.

Weitzman, M. 1982. Increasing returns and the foundations of unemployment theory. *Economic Journal* 92:787–804.

———. 1983. Some macroeconomic implications of alternative compensation systems. *Economic Journal* 93:763–83.

———. 1984. *The share economy.* Cambridge: Harvard University Press.

———. 1985. The simple macroeconomics of profit sharing. *American Economic Review* 75:937–53.

Discussion

In replying to Russell Cooper, Weitzman agreed that it would indeed be desirable to build a general model from which both the wage system and profit sharing can be derived, but that the task is very difficult, and that consideration of the profit-sharing system cannot wait for that. The effects of profit sharing on the natural rate of unemployment would depend on the underlying causes of normal unemployment, though he speculated that profit sharing will never produce a higher natural rate than the wage system. Profit sharing will lower the natural unemployment rate in models where sector-specific shocks, or insider-outsider distinctions, or inertia, drive the unemployment rate.

He did not think the analogy of labor unemployment under profit sharing with unemployment of capital at present, when capital receives 100 percent of profits, was relevant. Capital is often unemployed despite receiving 100 percent of profits because there are fixed coefficients in the short run. This explanation did not satisfy Lawrence Summers, who did not see why labor under pure profit sharing would be in any different position than capital at present. He suspected that who gets the residual claim in the economy is very important.

Robert Hall questioned Weitzman's theme, that the optimal system fully stabilizes employment in the face of shocks. Stabilization can go too far. Sometimes shocks (especially idiosyncratic ones) call for changes in employment.

The equivalence of the Japanese bonus system with profit sharing was doubted by Takatoshi Ito. The bonus is usually negotiated, expected, and stable, and does not show much cyclical fluctuation. He also commented that the use of overtime work rather than the bonus system was responsible for the stability of Japanese employment.

Arnold Kling pointed out a cost of the share economy, which is ignored in Weitzman's article. Since pay now depends on the profitability of the firm, workers will have to obtain far more information about the firm for which they choose to work, both in looking for a job and after they take one, than they do at present. This is a cost for the worker that is absent in the wage system.

Given that the industrial wage structure has existed for two centuries, Robert Gordon wondered why profit sharing had not been introduced earlier if it was thought to be such a good idea. He saw it as having several disadvantages. First, its introduction can be contrary to the senior worker's vested interest, which is the reason the two-tiered system rather than profit sharing has become popular. Second, in the share economy, a worker's pay is tied to his own firm. This may lower the welfare of the worker compared with, for example, wage indexation to nominal GNP.

Weitzman concluded the discussion by answering Summers. He commented that it is not clear that capital in the present system has the same characteristics as labor would under profit sharing. At present labor can in some sense be thought of as the residual claimant, with some workers taking their share in the form of unemployment. Other comments, he thought, had failed to distinguish between private and social optimality. He stressed that the issue is social rather than private optimality. It is true that there are strong private incentives for the continuation of the wage system, but that does not necessarily make it socially optimal—and this is the issue he is addressing.

Martin S. Feldstein
HARVARD UNIVERSITY AND NBER

The Budget Deficit and the Dollar

The dramatic surge in the dollar's value relative to major European currencies was probably the most important economic event of the period between 1980 and 1984. The dollar's value rose from 1.8 German marks in mid-1980 to a peak of more than 3.3 marks in February 1985. More generally, the multilateral trade-weighted real value of the dollar rose by 70 percent between 1980 and the first quarter of 1985.

The rise of the dollar produced an unprecedented merchandise trade deficit that increased to 3 percent of GNP by 1985, hurting a wide range of American industries and creating a political receptivity to protectionism that still threatens to reverse the progress of the past half-century in liberalizing world trade. The trade deficit and the associated current account deficit transformed the United States from a net capital exporter in 1980 to a country that by 1984 had a large enough capital inflow to finance 55 percent of the nation's total net fixed investment. In addition, the sharp rise in the dollar not only increased Americans' real incomes but also contributed significantly to the decline of inflation.[1]

In Europe and Japan, exports rose sharply and the current account moved into substantial surplus; for the European Economic Community as a whole, the trade balance with the rest of the world improved by more than $50 billion between 1980 and 1984. But at the same time, the rise in the dollar induced foreign central banks to increase their interest rates in order to prevent their currencies from falling even further.[2] On balance, despite the increase in exports, the induced rise in interest rates may have depressed aggregate demand in Europe by enough to make the dollar's rise a net contributor to the stubbornly high level of unemployment.

1. On the impact of the dollar's rise on U.S. inflation, see Sachs (1985) and Sinai (1985).
2. This idea of an induced monetary policy response is discussed in Feldstein (1985, 1986a). This provides an alternative to the Blanchard and Summers (1985) explanation of the high level of world interest rates.

The present study focuses on the real exchange rate between the dollar and the German mark from the beginning of the floating exchange rate regime in 1973 through 1984. The mark is not only very important in its own right but is representative of the exchange rate between the dollar and the other European countries, since the mark is the dominant currency in the European Monetary System.

1. *Alternative Explanations of the Dollar's Rise*

The basic cause of the dollar's sharp increase still remains a very contentious subject. I have argued since 1982 that the dollar's rise could be traced primarily to the increase in current and expected structural deficits in the federal budget and to the shift to an anti-inflationary monetary policy.[3] This view was also elaborated in the *Economic Reports of the President for 1983 and 1984*.

Increases in the federal budget deficit raise real long-term interest rates and these higher rates attract funds to the United States. The dollar's rise is necessary to create the trade deficit and associated current account deficit that permits the desired net inflow of foreign capital. Moreover, to achieve portfolio equilibrium, the dollar must rise by enough so that its expected future fall just offsets the nominal yield differential between dollar securities and foreign assets. This is discussed in Branson (1985) and Frenkel and Razin (1984). The budget deficit may also raise the dollar more directly by changing the relative demand for U.S. and foreign goods (Dornbusch 1983, Obstfeld 1985).

The effect on the dollar of the rising level of structural budget deficits was reinforced by the change in monetary policy that began in October 1979. The contractionary shift of Federal Reserve policy caused a short-term spike in real interest rates that temporarily increased the attractiveness of dollar securities. More fundamentally, the new Federal Reserve policy also caused a more sustained increase in the confidence of investors worldwide that the value of the dollar would not soon be eroded by a return to rising inflation in the United States. This reduction in the risk of dollar investments reinforced the attractiveness caused by the deficit-induced rise in the expected real interest rate.

Other economists and policy officials have offered quite different explanations of the rise in the dollar. The *Economic Report of the President for 1985* concludes that the most important reason for the rise in the dollar between 1980 and 1982 was the rise in the after-tax return on new busi-

3. See, e.g., Feldstein (1983).

ness investment caused by the combination of the Economic Recovery and Tax Act of 1981 and the reduced rate of inflation. The tight money policy is also seen as a cause of the dollar's rise in this period. But the authors conclude that although expanding budget deficits in this period "may also have raised the level of U.S. real interest rates and helped to strengthen the dollar . . . the extent of upward pressure on real interest rates and on the dollar through this channel is uncertain, and numerous studies have failed to uncover significant effects" (p. 105).

The report's authors also note that after 1982 the differential between U.S. three-month real interest rates and a trade-weighted average of three-month real interest rates in six other industrial countries (calculated using OECD inflation forecasts) narrows to zero and is occasionally negative. They conclude from this that "other factors have continued to push up the demand for dollar assets" and suggest that the dollar's strength since 1982 has been due to "the combination of increased after-tax profitability of U.S. corporations, demonstrated strength of the U.S. recovery, reversal of international lending outflow from U.S. banks, and generally more favorable longer run prospects for the U.S. economy. . . ." (pp. 105–6).

Another commonly expressed opinion is that the rise in the dollar since the summer of 1980 reflected growing confidence in the United States as a "safe haven" for investments by foreigners who believed that the election of Ronald Reagan would make their assets safer in the United States than elsewhere in the world. There is also the view, identified most strongly with Ronald McKinnon (e.g., 1984), that the strong dollar does not reflect any "real" phenomena (budget deficits, increased profitability, alternative tax rules) but is solely an indication that monetary policy in the United States is too tight.

At a more fundamental level, any role for the budget deficit in explaining the rise of the dollar must be rejected by those economists who believe that deficits do not raise real interest rates because they induce an equal offsetting rise in private saving (e.g., Barro 1974). Evans (1986) extended the procedure of Plosser (1982) to study the relation between unexpected changes in budget deficits and the dollar and concluded the dollar exchange rate is not affected by changes in the budget deficit. I return below to the deficiencies of this type of analysis.

Although there may be some element of truth in each of the alternative explanations of the dollar's rise, my own judgment is that they are not as important as the increase in expected structural budget deficits and the shift to a less inflationary monetary strategy. This is supported by the econometric evidence presented in sections 4 through 6. The estimated effects of the expected deficits and of the rate of growth of the money supply are economically important and statistically significant. In contrast, the increase in profitability induced by the tax changes in the first half of the 1980s did not have a significant effect on the exchange rate in the equations presented below. The strong statistical evidence of a link between the expected structural budget deficits and the value of the dollar is direct evidence against the Barro hypothesis that budget deficits have no real impact. The implied impact of the expected budget deficits also contradicts the McKinnon hypothesis that the rise of the dollar was due only to a tight monetary policy.

Before I turn to that econometric evidence, I think it will be useful to consider some further reasons for rejecting the arguments of those who claim that neither increased real interest rates nor budget deficits was responsible for the dollar's rise.

The evidence presented in the *1985 Economic Report of the President* (and elsewhere) that there is no longer a difference between the three-month real interest rate in the United States and in other industrial countries is essentially irrelevant since the theory implies that the equilibrium relation between the exchange rate and the difference in *long-term* real rates is much larger than the relation with the difference in *short-term* real rates. It is easy to see why this is true. Consider the situation in which the U.S. three-month real rate is four percentage points above the three-month rate on foreign securities but there is no interest differential for intervals beginning after three months. Thus the six-month interest rates differ by only two percentage points, the one-year rates differ by one percentage point, and so on. The value of the dollar can be one percentage point above its equilibrium value since the interest rate differential is enough to compensate for a one percent decline in the dollar, regardless of whether this happens in three months, six months, a year, or longer. But with the differential in real rates concentrated only in the three-month maturity, any greater overvaluation of the dollar would imply an expected future decline not compensated by the difference in interest rates.

In contrast, consider the situation in which the real interest rate on the U.S. 10-year bond is 4 percentage points above the real yield on foreign 10-year bonds with no interest differential for intervals after ten years. Then the real value of the dollar can fall by 4 percent a year for ten years and still leave an investor indifferent between having purchased dollar bonds and foreign bonds. This implies that a 4 percent real interest differential on 10-year bonds can support a 48 percent initial overvaluation of the dollar.

It is noteworthy therefore that, although the three-month real yield differential reached zero by the end of 1982 and hovered around that level thereafter, the long-term real interest differential at the end of 1983 was in the range of two to four percentage points, depending on the method of forecasting future inflation.[4] The observed real interest differential was therefore quite consistent with the observed rise in the dollar's real value. I will return later to the more formal evidence on the link between the dollar and the real interest differential.

While the change in U.S. monetary policy after October 1979 may have reduced the inflation risk in U.S. fixed-income securities, the notion that the dollar rose in the 1980s because the United States capital market is a *political* safe haven for foreign funds seems doubtful. Although the United States does offer a politically safe environment, it is hard to see a rise in U.S. political stability vis-à-vis Switzerland or other major countries between the late 1970s and the early 1980s. Moreover, if there had been a shift in the worldwide portfolio demand in favor of U.S. assets, U.S. interest rates would have declined. The sharp rise in real rates suggests that any "safe haven" increase in the demand for dollar assets was overwhelmed by the increased supply of those assets. It is also doubtful that the declines of 25 percent or more between February 1985 and February 1986 in the value of the dollar relative to the German mark, the Swiss franc, and the Japanese yen reflects any deterioration in the relative political stability and security of the United States.

Those who point to the reduced lending of U.S. banks to the Latin American debtor nations after fall, 1982, as an example of the safe haven effect misconstrue the portfolio effect of that lending. That change in lending did not represent a change in U.S. demand for assets denominated in foreign currencies since those loans were all denominated in dollars. Moreover, the loan proceeds were used by the borrowers either to purchase imports or, through capital flight, to make deposits or purchase assets in the United States.

There are two problems with the argument that the dollar rose because the strength of the recovery attracted investments seeking to share in U.S. profitability. First, the real value of the dollar rose through the recessions of 1980 and 1981 and was 36 percent higher at the trough of the second recession (in the final quarter of 1982) than it had been in 1980. Real interest rates and projected budget deficits were rising during this period even though the economy was sagging. Second, most of the capital inflow to the United States was in the form of bank deposits or pur-

4. This is shown on p. 52 of *The Economic Report of the President for 1984*.

chases of short-term fixed income securities and only about one-third was in the form of portfolio equity purchases or direct investment. In 1982 and 1983 combined, there was a $192 billion increase in foreign private assets in the United States but direct investments were only $27 billion and stock purchases were only $33 billion.

In short, there are good reasons to reject the arguments of those who say that the dollar's rise cannot be due to higher real rates because the interest differential disappeared long ago and who attribute the dollar's rise to the attractiveness of U.S. financial markets as a safe haven for foreign investors and as a place in which equity investments can participate in the profitable recovery. Although the improved tax climate for investment should in principle have raised the value of the dollar, the evidence presented below indicates that this effect is too weak to discern statistically.

The study by Evans (1986) is unpersuasive for quite a different reason. Evans's basic procedure is to relate quarterly movements in the exchange rate to the quarterly "surprises" in the deficit, in government spending, in monetary policy, and the like. These "surprises" are calculated as the residuals from vector autoregression predictions of the deficit and other variables. The fundamental problem with this procedure is that it assumes that the deficit variable that might influence the exchange rate is the concurrent deficit, when theory implies that it is the sequence of expected future deficits that influences the long-term real interest rate and the exchange rate.[5] There is no reason for the surprises in actual current quarterly deficits to be related to the expected future deficits.[6]

Finally, the evidence presented below supports the importance of the increased budget deficits as the primary cause of the rise in the dollar and thereby refutes both the Ricardian-equivalence proposition that budget deficits have no real effects and the position of McKinnon and others who attribute all of the dollar's rise to tight monetary policy in the United States.

2. *Studies of the Dollar and the Interest Differential*

Except for the study by Evans (1986), the empirical research on the determination of exchange rates has focused on the relation between the

5. The importance of expected future deficits was emphasized in Feldstein (1983) and analyzed more formally in Frenkel and Razin (1984), Blanchard (1985), and Branson (1985).
6. The same criticism also applies to Plosser's (1982) claim that budget deficits do not influence the level of interest rates.

exchange rate and the real interest differential.[7] Although the equilibrium relation between the exchange rate and the interest differential is a fundamental characteristic of portfolio balance in foreign exchange markets (Dornbusch 1976, Frankel 1979), there are four serious problems in estimating an equation relating the exchange rate to the real interest differential in order to understand the causes of variations in the real exchange rate and, more specifically, to assess the role of the budget deficit as a cause of changes in the exchange rate.

First, the critical interest rate variable is very difficult to measure with any accuracy. The difference in real long-term interest rates is equal to the difference in nominal long-term interest rates minus the difference in expected long-term inflation rates. It is clearly very difficult to measure with any accuracy the difference between the long-term expected inflation rates in the two countries. These expectations depend not only on the history of inflation in the two countries but also on the credibility of government and central bank policies. The critical real interest differential is therefore subject to substantial measurement error that will tend to bias the coefficient toward zero and to reduce the statistical significance of its effect.[8]

Second, changes in the level of the real interest rate in each country

7. Although measures of the money stock, inflation, and real activity have sometimes been included among the regressors, neither the budget deficit nor the effect of changes in tax rules has been included. See Frankel (1979) for a relatively early study of this form and Hooper (1985), Meese and Rogoff (1985) and Sachs (1985) for more recent examples; Obstfeld (1985) provides a very useful survey of recent research on this subject. Hooper allows budget deficits and tax rules to affect the exchange rate as part of a large econometric model but the estimated effect is only through their impact on the real interest differential. Moreover, since Hooper uses only the current budget deficit (rather than expected future deficits) it is not surprising that he estimates only a relatively small effect of the deficit on the exchange rate.

After this paper was written, I received a copy of Hutchinson and Throop (1985); the authors provide a very careful analysis that shows that the trade-weighted real value of the dollar can be explained by an equation that combines the real interest differential between the United States and the seven major industrial countries and a corresponding one-year expected structural budget deficit differential. Both the interest rate and the deficit differential are significant in this formulation. They present no evidence about monetary policy or tax policy.

8. A review of the papers that use a "real interest differential" to explain exchange rate variations shows the potential seriousness of this problem. For example, Frankel's 1979 paper used the short-term German-U.S. interest differential instead of the long-term differential and measured the difference in expected long-term inflation rates (a separate variable in his formulation) by the difference in long-term bond rates. Meese and Rogoff (1985), in an otherwise very sophisticated paper, also generally use the three-month interest rates; when they do use long-term bonds, they take inflation during the most recent twelve months as a proxy for long-term expected inflation. Hooper's analysis is perhaps most satisfactory but uses only a three-year moving average of inflation rates.

reflect changes in the risk premium required to get investors to hold the debt denominated in that currency. These changes reflect variations in the perceived risk of fluctuations in the interest rate and the exchange rate as well as variations in the relative quantities of the assets denominated in that currency. An increase in the level of the real interest rate from a change in the risk premium can occur with no change in the exchange rate.

Third, the real interest rates in the two countries are endogenous variables, responding to changes in the exchange rate in a way that causes the direct structural effect of the interest rates on the exchange rate to be underestimated. Thus, a strong dollar implies a reduction in net exports, which depresses aggregate demand in the United States and therefore tends to lower the U.S. real interest rate. In addition, the strong dollar reduces U.S. net exports, thereby increasing the net capital inflow to the United States; the increase in the current and projected net capital inflow also tends to lower U.S. real interest rates. The stronger dollar may at times induce a more lax monetary policy than would otherwise prevail, temporarily reducing the real interest rate. These inverse effects of the dollar on the level of interest rates attenuates the measured direct effect of the interest rate on the level of the dollar.

An increase in the dollar-DM rate also tends to raise the real interest rate in Germany through the same three channels that cause it to lower the real interest rate in the United States. The weaker mark increases economic activity in Germany and this raises the real interest rate. The current and projected outflow of capital from Germany that accompanies the trade surplus raises the equilibrium real interest rate. And recent experience indicates that a fear of the inflationary consequences of a declining mark caused the Bundesbank to tighten monetary policy as the mark fell relative to the dollar.[9]

In the econometric estimates of the relation between the exchange rate and the interest rate presented in section 6, I use an instrumental variables procedure that treats the interest differential as endogenous. The instrumental variables are the budget deficits of the two countries, the past growth of the monetary base, and the past rates of inflation. The use of the instrumental variable procedure may also reduce the bias that results from the difficulty of measuring expected inflation. However, despite its desirable large-sample properties, the instrumental variable procedure is of only limited comfort with the small sample available in the present study.

9. On the induced change in Bundesbank policy, see Feldstein (1986a) and Feldstein and Bacchetta (1986).

In addition to the statistical problems of estimating the direct effect of exogenous shifts in the real interest differential on the exchange rate, there is the more fundamental issue that evidence on the dollar's response to changes in the real interest rate does not resolve the issue of the relative importance of changes in the budget deficit, in tax policy, and in monetary policy. Although that could in principle be obtained by estimating a separate equation relating the real interest rate to the budget deficit, tax, and monetary variables,[10] that two-equation specification implicitly assumes that these variables affect the exchange rate only through the real interest differential. At a minimum, changes in monetary, tax, and budget policies may affect the expected rate of inflation and the uncertainty about future real interest rates in ways that are not captured by the measured values of the real interest rates. In addition, as Dornbusch (1983) has noted, the budget deficit can have a direct effect through the relative demand for domestic and foreign goods.

This article therefore focuses on estimating a reduced-form specification that relates the dollar-DM exchange rate to four key variables: expected future budget deficits; tax-induced changes in the profitability of investment in plant and equipment; past inflation; and changes in monetary policy. The specification is also extended to include other variables such as the net U.S. stocks of international investment and the rate of growth of real GNP. A dummy variable is also used to evaluate whether the dollar's exchange value was higher in the period 1980–84 for some other unmeasured reason such as an increased attractiveness of the United States as a "safe haven" for foreign funds or international investors' greater faith in the Reagan administration. In addition to these reduced-form equations, the paper also reports estimates of equations relating the dollar-DM exchange rate to a measure of the real interest rate differential, using an instrumental variable procedure to reduce the statistical bias that might otherwise result from the endogeneity of the interest rates and the errors of measurement.

The next section describes these key variables and their construction in more detail. The estimated equations are then discussed and presented in sections 4 and 5.

3. *The Key Variables of a Reduced-Form Specification*

The dependent variable of the equations presented below is the real exchange rate between the dollar and the German mark calculated as the nominal exchange rate multiplied by the ratio of the GNP deflators. The

10. This is done in Feldstein (1986b).

exchange rate is stated as the number of German marks per U.S. dollar; a rise of the dependent variable is thus a rise in the real value of the dollar.

The key variables of the reduced-form specification described above cannot be observed directly but must be constructed. Here I describe the rationale for these variables and the way that they have been constructed for the current study. The regression equations reported later are estimated with annual observations for the period 1973 through 1984. The analysis uses annual observations because quarterly or monthly observations on variables like the expected future budget deficits and the tax-induced changes in profitability would probably contain much more measurement error with little or no increase in actual information.

3.1. EXPECTED U.S. BUDGET DEFICITS

It is the path of expected future budget deficits rather than simply the current year's deficit that influences the level of real interest rates and the exchange rate. In 1983 testimony (Feldstein 1983) I emphasized this link of the exchange rate to expected future budget deficits as follows:

That is the essential explanation of the strong dollar: the high real long-term interest rate in the United States, combined with the sense that dollar investments are relatively safe and that American inflation will remain low, induces investors worldwide to shift in favor of dollar securities. Moreover, the unusually high real long-term interest rate here relative to the real rates abroad is now due primarily to the low projected *national savings rate caused by the large* projected *budget deficits [emphasis added].*

To clarify the importance of the long-term projected deficits rather than just the current year's deficit, I noted:

Net national saving fell from its customary 7 percent of GNP to only 1.5 percent of GNP in 1982 and 1.5 percent of GNP in the first three quarters of 1983. Moreover, and of particular importance in this context, the large budget deficits that are projected for the next five years and beyond if no legislative action is taken means that our net national saving rate will continue to remain far below the previous level.

If government borrowing is high for only a single year, the additional government debt can be absorbed by temporarily displacing private investment with little effect on long-term interest rates. In contrast, the expected persistence of budget deficits in the future implies a larger increase in the stock of debt that must be sold to the private sector and a persistent displacement of private investment that must be achieved to accommodate the government's borrowing. Future budget deficits also mean future increases in potential aggregate demand that will lead to higher future short-term interest rates and therefore to higher current long-term rates. All of these considerations imply that the dollar exchange rate should be more sensitive to expected future deficits rather than to the current year's budget deficit.

Blanchard (1985) emphasized the importance of expected future deficits in the determination of current long-term interest rates and Frenkel and Razin (1984, 1986) and Branson (1985) emphasized the importance of expected future deficits in exchange rate determination.

The expected persistence of structural budget deficits also increases the risk that political pressures will lead to an inflationary monetary policy. To this extent, expected high future deficits may raise nominal interest rates but reduce the exchange value of the dollar by making dollar-denominated fixed income securities more risky.

Neither of the studies that explicitly looks at budget deficits considers the expected sequence of future budget deficits. I have already commented on the fact that Evans's (1986) procedure is based on the difference between the budget deficit in the current quarter and the deficit predicted by a VAR equation for the current quarter. There is no attention to expected future deficits. Hooper's (1985) analysis is also in terms of the current quarter's budget deficit with no attention to expected future deficits. As a result, I am not inclined to give any weight to Evans's negative conclusion or to Hooper's conclusion that budget deficits had only a small effect on the dollar exchange rate.

The variable used in this study to represent the anticipated future budget deficit (DEFEX) is an estimate of the average ratio of the budget deficit to GNP for five future years. Since the five-year deficit forecast is used as a proxy for the long-term expected deficit, it is appropriate to eliminate the cyclical component of the deficit and focus on the structural component of the deficit relative to an estimate of potential or full-employment GNP. The structural deficit is calculated from the observed or projected deficit and an estimate of the difference between the actual GNP and potential GNP. The details of this calculations and of the derivation of potential GNP are described in Feldstein (1986b).

Although five-year forecasts of the deficit and of GNP have been made in recent years, they are not available for the entire sample period. The analysis therefore assumes that, for the years for which it is observable, the actual deficit and the actual GNP are the best estimates of the values that financial market participants previously anticipated. For the years 1985 and beyond, the expected deficit and expected GNP are measured by the projections published in July 1985 by Data Resources, Inc. The

Data Resources deficit projections reflect anticipated policy developments as well as existing tax and spending rules; they are therefore taken as an indication of the view of sophisticated financial market participants. The actual and projected deficits are then adjusted to obtain structural deficits and full-employment GNP. Note that this implies that for recent years the expected deficit variable is a combination of actual deficits and projected deficits; e.g., the 1983 expected future deficit variable includes the observed deficit and GNP variables for 1983 and 1984 but the DRI projections for 1985 through 1987.

The anticipated deficit variable has been constructed in a way that, as far as possible, avoids discretionary decisions in order to eliminate any suspicion that the deficit variable has been modified to obtain a variable that can explain the variations in the exchange rate. Avoiding discretion can, however, lead to implausible assumptions and several people commenting on an earlier draft of this article said that they were concerned about the implication that the financial markets anticipated the unprecedented growth of budget deficits in the 1980s even before the 1980 election of Ronald Reagan and the presentation of his 1981 budget.

I have therefore constructed an alternative expected deficit variable that differs from the standard expected deficit variable for the years 1977 through 1980. For those years, the alternative expected five-year average deficit ratio is calculated by assuming that the 1980 ratio of structural deficit to GNP persists. For example, the five-year average for 1978 consists of an average of the deficit-GNP ratios for 1978, 1979, and 1980 with 1980 getting 60 percent of the weight. This variable will be denoted DEFALT (alternative deficit variable). The empirical analysis shows that substituting this for my standard expected deficit variable improves the explanatory power of the equation but does not alter the estimated coefficient.

3.2. EXPECTED GERMAN BUDGET DEFICITS

Although the exchange rate between the dollar and the German mark might at first seem to depend symmetrically on the budget deficits of the United States and Germany, this is true only if the two countries are symmetric in all other relevant ways. There are, however, two major differences between the United States and Germany that imply that changes in German deficits have smaller effects on the exchange rate than changes U.S. deficits.

First, the German economy is less than one-third the size of the U.S. economy. An increase in the German deficit by 1 percent of GNP is therefore only one-third as large as 1 percent U.S. GNP deficit increase.

More important, the close links among the European economies, now formalized by the European Monetary System, means that European investors will frequently act as if exchange rates among the major European countries are fixed. To the extent that this is true, what matters is not the change in the German budget deficit as a percentage of German GNP but the change in the combined European (or EMS) budget deficits as a percentage of the combined GNPs of those countries. Although this idea will be the subject of further attention in a future study, the current article uses only the ratio of the German budget deficit to German GNP.

The German expected deficit-GNP ratio variable (DEFEXG) is constructed to be as close as possible in concept to the U.S. expected deficit variable, although differences inevitably remain. The basic source of the data is an OECD study of structural budget deficits (Price and Muller 1984) that provides estimates of the ratio of the structural budget deficit to potential GNP for each year from 1973 through 1984. Forecasts for 1985 and 1986 are obtained from the *OECD Economic Outlook* for December 1985. For the years through 1982, these data can be used to construct a five-year average by assuming that financial markets expected the deficit-GNP ratios that were subsequently observed (or, for 1985 and 1986, that were subsequently forecast by the OECD). For 1983 and 1984, we lack the necessary forecasts of the deficit-GNP ratio in the more distant future; we therefore assume that investors project the deficit-GNP ratio at the 1984 level.

It should be noted that there is a serious problem in defining the structural deficit for Germany since the German unemployment rate (defined to approximate U.S. standards) rose from less than 1 percent in 1973 to nearly 8 percent in 1984. There is substantial controversy about how much of this increase is cyclical and how much is structural. Although the present analysis adopts the deficit implicit in the OECD measure of the structural deficit, it is clear that there is substantial possible error in this variable.

3.3. TAX-INDUCED CHANGES IN PROFITABILITY

The after-tax profitability of new corporate investments in plant and equipment determines the corporate demand for funds. If the domestic supply of funds to the corporate sector is relatively inelastic, an increase in the corporate demand for funds will put upward pressure on real interest rates and attract an inflow of capital from abroad. In contrast, if the corporate sector is a relatively small part of the domestic capital market, an increase in the corporate demand for funds can probably be satisfied without a significant rise in the real rate of return and therefore with little effect on international capital flows and the dollar.

The difference between pretax and after-tax profitability depends on the corporate tax rate, the depreciation rules, the investment tax credit, and the rate of inflation. All of this can be summarized by the "maximum potential real net return" (MPRNR) that the firm can afford to pay to the suppliers of capital on a standard project.[11] In an economy without taxes, the MPRNR on a project would be the traditional real internal rate of return. With taxes and complex tax depreciation rules, the MPRNR is the maximum real return that the firm can afford to pay on the outstanding "loan" (of debt or equity or a combination of the two) used to finance the project and have fully repaid the "loan" when the project is exhausted.

The standard project for which this calculation is done is a "sandwich" of equipment and structures in a ratio that matches the actual equipment-structures mix of the nonresidential capital stock. Because the tax law specifies depreciation rules and interest deductibility in nominal terms, the expected real net return depends on the expected rate of inflation; a maximum potential nominal return is obtained using an expected inflation series generated by a "rolling" ARIMA forecast (described below) and then the real MPRNR is calculated by subtracting the average expected inflation rate from this maximum potential nominal return. Full details of the calculation are provided in Feldstein and Jun (1986) in which it is also shown that variations in the MPRNR have had a substantial effect on corporate investment in the past quarter-century.

The MPRNR represents a potential *net* return that the firm can provide in the sense that it takes into account the deductibility of interest payments. From the portfolio investor's point of view, what matters is not the MPRNR but the maximum market rate of return that the corporation can provide. This differs from the MPRNR essentially in the fact that the portfolio investor receives gross interest while the MPRNR reflects interest net of the corporate deduction for that interest cost. The maximum real return depends on the mix of debt and equity that the firm uses to raise marginal increments to its capital stock. If we assume an average ratio of two-thirds equity and one-third debt and incorporate the average historical standard difference in the net returns of equity and debt, we can calculate "the maximum potential real interest return" (MPRIR).[12]

The MPRNR measure of real net profitability remained at approximately 6.0 percent during the years 1973 through 1984 and then rose to approximately 7.3 percent in the early 1980s. The behavior of the

11. This MPRNR measure is very closely related to the MPNR and MPIR values calculated in Feldstein and Summers (1978) and updated with some improvements in Feldstein and Jun (1986).

12. See Feldstein (1986b) for an explanation of how the related nominal MPIR is calculated. The MPRIR is obtained from the MPIR by substracting the same average projected inflation rate used to generate the MPNR and MPIR values.

maximum potential real interest rate was quite different. Since nominal interest rates are deductible in calculating the taxable profits of the corporation, a one percentage point decline in expected inflation reduces the maximum potential nominal interest rate by more than one percentage point and therefore reduces the maximum potential real interest rate. The MPRIR measure of the maximum real net interest rate rose significantly between 1973 and 1981 (because of the rising expected rate of inflation) and then came down significantly in the 1980s. Both variables are studied in the empirical section.

3.4. EXPECTED INFLATION

The expected inflation rate has no direct role in a simple model of exchange-rate determination since the exchange rate depends only on the difference in real rates. However, as Frankel (1979) has emphasized, a rise in expected inflation may temporarily depress real interest rates (because nominal rates do not adjust rapidly enough) and therefore the exchange rate. In addition, financial investors may regard a higher inflation rate as inherently more uncertain; a government that has allowed its inflation rate to get to (say) 10 percent may be less able to control it in the future than a government that has kept its inflation rate under 5 percent. The uncertainty of future inflation makes the future value of the currency more uncertain and therefore depresses the demand for the currency.

The expected rate of inflation is not only unobservable but depends on a large number of variables: past rates of inflation; past increases in monetary aggregates; projected structural budget deficits; changes in energy prices; the current level of capacity utilization; etc. Although it is not possible to combine all of these factors to obtain a single operational measure of expected inflation, the exchange-rate equations presented below include many of these variables. The proper interpretation of the projected structural budget deficit variable, for example, is therefore a combination of the direct effect of the deficit on real interest rates and any effect that operates through expected inflation and inflation uncertainty. It is not possible to identify these separate effects but only to quantify the net impact of expected deficits on the exchange rate.

Although this approach is satisfactory as a general way of dealing with the effect of expected inflation on the dollar's value, it cannot be used for quantifying the effect of the tax-inflation interaction on the maximum potential real interest rate. For that purpose, we require an explicit year-by-year forecast of inflation over the future life of the standard investment project. To do that, we estimate a series of first-order ARIMA models using quarterly data on the GNP deflator with observations through each year and use these models to forecast future inflation rates for the 30-year life of the standard investment project. The algorithm calculates nominal values of MPNR and MPIR using the entire set of thirty years of inflation rates. These nominal returns are then converted into real returns by subtracting a weighted average of the projected future inflation rates.

This "projected inflation variable" (INFEX) is also used as a separate explanatory variable in the exchange-rate regressions to summarize the past rates of inflation. As an alternative, equations are also presented with a polynomial distributed lag on past rates of change of the GNP deflator.

3.5. OTHER VARIABLES

The other variables that are included in some or all of the estimated exchange-rate equations can be easily described.

The basis measure of U.S. monetary policy in this study is the rate of change of the monetary base (MBGRO). As an alternative, equations are also estimated with the rate of change of M1 (M1GRO). Variables such as the ratio of money to GNP or the interest rate would clearly be endogenous in a way that would be inappropriate for the current specification.

For Germany, equations are presented with the rate of change of the Central Bank money stock (MBGROG). There is, however, a problem of interpreting this variable if, as I believe, the Bundesbank altered the growth of its monetary base in response to variations in the dollar-DM ratio. A strong dollar and declining mark created potential inflationary pressures that caused the Bundesbank to reduce the growth of the monetary base, thereby introducing an offsetting negative correlation between the growth of the German monetary base and the strength of the dollar.

Much of the financial market discussion of short-term changes in exchange rates focuses on changes in the pace of economic activity, presumably as an indicator of future changes in real interest rates. Dornbusch (1983) and Obstfeld (1985) also show how changes in domestic demand can alter the exchange rate by changing the relative demand for domestic and foreign goods. The current analysis uses the change in real GNP (GNPGRO) as a measure of economic activity.

Some of the equations also include a dummy variable for the period beginning in 1980 (DUM80+) to see whether the effects attributed to the rising budget deficit are due simply to some other unidentified or unmeasured character of the period since 1980, such as the altered nature of monetary policy or the strengthened political "safe haven" quality of the dollar.

Finally, some of the equations include the net international investment position (NIIP) of the United States, i.e., the excess of U.S. investments abroad over foreign investments in the United States. If U.S. securities are not a perfect substitute for foreign securities, an exogenous increase in the net international investment position of the United States should strengthen the dollar by reducing the demand for additional foreign securities by U.S. investors. Similarly, an exogenous rise in the foreign holding of U.S. securities (a decrease in the U.S. net international investment position) should reduce the value of the dollar by reducing the demand for dollar securities.

Since the NIIP of the United States reflects past current account deficits, the level of the NIIP will not be exogenous if the residual in the current account equation or in the equation for the exchange rate is serially correlated. For example, an increased taste for investing in dollar securities will strengthen both the dollar and, after a lag, reduce the U.S. net international investment position. Since the taste shift is unobservable, the coefficient of the NIIP of the United States will be biased downward toward zero. Although it would be desirable to develop a more complete analysis of this issue with which to model the process of portfolio satiation, the current research settles for only a very simple extension of the basic specification to include the NIIP variable.

4. *A Summary of the Reduced-Form Estimates*

It is useful to begin with a summary of the estimated reduced-form equations and a commentary on the magnitude of the estimated coefficients. The individual estimated equations are presented and discussed in section 5. The equations relating the exchange rate to real expected interest rates in the United States and Germany are discussed in section 6.

The dependent variable of all of the estimated equations is the real dollar-DM exchange rate, defined as the number of German marks per dollar, adjusted for the level of the GNP deflator of the two countries and normalized to 1.0 in 1980. This variable declined erratically from 1.21 in 1973 to 0.97 in 1979 and then climbed to 1.72 in 1984. Individual annual values are shown in appendix table A-1, together with the annual values of all other variables used in this study.

The basic equation relates the real dollar-DM exchange rate to the expected structural deficits as a percentage of GNP (DEFEX), the maximum potential real interest rate that can be supported by a standard investment project given the concurrent tax rules and expected inflation (MPRIR), the rate of growth of the monetary base (MBGRO), and the average future GNP inflation projected by a rolling ARIMA model

(INFEX). To test the sensitivity of the estimated effect of the expected deficit variable to the specification of the exchange rate equation, a large number of variants of this basic specification have been estimated. These variations omit some of the basic variables, replacing the basic variables with other closely related variables (e.g., replacing INFEX by a polynomial distributed lag on past changes in the GNP deflator) and adding additional variables.

Several results are very robust with respect to alternative specifications. The coefficient of the expected future budget deficits is always positive, substantial, and almost always statistically significant. The point estimate generally varies between 0.25 and 0.40. To appreciate the magnitude of this coefficient, it is useful to recognize that DEFEX rose from 1.58 (percent of GNP) in 1978 and 1.79 to 3.38 in 1983 and 3.33 in 1984. Comparing the average of the first two years with the average of the last two years implies an increase of 1.67 percent of GNP. A coefficient of 0.25 implies an increase of the dollar-DM exchange rate index of 0.42 while a coefficient of 0.40 implies an increase of the dollar-DM index of 0.67. Since the dollar-DM index rose from 0.99 in 1978–79 to 1.61 in 1983–84, the rise in the expected budget deficit can account for between two-thirds of the dollar's rise (0.42/0.62 = 0.677) and slightly more than 100 percent of the dollar's rise (0.67/0.62 = 1.08).

The coefficient of monetary base growth is always negative and generally statistically significant. A negative coefficient implies that a faster growth of the monetary base depresses the value of the dollar. This may be because an increase in the monetary base temporarily increases the liquidity of the banking system and therefore reduces interest rates or, more generally, because it causes nominal interest rates to decline. Alternatively, more rapid growth of the monetary base may raise expected inflation or inflation uncertainty, thereby making dollar securities more risky.

The value of the coefficient of the annual growth rate of the monetary base is approximately −0.06. Although the implied effect of monetary policy can explain relatively little of the dollar's rise from 1980 to 1984, it does indicate an important effect during the early part of the period. The annual rate of growth of the monetary base fell from 8.8 percent in 1978 and 1979 to a low of 6.4 percent in 1981. The coefficient of 0.06 implies a rise in the DM-dollar exchange rate index of 0.144 between these years. Since the actual exchange rate index rose from 0.99 to 1.31, the tighter money can account for nearly one-half of the observed rise (0.144/0.32 = 0.45) from 1978–79 to 1981. However, since the expected budget deficit increased during the same years from 1.68 percent of GNP to 2.82 percent of GNP, the implied rise in the DM-dollar index was about twice as large as the rise implied by the change in monetary policy and the two together account for more than the entire rise, implying that other factors depressed the dollar's value during this period.

By 1984, the annual rate of increase of the monetary base was back up to 8.1 percent, implying that the change since 1978–79 could only explain about 0.05 points of the 0.73 point rise in the real dollar-DM ratio.

The coefficient of the MPRIR tax variable was frequently insignificant and generally had the wrong sign (implying that increases in the maximum potential real interest rate that resulted from changes in ex ante effective tax rates depressed the value of the dollar). The coefficient of the MPRNR variable also generally had the wrong sign but was almost always insignificant. While a negative coefficient cannot be reconciled with the theoretical expectations, the insignificant coefficients are consistent with an earlier finding (Feldstein and Summers 1978) that shifts in the MPIR had only a small effect on market interest rates, a result that was obtained more recently (Feldstein 1986b) in an even stronger form. The small and insignificant effect of the MPRIR and MPRNR on the financial variables stands in sharp contrast to their powerful effects on real investment reported in Feldstein (1982) and Feldstein and Jun (1986).

The insensitivity of the real interest rate and the real exchange rate to the rate that corporate borrowers can afford to pay on a standard investment project may simply reflect the fact that corporate borrowers represent only a small part of the funds raised in credit markets. Between 1980 and 1984, corporate borrowing was only 20.5 percent of the total funds raised in the credit markets by all of the public and private nonfinancial borrowers combined. Even a substantial shift in the demand curve represented by this 20 percent need not cause an appreciable rise in the interest rate if the additional funds are easily attracted from the other borrowers, from potential savers, or from the rest of the world.

Negative coefficients of the MPRIR and MPRNR variables cannot be given a structural interpretation. They may represent the correlation of this variable with other omitted variables that depress the value of the dollar. While this leaves some residual doubt about the actual impact of the tax changes, it is important to note that including, excluding, or changing the specification of the tax variable does not alter the conclusions about the expected budget deficit variables.

The inflation variables had a negative coefficient, implying that a higher rate of predicted (or past) inflation depressed the relative value of the dollar. This may reflect a failure of the nominal interest rate to adjust quickly enough to changes in the expected rate of inflation. Alternatively, if there is a positive correlation between the inflation level and inflation uncertainty, the higher level of predicted inflation may make the dollar a riskier asset for investors and therefore an asset of lower value.

Although the inflation coefficient was always negative, the magnitude of the coefficient varied substantially from one specification to another and was not always statistically significant. In interpreting the coefficient, it should be borne in mind that INFEX rose from 6.7 percent in 1978–79 to 8.1 percent in 1981 and fell to 5.5 percent in 1984. A coefficient of −0.04 on this variable would imply a decline of 0.06 points on the dollar-DM index between 1978–79 and 1981, followed by a rise of 0.10 points between 1981 and 1984. This increase represents about one-fourth of the rise in the dollar-DM index during those years.

The estimated coefficients of the expected German budget deficits are always insignificant. This may reflect the difficulty in measuring the German structural deficit accurately or it may reflect the fact that the close links among the European economies mean that the dollar-DM ratio is not sensitive to German deficits per se. Only future work will clarify this. It is important to note, however, that the inclusion or exclusion of this variable has essentially no effect on the coefficient of the U.S. budget deficit variable.

5. The Estimated Reduced Form Equations

Table 1 presents the basic reduced-form equation and a number of variations on this specification. In equation (1.1) the coefficient of the expected deficit variable (DEFEX) is 0.375 with a standard error of 0.071, implying that each percentage point increase in the ratio of expected structural deficit to GNP raises the real dollar-DM index by 0.375 points. As noted above, the real dollar-DM index rose from 0.99 in 1978–79 to 1.72 in 1984 while the expected deficit rose from 1.68 percent of GNP to 3.35 percent of GNP. The coefficient of 0.375 implies that the rise in DEFEX accounts for 63 points of the 73-point rise in the index.

The coefficient of the tax variable, the maximum potential real interest rate (MPRIR) supportable by a standard project, has the wrong sign. I will return later to this and to its sensitivity to specification.

The coefficient of the ARIMA inflation projection (INFEX) is negative but is only −0.010 and much smaller than its standard error of 0.029. It is useful to reiterate a point made earlier that this ARIMA variable should not be regarded as equivalent to inflation expectations since inflation expectations at any time will also reflect the growth of the monetary base, the size of projected budget deficits, and many other political and economic factors.

Table 1 EFFECTS OF EXPECTED BUDGET DEFICITS AND OTHER VARIABLES ON THE DM-DOLLAR EXCHANGE RATE: BASIC SPECIFICATIONS

Equation	*DEFEX* (1)	*DEFALT* (2)	*MPRIR* (3)	*MPRNR* (4)	*MBGRO* (5)	*INFEX* (6)	*PDLINF* (7)	*CONST.* (8)	U_{-1} (9)	U_{-2} (10)	$\bar{R}^2$ (11)	*DWS* (12)
1.1	0.375		−0.095		−0.061	−0.010		1.47			0.78	1.68
	(0.071)		(0.038)		(0.042)	(0.029)						
1.2		0.385	−0.093		−0.044	0.005		1.21			0.95	1.76
		(0.031)	(0.017)		(0.019)	(0.014)						
1.3	0.387		−0.102		−0.058			1.39			0.81	1.72
	(0.059)		(0.031)		(0.038)							
1.4	0.254		−0.016		−0.068		−0.098	1.99			0.84	1.78
	(0.118)		(0.077)		(0.050)		(0.082)					
1.5	0.234				−0.036	−0.048		1.32			0.64	0.76
	(0.056)				(0.052)	(0.032)						
1.6	0.236				−0.060	−0.020		1.34	1.23	−0.68	0.84	2.22
	(0.193)				(0.023)	(0.017)			(0.33)	(0.45)		
1.7	0.223				−0.057			1.21	1.21	−0.69	0.83	2.13
	(0.161)				(0.024)				(0.29)	(0.38)		
1.8	0.343			−0.110	−0.054	−0.070		2.07			0.64	1.11
	(0.123)			(0.111)	(0.055)	(0.039)						
1.9	0.246			0.023	−0.043	−0.027		1.09	0.72		0.73	0.87
	(0.201)			(0.108)	(0.041)	(0.033)			(0.53)			
1.10	0.283			−0.106	−0.097		−0.084	2.63			0.86	2.48
	(0.075)			(0.108)	(0.052)		(0.046)					
1.11	0.367		−0.081			−0.000		0.86			0.75	1.59
	(0.076)		(0.040)			(0.030)						
1.12	0.339		−0.053		−0.027	−0.023		1.10			0.76	1.16
	(0.079)		(0.046)		(0.023)	(0.036)						

The dependent variable is the real DM-dollar exchange rate (DMs per dollar, adjusted for GNP deflators) normalized at 1.0 = 1980. Equations estimated for 1973 to 1984. Standard errors are shown in parentheses. See text for explanation of variables. In equation (1.12), the growth of the monetary base is replaced by the growth of M1.

Finally, the rate of growth of the monetary base has a coefficient of −0.06 (with a standard error of 0.042), implying that a faster rate of monetary growth depresses the value of the dollar.

The adjusted $\bar{R}^2$ of 0.78 implies that the equation explains the variations in the dollar-DM ratio quite well and the Durbin-Watson statistic of 1.68 indicates that there is little serial correlation of the residuals.

Equation (1.2) replaces the basic DEFEX variable with the alternative DEFALT variable (described in section 3.1) that was constructed to avoid the assumption that financial market participants anticipated the large budget deficits before 1981. The coefficient of DEFALT is 0.385 and therefore almost identical to the 0.375 coefficient of DEFEX reported in equation (1.1). The standard error of DEFALT is, however, only 0.031 or less than half of the standard error of the coefficient of DEFEX, reflecting the fact that the alternative variable has far less "noise" in it. This is also seen in the sharp rise of the corrected $\bar{R}^2$ from 0.78 in equation (1.1) to 0.95 in equation (1.2). The other coefficients are not changed in any substantial way. Although DEFALT seems clearly to be a better variable than the DEFEX variable, the latter does have the virtue that its construction involved less discretion and I will continue to present results for DEFEX.

Because the coefficient of the inflation variable is much smaller than its standard error, it is desirable to conserve the very scarce degrees of freedom by reestimating the equation with the INFEX variable omitted. This is done in equation (1.3). None of the remaining coefficients or standard errors changes appreciably.

Instead of omitting the rolling ARIMA forecast variable, equation (1.4) replaces it with a polynomial distributed lag on the annual changes of the GNP deflator. The distributed lag coefficients are constrained to satisfy a third-order polynomial on six lagged values of the annual rate of change of the GNP deflator with no restriction on the final weight. The sum of the implied coefficients is −0.098 with a standard error of 0.082. The monetary base variable remains essentially unchanged with this respecification. The coefficient of MPRIR drops to −0.016 and is completely insignificant (standard error 0.077); this is reassuring since an insignificant coefficient is quite plausible while a significantly negative one cannot be justified. Finally, the coefficient of DEFEX drops to 0.254 but remains both statistically significant and economically very powerful. The corrected $\bar{R}^2$ statistic of 0.84 shows that the polynomial distributed lag specification has slightly greater explanatory power than the more constrained INFEX specification.

Since the MPRIR variable is either insignificant or significant with the wrong sign, it is useful to see the implications of omitting it from the specification. This is done in equation (1.5). The coefficient of the DEFEX variable is 0.234, indicating that the decline in the coefficient value observed in equation (1.4) was due to the small size of the MPRIR coefficient rather than to the change in the inflation variable per se. This specification is clearly inferior to the previous ones, with a much lower corrected $\bar{R}^2$ and a very much lower Durbin-Watson statistic.

To deal with the low Durbin-Watson statistic, equation (1.5) was reestimated with a first-order transformation. Since this still had a low Durbin-Watson statistic, a second-order autocorrelation correction was used. This is shown in equation (1.6). The DEFEX coefficient has remained essentially unchanged at 0.236 and the MBGRO coefficient has returned to −0.060. The inflation coefficient is now the same size as its standard error. This variable is dropped in equation (1.7) where the other coefficients remain essentially unchanged.

The specification of the MPRIR variable requires assuming a particular marginal debt-equity ratio and a particular yield difference between equity and debt. An alternative measure of the effect of changes in tax rules and in the tax-inflation interaction is to use the less restricted variable MPRNR, the maximum potential real net return. This alternative is used in equations (1.8) through (1.10).

Equation (1.8) parallels (1.1) except for the substitution of MPRNR for MPRIR. The DEFEX variable is essentially unchanged (0.343 with a standard error of 0.123) while the MPRNR is statistically insignificant. MBGRO is similar to its earlier value (−0.054) and the INFEX variable is now nearly twice its standard error (−0.070 with a standard error of 0.039). A first-order autocorrelation correction actually lowers the Durbin-Watson statistic.

A far better specification is obtained by substituting the polynomial distributed lag for the INFEX variable (equation 1.10). This combination of variables has the highest corrected $\bar{R}^2$ statistic (0.86) of all the regressions that include the DEFEX variable and a Durbin-Watson statistic of 2.48. The coefficient of the DEFEX variable is 0.283 with a standard error of only 0.075. MBGRO and PDLINF are both negative and nearly twice their standard errors while the coefficient of MPRNR is satisfactorily less than its standard error.

Equation (1.11) is similar to (1.1) but constrains the monetary base growth not to appear in the equation. Although the resulting specification is not very satisfactory, the coefficient of DEFEX remains almost unchanged from equation (1.1).

Finally, equation (1.12) substitutes the rate of growth of M1 for the rate of growth of the monetary base. The coefficients are generally similar to those of equation (1.1) but the overall goodness of fit is slightly worse.

A variety of additional sensitivity tests are presented in table 2. These

Table 2 EFFECT OF ADDITIONAL VARIABLES ON THE ESTIMATED EFFECT OF THE EXPECTED BUDGET DEFICITS ON THE DM-DOLLAR EXCHANGE RATE

Equation	*DEFEX* (1)	*MPRIR* (2)	*MPRNR* (3)	*MBGRO* (4)	*INFEX* (5)	*PDLINF* (6)	*DUM80+* (7)	*GNPGRO* (8)	*NIIP* (9)	*CONST.* (10)	$\bar{R}^2$ (11)	*DWS* (12)
2.1	0.525	−0.073		−0.065	−0.012		−0.283			1.17	0.84	1.77
	(0.099)	(0.034)		(0.035)	(0.025)		(0.147)					
2.2	0.539	−0.081		−0.061			−0.281			1.07	0.86	1.77
	(0.089)	(0.028)		(0.032)			(0.138)					
2.3	0.454	−0.059		−0.057		−0.032	−0.224			1.31	0.86	2.33
	(0.185)	(0.078)		(0.047)		(0.091)	(0.167)					
2.4	0.484			−0.048	−0.037		−0.386			0.95	0.77	1.46
	(0.119)			(0.042)	(0.026)		(0.170)					
2.5	0.553		−0.084	−0.062	−0.055		−0.365			1.54	0.76	1.43
	(0.142)		(0.092)	(0.045)	(0.033)		(0.173)					
2.6	0.343			−0.067		−0.094	−0.174			1.73	0.87	1.72
	(0.107)			(0.043)		(0.037)	(0.146)					
2.7	0.429		−0.173	−0.077	−0.029			0.034		2.09	0.71	1.05
	(0.122)		(0.107)	(0.051)	(0.043)			(0.021)				
2.8	0.365		−0.183	−0.103		−0.054		0.017		2.72	0.86	2.34
	(0.111)		(0.133)	(0.053)		(0.055)		(0.017)				
2.9	0.642		−0.147	−0.085	−0.014		−0.368	0.634		1.56	0.87	1.56
	(0.110)		(0.072)	(0.034)	(0.029)		(0.127)	(0.014)				
2.10	0.547	−0.069		−0.072	−0.022		−0.301	0.022		0.88	0.89	1.63
	(0.085)	(0.029)		(0.030)	(0.028)		(0.125)	(0.012)				
2.11	0.241			−0.069		−0.113		0.004		2.01	0.84	1.51
	(0.070)			(0.050)		(0.038)		(0.016)				
2.12	0.346		−0.100	−0.049	−0.068				0.003	1.92	0.59	1.12
	(0.135)		(0.147)	(0.070)	(0.045)				(0.027)			

The dependent variable is the real DM-dollar exchange rate (DMs per dollar, adjusted for GNP deflators) normalized at 1.0 = 1980. Equations estimated for 1973 to 1984. Standard errors are shown in parentheses. See text for explanation of variables.

tests involve adding several new variables as well as considering some of the variations discussed in table 1. All of the results again support the conclusion that the coefficient of the expected deficit is statistically significant and economically powerful.

Equation (2.1) starts with the basic specification of equation (1.1) and adds a dummy variable equal to one for the years 1980 through 1984 and zero for the previous years. The purpose of the dummy variable is to test whether the dollar was strong in the 1980s for any of a variety of otherwise unspecified reasons (the new monetary policy regime that began in October 1979; the Reagan presidency; the increased importance of the United States as a political safe haven for foreign capital). If some combination of omitted variables did indeed raise the dollar in the 1980s above what it would otherwise have been, the equations of table 1 might have imputed this to the large expected deficits or to some other variable that distinguished the 1980s from previous years. Including a specific dummy variable should eliminate this source of bias.

Rather surprisingly, the coefficient of the dummy variable for the 1980s (DUM80+) is negative, about twice its standard error and quite large in absolute size (about −0.25). This implies that the unspecified factors at work in the 1980s had the effect of lowering the dollar relative to the German mark in comparison to the earlier years. Faced with the negative coefficient, it is of course possible to identify possible explanations. For example, the decline in OPEC financial assets during most of the 1980s reduced the demand for dollar securities relative to DM securities. The conservative political victories in Germany and Britain, and the switch in French economic policy, may have revived the demand for portfolio investment in Europe.

The important point to note about these arguments is that they imply that the actual rise of the dollar in the 1980s is even more surprising and that the combined role of those factors that systematically raised the dollar was even stronger. The other coefficients of equation (2.1) show that the primary effect of including DUM80+ is to raise the coefficient of DEFEX from 0.375 to 0.525.

The DUM80+ variable appears in most of the specifications of table 2. Its coefficient is almost always about twice its standard error and it has the effect of raising the coefficient of DEFEX to 0.5 or above. Although it is of course possible that the DUM80+ variable is spurious, it is not necessary to decide this question in order to say whether the rise in the expected budget deficit was an important cause of the increase in the dollar. That is clearly an implication of the specifications of tabel 1 without the DUM80+ variable as well as of the equations in table 2 with the DUM80+ variable.

Equation (2.2) drops the INFEX variable and equation (2.3) replaces it with the polynomial distributed lag. Equation (2.4) omits the tax variable while equation (2.5) switches to the relatively unconstrained MPRNR specification. Equation (2.6), with no tax variable and with the distributed lag specification of the inflation variable is one of the few specifications in which the coefficient of the DUM80+ variable is only slightly greater than its standard error. In this specification, the coefficient of the DEFEX variable is reduced to the level of 0.343, approximately its value in the equations without the DUM80+ variable.

Equations (2.7) through (2.11) include the annual growth of real GNP (GNPGRO) as an additional explanatory variable. When the DUM80+ variable is not present (equations 2.7 and 2.8), the GNPGRO variable is only slightly greater than its standard error. The DEFEX coefficients are raised by a small amount and the inflation variables are insignificant. When the DUM80+ variable is present, the GNPGRO coefficients are quite significant and the DEFEX coefficients are increased to more than 0.5.

Finally, equation (2.2) adds the net international investment position of the United States as a percent of GNP (NIIP). Its coefficient is very much less than its standard error and the remaining coefficients are very similar to the coefficients of equation (1.8) (which has the same specification except for the NIIP variable). The statistical insignificance of this coefficient should not be overinterpreted. As I noted above, the net stock of accumulated assets may not be truly exogenous since the decline in NIIP in the 1980s has been the cumulative result of the high value of the dollar and the resulting current account deficits.[13]

Table 3 extends the analysis of tables 1 and 2 to include the German deficit and monetary base variables. For reference, the basic specification of equation (1.1) is repeated in equation (3.1). Adding the variable that measures the ratio of expected German deficits to GNP (DEFEXG) and the growth of the German monetary base (MBGROG) does not alter the other coefficients subtantially but does cause the standard errors to become quite large (equation (3.2)). The additional variables also leave the corrected $\bar{R}^2$ unchanged.

The increased standard errors are perhaps not surprising since equation (3.2) has six coefficients and a constant term to estimate with only twelve observations. Dropping the German monetary base variable

13. When equation (2.12) was estimated with the stock of foreign private assets in the United States as a percentage of GNP instead of NIIP, its coefficient had the wrong sign (positive) and was statistically significant. This again no doubt reflects the fact that foreign private investment in the United States grew in the 1980s because of the high dollar.

Table 3 EFFECTS OF US AND GERMAN EXPECTED BUDGET DEFICITS AND OTHER VARIABLES ON THE DM-DOLLAR EXCHANGE RATE

Equation	*DEFEX* (1)	*DEFALT* (2)	*MPRIR* (3)	*MBGRO* (4)	*INFEX* (5)	*DEFEXG* (6)	*MBGROG* (7)	*CONST.* (8)	U_{-1} (9)	U_{-2} (10)	$\bar{R}^2$ (11)	*DWS* (12)
3.1	0.375		−0.095	−0.061	−0.010			1.47			0.78	1.68
	(0.071)		(0.038)	(0.042)	(0.029)							
3.2	0.344		−0.100	−0.081	0.028	−0.055	0.040	1.22			0.78	1.85
	(0.491)		(0.044)	(0.046)	(0.051)	(0.217)	(0.030)					
3.3	0.323		−0.093	−0.062	−0.007	0.022		1.58			0.75	1.64
	(0.521)		(0.047)	(0.047)	(0.047)	(0.218)						
3.4		0.414	−0.092	−0.045	0.010	0.007	0.009	1.06			0.94	1.76
		(0.103)	(0.018)	(0.025)	(0.023)	(0.055)	(0.509)					
3.5		0.202		−0.029		−0.173		1.15	1.73	−0.94	0.95	2.11
		(0.058)		(0.012)		(0.087)			(0.11)	(0.09)		
3.6		0.212		−0.034	−0.016	−0.067		1.21	1.60	−0.91	0.96	1.84
		(0.070)		(0.016)	(0.013)	(0.154)			(0.37)	(0.15)		

The dependent variable is the real DM-dollar exchange rate (DMs per dollar, adjusted for GNP deflators) normalized at 1.0 = 1980. Equations estimated for 1973 to 1984. Standard errors are shown in parentheses. See text for explanation of variables.

(equation (3.3)) leaves the coefficients of the four U.S. variables very similar to the basic specification of equation (3.1) but with very large standard errors. The coefficient of the German deficit variable is small and only about one-tenth of its standard error.

In an attempt to reduce the problem of the large standard errors, these equations are repeated with the standard U.S. DEFEX variable replaced by the alternative DEFALT variable in which the observations for 1977 through 1980 are modified to assume that the 1980 deficit-GNP ratio was projected forward until after the 1980 election. Equation (1.2) indicated that this substitution leaves the coefficient of the deficit and other variables essentially unchanged while reducing their standard errors. The effect is similar in equation (3.4). The coefficient of DEFALT is 0.414 with a standard error of 0.103. The coefficients of MPRIR and MBGRO are very similar to their values in equation (3.1) but with smaller standard errors. The coefficient of INFEX remains very much smaller than its standard error. The coefficients of the two German variables are again much smaller than their standard errors.

Dropping the insignificant MBGROG and INFEX variables and the MPRIR variable which has an inadmissible sign lead to equation (3.5) in which the three remaining variables are statistically significant and have the correct sign. In this equation, which is estimated after a second-order autocorrelation transformation, the coefficient of DEFALT is 0.202 (with a standard error of 0.058) and in which the coefficient of the German deficit variable is −0.173 with a standard error of 0.087.

This coefficient structure is, however, quite fragile. Adding the INFEX variable produces a coefficient of −0.016 with a standard error of 0.013 while the coefficient of the German deficit variable drops to −0.067 and less than half of its standard error.

In short, it seems from table 3 that the German deficit variable does not have a significant or stable relation to the dollar-DM ratio and that the decision of whether or not to include it does not alter the point estimate of the U.S. deficit variable. Future work will be needed to assess whether some combination of German and other European deficits is significant and whether its presence alters the coefficient of the U.S. budget deficit variable.

It is, of course, unfortunate that the history of the floating rate period gives us only twelve years of experience to analyze. Although more data points could be created by using quarterly observations, I believe very little (if any) additional information on DEFEX and MPRIR would actually result. Instead, there would be more measurement error in the "expectations" variables (DEFEX, INFEX, MPRIR) relative to the actual variation. Looking back before 1973 is inappropriate because the quasi-fixed rate system that existed then would imply very different exchange-rate dynamics and might be expected to have very different monetary policy responses as countries tried to maintain their currencies at the fixed parities. Expectations would also be formed differently in a regime in which governments were committed to maintaining fixed exchange rates and in which the United States appeared willing to accumulate overseas investments or run down its assets in order to maintain that fixed rate system.

6. *Effects of the Interest Differential*

I have already commented (in section 2) on the difficulty of assessing the structural relation between the exchange rate and the difference in expected real interest rates. The expected inflation rate, which is a very critical component of the calculation, is difficult to measure and the real interest rates themselves are endogenous variables.

Despite these difficulties, it is worth devoting some attention to the estimation of a structural equation linking the exchange rate to the real interest differential because it is the operational link between budget deficits and the exchange rate in several analytic models. The problems of measurement and of endogeneity can be mitigated by using an instrumental variable procedure with the DEFEX, MBGRO, and INFEX variables as the instruments. The results indicate that the use of an instrumental variable procedure is important and that, when it is used, the evidence shows a substantial effect of the real interest differential on the exchange rate.

Equation (4.1) of table 4 presents an ordinary-least-squares regression of the exchange rate index on the difference between the real long-term interest rate in the United States and a corresponding real long-term interest rate for Germany. The nominal U.S. rate is the yield on Treasury bonds with five years to maturity. The real rate is calculated by subtracting the ARIMA projection (INFEX) from this nominal rate. The nominal German rate is a rate on long-term German government bonds.[14] The real rate is calculated by subtracting an ARIMA estimate of future German inflation calculated by the same process used for the U.S. ARIMA forecast of inflation. Annual values of these variables are shown in appendix table A-2.

The coefficient of the real interest rate differential is 0.042 with a standard error of 0.025. The Durbin-Watson statistic is very low and the

14. The German interest rate was provided by Data Resources, Inc. and is identified by Data Resources as RMGBL@GY.

Table 4 REAL INTEREST* DIFFERENTIALS AND THE DM-DOLLAR EXCHANGE RATE

			Interest Rates minus Predicted Inflation						$\bar{R}^2$	
Equation	*Estimation Method*	*Interval*	*RUS-RG* (1)	*RUS* (2)	*RG* (3)	*Constant* (4)	U_{-1} (5)	U_{-2} (6)	*(SER)* (7)	*DWS* (8)
4.1	OLS	1973–84	0.042			1.24			0.14	0.41
			(0.025)						(0.21)	
4.2	OLS	1973–84	0.032			1.32	0.81		0.63	0.90
	AR1		(0.023)				(0.19)		(0.13)	
4.3	OLS	1973–84	0.034			1.26	1.27	−0.59	0.74	2.13
	AR2		(0.022)				(0.29)	(0.31)	(0.11)	
4.4	IV	1973–84	0.082			1.25			NA	0.53
			(0.035)						(0.23)	
4.5	IV	1973–84	0.054			1.26	0.75		NA	1.18
	AR1		(0.023)				(0.18)		(0.15)	
4.6	OLS	1973–84		0.051	0.003	1.08			0.23	0.48
				(0.024)	(0.037)				(0.19)	
4.7	OLS	1973–84		0.038	0.011	1.10	1.38	−0.75	0.80	2.08
	AR2			(0.019)	(0.034)		(0.28)	(.028)	(0.10)	
4.8	IV	1973–84		0.080	−0.005	1.17			NA	1.05
				(0.034)	(0.061)				(0.16)	
4.9	IV	1973–84		0.046	−0.037	1.23	0.74		NA	1.05
	AR1			(0.024)	(0.024)		(0.18)		(0.16)	

*Real interest is interest minus ARIMA predictions of inflation.

The dependent variable is the real DM-dollar exchange rate (DMs per dollar, adjusted for GNP deflators) normalized at 1.0 = 1980. Standard errors are shown in parentheses. See text for explanation of variables.

equation is therefore reestimated with an autocorrelation transformation. A first-order transformation (equation (4.2)) is inadequate so the final result (presented in equation (4.3)) has a second-order autocorrelation correction. In this form, the coefficient of the interest differential is 0.034 with a standard error of 0.022.

When the equation is estimated by an instrumental variable procedure (equation (4.4)), the coefficient of the interest rate differential becomes much larger (0.082) and more than twice its standard error. The Durbin-Watson statistic is, however, very small (0.56). When Fair's method is used to obtain an instrumental variable estimate with a first-order autocorrelation correction, the coefficient falls to 0.054 with a standard error of 0.023. In short, the instrumental variable procedure results in a slightly larger coefficient than the OLS procedure. It might also be noted that these coefficient estimates are similar to the estimates of approximately 0.06 obtained by Sachs (1985) and Hooper (1985).

Before looking at any further equation estimates, it is helpful to consider the implications of a coefficient of approximately 0.04 to 0.06 on the interest rate differential. In 1978–79, the estimated real long-term U.S. rate exceeded the corresponding German rate by 0.7 percent; by 1983 the differential was 1.4 percent and by 1984 it was 2.8 percent. Even a coefficient of 0.06 implies a rise in the dollar-DM real exchange rate of 0.042 between 1980 and 1983 and of 0.126 between 1980 and 1984. Since the actual exchange rate rose by 0.72 points over this period, the equation can account for at most one-fifth of the actual rise.

The estimated coefficient is far less than theory suggests. An increase of one percentage point in the difference between U.S. and German 10-year real interest rates should increase the dollar-DM exchange rate by about twelve percentage points, not the four to six percentage points estimated here and in previous studies. This implies that the coefficient may be grossly underestimated because of the measurement and simultaneity problems referred to above.

When the interest differential is split into two separate interest rates and the equation estimated by ordinary least squares, only the coefficient of the U.S. rate is statistically significant. This remains true when the equation is reestimated with a second-order autocorrelation correction (equation (4.7)) and by an instrumental variable procedure (equation (4.8)).

However, the combination of instrumental variable estimation and a first-order autocorrelation correction (Fair's method) does result (equation (4.9)) in coefficients for the U.S. and German interest variables that are both absolutely about 0.04 but with the appropriate opposite signs. More specifically, the coefficient of the real U.S. rate is 0.046 (with a standard error of 0.024) while the coefficient of real German rate is −0.037 (with a standard error of 0.024).

As an alternative to the rolling ARIMA procedure, I have also used a simpler method that may correspond more closely to the way that market participants used past inflation experience to form judgments about the future. In place of the ARIMA estimate of inflation, I use a weighted average of inflation, giving a weight of 0.5 to the most recent year's inflation, of 0.33 to the inflation of the previous year's inflation and of 0.17 to the inflation of the year before that. On that basis, the expected inflation came down gradually in Germany from 4.5 percent in 1980 to 4.3 percent in 1981 and 1982, 3.8 percent in 1983, and 2.8 percent in 1984, and real German long-term rates in the 1980–84 period stayed between 4.0 and 5.0 percent except for a 6.1 percent rate in 1981.

Table 5 presents the results based on this simpler specification of expected inflation. The OLS estimates (equations (5.1) and (5.2)) are similar to the estimates with the ARIMA inflation forecast: a coefficient of 0.055 with a standard error of 0.035. The instrumental variable estimates (equations (5.3) and (5.4)) show a more substantial coefficient and a smaller standard error of regression measures than the ARIMA forecast. With the AR1 correction (i.e., using Fair's method), the coefficient of the interest differential is 0.081 with a standard error of 0.031. This is approximately twice the typical estimate based on the ARIMA inflation forecast. Dividing the interest differential into a real U.S. rate and a real German rate (equation (5.5)) results in a coefficient of 0.072 (with a standard error of 0.025) for the U.S. real rate but a very small and statistically insignificant coefficient of 0.003 (with a standard error of 0.032) for the German real rate, possibly because there was very little variation in the measured real rate for Germany.

In short, the different specifications of the real interest differentials and the different estimation methods indicate that each percentage point difference in real interest rates raises the real exchange rate by between 0.04 and 0.08 points, an impact that accounts for only a small part of the rise in the exchange rate that actually occurred in the 1980s and also only a small part of the rise in the exchange rate that is predicted by the changes in the expected budget deficits and in monetary policy. It is difficult to tell whether this is because the real interest differential is measured very badly (causing a substantial underestimate of the true coefficient) or because the budget deficit and monetary policy have direct effects on the exchange rate that are not channeled through the real interest differential.

Table 5 REAL INTEREST* DIFFERENTIALS AND THE DM-DOLLAR EXCHANGE RATE

		Interest Rates minus Predicted Inflation						
Equation	*Estimation Method*	*RUS-RG (1)*	*RUS (2)*	*RG (3)*	*Constant (4)*	U_{-1}	$\bar{R}^2$ *(SER)*	*DWS*
5.1	OLS	0.055			1.31		0.45	0.84
		(0.035)					(0.16)	
5.2	OLS	0.055			1.32	0.69	0.62	1.36
	AR1	(0.035)				(0.78)	(0.14)	
5.3	IV	0.097			1.32		NA	0.91
		(0.029)					(0.17)	
5.4	IV	0.081			1.33	0.58	NA	1.50
	AR1	(0.031)				(0.24)	(0.15)	
5.5	IV		0.072	0.003	1.04	0.75	NA	0.83
	AR1		(0.025)	(0.033)		(0.17)	(0.12)	

*Real interest is interest minus distributed lag inflation.

The dependent variable is the real DM-dollar exchange rate (DMs per dollar, adjusted for GNP deflators) normalized at 1.0 = 1980. Equations estimated for 1973 to 1984. Standard errors are shown in parentheses. See text for explanation of variables.

7. Concluding Comments

The findings of the current research can be summarized briefly. The estimated reduced-form equations for the dollar-DM real exchange rate imply that the rise in the expected future deficits in the budget of the U.S. government had a powerful effect on the exchange rate between the dollar and the German mark. Each one percentage point increase in the ratio of future budget deficits to GNP increases the exchange rate by about thirty percentage points.

Changes in the growth of the monetary base also affect the exchange rate, but the estimated effect of the deficit does not depend on whether this is taken into account in the estimation procedure.

The analysis also indicates that the changes in tax rules and in the inflation-tax interaction that altered the corporate demand for funds did not have any discernible effect on the exchange rate. The presence or absence of alternative tax variables did not alter the estimated effect of the budget deficit.

The estimated effect of the budget deficit is also relatively insensitive to the other variables that were included in the regression equation.

As I have emphasized elsewhere in a different context (Feldstein 1982), all models are "false" in the sense that they involve substantial simplifications that can lead to incorrect inferences. It is impossible to relax all of the specification constraints or include all of the plausible variables in any single model. We learn about reality only by examining a variety of alternative false models to see which implications of these models are robust. In the present study, I was eager to focus on the question of whether changes in the expected budget deficit could account for shifts in the real exchange rate and, if so, whether this was a spurious relation that was really reflecting a more fundamental relationship between the exchange rate and tax rules, monetary policy, inflation, German budget deficits, or unobservable characteristics of the 1980s that strengthened the dollar. Although any econometric study leaves room for doubt and uncertainty, I believe that the current evidence shifts the burden of proof to those who would claim that deficits do not matter or that tax, monetary, or "confidence" variables were the real reasons for the dollar's strength since 1980.

There are of course a number of things that have been omitted from the analysis that deserve attention in future studies. It would be good to model the changing behavior of expected European budget deficits or, even more generally, the changing balance between the supply and demand for funds in Europe. There are a number of difficulties in doing so, including the problem of establishing the "full employment" level at which to estimate structural deficits in the face of Europe's rapidly rising unemployment and the much larger and more ambiguous role of public investment in Europe.

U.S. budget deficits have been defined without correction for the inflation erosion of the public debt on the implicit assumption that, at the observed rates of inflation, individuals did not adjust their saving but treated the inflation component of the interest on the public debt as income.

Shifts in the price of oil were ignored in the present study although they presumably affected the equilibrium exchange rate between the DM and the dollar. It should be possible to extend the analysis to include the price of oil and other raw materials.

Finally, in future work I plan to extend the analysis to include 1985 and the decline of the dollar. The sharp rise in the dollar-DM ratio that climaxed in the early spring of 1985 may have had some unsustainable speculative element (as Krugman's 1985 analysis implies) but the decline of more than 20 percent in the dollar-DM ratio between mid-1984 and the present time is, I believe, quite in line with what would have been expected on the basis of the fall in expected future budget deficits.

As participants in financial markets studied the action of Congress in the spring and early summer of 1985, there was growing confidence that some significant action would be taken to reduce future budget deficits. The Congressional Budget Office summarized this in August when it contrasted the current services deficits of 5.1 percent of GNP each year from 1986 to 1990 with the results of the Congressional Budget Resolution that brought the projected deficits onto a path that declined to 3.0 percent of GNP in 1988 and 2.1 percent in 1990. The Gramm-Rudman amendment gave the markets even greater confidence that budget deficits would continue to decline in the future.

The estimated ratio of the expected 5-year structural deficit to potential GNP has declined from 3.3 percent in 1984 (the last observation in the sample) to about 2.6 percent in early 1986. An estimated coefficient of 0.25 to 0.40 would imply a decline in the dollar from this source alone of between 18 and 28 points. In fact, as of mid-February 1986, the dollar-DM ratio was down 23 points in comparison to its 1984 average value and 32 points from its high in early 1985.

There is substantial room for additional research on the determinants of the exchange rate. But the massive fiscal experiment of the past six years should have convinced us that sustained shifts in the federal government's deficit have powerful effects on the value of the dollar.

Table A-1 TIME SERIES REGRESSION VARIABLES

Year	*DM-Dollar Index (1)*	*DEFEX (2)*	*DEFALT (3)*	*MPRIR (4)*	*MPRNR (5)*	*MBGRO (6)*	*MIGRO (7)*	*INFEX (8)*	*GNPGRO (9)*	*NIIP (10)*	*DEFEXG (11)*	*MBGROG (12)*
1973	1.208	1.802	1.802	3.500	5.800	8.348	5.756	4.500	5.198	11.659	−1.220	10.637
1974	1.189	1.829	1.829	4.100	5.000	8.091	4.761	7.500	−0.539	10.893	−1.820	6.121
1975	1.166	1.808	1.808	5.300	5.100	7.681	5.014	9.700	−1.257	11.171	−2.180	7.843
1976	1.211	1.651	1.651	4.400	6.000	7.520	6.141	5.800	4.887	10.251	−2.000	9.245
1977	1.140	1.519	1.623	4.400	6.000	8.045	8.122	6.000	4.666	8.453	−2.040	8.975
1978	1.015	1.577	1.615	4.600	5.900	9.302	8.222	6.400	5.293	6.793	−1.960	8.468
1979	0.968	1.790	1.636	5.500	6.100	8.368	7.532	7.000	2.478	6.053	−1.520	8.485
1980	1.000	2.335	1.753	6.000	5.900	8.169	7.477	7.600	−0.166	5.626	−0.720	4.831
1981	1.310	2.821	2.821	8.300	7.200	6.432	5.134	8.000	1.936	5.243	0.220	4.421
1982	1.430	3.247	3.247	7.700	7.500	6.852	8.747	7.000	−2.549	4.801	1.240	4.933
1983	1.511	3.377	3.377	7.100	7.500	9.483	10.387	5.600	3.449	3.116	1.960	7.309
1984	1.716	3.330	3.330	4.900	7.300	8.142	5.221	5.500	6.619	−0.036	2.400	4.769

Table A-2 INTEREST AND INFLATION TIME SERIES OBSERVATIONS

Year	*IUS* (1)	*IG* (2)	*INFPUS ARIMA* (3)	*INFPG ARIMA* (4)	*INFPUS PAST* (5)	*INFPG PAST* (6)
1973	6.868	9.323	4.500	4.869	5.093	6.313
1974	7.802	10.383	7.500	5.494	7.037	6.555
1975	7.766	8.483	9.700	6.101	8.535	6.405
1976	7.179	7.800	5.800	6.125	7.173	4.982
1977	6.990	6.158	6.000	5.603	6.193	4.062
1978	8.318	5.733	6.400	5.284	6.500	3.990
1979	9.518	7.425	7.000	4.902	7.770	4.053
1980	11.478	8.500	7.600	4.812	8.725	4.462
1981	14.236	10.383	8.000	4.495	9.324	4.288
1982	13.006	8.950	7.000	4.050	7.751	4.320
1983	10.796	7.892	5.600	4.048	5.520	3.802
1984	12.241	7.775	5.500	3.874	4.159	2.771

IUS = yield on 5-year government bonds;
IG = yield on long-term German government bonds;
INFPUS (ARIMA) = U.S. inflation predicted by ARIMA method;
INFPG (ARIMA) = German inflation predicted by ARIMA method;
INFPUS (PAST) = U.S. inflation predicted by average of past values;
INFPG (PAST) = German inflation predicted by average of past values.

I am grateful to Andrew Berg for help with this work and to Rudiger Dornbusch, Jeffrey Frankel, Paul Krugman and Jeffrey Sachs for discussions about this subject.

REFERENCES

Barro, R. 1974. Are government bonds net wealth? *Journal of Political Economy* (November). 82: 1095–118.

Blanchard, O. 1985. Debts, deficits and finite horizons. *Journal of Political Economy* 93 (April): 223–47.

Blanchard, O., and L. Summers. 1985. Perspectives on high world real interest rates. *Brookings Papers on Economic Activity* 273–324.

Branson, W. 1985. Causes of appreciation and volatility of the dollar. NBER Working Paper 1777.

Dornbusch, R. 1976. Expectations and exchange rate dynamics. *Journal of Political Economy* (December). 84: 1161–76.

———. 1983. Comment on floating exchange rates after ten years. *Brookings Papers on Economic Activity* 1983: 1

Evans, P. 1985. Do large deficits produce high interest rates?" *American Economic Review* 75 (March): 68–87.

———. 1986. Is the dollar high because of large budget deficits? *Journal of Monetary Economics.* Forthcoming.

Feldstein, M. 1982. Inflation, tax rules and investment: Some econometric evidence. (The 1980 Fisher-Schultz Lecture of the Econometric Society), *Econometrica* 50(4): 825–62.

———. 1983. Why the dollar is strong. In *Foreign Exchange Value of the Dollar,*

Hearings Before the Committee on Banking, Finance and Monetary Policy, House of Representatives, October 1985 (reprinted in *Challenge Magazine*, 1984).
———. 1985. American economic policy and the world economy. *Foreign Affairs* 63 (Summer): 995–1008.
———. 1986a. U.S. budget deficits and the European economies: Resolving the political economic puzzle. *American Economic Review* 76 (May).
———. 1986b. Budget deficits, tax rules and real interest rates. NBER Working Paper (Forthcoming).
Feldstein, M., and P. Bacchetta. 1986. U.S. budget deficits and European unemployment: The German experience. Forthcoming.
Feldstein, M., and L. Summers. 1978. Inflation, tax rules and the long-term interest rate. *Brookings Papers on Economic Activity* 1 (January): 61–99.
Feldstein, M., and J. Jun. 1986. The effects of tax rules on nonresidential fixed investment: Some preliminary evidence from the 1980s. Forthcoming in M. Feldstein, ed., *Taxation and Capital Formation*.
Frankel, J. 1979. On the mark: A theory of floating exchange rates based on real interest differentials. *American Economic Review* 69 (September): 610–22.
———. 1982. A test of perfect substitutability in the foreign exchange market. *Southern Economic Journal* 49 (October): 406–16.
———. 1985. Causes of appreciation and volatility of the dollar. NBER Working Paper 1377.
Frenkel, J., and A. Razin. 1984. The international transmission of fiscal error and budget deficits in the world economy. NBER Working Paper 1527.
———. 1986. The international transmission and effects of fiscal policies. NBER Working Paper 1799.
Hooper, P. 1985. International repercussions of the U.S. budget deficit. Brookings Discussion Paper 27 (February).
Hutchinson, M., and A. Throop. 1985. U.S. budget deficits and the real value of the dollar. *Economic Review of the Federal Reserve Bank of San Francisco*, Fall.
Krugman, P. 1985. Is the strong dollar sustainable? NBER Working Paper 1644.
McKinnon, R. 1984. *An international standard for monetary stabilization*. Policy Analyses in International Economics No. 8, *Institute for International Economics*.
Meese, R., and K. Rogoff. 1983. Empirical exchange rate models of the seventies: Do they fit out of sample? *Journal of International Economics* 14: 3–24.
———. 1985. Was it real? The exchange rate–interest differential relation, 1973–1984. NBER Working Paper 1732.
Obstfeld, M. 1985. Floating exchange rates: Experience and prospects. *Brookings Papers on Economic Activity* 2: 369–450.
Plosser, C. 1982. Government financing decisions and asset returns. *Journal of Monetary Economics* 9 (May): 325–52.
Price, R. W. R. and P. Muller. 1984. Structural budget indicators and the interpretation of fiscal policy stance in OECD economies. In *OECD Economic Studies* 3 (Autumn).
Sachs, J. 1985. The dollar and the policy mix: 1985. NBER Working Paper 1636. Forthcoming in *Brookings Papers on Economic Activity*.
Sinai, A. 1985. The dollar and inflation. *Economic Studies Series*, Shearson Lehman Brothers, Inc. (November). (Reprinted from the *Eastern Economic Journal*, Proceedings: Eleventh Annual Conference, July/August 1985.)

Comment

RUDIGER DORNBUSCH
Massachusetts Institute of Technology

In the area of international economics Feldstein never fails to be provocative. In his analysis of the integration of international capital markets (Feldstein and Horioka (1980)) he posed a puzzle that still stands unanswered. This article is in much the same tradition: it explores the Feldstein doctrine according to which budget deficits translate into currency appreciation, the Mitterand experiment notwithstanding. Of course, this time the shock is more on Washington rather than the professional audience. The effect is familiar from the Mundell-Flemming model (Mundell (1963)) which remains, with suitable extensions, the ruling paradigm of textbook open-economy macroeconomics.

Feldstein's article takes the Mundell-Flemming paradigm and tries to quantify it in the context of the dollar-DM exchange rate. What is the impact on the level of the exchange rate of an extra dollar of prospective budget deficits? Are budget deficits, not safe haven and monetary effects, the primary explanation for the strong dollar in 1981–85? This is really an important issue, one that quantitative international economics has simply failed to address. Almost all the work concentrates on interest rates and money, and virtually no one has paid attention to the quantitative plausibility of the Mundell-Flemming result, even in those cases where the policy mix is in fact the central focus of the analysis.

HYPOTHESES

Feldstein reviews four hypotheses for the strong dollar: safe haven arguments, interest rate differentials, capital investment profitability effects and the proper Feldstein doctrine. *Safe Haven:* Feldstein does not think much of the safe haven hypothesis. The evidence is primarily anecdotal: what changed between Carter's hostage crisis and the U.S. invasion of Grenada? Is the perception that Carter was a loser and Reagan a winner at all relevant to international portfolio choice? It seems to me that the relevant question must be what, if any, the link between these political perceptions and the dollar would be. Suppose that in fact the United States was perceived as the place in the sun, does that necessarily mean a stronger dollar must result? Is the implication of a politically stronger United States that people will shift into nominal dollar assets at a reduced risk premium, or into U.S. stocks, or that they choose to locate their assets in the U.S. jurisdiction? And does a stronger United States mean that the allies—Germany and the U.K., for example, are weaker?

The answers to these questions are not obvious. It certainly is not the case that the risk premium on U.S. assets fell in this period. On the contrary, the relative rates of return in the United States increased. But Feldstein apparently does not see the one point where safe haven effects are in fact appropriate. He argues that the absence of large shifts in direct investment and the predominance of a reversal of banking flows argues against the safe haven hypothesis. However, banking flows are the only area where safe haven arguments really apply: LDC loans were becoming politically risky when it beame conceivable that insolvent debtors might elect to default.

Although I also do not have any evidence to support my belief I do agree with Feldstein that interest rates and fundamentals remain the chief magnet for capital flows, particularly for crazy money. There is really no difference between the Argentine experience under Martinez de Hoz and our own under Secretary Regan.

Real Interest Rates Feldstein makes much of the point that theory establishes a link between *long-term* real interest differentials and the exchange rate, not short-term differentials. That point is, I think, exaggerated or actually wrong, depending on the vigor with which it is advocated. If capital mobility is taken to be perfect, portfolio holders will bring about equalization of nominal rates adjusted for anticipated depreciation:

$$i = i^* + e \quad (1)$$

where i, i^* and e denote home and foreign nominal interest rates and the anticipated rate of depreciation. Subtracting national inflation rates (π^*, π) on both sides and using the definition of the rate of change of the *real* exchange rate, $\dot{q} \equiv \dot{e} + \pi^* - \pi$ we have a relation between real interest rates:

$$r = r^* + \dot{q}. \quad (2)$$

We supplement this model with an adjustment equation for the actual real exchange rate to the long-run equilibrium rate, $\bar{q}$,

$$\dot{q} = \alpha(\bar{q} - q). \quad (3)$$

Such an equation arises in models such as Dornbusch (1976) from the gradual adjustment of prices. Combining equations (2) and (3) then yields the link between the real exchange rate and real interest rates:

$$q = \bar{q} - \beta(r - r^*); \beta \equiv 1/\alpha. \quad (4)$$

This model thus establishes a link between the movement of the equilibrium real exchange rate and the real interest differential over time. The more rapid the adjustment of the real exchange rate as measured by the size of α the smaller the impact of short-term real interest rate disturbances on the equilibrium real exchange rate. Clearly the theory can be stated in terms of short-term differentials.

But it is essential to recognize that the model developed here emerges when we consider exclusively the path of real interest rates and real exchange rates in response to a permanent monetary disturbance. When fiscal disturbances are considered, equation (4) no longer applies. This point is easily sketched for the case of a transitory fiscal expansion in the extended Mundell-Flemming model.[1] Figure 1 shows the schedule $\dot{e} = 0$ along which the price level is such that home real balances are at a level at which the equilibrium interest rate is equal to that abroad. Along $\dot{p} = 0$ the goods market clears with government spending at its long-run level. An unanticipated, transitory increase in demand for dometsic goods due to higher government spending leads to an immediate appreciation from E to E'. Then, over time, as government spending falls off the real exchange rate depreciates until in long-run equilibrium it returns to its initial level.

Note that now there is no longer a simple link between interest differentials and the *level* of the real exchange rate as in equation (4). The initial level and the pace of decline of the level of government spending will appear as determinants of the real exchange rate. In fact, at point E' the real interest rate at home has declined while the level of the real exchange rate has appreciated and is appreciating. The real exchange rate in this extended model then becomes a function not only of monetary variables but also of the prospective path of fiscal variables.

The problems encountered in identifying an interest differential–exchange rate relation in empirical work presumably reflects the role played by other variables, including fiscal shocks, in the exchange rate–interest rate relation. This point is, of course, reinforced if imperfect sub-

1. The model explored here is Dornbusch (1976) with the addition of an equation for real government spending on domestic goods. It is assumed that government spending follows the simple rule $g = -\rho(g - g)$ where g denotes long-run government spending.

stitutability between assets is the rule, as Feldstein believes is the case. In that event interest rate movements may simply represent risk premiums rather than excess returns. They tell us little except that their determinants—relative asset supplies and the stochastic structure—are a necessary part of the model.

Channels of Transmission Feldstein's article leaves no doubt that fiscal deficits will lead to appreciation of the real exchange rate. But little effort is made to identify the exact channels that bring about this result.

In the argument above, fiscal policy affects the real exchange rate *exclusively* via its effect on demand. There is no room for the impact of debt accumulation, debt service, crowding out, or all the other possible chan-

Figure 1 THE EFFECTS OF TRANSITORY GOVERNMENT SPENDING

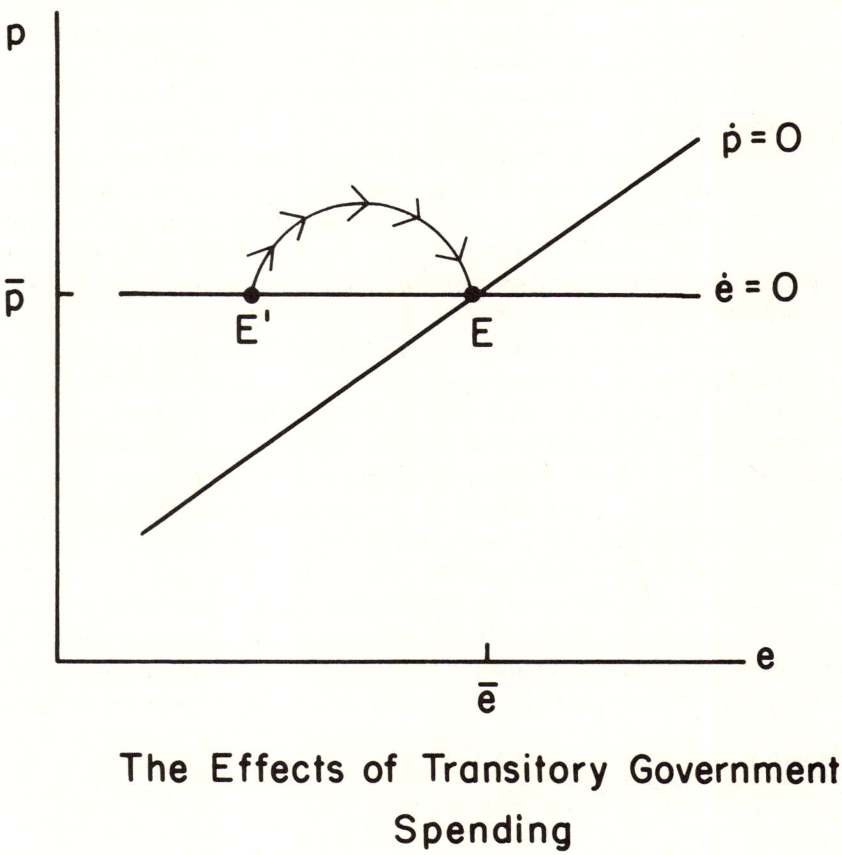

nels. In this very simplified model fiscal policy has entirely unambiguous effects. But once we go to more complicated models that is no longer the case.

Work by Dornbusch and Fischer (1980), Hooper and Morton (1982), Sachs and Wyplosz (1984) and Frankel (1982) has focused on other channels. First, the accumulation of debt will bring about a future service burden. While current resources are attracted from abroad to meet an increase in demand, and thus lead to appreciation, in the future demand will be reduced and accumulated debt will require servicing. Thus in the future there will be real depreciation. This consideration brings up the question of the persistence of the initial real appreciation.

In forward-looking asset markets more persistent deficits require ultimately larger trade surpluses and thus, other things being equal, larger real depreciation. But forward-looking asset holders also recognize that more persistent deficits imply ultimately larger taxes and that might dampen their current spending, reducing the need for crowding out via the real exchange rate. On the other hand, if they are Blanchard-style taxpayers they expect that more distant fiscal correction means that most of the bill ultimately will be paid by someone else, thus reducing the offsetting impact of prospective taxes on demand. Does the conjunction of all these channels mean that the initial real appreciation will be smaller the more persistent the fiscal expansion?

So far nothing has been said about the impact of debt accumulation per se on interest rates. Feldstein makes much of this point, but it is not obvious where it comes from. Is it that government deficit finance raises the *relative* supply of domestic securities and hence the required risk premium? Or is the increase in interest rates the result of increased demand at full employment in a world of perfect asset substitution? The answer is very important. It is quite possible that deficit finance may not involve any appreciation if, in one case, the financing is done by issuing foreign debt, and in the other, if the deficit involves increased demand for foreign goods. If the deficits vary significantly in their makeup, financing, and persistence it might be hopeless to get any significant relation between deficits and exchange rates.

The same considerations apply to Feldstein's argument that increased profitability of investment should lead to appreciation. Does the increased spending fall on domestic or foreign goods? What is the distribution of adjustment between world interest rates and real exchange rates? If the investment opportunities increase the future supply of U.S. output beyond the increase in demand, they will bring about an ultimate real depreciation. Why then should the adjustment be one of appreciation followed by depreciation rather than a sharp increase in world interest rates even combined with an initial real depreciation? Theoretically there is absolutely no presumption unless one believes that current demand effects dominate because goods are very imperfect substitutes and demand in each country falls nearly exclusively on domestic goods so that transfer problems predominate. But such a world where the future matters very little is clearly not one that would be very congenial to Feldstein. All this is to say that while he has an unshakeable faith in the budget-exchange rate link, theory is not so firmly on his side although the facts may well be.

EMPIRICAL EVIDENCE

The central point of the article is the empirical evidence in support of the Feldstein doctrine. Here it is shown that a five-year forward-looking measure of U.S. budget deficits appears as a sturdily significant explanatory variable in a dollar-DM real exchange rate equation. Other explanatory variables such as the Reagan-Dummy, the net foreign investment position, money growth and inflation forecasts round out the equation, though with less striking significance. If the point of the article is to demonstrate *the* central role of budget deficits in explaining the dollar appreciation a full success might be claimed.

I will not dwell on the obvious problems: the U.S. foreign investment position, counting direct investment at book value, makes little sense and changes in it are hard to link to the exchange rate. Monetary growth certainly is not exogeneous and certainly is not a good predictor of inflation in periods of vast velocity shocks.

The chief problem of the empirical tests is the predominant use of U.S. variables alone to explain the dollar-DM rate. European deficits too should affect the exchange rate. Why then not introduce symmetry at least? This point is obvious. No one would argue that the steep appreciation of the dollar in 1923 was due to the Mellon tax cuts rather than the German hyperinflation. It might be argued in the present context that concentration on the United States and omission of Europe (except for Germany in Feldstein's table 3) is justified because one is studying the *real* exchange rate and because disturbances are primarily those in the United States. But of course that is completely wrong. Fiscal disturbances abroad were almost as large as in the United States, but of opposite sign. Table 1 shows the changes in cyclically adjusted budget deficits for Germany, the U.S. and Japan in the past five years.

The Feldstein doctrine is certainly reinforced if we look at our deficits and those abroad. It would have been an embarrassment if table 1 had showed that there were even larger shifts in structural deficits abroad in the *same* direction as in the United States. Of course, data problems with past, current, and future structural deficits especially in Europe make it difficult to test the hypothesis in a more symmetric fashion, but the point cannot be neglected. This would be far more important at the present time than the odd one- or two-percentage-point differential in inflation or the prospective changes in the profitability of investment.

The fact that foreign deficits (not only German) matter just as much as our own is brought out in the research by Hutchinson and Throop (1985) which pursues exactly the same issue of a deficit-exchange rate link. Table 2 shows their results for the multilateral U.S. real exchange rate (REX), using the real interest differential, $R - R^*$, and U.S. as well as foreign structural budget deficits, B and B^* respectively, as explanatory variables.

The results in table 2 strongly support the Feldstein doctrine. A rise in U.S. deficits leads to real appreciation of the *multilateral* real exchange rate, a rise in foreign deficits to real depreciation of the dollar. The real interest differential also appears as a significant determinant of the real exchange rate. It is interesting to note from table 2 that the results do not come exclusively from the post-1980 period of U.S. fiscal expansion. The results are present also for the shorter sample period ending before the Reagan deficits got under way. Moreover, the coefficients do not change much between these periods.

Table 1 CUMULATIVE CHANGE IN ADJUSTED BUDGET DEFICIT: 1980–85 (Percent of GNP)

Germany	*Japan*	*United States*
−4.2	−3.2	4.5

Source. OECD *Economic Outlook,* various issues.

Table 2 THE HUTCHINSON-THROOP FINDINGS ($REX = a_0 + a_1 (R^* - R) + a_2B + a_3B^*$)

Period	a_0	a_1	a_2	a_3	R^2	Rho
1974–81:4	4.59	3.4	−4.3	2.96	0.88	0.59
	(85.4)	(3.7)	(−3.05)	(2.11)		
1974–84:3	4.61	3.46	−4.48	3.22	0.97	0.62
	(191.4)	(4.49)	(−7.6)	(3.12)		

t-statistics in parentheses.

Source. Hutchinson and Throop (1985, p. 36)

The reason for the good performance in the earlier period is in part the behavior of the yen and Japanese deficits. In the period 1975–78 the yen appreciated relative to the dollar in real terms by 40 percent as a result (among other factors, perhaps) of a shift in the Japanese structural budget toward deficit in the cumulative amount of 5.7 percent. In the following period, 1979–84, the Japanese structural budget improved by 3.5 percent accompanied by a 33 percent appreciation.

The case of Japan, and no doubt others, raises interesting questions about the multilateral effects of a country's fiscal policies: Does a Japanese fiscal expansion lead to an across-the-board appreciation against all currencies in roughly the same proportion or are there significant intercountry differences? In the U.S. case that question is of interest because in 1982–84 the yen remained relatively constant, our fiscal expansion notwithstanding. This point is well worth exploring in an explicit multicountry estimation where a number of countries' real exchange rate responses to fiscal shocks of other countries would be studied.

This then raises the research agenda of testing the multilateral fiscal effects by looking at the real exchange rate equations of various countries, perhaps in a seemingly unrelated regression to see whether fiscal policies have significant effects on the pattern of multilateral rates or merely a uniform impact on the rate of the expanding or contracting countries. To some extent such work is already implicit in the Federal Reserve's multilateral exchange rate model and in other aggregative models of the world economy.[2]

A second question of great interest is to know why real exchange rate movements are so closely associated with current shifts in fiscal policy. Why did the dollar decline in 1985, as Gramm-Rudman got under way, and not in 1984 when the recognition of unsustainable deficits was dawning? In the same way why did the yen appreciate right up to 1978, until fiscal policy turned around, rather than stopping much earlier in recognition that deficits will ultimately be trimmed? Does this suggest that the current demand aspect is very important or does it tell us something of the way people form expectations about the prospective path of deficits? This, of course, is an important issue and one would have liked some more exploration in Feldstein's empirical analysis. The five-year rule that he has imposed on the deficit variable is short if reckoned by one's expected lifetime as a taxpayer and long if judged by short-run Keynesian considerations.

2. See Hooper (1985), Masson et al. (1985), Masson and Knight (1985) and van Wijnbergen (1985).

CONCLUDING REMARKS

Two issues, I believe, receive inadequate treatment. The first concerns real interest rates. The high level of domestic long-run real interest rates is attributed to fiscal expansion. The alternative hypothesis is that monetary stabilization has frozen real balances at low levels. In the Volcker deflation monetary growth was not allowed to blip the real money stock back to normal levels. Moreover such blips are not anticipated and hence the entire time path of future real interest rates is affected by the recent past of monetary policy. In this view fiscal policy is less important for real interest rates and price stickiness assumes central importance for real exchange rates and the current account.

The other point concerns Feldstein's research methodology—testing "false" models. At one level this is inevitable. We will never be able to test the complete, all-encompassing model. Hence *any* econometric work in fact is testing false models. But there must be lower bounds on such testing. Without such minimal standards we really have absolutely no idea what the estimated coefficients might mean.

It is comforting to know that there is empirical support for the Feldstein doctrine. Mundell's research strategy was to judge the empirical success of a theory by its theoretical plausibility. Feldstein comes from the other side and has offered support for the openness of the U.S. economy. This opens up the task of identifying in much greater detail the particular channels of these fiscal effects.

REFERENCES

Dornbusch, R. 1976. Expectations and exchange rate dynamics. *Journal of Political Economy* (December). 84: 1161–76.

Dornbusch, R. and S. Fischer. 1980. Exchange rates and the current account. *American Economic Review* (December)

Feldstein, M. and C. Horioka. 1980. Domestic saving and international capital flows. *Economic Journal*

Frankel, J. 1982. A test of perfect substitutability in the foreign Exchange market. *Southern Economic Journal* (October)

Hooper, P. 1985. Summary description and analysis of comparative model simulations. Board of Governors of the Federal Reserve System. Manuscript.

Hooper, P. and J. Morton. 1982. Fluctuations in the dollar: A model of nominal and real exchange rate determination. *Journal of International Money and Finance.*

Hutchinson, M. and A. Throop. 1985. U.S. budget deficits and the real value of the dollar. Federal Reserve Bank of San Francisco, *Economic Review* No. 4, Fall.

Masson, P. et al. 1984. Domestic and international effects of government spending under rational expectations. *OECD Economic Studies*, No. 3, Autumn.

Masson, P. and M. Knight. 1985. Fiscal policies, net saving and real exchange

rates: The United States, the Federal Republic and Japan. Paper presented at the NBER Conference "International Aspects of Fiscal Policy."
Mundell, R. A. 1963. Capital mobility stabilization policy under fixed and flexible exchange rates. *Canadian Journal of Economics* (November)
Sachs, J. and C. Wyplosz. 1984. Real exchange rate effects of fiscal policy. NBER Working Paper 1255.

Comment

ALAN C. STOCKMAN
University of Rochester and NBER

The thesis of Martin Feldstein's article is that current and prospective government budget deficits in the United States were the main cause of the appreciation of the dollar on foreign exchange markets from 1980 to 1985. According to him, the high budget deficits were responsible for high real interest rates in the United States, and a high real interest rate differential between the United States and the rest of the world. The appreciation of the dollar is supposed to have resulted from this interest rate differential.

The main evidence presented in the article consists of regressions of the real exchange rate (the exchange-rate-adjusted ratio of price levels, measured by GNP deflators) between the United States and Germany on a measure of the budget deficit in the United States and a set of other variables. The estimated effect of the deficit on the real exchange rate is strong and robust to inclusion or exclusion of other variables; the effects of other variables on the real exchange rate are weaker. The picture of a strong piece of evidence emerges. The major shortcoming of this evidence (acknowledged by Feldstein) is that the regression covers only twelve annual observations, from 1973 to 1984 (and only a single pair of countries, the United States and Germany).

I will argue in these comments that (1) the evidence presented by Feldstein may be spurious and is in conflict with other evidence; (2) the evidence regarding the effect of a budget deficit on the real exchange rate combines two different effects, one from changes in government spending and the other from changes in tax revenue; and (3) the theoretical argument outlined by Feldstein raises serious problems. Finally, one could be more confident in the empirical results if they could be replicated (a) over a longer period of time for the same country pair, (b) with time-series data for other country pairs, and (c) if they were consistent with cross-sectional evidence (i.e., if, at a given time, countries with larger budget deficits tended to have currencies that are valued above estimates from purchasing power parity). One could have greater confidence in the interpretation of the results—as a response to the deficit per se rather than to changes in government expenditure (regardless of the method of finance) or changes in tax revenue (regardless of the use of that revenue)—if the results were robust against separate inclusion of government spending (or tax revenue). I will argue that, based on these criteria, our confidence in the results and the interpretation must be low. Indeed, some evidence indicates a contrary result.

Spurious results are easy to obtain in a time series of twelve annual observations, particularly if—as in this case—the main variation in the data consists of a single change from a relatively stable real exchange rate between 1973 to 1980 and a fairly steady dollar appreciation beginning in 1980.

Feldstein uses a 5-year forward moving average of the (projected) budget deficit in his equations, on the ground that the real exchange rate and real interest differential are affected by long-run budget deficits and not simply by temporary deficits. This general point (insofar as it concerns the interest rate) comes from theoretical models such as Blanchard (1985). That model would predict something other than a 5-year moving average as the appropriate measure, but the difference is probably unimportant. The deficit, however, is highly correlated with changes in government purchases over this period of time, particularly national defense outlays. It is likely that defense outlays (or total government purchases) would provide about an equally good statistical explanation of changes in the value of the dollar over this period of time as does the deficit.

Government spending, or defense outlays, may not be merely a spurious variable. There are good theoretical reasons to expect that changes in government spending affect the real exchange rate. Moreover, some statistical evidence indicates that the effect is empirically important, and that it is changes in government spending rather than changes in the deficit that affect the real exchange rate.

Changes in government spending (such as defense spending) can have a direct effect on the real exchange rate by shifting demands from foreign to domestic goods (if that is what the government purchases) and thereby altering equilibrium relative prices. Because of the durability of many of the goods that the government purchases, an increase in anticipated future defense outlays will have an immediate impact on relative prices. This suggests that a longer-term moving average of government purchases (and not simply the level over a quarter or a year) would affect the real exchange rate. Therefore, a moving average of current and prospective future levels of defense spending, rather than the current annual level, might be the appropriate concept for empirical purposes.

Paul Evans (1986) has recently examined quarterly changes in the exchange rate between the United States and seven other OECD countries over the same time period as Feldstein's study. When changes in real government spending and the deficit are simultaneously included in an equation for the exchange rate, his estimates show a sizable and statistically significant effect of higher government spending, leading to real appreciation, and a coefficient on the budget deficit that is *opposite in sign* from Feldstein's estimates and sometimes statistically significant. Evans's results show a larger U.S. deficit, given real government spending, leading to a dollar *de*preciation. When Evans included foreign variables in his equations, he found that greater foreign government spending leads to dollar depreciation and greater foreign deficits lead to dollar appreciation, with the estimated effects of U.S. government spending and deficits remaining essentially unchanged.

Neither Feldstein nor Evans uses samples recent enough to include the 1985 depreciation of the dollar. One could argue that projections of a long-term fall in the deficit that emerged early in 1985 caused the depreciation. On the other hand, changes in prospective government spending, or in defense outlays alone, would probably also do as well as the deficit in explaining the depreciation of the dollar after February 1985. The fall in projected deficits, e.g., by the Congressional Budget Office, is predominantly a consequence of a fall in projected national defense outlays over the next five years.

Feldstein's equations, by including the budget deficit but not its separate components, confound changes in government expenditure, its composition, tax revenue, and the value of the existing stock of government debt due to changes in inflation and interest rates. Each of these components of changes in the deficit may have—in theory—different effects on the real exchange rate. As noted, there is some evidence that the difference in the effects of spending and deficits is empirically important.

Feldstein criticizes Evans for using unexpected changes (measured as residuals from a vector autoregression) in his analysis, and for considering only current budget deficits rather than prospective future deficits. While Feldstein is correct that, in theory, prospective future deficits are important, the high autocorrelation of structural budget deficits as a fraction of trend or potential GNP (used by both Feldstein and Evans) reduces the empirical importance of the point. Unexpected increases in the current structural deficit probably make fair proxies for near-future structural deficits as well.

Even if it were necessary to use a measure of the deficit that directly incorporates prospective future deficits, it would be important to control for the components of the deficit in order to estimate a coefficient that has any chance of remaining stable over time and being subject to an unambiguous interpretation. A second piece of evidence, though, casts doubt on the importance of expected future deficits in an equation for the exchange rate: Evans found no evidence that changes in expected future deficits have an independent effect on the exchange rate.

The evidence for the period since 1973, therefore, does not necessarily support Feldstein's hypothesis. Furthermore, there is little reason to restrict ourselves to the period of flexible exchange rates to examine these issues. The effects of government budget deficits (or, more precisely, the effects of changes in government spending, tax receipts, etc.) on the *real* exchange rate can be examined using data over much longer periods of time and over a much larger cross-section of countries. The theories generally postulated, and outlined in Feldstein's article, about the effect of budget deficits on the real exchange rate, do not refer specifically to a regime of flexible *nominal* exchange rates. In particular, the postulated effect of U.S. government budget deficits on real interest rates in the United States is independent of the exchange rate system. Greater government borrowing to finance the deficit adds to demand on credit markets—and in the absence of Ricardian equivalence, raises the real interest rate—irrespective of the exchange rate system. Empirically, the existing evidence on Ricardian equivalence, i.e., the evidence regarding the effects of changes in the timing of taxes (holding fixed the path of spending) on interest rates, is mixed. The existing evidence regarding the effects of the timing of taxes on international interest rate differentials is even weaker.

In the theory outlined by Feldstein, high U.S. budget deficits raise real interest rates on dollar-denominated securities. These are imperfect substitutes for securities denominated in foreign currencies. So the interest rate differential between dollar-denominated assets and other assets rises with the relative stock of dollar-denominated assets. I have no quarrel with these arguments in the absence of Ricardian equivalence, though it should be noted that a temporary budget deficit has a permanent effect on the relative asset supplies, so that a subsequent reduction in the deficit need not reduce the yield differential. The assumption of imperfect substitutability between assets denominated in different currencies is a reasonable one, because the real rates of return on these assets are affected by inflation rates in each currency. Imperfect correlation of inflation across countries gives different risk properties to assets denominated in different currencies, so a change in the net supply of dollar-denominated assets should (in the absence of Ricardian equivalence) raise the yield differential.

But, the theory continues, the increase in the yield differential raises the value of the dollar. As Feldstein puts it, "the dollar must rise by enough so that its expected future fall just offsets the nominal yield differential between dollar securities and foreign assets." Now, empirically, it is difficult to believe that markets expected a major fall in the value of the dollar when the dollar appreciated in this period. No evidence for expected depreciation shows up in futures markets or forward markets for currencies. But there are also theoretical problems with the argument. The increase in the yield differential, in this theory, reflects a change in the terms on which the new stocks of assets will be willingly held. The yield differential, therefore, does not provide new opportunities for arbitrage between securities or new incentives for capital flows. In that sense, the differential in this theory is an equilibrium phenomenon. The same risk premium embodied in the yield differential shows up in the forward premium. The dollar may appreciate if the yield differential were to rise, for some reason, above its equilibrium value. But that is not what is stated in the theory, nor is it very plausible that substantial yield differentials could exist very long on well-integrated international financial markets (particularly between countries like Germany and the United States), unless they reflect differences in risk premia, taxes, or transactions costs. So even if higher budget deficits in the United States lead to higher interest rates and a larger international yield differential, this does not imply that the dollar appreciates.

Nor does the theory suggest that economists should restrict themselves to periods of flexible exchange rates to examine these issues. Additional evidence can be obtained by examining longer periods of time, for many countries, with various exchange rate systems. Only if the exchange rate system itself plays some role in the argument would economists want to limit themselves to one system or the other. That would be the case if price levels were sticky, so that the real exchange rate moves sluggishly in response to a deficit under pegged exchange rates (when the entire change in the real exchange rate must come from a change in price levels), while the real exchange rate can respond more rapidly to deficits under flexible exchange rates (because the nominal exchange rate can adjust). But, as I have argued elsewhere, the near-random-walk behavior of real (and nominal) exchange rates is inconsistent with models that postulate sticky prices or other slowly adjusting state variables. So it seems reasonable to expect that any effects of deficits on real exchange rates would show up in the data under various exchange rate systems; empirical studies need not be limited to the small samples of flexible exchange rates.

Additional evidence on the type of theory outlined by Feldstein can also be obtained by examining its other implications. For example, if high deficits in the United States lead to dollar appreciaton, that appreciation should reduce the profitability of U.S. exporting firms and import-competing firms, and raise the profitability of foreign firms exporting to the United States or competing with U.S. exports in their home market. These changes in profitability should be reflected in stock market values for these firms. But the evidence indicates a zero correlation, at all leads and lags, between (changes in) stock prices or returns and real exchange rates (see, for instance, Wasserfallen (1985). The evidence from the stock market, therefore, does not support any theory in which changes in real exchange rates are systematically related to changes in profitability of foreign or domestic firms. The absence of any systematic relationship could be explained by a model in which changes in the real exchange rate reflect changes in equilibrium relative prices, and in which the underlying economic disturbances are mixtures of shocks to supply and to demand. In that case, profitability and relative price are not systematically related, because positive demand disturbances raise the relative price and raise profitability while negative supply disturbances raise the relative price but may lower profitability. The stock market evidence, then, would suggest that changes in real exchange rates are not caused by deficits but by disturbances to demands and supplies for various goods, some of which may be due to changes in government expenditure.

Cross-sectionally, differences in real exchange rates are closely related to differences in real incomes. Countries with higher real incomes have higher prices than those predicted by purchasing power parity, while those with lower real incomes have lower prices. The evidence on changes in real exchange rates over time should be consistent with the cross-sectional evidence. That evidence could be usefully exploited in future research to supplement time-series studies over longer periods of time and across more countries than the study by Feldstein.

REFERENCES

Blanchard, O. 1985. Debt, deficits, and finite horizons. *Journal of Political Economy* 93 (April): 223–51.

Evans, P. 1986. Is the dollar high because of large budget deficits? *Journal of Monetary Economics*. Forthcoming.

Feldstein, M. 1986. The budget deficit and the dollar. *NBER Macroeconomics Annual 1986*. 1:355–92. Cambridge, Ma.: The MIT Press.

Wasserfallen, W. 1985. Expected and unexpected changes in nominal and real variables—Evidence from the capital markets. Universitat Bern, Switzerland. Unpublished.

Discussion

Feldstein agreed with Stockman and Dornbusch on the importance of looking at a broader group of countries. He stressed the significance of long-term interest rate differentials for exchange rates. Certainly all rates matter, but if interest rate differentials hold only at the short end, expected exchange rate changes will be very small. He would have preferred running nested hypothesis tests, but that was difficult with only fourteen observations. In answer to Dornbusch, he commented that the results on the effects of expected deficits are remarkably insensitive to the choice of the horizon, whether three, five, or seven years.

Jacob Frenkel questioned the justification for constraining government spending and taxes to enter only through the budget deficit. He pointed out the importance of the timing of government spending. An increase in current spending increases current demand and leads to a higher interest rate, but an increase in future spending leads to a lower interest rate now. He also expressed doubt that it was necessary to focus on the interest rate differential as the mechanism through which government spending and perhaps taxes affect the exchange rate.

Maurice Obstfeld commented that the interest rate differential and the exchange rate are both endogenous; in response to different shocks they may move to differing relative extents. He agreed with Feldstein that the safe haven argument was inadequate, citing against it the strong correlation of stock prices in the United States, Japan, and Germany. He also argued that changes in government spending cause a transfer problem that can move the exchange rate whether Ricardian equivalence holds or not. Finally, he remarked that the recent fall in the dollar can be explained by changes in expectations of future budget deficits as well as in monetary policy.

Robert Hall argued that the relation between the expected budget deficit and the exchange rate should be a short-run one. In an extreme case, over an infinite horizon the expected budget deficit has to be nearly zero. He also suggested that the right version of "safe haven" is that the United States became a safe haven for Latin-American investors.

The construction of the expected budget deficit varibles was criticized by Robert Barro. He recommended the use of Blanchard-like measures that look over a longer horizon and include the variables that might cause Ricardian equivalence to fail. He added that Ricardian equivalence does not imply that the interest rate is not affected by a temporary change in government spending, which is in practice correlated with the budget deficit.

Olivier Blanchard questioned the specification of the regressions with the level of the exchange rate as the dependent variable. It is well known that the exchange rate follows a random walk. The regressions should therefore be run in first differences. He was puzzled, however, by the ability of the regressions to explain expected movements of the exchange rate.

Takatoshi Ito expressed doubt that the budget deficit affects the real exchange rate. He had examined the behavior of the yen-dollar exchange rate using four daily observations for 1500 days. He found that news about the deficit had no effect on the exchange rate. Large changes in the exchange rate are associated not with the deficit but with monetary news. Ben Bernanke argued that an events study of the type done by Ito might be a more promising direction of research than the type of regression in Feldstein's article, because the statistical expectations used by Feldstein are inevitably poorer than those of the market.

Dornbusch found disturbing the insensitivity of Feldstein's results to the length of horizon used to construct expected deficits. Surely the turning points of expected deficits must differ depending on the horizon; if those differences do not affect the empirical results, something other than expected deficits may be producing the results.

Lawrence Summers said that the budget deficit story is oversold in this article relative to alternative theories. In particular, the roles of tight money and tax effects were not treated adequately. The monetary base does not capture the tightness of monetary policy since it does not reflect velocity shocks. Tax incentives for investment affect the investment-saving gap, hence the current account, and thus should affect the exchange rate. This effect may be smaller than that of the deficit, but must be significant.

Martin Feldstein concluded the session by answering some of the comments. He suggested that the small interest-rate effect on the exchange rate was probably due to downward bias due to simultaneity and measurement error. In response to Robert Barro, he said that his results are not sensitive to the method of construction of the budget deficit variable. He did not want to work with first-differenced data since that was likely to raise the noise/signal ratio. He agreed with Summers that the tax effect should enter positively in a regression, but had found that the effect is very small.